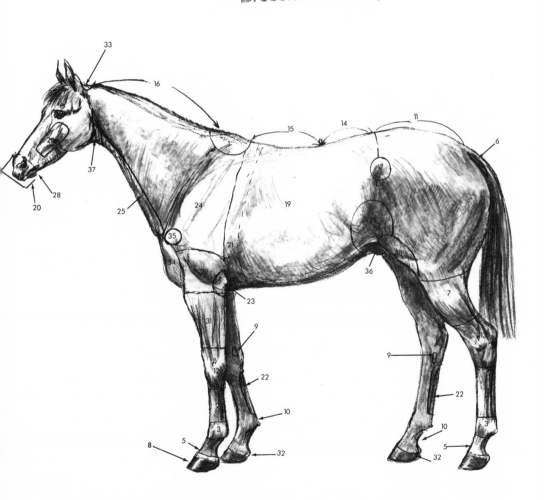

a horse around the house

a horse around the house

NEW, REVISED, AND EXPANDED EDITION

BY PATRICIA JACOBSON
AND MARCIA HAYES

ILLUSTRATED BY PAT KELLY

CROWN PUBLISHERS, INC., NEW YORK

© 1978 by Patricia Jacobson and Marcia Hayes

Manufactured in the United States of America

Designed by Ruth Smerechniak

Library of Congress Cataloging-in-Publication Data

Jacobson, Patricia.
  A horse around the house.

  Bibliography: p.
  Includes index.
  1. Horses. I. Hayes, Marcia, joint author.
II. Title.
SF285.3.J3 1978   636.1'08   78-529
ISBN 0-517-53166-6

10   9   8

FOR
mother and dad

ACKNOWLEDGMENTS

Special thanks and appreciation are owed to those who introduced me to riding, guided me through the early stages of learning, and made me aware of a seemingly limitless potential for enjoyment and enrichment.

In the beginning there was Margaret Cabell Self, Felicia Townsend, and Otto Heuckeroth. Later my awareness and appreciation for the art of riding was awakened and stimulated by Walter Staley, Gordon Wright, Frank Carroll, and George Morris.

Thanks are due to Faizig Tipton Auctioneers, who provided up-to-date record sales figures; to Dr. Helmut Nickel, Curator of Arm and Armaments at the Metropolitan Museum of Art, who dispelled a lot of myths and supplied interesting new details on the origins of the modern Western and English saddle.

I am particularly indebted to the following people for contributing their specialized knowledge to this book: to my neighbor Vernon Barnhardt, who gave me information on types of hay and how to grow them; to Katherine Boyer, who patiently answered my dozens of questions; to Ava Chavez, who contributed information on the American mustang; to my blacksmith Charlie Kinkade, who has practiced horseshoeing for over forty years; to Dr. Paul Mountan, D.V.M. and Equine Practitioner, who read, corrected, and suggested additions to the technical information in the chapters on health and the hoof.

I also want to thank Mrs. Amos Newcombe, who furnished information on Pony Clubs; to Linda Salwen, who lent me materials and answered questions about the Morgan, driving, carts, and harness; and to Louise Van Wagonen, my main source for information on Western equipment, attire, and grooming.

A special thanks to Pam Mulligan who started as a student and has been groom, fence-fixer, instructor, babysitter, and loyal friend.

To my students whose questions and problems have been a continual source of stimulation and the motivation for writing this book, I am particularly grateful.

Finally, to my daughter, Jackie, a young equestrian, and my husband Bob, a non-equestrian, my love and appreciation for helping me and encouraging me in what at times seemed an endless task.

Patricia Jacobson
Kripplebush, N.Y.

contents

INTRODUCTION

While I have been riding and traveling with horses throughout the world, my home state of New Jersey has been adding to the population explosion—in horses. Ten years ago, I knew just about every horse owner in the state. Since then, New Jersey's horse population has more than doubled—an increase greatly accounted for by owners of only one or two horses, and they keep them in their own backyards.

New Jersey is not unique. I fly a small plane. Within a sixty-mile radius of New York City I can see the countryside literally dotted with small backyard barns with some sort of little pasture adjoining.

Many states are experiencing a similar growth in horse population, according to Department of Agriculture statistics. Throughout the United States, people are turning to the horse for recreation, many with very little practical knowledge or experience, but impressed by and relying on horse sense acquired from movies, television, and other such unfortunate sources. Not surprisingly, many of these people are old hands around horses but have much unlearning to do—or reviewing of forgotten practices that make the difference between a happy owner and his horse and a short-lived relationship.

A HORSE AROUND THE HOUSE by Patricia Jacobson and Marcia Hayes does for horsemen and horsewomen what Dr. Spock has done for a generation of new parents. The authors have created an extensive horseman's guide, rich in content, redolent with the love and pleasure of horses, based on their practical, everyday experience. They not only cover step-by-step basic information one should know when buying a horse to taking care of it by oneself, with the minimum of effort and expense and a maximum of riding pleasure, but have extended their work to help one when one becomes more advanced and is ready to broaden one's knowledge.

I like the book's pointedness. What's the irreducible limit on equipment? The answer to that alone can salvage a down payment on a new horse. As in Spock, name your concern or let it come up, however unexpectedly, and it's covered—feeding, housing, medical care, equipment, attire, etc.—in readable, literate, droll fashion.

But I suggest one read it straight through, before making a move. I have had to catch myself (if ever I am to get my chores done around the house) from reading on and on just for the pleasure of the good vibrations that one gets from this book.

FRANK CHAPOT

1

horses aren't house pets

He was a no-count Buckskin,
Wasn't worth two bits to keep,
Had a black stripe down his backbone,
And Wooly like a sheep,
That Hoss wasn't built to tred the earth,
He took natural to the air,
And every time he went aloft
He tried to leave me there

—ANONYMOUS TRIBUTE
TO AN UNMANAGEABLE HORSE

There is a miniature horse on the market called a Falabella. It's an Argentinian breed that stands about two and a half feet high, weighs around 120 pounds, and only eats a few cups of oats a day. Falabellas look decorative running around the yard or sitting in the front seat of a car, and they can even be trained to a leash.

But the kind of horse one rides usually weighs anywhere from eight hundred pounds to half a ton and stands between 14.2 and 16.2 hands high—about five and a half feet from hoof to withers. He eats like a horse and he's no house pet.

Even a little Shetland pony, docile looking and cute as he may be, is able to pull, pound for pound, as much as the biggest Clydesdale

1

draft horse you can find. Just because you can look down on a horse doesn't mean you can ride him—or even lead him around.

Considerations of this sort are often overlooked by people about to buy a first horse. A childhood diet of romantic horse stories and TV westerns frequently leaves the impression that a horse is sort of like an oversized dog that you ride. It's easy to identify with the Virginian and imagine yourself astride a steady steed that responds to every spoken command, stops on a dime, and finds his own way to the barn.

Such notions are not only dangerous but ultimately discouraging. Quite understandably a prospective buyer is seduced by a horse's aesthetic and athletic appeal. But he will eventually have to face the fact that there is considerably more than that to owning a horse.

While hardy enough to winter out on a windy, subzero plain, horses can also be delicate, complex, and often eccentric creatures, with very special needs. In their domestic state, they are entirely dependent on their owners to meet these needs—all of which requires considerable time and effort.

There are great rewards in store for the dedicated horse owner. Nothing beats the experience of a trail ride on a crisp fall day when your horse is in good condition and fine spirits, responding to every command. And there can be a feeling of immense satisfaction on a cold winter night when you get him bedded down on fresh straw, happily munching on a hot bran mash. If your horse is given proper care and schooling, a rapport will develop between you that you wouldn't trade for anything in the world.

But like anything worthwhile, this doesn't come easily. It involves lots of time, dedication, and hard work. You may not be aware, for instance, that a responsible horse owner spends more time caring for his mount than riding him. Horses need regular care, day in and day out, twelve months a year. They can't be taken to a kennel when you want to go on vacation, and a month at a boarding stable can cost as much as a month's rent for a one-bedroom city apartment. In fact, unless you have a pasture with a constant supply of fresh water, you won't be able to leave your horse alone for more than a day.

Horse owners who live in temperate climates and don't have access to an indoor ring, or who don't like to ride in the snow, will only be working their mounts regularly for six or seven months of the year. This leaves a long, cold, dark period when the only reward for all your efforts will be a friendly whinny as you open the feedbox with numbed hands.

Caring for a horse involves more than throwing a bale of hay in the stall twice a day. Feeding a horse takes time. Hay has to be shaken out to get rid of dust and other particles that could be harmful if

inhaled. And feed must be carefully measured.

When a horse is stabled, he should be groomed daily, not just for appearances but to ensure cleanliness and to keep up the animal's circulation and muscle tone. A good grooming job usually takes at least a half hour, and it's hard work.

A horse's hoofs need daily care, too. They look strong, yet they are probably the most vulnerable part of the animal. Hoofs must be trimmed and shod at least every six weeks, preferably once a month, by a *good* blacksmith. They should be picked out daily and checked for various irregularities, particularly thrush, a hoof disease.

Perhaps the hardest task of all is cleaning, or mucking out, the stalls. If a horse is outside during the day, the stall need only be tended in the morning and evening. But if the animal is stabled, his stall should be picked out three or four times a day. Normally the whole job takes about half an hour.

Tack—riding equipment—should be cleaned regularly—ideally every time it's used, but, more realistically, at least twice a month.

Apart from matters of maintenance, there's money. It's far wiser to face the hard economic facts before you get your horse in your barn.

There will be the initial purchase price, which can range anywhere from $500 to $9 million (but I'm assuming you won't be buying The Minstrel). When you get him home, you'll have a monthly blacksmith's bill—usually $24 to $36 per horse. Add to this the cost of bedding for the stall (straw costs about $2.50 per bale, depending on size and you may need about four per week), grain at approximately $8.50 to $10 a bag, hay at $65.00 a ton and up, tack, blankets, medicines, and materials for building and maintaining a

3

stable, paddock, and pasture—if you haven't got them already. While a stable can be as simple as an open shed, and a fence a single strand of electric wire, it still adds up. And up. And that's not counting the vet's bills. Even a healthy horse will need to be checked for worms several times a year. And his teeth should be looked at and floated (filed) if necessary.

Clothes should be figured into your overall budget. Even for casual English riding, you will need breeches, or jodhpurs, boots, gloves, and a hard hat if you're jumping. And, if you will be showing in English classes, add to that a jacket, shirt, choker, or stock. Even if you can find these things secondhand, a total outfit for an English rider will probably run around $150 to $500 (western riders can get by more cheaply). And keep in mind that growing children will need most of their riding clothes replaced each year.

All in all, keeping your horse at home without skimping will run around $65.00 to $75.00 a month in northern rural areas of the United States, or slightly less than payments on a new car. It will cost considerably more in suburban areas and a good deal less in mild southern climates where horses can be pastured much of the year.

Money and maintenance aside, there is the matter of keeping your horse in condition. Like people, horses need exercise. *Regular* exercise.

This will require discipline on your part. If the weather is right, your horse should be exercised daily, and this deserves serious thought before you buy. Perhaps you won't be able to ride on Tuesdays or Thursdays, or most weekdays. Maybe you would prefer to go out for a long trail ride on Sunday afternoon and let your horse take it easy for the rest of the week.

This kind of casual approach to riding is an invitation to catastrophe. Even two hours of riding for an out-of-condition horse can result in strained muscles, saddle or girth sores, pulled tendons, colic, or, in extreme cases, founder—a serious and sometimes chronic disease of the hoof. Think about how you feel the day after you take your first long ride in the spring. That should give you a rough idea of how the horse feels. And *you're* riding *him*. Sunday riders who go in for long trail rides usually end up with very sick or sore horses on their hands.

If you can't ride your horse regularly, there are other ways of exercising him. But you or someone else will have to be there.

Up until now I've been taking it for granted that as a prospective horse owner you are able to ride. By riding, I don't mean the ability to rent a horse from a public hacking stable and bounce around on the trail. I mean knowing how to control your horse, how to signal him to canter on the correct lead, and how to post (if you ride in the English style) on the correct diagonal. Good riding is the ability to imperceptibly control your horse through a proper seat and firm leg pressure, not kicking or jerking on the reins. To do all this, you will need instruction.

As an unschooled rider you have a fifty-fifty chance of purchasing a horse you can mount and control. But if you don't know how to saddle, bridle, or halter the animal, and if you are ignorant of the correct riding aids, *any* previous training will be quickly nullified. I can guarantee that as time goes by you'll spend more time on the ground than in the saddle—either unable to get on, unable to stay on, or too frustrated to keep trying.

If you buy a horse without knowing how to ride, groom, and feed him, you're beaten before you start. I know several people who bought horses cold—always with distressing results.

One beginning pupil of mine came to my course on stable management to learn how to care for her first horse, a purebred Arabian stallion. Specifically, she wanted to know how to saddle and bridle him. But as the course wore on, it became apparent that the horse didn't even tie with a halter. Because stallions tend to be high spirited and unpredictable, the girl was afraid of getting too close to him. Consequently she couldn't groom her horse, let alone saddle or bridle him. And since she was unable to get a halter on, she couldn't lead him around. This meant the horse couldn't be taken outside, because there was no way of getting him back in.

The girl was reluctant to have the stallion gelded, arguing that it was unnatural and might hurt (it doesn't). But faced with the prospect of a long, hard winter and a spirited horse becoming more unmanageable by the day, she finally agreed to let him have the operation. She has since taken riding lessons, her horse is being trained, and she is starting to enjoy him.

Stallions, needless to say, are not normally suitable for riding. They are usually kept only for breeding purposes.

But this is the sort of dilemma anyone can get into if his knowledge

of horses is based on romantic fiction instead of fact. The incident is not isolated. I can think of dozens of similar stories. The first lesson to be learned from all of them is that ignorance of this dimension can be lethal.

Putting an untrained rider on a green horse is equivalent to sending a novice skier down the steepest slope at Whiteface Mountain or throwing a nonswimmer into deep water. No, it's not quite equivalent, because in the case of horse and rider, you're dealing with a very strong animal that has a mind of its own. Horses do think. Not very deeply, perhaps, but enough to get you into a lot of trouble.

Ignorance of the right way to handle and care for a horse can be equally dangerous. Did you know that some horses are trained to tie with a halter, others around the neck? If you tried to necktie a horse that has been trained to halter tie, he'll panic, pull back, and either rip the fence post out of the ground or choke himself. And although it's done all the time in the movies, horses should not be tied by the bridle —unless you want them to break it.

Everything a horse does, or doesn't do, is a matter of training. Horses are always learning, for better or worse. Well-trained horses have been taught to lead, tie, to stand for mounting, to behave in the stall, and to respond to the aids used in a particular riding style.

All horses are trained to be approached, mounted, and led from the *near* or left side—a custom derived from the military, who carried their swords on the left hip. If someone tries to approach or lead a trained horse from the *off* or far side, the animal will know something is wrong, become confused, and perhaps balk at being led.

When approaching a strange horse, be as wary as you would with a strange dog. Don't, for example, run up and pat him on the nose. Many horses dislike being touched on the nose. If you want to show your affection, speak to him, pat him briskly on the neck or shoulder on the near side, and always keep an eye on the set of his ears to see if he enjoys it.

I've often seen parents allow their children to pet a horse that has his ears laid flat back against his head and his mouth set in a menacing expression, apparently unaware that the horse's mood was anything but friendly.

Experienced horsemen never take even the most docile horse for granted, and they learn to anticipate a horse's reactions and interpret its moods.

Learning all these things will take time and training, and your first step should be to find a good instructor. This will be expensive, but your career as a horse owner won't progress far without it.

Once you have a good teacher, he or she will be a good person to take along when you go horse hunting. An instructor is best able to judge your riding potential and help pick the horse that is right for you. Also, he knows the local dealers.

But not all teachers will instruct you in horse care and stable management in addition to riding. If you have one that doesn't, there are alternatives. (*See* chapter 10.)

Now that I've summarized the basic problems a novice horseman might face, if you're still set on owning a horse, you might ask yourself these few leading questions before turning to the classified ads:

—Are you willing to get out of bed at 2:00 A.M. during a cloudburst to retrieve your horse from a neighbor's yard (usually a terrified, angry neighbor) and then mend the fence he escaped through?

Not all horses are trained to tie by the neck

—When it's twenty below and all the water pipes to your barn have frozen, how will you feel about carting two or three pails of water a day two hundred yards from your house to his stall?

—Would you have the stomach to hold your horse's tongue over on the side of his mouth (horse's tongues are very large) while you pour a half bottle of milk of magnesia down his throat to cure the colic (his kind of stomachache)? And after that, can you feature walking him around the paddock for an hour when all he wants to do is lie down?

—Can you help your horse up from a stall when he's tried to roll and gotten himself pinned against the wall (cast) and is panicked and thrashing about?

—Are you willing to chip frozen manure from the floor of the stall and then dig a path through two feet of snow to the manure pile?

I could go on. And on. But I'm sure you get the idea. And these situations aren't exaggerated. I face all of them at least once a year. If you're planning on getting more than one horse, problems like these tend to multiply in proportion to the occupants of your stable.

But if you are able to confront these prospects with equanimity, I'd say you have the stamina and dedication necessary for happy and successful horse ownership. That being settled, we can get down to the business of choosing the horse you would like to own.

2

hunting for a horse

Round-hoofed, short-jointed, fetlocks shag
and long,
Broad breast, full eye, small head, and
nostril wide,
High crest, short ears, straight legs, and
passing strong,
Thin mane, thick tail, broad buttocks,
tender hide.
Look, what a horse should have he did
not lack
Save a proud rider on so proud a back.

—SHAKESPEARE:
Venus and Adonis (49, 50)

Buying a horse is not something to let yourself be rushed into, either by personal whim or pleading children. The first horse you see may capture your heart at three hundred yards, but don't reach for your checkbook until you've closely examined this prospective purchase for soundness, schooling, manners, temperament, conformation, and breeding. If not cautious, you're liable to end up getting stuck—like the person who bought the horse advertised below:

For Sale: Alert young trailhorse for experienced rider. Gorgeous Chestnut mare with white blaze. Goes English or Western. Sacrifice Cheap. Will Deliver.

Once you understand what to look for in a good horse, you'll never get excited by an ad like this. Reading between the lines, you'll suspect that "alert" ("spirited" is more like it) is a euphemism for spooky or unmanageable. A horse that "goes English or Western" probably just goes, period; and an "experienced rider" is likely to be the only kind who could stay on for the trip. Low price tags ("Sacrifice Cheap") are often a signal of serious personality and behavior problems, and the offer of free delivery probably means she is impossible to load.

Remember too that handsome is as handsome does. Good looks are only important in a mature riding horse when accompanied by good training. A horse that is absolutely beautiful and absolutely unmanageable is absolutely worthless—except, perhaps, for breeding.

WHERE TO LOOK

If you are relatively inexperienced with horses, it's a good idea to take an experienced person with you when you look for a first horse. Horses can be found successfully through ads, if you know how to read them, through camp sales, at breeding farms, or through a dealer.

Auction sales are not a good place for a beginner to buy a horse. Bargains have been gotten at sales, of course. Some of the top horses in the country have been picked up for a song, but *always* by people who know what to look for. Gordon Wright, a former coach of the U.S. Olympic team, got his famous open jumper Sonny at a sheriff's auction for sixteen dollars. The horse had been found wandering along some back roads in Westchester County, and no owner had come to claim him.

Greyhound, a Standardbred racer whose 1938 record was unbroken for years, was purchased for under a thousand dollars. And a horse named Sinjon, who was sold for $185 because of his reputation as a weaver, cribber, and general nuisance, went on to become the prize-winning mount of U.S. Olympic teamers George Morris, Kathy Kusner, and Bill Steinkraus. Before his retirement Sinjon had helped Steinkraus win a fourth at the 1960 Rome Olympics, had made seven trips to Europe, and finally was rewarded with the coveted King George V cup, presented by Queen Elizabeth.

The Angel, a famous open jumper who won hundreds of ribbons at every top show in the country and holds the Haymond record for winning Horse-of-the-Year four times in a row, was discovered standing knee deep in manure in a milkman's broken-down barn. His stall was so dark that when The Angel was taken outside he was temporarily blinded and stumbled into the barn door. But treatment by a veterinarian restored his vision, and he went on to become a champion.

Probably everyone has heard of another famed open jumper, Snow Man, who began life as a plowhorse and was bought by Harry de Leyer just as he was being loaded on a truck bound for the dog-food factory. This eighty-dollar bargain, sold because he kept jumping out of his pasture, became the winner of the National Horse Show Crown as well as the Professional Horsemen's Association Champion, and De Leyer later turned down an offer of fifty thousand dollars for him.

Canonero II, winner of the 1971 Kentucky Derby, was purchased for fifteen hundred dollars—a low price for a racehorse—and sold at stud for over a million dollars.

But don't get your hopes up. All these buyers were very experienced horsemen, and the chances of a beginner getting a steal like these are very slim.

Dealers can be tricky, and you shouldn't go to one without professional help. While most are very aboveboard and reliable, there are still a few around who are definitely not, and a professional will know which is which. Some dealers will take a hot horse out and ride him for three or four hours and then pass him off as a quiet mount when he's so exhausted he can barely walk. They have been known to give sick horses stimulants, antibiotics, or tranquilizers to make them appear normal. Or they may give medications for various lamenesses that will work a cure temporarily. Butazolidin (Bute), which is one of the most effective coverups, is commonly used to obscure problems of the feet. If there's reason to suspect that a horse is under the influence of a drug, ask your vet to do a urine chemistry. Or try to take the horse home for a seventy-two-hour trial period, during which time any drug will wear off. Beware of Butazolidin under any circumstances where a dealer or stable owner stands to gain a great deal by peddling an unsound horse. One girl I know bought a horse from the riding stable where she took lessons, never getting a hint that the horse was unsound, although she rode him several times a week. When the stable was sold to another owner some months later, she found that she had a thirty-five-hundred-dollar lame horse on her hands. The former owner had been putting a dose of Bute in her horse's food every morning. Reputable dealers, however, depend on their good reputations and will often guarantee a horse's soundness by paying for examination by a vet of your choice.

WHAT WILL YOU BE USING HIM FOR?

It will help to ask yourself a few questions before starting out on your quest. Will you be riding only for pleasure, either English or Western? If so, will you be riding mostly on the trail in the company of other

horses? Will you be showing? Will the shows be small local affairs or large ones, recognized by the American Horse Show Association? Will you be specializing in some particular seat, like saddle seat, or do you want to hunt? If you ride Western, will you be using your horse for cutting or reining classes?

All these things will determine the kind of horse you buy. A good trail horse, for example, ought to be able to get along with other horses in close quarters—something not all horses do well. He should be tractable (well mannered) and not too high strung. If you'll be showing in recognized shows, you will probably want to choose a purebred (if you want to place, that is). Saddle-seat riders will find that American saddle breds, park-type Morgans, or Arabians will be the most suitable mounts for them.

The rider who wants to hunt should choose a horse suited to the country he'll be riding through and one suited to him in size. Good hunters should be even tempered and should enjoy jumping as well as excelling at it. Half-breds and cross-breds are usually excellent for this purpose because of their even disposition and more rugged constitution. (Conformation hunters used for show, however, are almost always Thoroughbreds and are rarely used for real hunts outside the ring.) To get the right horse, you should be acquainted with the different breeds. (See Chapter 3.)

WHAT SIZE AND HOW OLD IS HE?

The size of the horse is obviously important. A short person will be out of place on a burly hunter. And a child who will be caring for his own horse should have one that he can easily saddle, bridle, and groom.

Age must be considered. Everyone has heard the cautionary "never look a gift horse in the mouth." It's based on the fact that dental structure is the only precise indicator of a horse's age, a factor in determining suitability.

Horses, like people, lose their baby teeth (milk teeth) in a certain sequence. Their permanent teeth grow in the same order. Depending on the construction of the jaw, the mature teeth are then ground down in a fairly predictable way. The wearing surface, viewed from above when the jaw is open, is more or less horizontal in a young horse and becomes triangular with increased age. Older horses lose the "cups" on teeth at about seven years and acquire the dental star in their central incisors at about eight years. The star becomes larger and more centrally located with age. Also, the angle at which the teeth meet increases with age. In young horses, it is close to a right angle; with older horses, more acute. Although it's fairly easy to tell the age of a horse seven or under, after that it gets tricky. So if you don't have a professional along, you could buy a so-called eight-year-old and find out later that he's actually eighteen.

When a rider is inexperienced, a horse between the ages of seven and ten is a good choice. By that time he has had schooling (if he hasn't, forget it, unless you're a highly experienced horseman) and his temperament is stabilized. Properly cared for, a ten-year-old horse will be ridable into his late teens. The Russians' 1972 Olympic gold medal winner in dressage—Pepal—was sixteen years old at the time of

1 year   4 years   6 years   8 years   10 years   15 years

Wearing surface of teeth, as in this right front central tooth viewed from above, is more horizontal in a younger horse, becoming triangular with age.

Cross-section side view of permanent front tooth

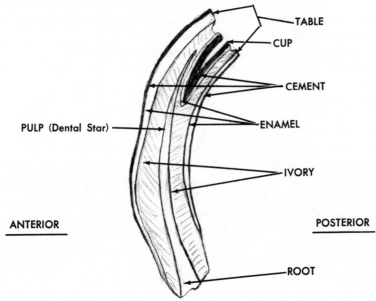

TABLE

CUP

CEMENT

PULP (Dental Star)

ENAMEL

IVORY

ANTERIOR

POSTERIOR

ROOT

his victory. A seven-year-old horse given good care and kept in condition can be expected to give at least a decade of pleasure.

Unless a rider is very inexperienced, I wouldn't recommend an animal much over eleven years old. While older horses are more gentle, they tend to break down with increasing age—like a used car. The wear and tear begins to show up in the weaker parts of the animal, and he is more liable to age-linked ailments like arthritis. It's essential that a vet check out the prospective purchase for soundness.

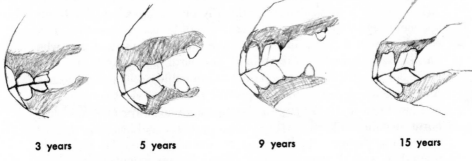

3 years   5 years   9 years   15 years

Side view—angle of incidence

If you spend more than a thousand dollars on a young horse or a middle-year horse, protect your investment by having at least the front feet x-rayed. Professional horsemen who deal in the sale of show horses and hunters always do this. And on the track, the knees and hocks of young racehorses are commonly x-rayed to see if the growth plates have matured and if the horse is ready for racing.

Should the X rays show anything doubtful—like a splint or a joint enlargement (see Chapter 8)—then have additional X rays in those areas.

Knee and ankle problems are more common in horses that come off the track, so be sure to examine these areas in any horse that's tattooed (a sign he's been on the track). Things like chip fractures of the knee and ankle are often impossible to detect without an X ray.

A complete set of X rays, which are usually unnecessary, can cost as much as three hundred dollars. Not only is such thoroughness expensive, but pointing up every minute problem in leg conformation can be confusing. Instead, pay special attention to feet, ankles, knees, hocks, and stifles. And don't bother to X ray at all if you're buying an inexpensive young horse or an aged horse (over twelve) that your vet has checked out as sound. As long as a urine chemistry has ruled out the possibility of painkillers, the extra expense isn't worth it.

WHAT TO SPEND?

It's practically impossible to find the perfect horse at any price. So aim for one that comes as close to your ideal as you can find—at a price you can afford. Unless this ideal is realistically within your means, you'll spend a long time looking. The chances of finding a purebred Arabian for a few hundred dollars are minuscule.

First of all, decide what you will spend. It is hoped that this will be a minimum of around five hundred to seven hundred dollars, because in most parts of the country you can't get much of a horse for less.

The cost of a horse depends primarily on his breeding. **Purebreds** are more expensive than **cross-breds** or **half-breds.** A cross-bred is a combination of different breeds, like the Morab, a half-bred, one who has a parent that is a Thoroughbred, Standardbred, or Arabian.

Grades are horses of uncertain and probably accidental ancestry. And there are fewer of the inexpensive horses around for two major reasons. First, it doesn't pay in a competitive and expensive field like horse breeding to keep anything but a purebred stallion. The expense of feeding, training, stabling, and maintaining a horse is high, and grade horses don't give a good return on the investment.

Another reason, a grim one, for the decline in inexpensive stock is the growing human appetite for horsemeat. There's more of a demand for grade horses on the plate than on the hoof, and meat buyers currently outbid everyone else at horse auctions where grade stock is sold. The French have always been big consumers of horsemeat, and (at this writing) it's cheaper for them to buy it at American prices. (The spiraling cost of beef in this country has converted many Americans to *viands de cheval*.)

More than twenty thousand horses a month end up on the butcher's block in this country, and there's nothing illegal about it because other domesticated animals are part of our food supply. Wild horses, however, are protected by federal law.

As a consequence, grade horses are priced too high for the backyard buyer, and the entire horse industry has felt the effect. Novices who would once have bought a grade horse as a safer mount of steady disposition are now forced to purchase half-breds and purebreds at higher prices.

A half-bred is a good choice for a first horse. They are frequently good looking, reasonably priced, and often of a quieter disposition than purebreds. They are likely to go between eight hundred and fifteen hundred dollars and up, depending on schooling. (Half-bred hunters that look like Thoroughbreds can go for as much as seven thousand dollars.)

The term purebred, by the way, is not to be confused with Thoroughbred, a definite breed developed in England for racing. A purebred is any horse of distinct breed, from the Arab to the Peruvian Peso, whose sires and dams are all registered in the same studbook and who have papers to prove it. Breeds, like some human families, have long and intricate genealogies.

A **hotblood** usually is a horse whose ancestors came from the Orient, the Mideast, or North Africa. The term refers to a horse who is either pure Thoroughbred, Standardbred, or Arabian and is interchangeable with **full-blood. Cold-blooded** refers to horses that have one of the draft breeds somewhere in their ancestry. These designations have been used to denote a class of horses by temperament. Hotbloods tend to be more high-strung, nervous, mischievous, and playful. Cold-blooded horses keep calm longer in stressful situations. But they may also be rather dull-witted and sluggish.

Warm-bloods are horses without any cold blood in their ancestry but who could be a cross between a warm-blood and a full-blood. Many German breeds are warm-bloods, among them Hanoverians, Holsteiners, and Trakehners.

Centuries ago, to improve each strain, breeders began crossing coldbloods and hotbloods with horses of better disposition and greater size and stamina. For years the best Irish hunters were a mixture of seven-eighths Thoroughbred and one-eighth draft horse—a perfect blend for the rugged country where they worked.

Half-breds like the half-Percheron-half-Thoroughbred have been developed in this country because they're sound, good-tempered and easy to keep. They're also relatively inexpensive, going easily for three thousand dollars in their prime.

A horse's breeding potential will also affect his price. Thus a pure-bred stallion, which would be unsuitable in any case for anyone but an experienced rider, will be priced far above a mare or gelding. Again, because of her ability to reproduce, the mare would cost more than a gelding. And in the case of a purebred mare, her conformation will consequently be important. The better looking she is, the more likely it is that her foals will be good looking, therefore, the price will be higher. Mares, however, tend to be unpredictable and sometimes irritable and untrustworthy, especially when they're in season (in heat).

If you have your heart set on a purebred, your best bet is a breeding farm. To shop and compare, go to more than one place. Since the sole purpose of these farms is to develop a particular breed, you're more likely to find a sound, attractive specimen.

If you're working on a limited budget and can't afford a purebred, you may eventually want to consider a half-bred mare of reasonable conformation with the idea of breeding her with a registered stallion and raising a colt of your own. But I recommend getting a few years of horse management under your belt before doing this.

A gelding, by far the most popular horse for riding, is generally more dependable and quieter than a stallion or mare. Geldings are very economical, in all a good choice for a first horse. Once again, cost will be determined by breed. A registered gelding will cost less than a registered stallion or mare. Half-bred gelding prices depend on con-formation, schooling, and age.

Incidentally, the time of the year that you buy will influence the price of a horse. They are generally most expensive in the spring when every-one yearns to get out and ride and there is a summer of green pastures ahead. In the late fall in northern climates horses are sold far cheaper. But remember that a long period awaits you when the horse can't be ridden but has to be fed. The lower purchase price may be offset by feeding bills.

Age is also a price factor. As I mentioned before, a young horse is not a good idea for a first-horse owner. It will need training by an ex-perienced horseman to develop into a well-trained mount, and this could run into several thousand dollars a year if the cost of boarding out and feeding are figured in. This varies, of course, with locale. An untrained horse will be cheaper initially, however, because he hasn't had any schooling.

A schooled horse can be expected to cost more (a good deal more in the case of a purebred), and his price will be highest between five and nine years of age. Most breeds reach full maturity at five, when they should have finished their education and be ready for a full working schedule.

By the time a horse is seven, he should be finished with his education. While it isn't impossible to teach an old horse new tricks, it takes more time and patience than most riders will care to expend. A horse's body is "set in its ways" by the age of seven. His muscular system has developed according to the way he's been carrying and using himself for those years, and it's a slow and difficult task for him to change it.

If a horse has been shown in a particular field, it will enhance his price. Obviously, the category and type of show or competitions he's placed in will influence this. If you have the money, it makes the most horse sense to get a mount who is most talented at what you want to use him for.

Size and color have more to do with individual suitability and preference than price, except in the case of those purebreds that must conform to size and color requirements. Ponies tend to be cheaper as they get smaller, because their utility will be limited to a few years (unless you plan to have a large family).

Colors are costly only where particular breeds are concerned like registered albinos, Appaloosas, palominos, pintos, and buckskins, all of which are bred especially for color.

Every passing decade has seen a new color trend. In 1900, most Arabians were bays. Today, only one out of four Arabs is a bay. Chestnuts were the preferred color for this breed in the fifties, yet only one out of three Arabians today is chestnut, gray being the preferred color. The only breeds that have remained color constant are the Thoroughbred, Standardbred, and quarter horse.

Even in pleasure horses, one color may give an owner more pleasure. A chestnut horse with four white stockings and a blaze is obviously more interesting looking and will command a higher price than a plain chestnut of the same conformation.

The trend in size has changed too, with almost everyone seeking a larger mount—particularly those who want hunters. A small (fifteen-hand) Thoroughbred is going to sell for less than one a hand larger.

The value of certain breeds will also vary considerably from area to area. A Tennessee Walker, for example, might go for a third of his home-state value up north. A Thoroughbred could go for a song in cattle country, where ability to work with stock is considered a horse's greatest attribute.

Always buy the best horse you can afford. Remember that a poor horse costs as much to feed as a good one.

LOOKING HIM OVER

Obviously you want to get the most for your money, meaning that you will search for a horse with a good conformation (the total physical attributes of an animal and the relationship of one part to another). Beauty is definitely functional where horses are concerned. A good-looking horse is generally a good mover, while one that is badly put together is often awkward in action as well as appearance and is more likely to develop unsoundness. (Unsoundness is an abnormal deviation in the horse's form or function that affects his way of going.)

There are some conformation faults that will not interfere with a horse's going or his life of service. Some faults are important only if present to a large degree. Others can't be accepted at all. Some unsoundnesses can be treated, some can't. These are not to be confused with blemishes, like scars that don't interfere with ability. A Thoroughbred with a bad leg scar, for example, has lost his value in the show ring, yet he might be an excellent buy as a hunter. But an unsound horse, say one with chronic founder, is worthless.

When you're actually out there in the stableyard viewing your prospective horse for the first time, stand back and inspect him from the side at a distance of twenty or thirty feet. This will give you a whole picture of how the horse fits together. Are the legs placed square, as they should be, on all four corners? Does the forehand look too large for the rear? Or does the rump look as if it belonged on a large workhorse and the shoulders on a pony?

While still viewing the horse from the side, notice the topline, from the top of the ears to the tail. This line should curve gently, and not run off into sharp bumps and angles. Ideally the bottom line should

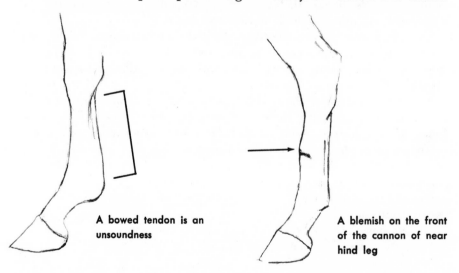

A bowed tendon is an
unsoundness

A blemish on the front
of the cannon of near
hind leg

At twenty to thirty feet, view as a whole

not have more daylight showing than the measure of the width of the girth—the widest part of his barrel. A long underline affects the freedom of the leg movements, while a short underline could indicate a close, short stride and gait problems.

The next step will be to see the horse move out, first at a brisk walk, then at a trot. It's a good idea to have someone with you to lead him for you at these gaits. If you don't, ask the seller if he wouldn't mind leading him. Does he move out with a long, straight, well-coordinated stride, or is there a great deal of side movement of the feet and body that looks clumsy? To judge this properly, watch both gaits—from the back and front particularly.

Be sure to try out the horse at all gaits in both directions. Before mounting, always try to saddle, bridle, halter, and tie him. Assuming he gives you no trouble, ride him. Canter him for a couple of turns around the ring, stop him, and listen to his wind. If he makes strange noises, he may be suffering from roaring or whistling (*see* chapter 8 on ailments). Or, if his nostrils are extremely dilated, if his sides heave, or if he coughs, these could be indications of other respiratory unsoundness. Ride him on the trail and on the road if possible until you're satisfied.

To get the most out of a horse, you'll want to be able to truck him. So it's best to see him loaded into a trailer if you can. A balky loader can cause a lot of headaches and frustration.

Observe the horse's behavior closely. Does he respond well to your signals? Does he tend to shy at familiar objects—around cars or bridges? Does he throw his head back when bridled or back away as you try to mount? All of these things are bad habits or character traits that take a lot of time and know-how to correct. You should be wary of all of them. And if the person selling the horse seems reluctant to let you do all or any of the things mentioned above, you can be sure something is awry.

Naturally, you'll try out a number of horses to find out what you like and don't like. (I'm still assuming that you ride, and know how a well-trained horse should behave.)

There is no excuse except structural for bad action (movement) in a horse, and none should be accepted from the seller: "He was worked hard yesterday, and he's tired," or "I think you must be watching from a funny angle."

If you're satisfied with your prospective horse up to this point, move in for a closer examination of his individual parts. Begin with the feet, which you should pick up—one at a time—and hold for a few seconds. It's a good idea to tap them with something to detect signs of black-smith resistance (*see* chapter 7).

Feet

Veterinarians will tell you that 90 percent of all lameness occurs in the feet. This is one place where no irregularities are acceptable. Read through chapter 7 on the hoof to avoid making any mistakes in this area. Remember to check the feet for ridges that circle the hoof beginning at the center and curving down to the heel—an indication of founder (*see* chapter 8).

A dropped sole or separation of the sole from the wall is another indication of severe founder, which will cause lameness and an awkward stance. When a horse stands on the heels of his front feet to relieve soreness (called pointing), he may be foundered or suffering from some other unsoundness of the front feet.

Check the frog of the foot to see that it's healthy and large, not small and shrunken or drawn up. Look to see if there are signs of thrush. Then feel around the coronet for sidebones and around the pastern for ringbone.

The **pastern** and the angle of each hoof should be approximately the same—at about a 45-degree incline. Since the pastern functions much like a spring, it's a key point to notice. Faults here influence the gait and are a weak point of stress—a source of potential trouble. Short, straight pasterns usually indicate a rough, jarring gait. Very sloped

Conformation of front legs—front view

Narrow chest

Full chest

Wide chest

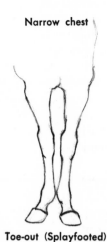

Toe-out (Splayfooted)

Good

Toe-in (Pigeon-toed)

pasterns are weak and likely to affect the tendons and joints. Sloping pasterns should definitely be avoided in a horse doing any hard work.

The **cannons** should be short, clean, and vertical. Small splints (calcified growths on the ligament connecting the splint bones) are usually not harmful to action unless they interfere with the joint or tendon.

The **tendon** should stand out like steel cord and not bow out or tie in behind the knee. Either of these would be a weakness, but the bow is unacceptable in such an essential part.

Viewed from the front, the feet shouldn't toe in or toe out. Toeing-out (splayfoot) puts a greater stress on the inside of the legs and is generally a worse fault than toeing-in. The former causes action faults called winging and dishing, which look very much as they sound. Toeing-in (pigeon-toed) causes a horse to paddle, making him look something like an eggbeater when he trots. A horse that toes in is less apt to brush in front than a horse that toes out.

Knees

Seen from the side, the knees should be large and flat and predominant. They should provide sufficient surface for the support and proper functioning of those muscles and tendons that control leg movements, which end at the knee. Calf knees put strain on tendons and pasterns. A horse with calf knees is obviously weak in this area and should be avoided. A horse who is over at the knee may have been worked too hard at an early age. The latter fault, depending on its severity, may not affect his way of going.

Conformation of front legs—side view

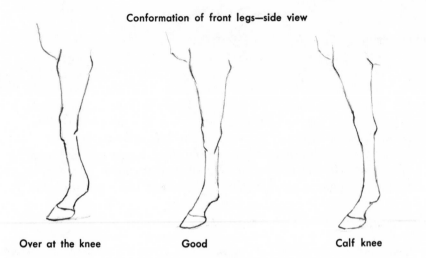

Over at the knee   Good   Calf knee

Chest

When looking at a horse from the front, make sure he stands square with his legs vertical. His chest should be generous enough to have room to spare for heart and lungs. If a horse is too narrow in the chest, the saddle will constantly be sliding forward, and riding downhill will be a frightening experience—either you or the saddle will end up on his neck.

One very narrow-chested pony I'd borrowed for my daughter for the riding season had this problem. After every trek downhill on our trail rides, we had to stop, dismount, undo the girth, and slide the saddle back into position. Once when the pony tried to drink at a very full stream my daughter ended up head first in the water.

A horse that is too wide in front, however, can be considered. By itself this isn't a serious fault, although the horse will look awkward and will probably have a rolling, lumbering canter and gallop.

Barrel and Withers

Viewed from the side, the barrel should be wide at the girth to allow room for all the internal organs. The withers should be prominent and distinct and should drop toward the back. It's better to have high withers than indistinct, fat ones (mutton withers). On a thick-withered horse you never feel that the girth is secure, and the saddle, which is placed behind the withers, always seems to be about to slip to the side. Thick-withered horses often have a short stride, while well-developed withers usually go with the graceful, flowing stride so evident in many famous racehorses and jumpers.

Back and Loins

The back and loins carry the weight of the rider in the saddle and act as a junction between the forehand and hindquarters. Consequently they should be short and well muscled. This varies, of course, according to breed specifications. Theoretically a short back is a better weight carrier and a long back is weak. But many excellent jumpers have long backs, often accompanied by a hump at the top of the pelvis. It's difficult to set hard and fast rules about this conformation area.

The long-backed horse *usually* has a smoother, longer gait and more flexible spine. He will not be an efficient weight-carrier, however. A heavy person ought to select a short-backed horse like a quarter horse.

Ribs

The ribs should be long and deep and well sprung or arched out with plenty of room for the digestive system and good breathing. Narrow ribs will cause the saddle to slide back on a horse.

Croup

The croup should generally be long and wide, the levelness varying greatly with every breed. Usually a level croup is an indication of a long, smooth stride and an ability to maintain speed for long distances. A more rounded croup indicates powerful hindquarters, allowing a horse to get his legs well under him—for power in the case of a draft horse, or for quick burst of speed, like a quarter horse.

Gaskin

The gaskin should have good muscling. These outer muscles propel the back legs, and a good long muscle here gives a long, powerful stride. Shorter, more bunched muscles give strength for turning and pivoting, desirable in polo ponies and quarter horses.

Hocks

Hocks should be large and wide from front to back. Because they are such an important joint, hocks should be clean and free of blemishes, not boggy (spongy), bony, capped, or curbed (*see* chapter 8 on ailments).

Hindquarters

Viewed from the side, hindquarters should be well under the horse. If

Conformation of hindquarters

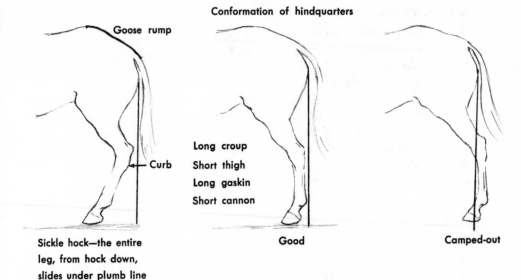

Goose rump

Curb

Long croup
Short thigh
Long gaskin
Short cannon

Sickle hock—the entire
leg, from hock down,
slides under plumb line

Good

Camped-out

sprung out or camped out, they display a lack of handiness and push and probably foretell an awkward way of going. A horse with this conformation defect will have difficulty balancing himself; and collecting him properly will be a frustrating experience because it will be almost physically impossible for him to get his hind legs under him.

As a whole, the croup should be long, the thighs short, the gaskin long, and the cannon short.

Conformation of rear legs

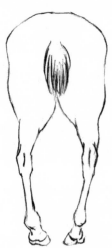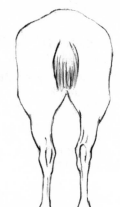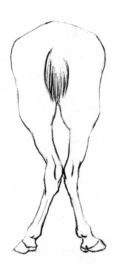

Toe-in

Good

Toe-out (cow hocks)

Seen from behind, the hind legs should be parallel, not turning out or in, with the greatest width at the stifle. A cow-hocked horse is easier to collect because he already tends to have his legs under him a bit. You collect a horse when you balance him by bringing his hindquarters well under him. He is collected when you feel him become lightened in the forehand. On the other hand, a horse that travels wide behind (his legs are too far apart) will tend to have a more rolling gait. Unless his feet interfere with each other, however, rolling is acceptable.

Neck, Shoulder, etc.

The neck, shoulder, arm, and forearm are all interrelated. The neck should have a slight arch to the top and be clean-cut at the throatlatch, which in turn should be free of fatty tissue to allow movement of the head and poll and proper breathing. The neck of a young, untrained horse will be thinner and lack the curved upper crest and strong balancing muscles of a mature horse. A good arch at the poll in an older horse may be an indication of good schooling.

A short, thick neck is usually associated with a hard (insensitive)

1 . Ewe-neck, Roman nose, pig eye—signs of uncertain breeding
2 . Short, thick neck, heavy through the throatlatch
3 . A well-crested neck with a good arch at poll and concave profile—signs of good breeding

Neck muscles and how they are connected with shoulder, arm, and forearm movement

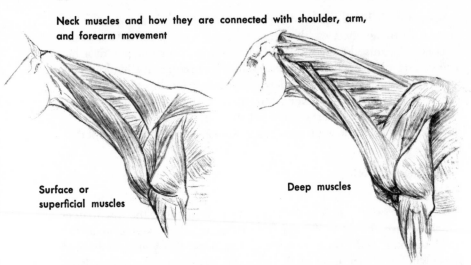

Surface or superficial muscles

Deep muscles

mouth. A bullnecked horse has a tendency to pull—in other words to be very heavy in the hands—a reflection of his physical heaviness in the forehand. A horse normally carries two-thirds of his weight on his forehand anyway. Because the neck aids the head in balancing the horse's body, a short neck would indicate a tendency toward slow, awkward turns.

The major neck fault to be avoided is a ewe-neck (which looks like a "u") or upside-down neck. The underside bulges out, causing a horse to carry his head too high. This, in turn, usually leads him to avoid the bit, requiring either a martingale or tie-down to keep the head in position. It is almost impossible to get good flexion at the poll and jaw with this type of neck. (When he flexes, he relaxes at the poll and jaw and becomes more manageable.)

The length of the neck plays an important part in the length of the horse's stride because of the interrelationship of the several layers of muscles over the side of the neck to the shoulder blade, the arm and, indirectly, the forearm. These muscles which control the leg movements end at the knee. (All action below the knee is controlled by ligaments and tendons.) Large side neck muscles allow more muscle contraction, permitting the arm to extend farther and the forearm to raise higher—resulting in a longer stride. Other muscles, at the front of the neck, extend to the shoulder blade. Long muscles here give the shoulder more freedom of movement resulting in a longer stride.

Compare the conformation of the Thoroughbred to that of the Morgan. The Thoroughbred has been bred to race while the Morgan was bred as a pleasure horse.

Shoulders also have a vital influence on stride; their slope should correspond to the angle of the pastern (45 degrees). Muscles here should be long, flat, and smooth. A straight shoulder will signal a rough ride, while its length indicates a long or short stride.

In other words, long, large neck muscles and long shoulder blades equal a long stride, and vice versa. The ideal side view should show a long shoulder and short arm, long forearm and short cannon—for the smoothest gaits.

Head

I've purposely left the head until last because it is the most obvious indicator of quality and breeding or lack of it. All light horse breeds (horses bred especially for riding) have a sizable infusion of Arab blood somewhere in the family tree, reflected in the chiseling of the facial features and the thin skin and fine hair covering the body.

The head relates to the rest of the body in structure. A long, narrow head is normally followed by a long, shallow body. A coarse head is followed by a coarse body. Any other combination would look odd. In most breeds a small head is desirable, short in length with a straight or slightly concave profile ending in a relatively square muzzle. Roman noses and large heads suggest poor ancestry.

The muzzle, ideally, should be small, with wide flaring nostrils capable of expansion when the horse is working hard and fast. Since horses can't breathe through their mouths, nostril size is very important. The jaw should be large enough to allow substantial room for the larynx and proper neck flexion.

A horse's face is ennobled by his ears and eyes. Ears should be set well on the head at about a 45-degree angle and should be alert when he's interested. Medium-sized ears are desirable in most breeds. With few exceptions, eyes should be dark; and, in all cases large and clear, with no cloudiness. When a hand is waved in front of a horse's eyes, he should blink immediately.

Small, narrow eyes—called pig eyes—are associated with poor breeding. This fault supposedly denotes a sluggish disposition. But I've had some excellent, highly responsive horses who were pig-eyed.

GENERAL CONDITION

Unless a horse is extremely run-down or seriously or incurably ill, his general condition is not as large a consideration for purchase as an amateur might think. Of course improper nutrition over a long period will cause serious bone damage and internal problems. But a short period of being off his feed and sloppily cared for will generally not produce problems.

I'd much rather view an underweight horse as a potential buy than one rolling in fat. While a thin horse's conformation—and faults, if any —are very evident, a fat horse has all his anatomy hidden under layers of lard. At yearling sales, it's standard practice to fatten up the horses before auction time.

A thin horse might just be a victim of a recent long, nerve-racking journey or a hard winter, or both. Frequently an animal newly arrived at a dealer's has spent a number of arduous days of travel on a van or truck and may have picked up shipping fever. If he's at all high strung, this will probably make him nervous and affect his appetite adversely. Or, he might have just come through a rough winter at a stable where the owner was cutting corners on feed. In either case, a few months of good care and feeding should fix him up. It's always wise to ask what a horse's recent history has been. Naturally, such a horse should be checked by a vet for serious problems before you buy him.

A horse in superficially poor condition can be had for a lot less than he is worth in good flesh. I once took a prospective buyer to look at a lovely five-year-old Anglo-Arab gelding with obvious hunting potential. The horse suited the family to a T in every respect—except for his superficial appearance. We went to the dealer's in early March, a few days after the horse had arrived from the West. Before making the trip, he had been through a long winter in the field, his coat was long and dirty, and he was a little thin; but his conformation and way of going were superlative. Best of all, the price was only five hundred dollars.

Nonetheless, I was unable to persuade the family to look beyond the dirt and weight to what the horse could be in a few months' time. Instead, they settled, at the same price, for a half-bred of inferior quality, sleek and glistening with fat. She would never at her peak equal the potential of the gelding. The dealer kept the Anglo-Arab for a month while he shed his coat out, fattened him up, and sold him for $850 to a grateful couple from Virginia hunt country.

Tattooing

Although tattooing is used on the racetrack as a means of identification, it doesn't necessarily mean a horse has been *raced,* nor is it an absolutely foolproof I.D. The acid in horses' mouths can change or obscure numbers over a period of time. Because of this, the New York Racing Association prefers to use chestnuts (not a color here but an anatomical feature)—sometimes referred to as "night eyes" for identification. Like human fingerprints, chestnuts have a unique and unalterable pattern.

Tattooing is often used in conjunction with other visual references, like markings and chestnuts. It's used by a number of organizations, including the American Quarter Horse Association. The process isn't painful. These markings, in the form of letters and numbers, are made with a dye-filled needle just under the surface of the upper lip.

Doctor's Orders

Before buying a horse, make sure he's had the required shots and tests:

- A two-part flu shot to protect against rhinopneumonitis, with shots given six weeks apart.
- A current tetanus shot.
- A negative Coggins test proving that the horse is not infected with or carrying an incurable swamp fever. (In 1972, Coggins tests were required by every state. Since then the test has been the subject of considerable controversy and at this writing is no longer required in a few states. Check with your agent or vet to see if it's required in your area.)

Whether or not a prolonged trial period is granted, any seller should welcome a full examination, including X rays, by a vet of your choosing. You, of course, will foot the bill. The person from whom you're buying should provide you with the vet's certificates attesting that the horse has had all the necessary shots and tests. Also, you should receive a statement confirming the animal's soundness.

Vetting a horse out is always important—particularly if you're buying from a friend or acquaintance and wish to keep him a friend. If anything is wrong, you'll find out immediately and you won't be led to suspect he tried to put something over on you.

Taking a Horse on Trial

For obvious reasons, many sellers are loath to let their horses go home with prospective buyers for trial periods. It's a risk, which increases in proportion to the expense of the horse (unless you have the wherewithal to insure your horse with Lloyds of London), and the courtesy should be appreciated when granted. When an owner allows it, a week should be enough to determine a horse's merits.

Should you get the opportunity to try out a horse for a prolonged period or to take him hunting, be exceptionally careful. Cool him out with extra care after each ride. Fit him with brushing or galloping boots (see page 154) when riding, and be hesitant about turning him out in a pasture situation where the regulars might give him trouble.

Temperament

Your horse's temperament will be a major factor in your future together, and you should start analyzing it as soon as he steps out of the stall. Is he alert and quiet? Or is he playful, nervous, or suspicious? While it's not unusual for a horse to start at a strange object, if he reacts this way to something he sees every day, I'd suspect that he's a **spook**—a nervous, flighty, unreliable mount.

A horse with a nice disposition will be inclined to obey you when frightened, even though his natural instinct is to run away. A horse with a bad disposition will go ahead and run away, which obviously is dangerous.

Such horses are as likely to harm themselves as their riders and frustrate everyone in their company. Spooks should be restricted to advanced riders, who will be able to anticipate problems and handle them.

The basic makeup of a horse's disposition is hereditary and can't be changed by environment. With purebreds, the candidate's pedigree may reveal insights into his personality. Many purebreds are noted for their good or bad dispositions. Some have reputations for being particularly difficult—the Fair Play and Blenheim Thoroughbred lines, for example.

When buying a registered purebred, examine the papers before the sale is concluded, making sure they carry the official seal or the name of the studbook they're registered in. Papers should show the date of birth, and the horse's age—it should be verified by the vet—should correspond to the date on the papers. Color and markings should match exactly. Should the owner or agent tell you that the papers are lost, you can write the registry to validate them before you buy—assuming that the price is based on registration. Be cautious about taking anyone's word about registry. The papers might not exist, or they may have been withheld at the request of an owner or of a trainer at the track. In the case of a Thoroughbred racehorse, the owner might not have considered him racing-sound and withheld the papers to protect him against misuse. Or the trainer might have withheld them against the owner for nonpayment of bills. Sometimes the track itself withholds the papers for infringement of rules.

Of course the papers might really be lost, in which case you should send in the official registered name of the horse to the registry in question, along with a written affidavit from the person who last had the papers, attesting to their loss. The validation fee is usually five dollars.

In most cases, these problems won't arise. If they do, the time involved in checking out your prospective horse is worth it. Despite the red tape—and the personality quirks you may encounter in some blood lines—to own a registered purebred is a great pleasure.

3

picking
a purebred

Some fifty million years and four geological epochs before man came on the earthly scene, the horse's evolution began. His most ancient fossilized ancestor is the tiny four-toed Eohippus, a creature eleven inches tall with paws like a dog. Eohippus had a number of pint-sized successors with equally intriguing names (like the Protohippus, Meso-hippus, and Merychippus). Each of them grew a few inches and shed toes with the advancing epochs until the advent of the Pleistocene and the development of the fully hoofed Equus caballus.

Prehistoric man wasn't interested in horses, except as an occasional meal. And so, as Homo sapiens lumbered through the ages of stone and iron, the horse's natural development continued. Equi roamed

Equus Caballus vs. Eohippus

untamed through prehistory, forced to adapt to the environments around them or perish.

By the time man began thinking of domesticating the horse (about five thousand years ago, according to relics found in Southeast Asia), there already existed a great variation in the species, developed in response to different climates, terrain, and available food supplies.

For instance, the long head of the Iceland pony, with its long, large nostrils, evolved in response to the chill air of his native Norway. His large jaw was necessary to house the teeth so essential to chew the tough grasses of his homeland, and his short, stocky body made possible a minimum of food for survival. Because of all the climbing this pony does, he needs more weight in the forehand—the reason for the short, thick neck. His heavy mane and forelock developed as protection against the chill Norwegian wind, while hard hoofs were a necessity on the rocky terrain. And the pony's hardiness, high intelligence, and keen eyesight enabled him to cope with the harsh world he lived in, where only the fittest survived.

Icelandic Pony

The Arabian developed in a very different world. Survival in the hot, arid climate, amid warring tribes, depended on swiftness and the ability to exist with a minimum of food and water. Since these horses usually shared the tents with their nomadic owners, geniality was at a premium. The Arabians that survive all have remarkably good dispositions.

Modern horse breeds should thus be thought of as a combination of social and natural selection. In ancient times horse breeders couldn't import their stock. They had to depend on the animals they found around them. Working through selective breeding, they tried to bring out the best of the naturally developed characteristics.

Most breeds were developed for a specific reason. Consequently some are more suited than others to particular types of work.

Many of the earliest horses were used in war—from the sands of Arabia to the steppes of Mongolia. Speed was vital, and horses were selectively bred for it. Weight-carrying ability was important, and despite the Arab's relatively small size, his short back is adapted to carrying heavy loads. Many purebred Arabs have one less vertebra than other breeds.

By the Middle Ages, when knights fitted themselves out in hundreds of pounds of armor, larger horses were needed to carry their immense weight and to move with some agility.

Shire

The Shire was developed in England as a war-horse, after Henry VIII arbitrarily decreed that all horses under five feet (fifteen hands) had to be destroyed. Standing an average eighteen hands high (six feet) and weighing as much as twenty-two hundred pounds, Shires are still the largest draft horses in the world. The French developed the Percheron for the same bellicose purpose, while the Flemish horse became the Netherlands's answer to armor.

Later, as agricultural methods became more advanced and gunpowder replaced lances, war-horses became lighter. The larger horses that remained were used to pull plows. Some large breeds, like the Belgian, were developed solely for farming. Belgians are still in great use today (much to the distress of those Belgians who would like to see their country's farms modernized). One of every three Belgians owns a draft horse. And the land for growing food for these animals is almost as valued as land reserved for human benefit.

In the United States, horses played an important historical role as a working animal. The work they did varied widely—from the ponies who toiled their entire lives in the coal mines to the huge draft farm animals and everyday buggy horses used for transportation.

The driving horse, almost forgotten today, was the center of the horse market for centuries. Breeds like the Cleveland Bay, developed in Cleveland (England), and the Hackney were bred solely for driving. The Bay is since extinct, while the high-stepping Hackney has survived primarily as a show animal. But the best blood of both horses has been passed on selectively to other breeds.

THE ARABIAN

By retracing its history, through drawings and paintings, historians have established that the Arabian is the world's oldest breed possessing a definite name and registry. Its influence can be seen in almost every light-horse breed, all at one time or another crossed with Arabians to improve the strain. Thoroughbreds, Standardbreds, Hackneys, and Morgans can be traced directly to an Arab stud.

Bred carefully for extreme endurance, sound wind, strong legs, speed, and the ability to exist in heat and cold on a minimum of food, the Arabian is famous for its docility and good nature, developed over years of close association with man. Bedouins are fabled to have valued their horses more than their wives.

Because the walk and gallop were the most useful gaits on the desert, the trot wasn't really developed until the Arabian was exported to England, where the breed became the foundation of the racing Thoroughbred.

The strict breeding standards leading to the Arabian we know today were set by the Bedouins, who guarded the animal's purity fanatically. For centuries, a mare was considered tainted if she was bred to anything but an Arabian stud, and many good horses were sold incredibly cheaply abroad for this fatuous reason.

The ideal Arabian has a small head with a straight or preferably slightly concave (dished) profile, a small muzzle, large nostrils, and large round dark eyes with a short distance between the eye and the muzzle. Jowls are deep and ears small, thin, and well shaped. The long, arched, smoothly muscled neck is set high on the withers. He has a short back, level croup, and well-sprung ribs set off by clean legs with strong tendons. His tail is carried naturally high and "gaily," and he averages 14.1 to 15.1 hands. His skin is dark and his coat is fine. Arabians are found in all the solid colors. Black, rose-gray, and flaxen are less common colors peculiar to the breed.

Several types of Arabians have developed over the centuries, some preferred more by breeders than by others. The Pyramid Line refers to those Arabians of pure Egyptian blood. Other major types are the Polish Arab and the English Arab. The Polish type has been bred for performance, and his size, substance, and soundness attest to this. He lacks the classic beauty of the Egyptian Arab and is less short and stocky than the English Arab.

The Arab is increasingly popular in the United States. Because of his extreme intelligence, he is naturally suited for working cattle, while his even disposition and smooth gaits make him an ideal pleasure horse. Because of his grace the Arab excels at jumping and dressage; crossed with a Thoroughbred, resulting in an Anglo-Arab, he makes an excellent hunter. In the United States, the Arabian is the leading breed in all endurance and competitive trail rides.

If you're buying an Arabian with intent to breed it, look carefully into its records for any signs of foal deaths in the line. Some 2.5 percent of Arabian foals die before the age of five months because of a little-understood genetic disease called CID (combined immunodeficiency), in which insufficient antibodies are developed to combat infection. Two

CID positive parents will always produce a foal with this disease. At present, the only way positive parents can be detected, unfortunately, is after a foal has died of the disease. Research on CID is now being conducted at the University of Washington using a herd of horses that have all tested out as carriers of the disease.

THE THOROUGHBRED

The Thoroughbred was developed in England in the early seventeenth century for racing. The breed was founded on three imported Arabian sires: the Byerly Turk (1689); the Darley Arab (1706); and the Godolphin Barb (1724). These three studs are believed to have been bred to Oriental and English mares, with the aim of producing the racing Thoroughbred. Speed and endurance were the Thoroughbred's main characteristics, and the most famous racehorses—like the legendary Eclipse (1764)—can be traced directly to one of the founding lines. Eclipse derives from the Darley Arab.

Breeding is extremely important to Thoroughbred enthusiasts, who can quote pedigrees by the page. They may not know how to ride, but they can usually pick good bloodlines.

A Thoroughbred with good ancestry can command incredible prices at auction. The Minstrel was bought by a syndicate for $9 million—the highest price ever paid for a horse. This surpassed the $5.5 million record set previously by Nijinsky II. Promising yearlings also bring high fees. A colt by Secretariat out of Charming Alibi brought the highest price in history: $1.5 million, at a Keeneland sale.

Stud fees can be equally impressive. A good stud normally breeds with thirty mares a year at fifteen thousand dollars each. Often fertility continues strong past the twentieth year. Man o' War stood through twenty-five, and Bull Lea was bred until nearly thirty.

Thoroughbreds were imported to the colonies around 1730, when mile racing was starting to rival quarter-mile racing as a popular sport. The first noted stallion to come into the country was Diomed, sire of the first all-American Thoroughbred stud, Sir Archie.

Descendants of English Thoroughbreds were the foundation sires of several other American breeds. Messenger founded the Standardbred; Lexington was the foundation sire of the American saddle bred; while Janus and Sir Archie were the fathers of the quarter horse.

The Thoroughbred is built for speed and excels in racing on the flat or over fences. Because of his build, he's well adapted for jumping and excels as a show hunter and jumper. But the generations of inbreeding and the intense training imposed on this breed have made it unusually high strung and hot. One answer was to crossbreed with

Thoroughbreds range from fifteen to seventeen hands. The body is streamlined, with long flat muscles, the head wide between the ears, and the profile is either straight or dished, with nostrils capable of great expansion during exertion. Thoroughbreds have long, slender necks, withers are usually pronounced, with a good slope to the shoulder and considerable depth in the girth. The breed is quite long from hip to hock, with a generous gaskin. Legs are straight, with short, dense cannons, long forearms, and well-sloped, long pasterns—all built for speed. Colors are usually solid, predominantly chestnuts, bays, blacks, browns, and, occasionally, gray.

horses of steadier temperament to produce good hunters and junior, or a child's, horses. Anglo-Arabs make excellent hunters, and Thoroughbreds crossed with ponies make elegant junior horses.

Before 1800 it was customary to race mature horses over long distances carrying top weight. Today, because of the expense of training, two-year-olds are raced over short distances for an entire season with weight handicaps. The strain this puts on the immature animals' feet and legs is so severe that they are often crippled for life after one or two seasons.

THE QUARTER HORSE

Like the mustang, this is an all-American breed. Its origins can be traced to the Chickasaw Indian ponies of Carolina, Virginia, and Tennessee. All were noted for speed and stamina. To improve these characteristics, the colonists crossed the ponies with imported horses of English ancestry and began to develop the quarter horse into a racing breed. By 1690, matched races for sizable purses were being held on the main streets of dozens of eastern communities, and special quarter-mile tracks were hacked out of the wilderness. As this type of racing gained in popularity, the horses that excelled at it were given the name they still bear.

The Thoroughbred stallion Janus, foaled in 1750, was responsible for passing on many of the traits associated with the best quarter horses today. Descended from an English Thoroughbred imported to the United States, Janus was at the time considered something of a freak

The head of the quarter horse is short and wide and carried low, with small alert ear and a short, square muzzle. Because quarter horses work with the head low, there is a distinct space between the large jawbones to allow for unrestricted breathing. The neck is of medium length, with a slight arch, blending into deep-sloping shoulders. The chest is deep and broad, with large girth and wide-set forelegs. The breed's powerfully muscled forearms taper to the knee. Joints are smooth, cannons short, and pasterns are of medium length. The feet are strong and round with a well-opened heel. The back is short, close coupled, and very full with large muscles over the loins and well-sprung ribs.

because of his unusual conformation. His appearance led to his being formally disowned by the Thoroughbred register. But as the quarter horse gained in popularity, the Thoroughbred people relented and deigned to take credit for its development. In the decades after Janus, Thoroughbred blood passed selectively into the quarter horse, refining and improving it.

Quarter horses gradually moved west with the population, where they continued to be used for working cattle during the day and as racehorses in the evenings. The best racers were usually put to stud to improve the breed.

Among the outstanding western sires were Copperbottom (1832), who is credited with passing along a keen cow sense to the breed, and Steel Dust (1849). Both are associated with Texas where most of their get, or offspring, were foaled. Steel Dust, noted for his extreme speed, was such a famous sire that for years Western quarter horses were called Steel-Dusters.

The breed was officially established in 1941, with a quarter-horse registry. Today quarter horses are known for their outstanding ability, speed, disposition, and intelligence, traits that make them particularly well suited to working cattle. Apart from racing, they make excellent polo ponies. And their calm nature makes them particularly suited to pleasure riding.

The great popularity of quarter-horse racing, which now commands some of the highest purses in the country, has led to the infusion of more Thoroughbred blood into the breed, changing the heavy, blocky conformation of the old-type quarter horse into a leggier, more streamlined animal that averages 15.2 hands.

Because of the Thoroughbred influence, quarter horses are becoming increasingly popular as hunters and jumpers, particularly in the East, and as junior equitation mounts. They also make excellent eventing mounts. Some are even making a hit in the dressage arena. And the renewed interest in driving has put many quarter horses into harness, where their tractable disposition makes them excellent carriage horses.

THE AMERICAN SADDLE BRED

This breed originally was called the Kentucky saddle bred. The name was changed officially (1899) when seventeen foundation sires were selected. In 1908, all but the stallion Denmark (foaled in 1839) were eliminated from the registry, thus giving this horse the credit for the entire breed. Fifty-five percent of the entries in the first volume of the Saddle Horse Registry can be traced directly back to him. Most of the best show horses can be traced to Denmark, as well as to another Thoroughbred, Chief.

The saddle bred has a tapered head, with large wide-set eyes, a fine muzzle, and small, slender ears. The long, slender neck is well arched and the throatlatch fine. Shoulders are well muscled and chest wide, the back short and straight and the barrel rounded, with a good, deep girth. The croup is set nearly horizontal, probably the straightest of any breed except the Arab. The tail is naturally high, and the legs are fine and shapely with long, springy pasterns.

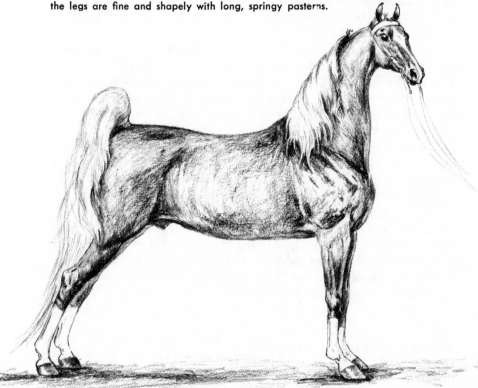

The saddle bred evolved from a potpourri of horses. Its ancestors include the Narragansett pacer, Canadian pacer, assorted Dutch horses, and the English ambler—many no longer in existence. Later on, Morgan and Standardbred blood were added to the blend.

From the beginning, the ambling, lateral gait was cultivated. Originally the saddle-bred horse was an all-purpose mount, strong and hardy as a working or driving animal and comfortable to ride. Ultimately, however, with the rise of the auto, the breed became primarily a show horse.

Although the easy gaits make saddle breds an extraordinarily comfortable pleasure horse, the majority today are shown at either three or five gaits. To accentuate the breed's flashy, high-stepping stride, they are subjected to a regimen more appropriate to a hothouse flower than a horse.

The hoofs are allowed to grow very long—as much as eight inches —and the shoes often weigh as much as twenty-five ounces each to encourage the high step and long, reaching stride. To keep the tail high for shows, the depressor muscles at the base of the tail are cut, and a tail set is used. Sometimes switches or falls are added for an extra flourish. The tail operation is painful, however, and it has been outlawed in many states.

Saddle breds can be shown in three different ways. The three-gaited types wear a roached mane with the top of the tail shaved clean and set, and the bottom pulled; five-gaited types are shown with a full mane and tail, a ribbon braided into both the forelock and the first section of mane, situated at the poll; a fine saddle-bred harness horse pulls a four-wheel cart, and also wears a full mane and tail.

The three-gaited saddle horse (often called a walk-trot horse) is shown at a **walk,** a **trot,** and a **canter,** all flourished with his high-stepping action. A five-gaited horse includes the above plus two additional gaits: the **slow gait,** a comfortable stepping pace; and the **rack** or single-foot, a very fast four-beat gait.

Kept in their natural state (with toes and tails allowed to develop normally), these horses are beautiful and can be used even as hunters. It's unfortunate that many saddle breds spend their entire lives stabled, unable to go barefoot or into the pasture for even a few days because they may chip their artificially long toes.

THE TENNESSEE WALKER

Like the saddle bred, this horse was developed for utility—as a combination riding and light harness horse that could be used occasionally for farm work. One of its natural gaits is the extremely comfortable **running walk.** Tennessee Walkers were often referred to as Plantation Walkers because their owners rode them between rows of crops to oversee their fields. The comfortable gait was prized and refined until the breed developed a natural tendency toward it. Although it is called the "slow" gait, some walkers can reach sixteen miles an hour at a running walk. But the most comfortable pace for the horse is around six miles an hour.

The Walker originated in the middle of his home state around 1850. Its background can be traced to the Thoroughbred, Standardbred, Morgan, and American saddle bred.

Walkers have also become primarily show horses. The three gaits they are famous for are the flat-footed walk, the running walk, and an easy, gliding canter. All the gaits are extremely comfortable.

The Tennessee Walker is a coarser, heavier horse than the saddle bred. It should have a balanced conformation, with clean, hard legs. Walkers come in a variety of colors, and it's not uncommon to see white markings on their faces and legs. They average 15.2 hands and weigh one thousand to twelve hundred pounds. The breed is generally shown with a full mane and tail, the latter broken and set. It is traditional to braid the top of the mane and forelock with three strands of ribbon.

THE STANDARDBRED

The best Standardbred trotters in the United States can all be traced to Messenger, a gray Thoroughbred stallion imported from England in 1788. **Trotting** is a natural two-beat gait in which the diagonal legs move in unison. Messenger was a successful racehorse and prepotent sire with an unusual ability to trot extremely fast. A now-extinct English breed called the Norfolk Trotter can also be traced to Messenger.

But the name most commonly identified with the breed is Hambletonian (foaled in 1849), who sired more than forty horses able to trot or pace a mile in better than two minutes thirty seconds; no less than 661 of his get have given record performances in their day. Some trotters have bloodlines indicating more than forty crosses of Hambletonian stock, so the breed could almost be called Hambletonian. One of the most famous trotting races, held in Goshen, New York, is named after the famous sire.

The Standardbred has a more angular, rugged build than the Thoroughbred, and he is closer to the ground. His long body and forearms are adapted to the long, flat stride needed for racing. The head is long and bony, and some have Roman noses.

Before the Civil War, Standardbreds were raced under saddle at a trot. Later, they pulled heavy sulkies with high wheels. Finally, around the end of the last century, the bicycle-wheeled sulky was introduced, and in 1889 a horse named Dutchman became the first Standardbred to win a mile race in light harness.

The first horse to trot a mile in under three minutes was a gelding named Yankee, who set a record of 2:59 at the Harlem racetrack in 1806. Today all Standardbred racehorses must be able to make a mile in 2:33 or better even to qualify.

Perhaps the greatest harness champion of all time was Dan Patch, who held the trotting record for thirty-three years—from 1905 to 1938 —performing more miles under two minutes than any horse since. After he broke the two-minute barrier, winners have had to do much better than that. The record against the clock for a Standardbred is one minute, fifty-four and four-fifths seconds, held by Nevele Pride (recently tied by Dayan). The record for the fastest clocked **pacing** mile (a pacer's front and hind legs on the same side move forward simultaneously) is held by Bret Hanover. Both horses also hold the record in competition, although the competing times are somewhat slower.

Because they were originally used as driving horses, the Standard-bred disposition is generally steady and tractable. The breed is often crossed with the Thoroughbreds, which results in good hunters. But because of their highly developed trot, pure Standardbreds are not comfortable to ride. A sorry result of their rough gait is that many of these fine animals are shipped to the slaughterhouse after their useful-ness on the track is exhausted.

THE MORGAN

The Morgan's genealogy is controversial, fans of the quarter horse recently claiming that a member of that breed was the founding Morgan

The Morgan profile is straight, with wide-set eyes, powerful jaws ending in a blunt muzzle, and short ears. The medium-sized neck is heavily muscled and crested, with the head carried high. The back is fairly short and powerfully coupled at the hips. The croup slopes slightly, and the shoulders are built up into the withers. The barrel is well rounded, set off by muscular thighs and gaskins. And the tail is set low but carried well. There is a great deal of width in the chest. The legs have considerable bone, with considerable length from elbow to knee and stifle to hock. Usually Morgans have a thick mane and tail. Their general appearance is powerful and stylish.

sire. This has caused a lot of anguish among Morgan people, who claim that it's actually the other way around—that a Morgan was founding sire for the quarter horse. Arguments about this controversy enliven the editorial and letters-to-the-editors columns of numerous horse publications.

While the ancestry of the foundation sire is somewhat uncertain, his identity is not. He was a small, dark, bay horse, a scant fourteen hands, foaled either in Massachusetts or Vermont around 1790. His most famous owner was Justin Morgan, who used him as a pleasure mount and workhorse as well as loaning him out for riding, hauling logs, and trotting races. Morgan's horse became legendary for his high intelligence and speed at the trot. After Morgan died, the little stallion changed hands many times and finally died of neglect. Whereas he had stood at stud, under the name of Figure (now known by his owner's name of Justin Morgan) for as little as two dollars, his prepotency was felt all over the East, where his get emulated his speed, stamina, and disposition. Some of the descendants were such outstanding trotters that their blood was used to improve the Standardbred line. They are also believed to have influenced the development of the saddle bred and the Tennessee Walker.

Throughout the last century, it was the Morgan that pulled the buggy to church on Sunday, and during the rest of the week was ridden, hauled logs, and raced.

Perhaps Morgans achieved their greatest fame as a cavalry remount horse. The entire Vermont cavalry, some eleven hundred, was composed of matched Morgans. General Phil Sheridan's favorite mount Rienzi was a Morgan; so was Stonewall Jackson's chestnut gelding Little Sorrel.

Morgans were used extensively in the Mexican War and the Civil War. The H Company of the 5th New York Cavalry, which rode only handpicked bay Morgans, met so much hardship in Civil War battles that their horses often remained saddled and without rations for three or four days at a time. Many were destroyed by their owners to keep them from falling into enemy hands. Of the H Company's 108 horses that went into battle, seven survived. Morgans were also used extensively during the Indian wars as cavalry mounts.

The invention of the auto led to a rift among Morgan fans. A sizable group felt that to keep up, the breed should be "upgraded," made into a more serviceable saddle horse by crossbreeding with saddle breds, which end they pursued. Opponents worked to keep the line free of five-gaited blood, and introduced as sires army remount Morgan stallions, several of which carried Thoroughbred blood. This faction of Morganites was interested in improving the existing breed, not changing it radically with saddle-horse blood. The argument, like that between Morgan and quarter-horse lovers, has became very spirited at times.

The division between the two Morgan types is pronounced. Park-type Morgans developed the high, reaching step of their saddle-bred relative and are shown with heavy shoes and five-inch toes. The traditional Morgan in many parts of the country is still used as the all-around breed it originally was intended for. Morgans make outstanding cow horses, hunters, jumpers, and workers, as well as good endurance and driving horses. For an easy-tempered family horse out on the trail, such a Morgan can't be surpassed.

THE MUSTANG

The history of this truly American horse begins with the descendants of horses brought to Mexico by Cortes (later to the southwestern states by Coronado). The mustang's distant ancestors were Arabs and Barbs, and possibly Andalusians.

By the end of the fifteenth century, there were numerous herds of horses in the West belonging to wealthy Spaniards. The Indians, who realized their potential, began stealing them and, in a short time, became highly accomplished horsemen. Riding without saddles and bridles, they became expert at controlling their horses by seat and leg pressure alone—leaving arms free for bows and arrows. The horses that escaped from the Indians were the ancestors of the wild mustang herds.

These horses remained unchanged in appearance from their Spanish ancestry until the arrival of the pioneers, who brought their draft horses with them. Cold-blooded stallions are thought to have mingled with mustang mares, and the breed gradually degenerated.

Excepting a few tribes, the Indians were indifferent to horse care and breeding; too many horses were available. Meanwhile, the wranglers, looking for mounts, were cutting the best horses out of the wild herds. One way was by "creasing" the horse with a bullet across the withers to bring him down—which killed a lot of good horses. Often, to bring in a herd more easily, cowboys would kill the lead stallion, further weakening the breed.

The Indians often selected mustangs in colors that aided camouflage, depending on season and terrain. Duns were ridden in the fall, white horses in the snow, and blue roans in the sage grass. Pintos and grays were smeared with paint to blend with just about anything.

An unusual Indian color was medicine hat (or warbonnet), consid-

Because of generations in which the best horses were destroyed or crossed with other less hardy or more cold-blooded breeds, mustangs can no longer be considered beautiful or as rugged as they once were. Still, only the hardiest have survived, and like the Arab the breed has remarkable endurance and an ability to live on the little land they have. Mustangs are small horses, not generally much over 14.2 hands, and they weigh about seven to eight hundred pounds. The most common colors are dun, roan, and grullo (pronounced gru-yo). They are tough and wiry, with sinewy muscles and hard hoofs that enable them to be ridden without shoes.

ered extremely lucky by Indians. Horses possessed of the coveted white coat with roan freckles scattered around the ears, neck, chest, and other parts of the body were considered invulnerable in battle. There are now fewer than seven thousand of these wild horses, which in 1900 exceeded two million. Until recently, in most states, no laws protected them. Planes ran them to exhaustion, after which the mustangs were herded into trucks, and slaughtered for dog food.

Those that have survived still make excellent cow ponies and are particularly outstanding as endurance horses. A Spanish mustang was a recent winner of the famed Tevis Cup, the toughest endurance ride in the country, where contestants ride from Lake Tahoe to Auburn, California—a distance of 100 miles in one day. Members of the breed have even been used successfully as hunters and jumpers.

Mustangs still run in Oregon, California, Nevada (with a national mustang refuge at Caliente), Arizona, Utah (with two small private refuges), Idaho, Wyoming (where most of the mustangs are still wild), and Montana (with one refuge). A few of the wild horses may be in Colorado and New Mexico.

The National Mustang Association is located in Caliente, Nevada. A registry of the Spanish mustang was opened in 1957 to keep track of pedigrees. Recently at a congressional hearing on the fate of the mustangs, children from all over the United States testified as part of a "children's crusade" to save the wild horses. In 1971, Congress finally passed a law giving the mustang national sanctuary against hunters. In the same year, an organization was formed to conduct its own surveillance of infractions. WHOA (Wild Horse Organized Assistance) adopts wild colts and places them with families throughout the United States who have the proper facilities for their care.

According to the Department of the Interior's Bureau of Land Management, an estimated fifty thousand wild horses now live in the Western United States, their numbers increasing by eight thousand to ten thousand animals a year. The BLM has also started its own horse adoption program, placing an average of two hundred mustangs a year in foster homes. The cost of transporting the animals is borne by the new owners. Anyone interested in becoming the foster parent of a mustang should write the Bureau of Land Management, U.S. Department of the Interior, Washington, D.C.

THE COLOR BREEDS

The Appaloosa

The name comes from a breed developed by the Nez Percé Indians in the Palouse region of central Idaho and eastern Washington. Horses bred there were referred to by the name of the region, which was gradually distorted to its present form. The Nez Percé raced the breed and used them for hunting; consequently they were bred for speed and endurance. This tribe was the first to practice selective breeding.

The speed of these Indian horses became legendary, and many settlers brought their horses west just to race against them. (The visitors usually lost.)

During the Indian wars, the U.S. Cavalry chased the peace-loving

With the revival of the Appaloosa, four types are recognized. Registered Appaloosas can be any of the four or mixed. The *Blanket Appaloosa* has a white area on the rump, dotted with elongated dark spots slightly larger than a fifty-cent piece. The *Leopard Appaloosa* is all white, with dark spots, while a type called the *Snowflake* is dark with splashes of white. *Marbleized Appaloosas* can be dark with light spots or vice versa. Roans seem to predominate. The skin of true Appaloosas should be parti-colored around the nose, lips, and genital area, and their hoofs should be striped.

Nez Percé toward the Canadian border, where the entire original breed was destroyed. The tribe, under the impression it had reached Canadian sanctuary, set up camp a few miles from the border on the United States side. They were met by the cavalry and slaughtered with their horses.

Appaloosas are said to stem from the Moroccan Barb and the Spanish Andalusian, and historians believe that the Chinese developed an identical color breed some three thousand years ago; pictures of it can be seen in ancient Oriental paintings.

Today Appaloosas are generally used as western utility and pleasure horses. They make good parade and rodeo mounts and are becoming increasingly popular with English riders for hunting and show. Registered Appaloosas cannot be less than fourteen hands. (For smaller specimens there is a new Appaloosa pony club.) To improve conformation, the breed is being crossed with Thoroughbreds.

Albinos

There is no recognized breed of pure albinos. Although they are pink

skinned, albinos must have large blue or dark eyes, and there are four different categories of hair color under which they can be registered, ranging from pure white to cream. For this reason the breed is often referred to as the dominant white horse, rather than albino.

The founding sire was Old King, foaled in 1906, and an albino registry was established in 1937. The national recording club keeps records of any solid-color offspring of albinos because they carry the gene and could produce an albino foal.

Albinos are popular as parade and circus mounts. And there is no reason why they can't be used for western or English pleasure or show —if you don't mind keeping them clean.

Pintos

These are the famous painted ponies of the West, prized by the Plains Indians for their brilliant colors, which were often accented with dye.

The mutations in pigment that cause the pinto's odd coloration can be traced to ancient times. Egyptian, Persian, and Chinese artists recorded pictures of pinto horses thirty-four hundred years ago.

Pintos may be any breed except Draft horse or Appaloosa. A paint horse on the other hand must have a sire or dam that is a registered thoroughbred, quarter horse, or paint to be registered in the American Paint Horse Association.

These are the two patterns of coloring: the Overo appears a solid color with white markings and the majority of the face white with blue, wall, or watch eyes. The Tobiano appears white with patches of color, usually a solid colored head with a mixed colored tail.

The Palomino

The breed's ancestry is believed to be Spanish. According to regulations, the color should be that of a newly minted U.S. gold coin, a difficult comparison to visualize because gold coins are no longer minted. The mane and tail are white, with no more than 15 percent dark hair allowed. And there can be no dark or light patches of hair on the dorsal area, no zebra stripes, and no white markings anywhere except on the face and legs. The eyes should be black, brown, or hazel.

Most registered palominos are quarter horses, with half-Arabs running second. The color is found in a few other breeds.

The Palomino Horse Breeders' Association requires that horses in its registry must also be listed with another breed registry—like the Quarter Horse Association, Arab, American saddle bred, Jockey Club, Tennessee Walker, or Standardbred, or else that the sire or dam be

registered with the PHBA. The association also allows only dark-skinned horses in its registry, and albino parents are not allowed in mares and stallions. (Geldings may have an albino parent as long as they meet color and conformation standards.)

Palominos bred with palominos many times produce an offspring of the same color. Sorrels bred with palominos or albinos with chestnuts offer a fifty-fifty chance of getting the desired result.

Buckskins

These horses are still in great demand in the Far West for their fabled resiliency. Buckskins have a legendary reputation for extreme endurance, and many cowboys have always preferred them. In 1962, the American Buckskin registry was opened, making the breed official.

The buckskin registry accepts all horses of good conformation that have no draft ancestry or no pinto or Appaloosa stock in them. Conformation is generally considered more important than color.

Buckskins can be registered with other purebred clubs, and the majority of them are quarter horses. There are three color types. The most common buckskin is a yellow brown, with black mane and tail, preferably with a zebra stripe down the back and zebralike barring on the legs. **Red duns** are reddish brown, with a dark red mane and

tail and dark red eel stripe. A gruella or **mouse dun** is quite rare; these buckskins are lavender or a bluish slate, with black points and a black eel stripe. All buckskins must have black skin and no white spots are allowed.

FOREIGN AND LESSER-KNOWN BREEDS

As air travel has made it easier for breeders and competitors to travel abroad, foreign breeds that were virtually unknown several years ago are turning up in greater numbers at American events. Not too many years ago the *Chronicle of the Horse* listed no Trakehners in its annual stallion issue. But now not only are there many Trakehners but dozens of other imported stallions, including Andalusians, Holsteiners, Hanoverians, Westphalians, and Dutch and Swedish warm-bloods.

German Breeds

German breeds are unique to the area where they originated, generally taking their name from it. They were developed according to the traits valued by the people of that region.

The Hanoverian (or Hannoverana). Hanover, Germany, where George II founded the state stud in 1735, is still the most important world center for this tall, powerful breed, which has become famous in world show-jumping. The foundation sires were Holsteiner stallions. Subsequently Norman and East Prussian blood were mixed with the breed, with the still-later infusion of English Thoroughbred.

Originally bred as farm horses and armoured mounts, the Hannoverana was modified in the eighteenth century as cavalry horses. The infusion of Thoroughbred blood has resulted in a handsome animal with an energetic trot and smooth, rhythmic canter that makes the breed most desirable as saddle and show horses. Hanoverians are also noted for their hardiness. Their heavier bone and conformation lend these horses well to eventing and dressage. The famous seventeen-hand Hanoverian Warwick Rex managed to negotiate the incredibly difficult course at the 1976 Olympics and win the gold medal for jumping despite a virus infection that left him jaundiced and without his usual form.

The consistently outstanding performance of this breed is a result of a rigorous testing program required of stallions before they are certified to stand at stud. Beginning at three years of age, Hanoverians must undergo an annual aptitude and achievement test, where their performance, appearance, and temperament are rated. Only certified stallions are sent to the official breeding farms or studs.

The Holstein (or Holsteiner). This breed originated in the thirteenth century, developed originally as workhorses and war-horses, pulling plows in peacetime and carrying their heavily armoured feudal lords to battle in time of war. After the Reformation, when lighter horses were needed for the cavalry, the breed was exposed to Oriental, Spanish, and Neopolitan blood. During this era, a stud was founded for the purpose of breeding war-horses, resulting in the typical Holsteiner still seen today—a strong, large-framed horse with powerful gaits and the characteristic Roman nose.

By the sixteenth century, the breed was in great demand and was exported throughout Europe for pleasure and cavalry horses. The high casualty rate of Prussian Army horses in the Napoleonic wars severely decimated the breed, but it was subsequently rejuvenated with the infusion of English Thoroughbred blood. By the end of World War II, Holsteiners had become much sought after as jumping and show horses. The world-famous German jumper Meteor was a Holsteiner; so was Tora, the 1936 Olympic gold medal winner in jumping.

As more Thoroughbred blood has passed into the breed, Holsteiners have become lighter, faster, and sportier looking. But they remain basically massive and muscular, with deep chest, strong limbs, and excellent character and temperament. Despite their size, they can be extraordinarily graceful, and they excel as dressage horses.

The Trakehner. In 1944, as the Russian advance threatened the Trakehner stud in East Prussia, hurried plans were made to evacuate the horses to the coast—an incredible 900-mile journey across snow and thawing ocean ice, through gunfire and bombing raids. Of fifty thousand horses, only one thousand broodmares lived to see the Baltic Sea. The official evacuation order was given in October of 1944 and the Prussians were given only three hours to organize the exodus. Because of Hitler's victory-or-death policy, no plans had been made to evacuate any of the population, let alone the horses. Because of the stress of the journey, most foals were born dead; and most of those who were tied beside their mothers to the field wagons couldn't survive the two-and-a-half-month ordeal. Already known for its endurance, the Trakehner breed was subsequently based almost exclusively on that hardy herd of mares who made it to the sea. Many countries of the world now have Trakehner studs, and the breed excels in all types of riding sports, in the harness, and on the farm.

Before being approved as studs and broodmares, Trakehners undergo a rigorous period of schooling and testing. At two-and-a-half years, stallions are expected to complete a timed three-day cross-country test, which is designed to show the prospect's potentialities, health, way of moving, and energy level. Testing of the mares is different because they are used for work, not sport. Mares are worked in the field while in foal and, later, with the foals by their side. Trakehners are currently in great demand, as they were before World War II when 30,000 were exported annually.

The infusion of Arab and Thoroughbred blood into the breed and over two hundred years of breeding have resulted in an all-round riding and driving horse, solidly built, with a medium-length back, medium bone structure, and round, full ribs. The head is noble and carried with style. Temperament and conformation are equally stressed in stallion selection. They are elegant movers, noted for their floating trot, and they are sought after in this country because they are excellent three-day and dressage prospects. Anglo Trakehners are used for the same purposes.

Other Foreign Breeds and Crossbreeds

The Andalusian. One of the oldest-known breeds in the world, the Andalusian dates from the eighth century during the period when the Moors invaded southern Spain. Finding that their small Barb horses were no match in battle against the nimble, Spanish horses, they crossed the desert breed with the lighter, more agile horses of the Iberian Peninsula. By the time the Moors were driven from Spain at the end of the fifteenth century, the Andalusian had been developed and perfected.

Andalusians first arrived in North America with the Spanish who accompanied Columbus on his voyage of discovery. Prized for its beauty, docility, and obedience, the Andalusian has influenced light-horse breeds of every country, with studs imported into Austria and Italy, where they were used to create special breeds like the Lippizan, the Neopolitan, and the Kladruper.

Andalusians stand from 14.2 to 16 hands and weigh from 800 to 1,200 pounds. White, gray, and bay are the most common colors for the breed, although some blacks and a few roans are registered. The only authentic registry for the breed in the United States, Canada, and Mexico is the American Andalusian Association, which registers both purebreds and horses with part Andalusian blood. In South America, the Andalusian Horse Registry of the Americas maintains genealogies based on a complete set of registration books brought to South America by the Spanish conquistadores. These horses are becoming more familiar in this country with the upsweep of interest in dressage.

The Bashkir Curly. How this unusual breed first arrived in the United States is a mystery its registry is still trying to unravel. Several experts on the history of this breed believe they came to North America by way of the Bering Strait, since they were first found running wild in the Northwest.

For centuries, horses with curly coats have been raised by the people of Bashkiria on the southern slopes of Russia's Ural Mountains, providing not only transportation but clothing, meat, and milk for their owners. Bashkirs were kept there in herds, like cattle, with mares yielding up to six gallons of milk a day. Besides yielding cream, butter, and cheese, the milk—when fermented—can be made into an alcoholic beverage called *kumiss.*

Because of their rugged build, stallions and geldings are prized for driving—they can pull the large Russian sleighs (*troikas*) up to seventy-five miles a day through the rugged Russian terrain.

An all-purpose breed for sure, and if its multitudinous uses astonish you, so will some of the unusual characteristics: a thick, curly coat that can take the form of tight ringlets or a crushed velvet effect, sheds completely in the summer, and grows back wavy; short, broad ears thickly lined with curls; and slanted eyes, which increase their range of rear vision. They are gentle and extremely friendly. When excited they move with head held high at a bold trot holding their tail absolutely straight in the air, making these horses easily identifiable in a herd.

The Lippizan. Although these famous dressage horses are identified with the Spanish Riding School, their origins are Austro-Hungarian. The original stud was the royal and imperial court stud of Lippiza, located in the mountainous Karst region, near what is now Trieste. When the Austro-Hungarian Empire was divided, some Lippizans went to Austria, others to Hungary, Yugoslavia, Czechoslovakia, and Romania.

The original breeding stock were nine Andalusian stallions and twenty-four Barb mares imported from Spain. Other breeds were later infused to obtain today's Lippizan, which is divided into six main lines: Conversano, Favory, Siglavy, Neopolitano, Pluto, and Maestoso.

Although born dark, most Lippizans gradually turn gray and then white between their fourth and seventh years. A few, particularly in the Neopolitano line, remain bay or black. Traditionally, one black or bay horse is included in each performance of the Spanish Riding School.

The American breeding of Lippizans has developed only recently, paralleling the rising interest here in dressage.

The Morab. Although Morgans and Arabs were probably crossed as early as 1800, the breed never really caught on until after World War I, when many people began experimenting with this versatile cross as a family pleasure horse and ranch horse. The registry was established in 1973 in Fresno, California, as the American Morab Horse Association.

The characteristics of the two breeds complement each other genetically, fusing into a distinct, versatile horse that incorporates the superior breathing system and tremendous endurance of both Morgan and Arab, along with their intelligence, spirit, flexibility, and easy-keeping qualities. One trait peculiar to the Morab is the strong, powerful hindquarters—a recessive Arabian trait synthesized with a dominant Morgan trait.

Mature Morabs range from 14.3 to 15.2 hands. They inherit their short back and refined beauty from the Arab and their strong, natural way of moving and muscular strength from the Morgan, with that breed's longer croup. Colors inherited from the Morgan side are bay, black, buckskin, chestnut, dun, and palomino, with grays, grullas, and roans drawn from the Arabian side.

PONIES

As horses gained in popularity, the pony population zoomed. Imported ponies come from all over the world, including the Dartmoor breed, the Dales, Fell, and the larger New Forest and Hackney from England. Everyone is familiar with the little Shetland from the Shetland Islands and the Welsh Mountain pony from Wales.

The Highland pony of Scotland is now widely used, and the Connemara pony from Ireland is popular as a children's hunter. Many of these larger ponies can be successfully crossed with Thoroughbreds or Arabians to produce a children's large show pony.

There are dozens of other pony breeds. One of the most unusual is the Pony of the Americas, established in Mason City, Iowa, in 1954. It fills the need for a large western pony for children who are too large for a small pony and not yet ready for a horse. PTAs have flashy col-

Purebred Ponies

Dartmoor

Pony of the Americas

Connemara

Shetland

Highland

Welsh

Hackney

oring that must meet the same requirements as the four Appaloosa types. The breed's foundation sire Black Hand was a white Appaloosa with black, egg-shaped markings on the loins, croup, and back. His dam was a Shetland mare.

The breed is used for racing, pole bending, barrel racing, and as all-around western horses. They are also beginning to show up as jumping and driving horses in English shows. At the moment, conformation varies, but the ideal is somewhere between an Arabian and a quarter horse.

The Halflinger (pony). This small Tyrolian breed, which averages fourteen hands, is heavyset and long-bodied with plenty of bone and a heavy head that is carried close to the ground while climbing. Tyrolians are small, surefooted, and make excellent packhorses, being widely used for that purpose by farmers and foresters. Most Tyrolians are palomino in color. They're raised in the central stud at Piber, Austria.

4
eating like a horse

In Ireland, the general feed is raw potatoes. In Iceland, dried fish is employed as a provender; while during the needy period of the Crimean campaign, the English horses devoured the tails of their stable associates. . . . Why, therefore, are oats preferred as the fittest food for horses? Nature has sent food in abundance and variety. Is man justified, when he opposes nature's obvious intention? When he first imprisons a life and then dooms it to subsist for the period of its being on a monotony of provender . . . ?

—DR. EDWARD MAYHEW, OF ENGLAND'S ROYAL COLLEGE OF VETERINARY SURGEONS, WRITING IN THE LAST CENTURY, WHEN VETS DIDN'T KNOW AS MUCH AS THEY KNOW TODAY

Real horses don't eat like proverbial horses. That is, they don't eat the way your great-uncle Ethan eats when he wades into a fourth helping at Thanksgiving dinner and your aunt says, "Ethan, you're eating like a horse." If a horse ate grain the way Ethan eats candied yams, it would kill him. His stomach isn't big enough to handle large amounts of food at one feeding.

While horses do eat a lot, it's important to remember that in their natural state they eat small amounts of food continually over a long period of time. These eating habits can be summed up in one simple statement: *Horses are grazing animals.*

Even those who have never seen a horse in the flesh know that grazing is one of the things horses do. But few owners bother to ponder the implications of this natural act when it comes to feeding their own horses.

In his wild state, a horse grazes continually, eating a little bit at a time, day and night. Horses have the smallest stomach of all farm animals, and they have a unique digestive system that functions best when it is constantly filled. Their stomachs are one-way organs, which means that they can't burp or vomit. If a horse tried to vomit, he might rupture his stomach—or the fluid could end up in his lungs. The point is that he has no control over the process.

Once you understand how the equine digestive system functions, you'll be less likely to abuse it or confuse it with the much more flexible human digestive system.

The teeth—and the condition they're in—are an essential first step in the digestive process. Horses grasp food with their upper lip, aided by the tongue or the front teeth, depending on the type of food involved. Grain or hay mixes with large quantities of saliva, produced by three large salivary glands that also produce a protein, which helps to break down the starches. The food moves back in the mouth, where the teeth grind it up, down, and sideways. This lateral movement of the teeth gradually wears down the enamel, creating sharp edges on the inside of the lower teeth and the outside of the upper. And because these edges can injure the tongue or the cheek, regular floating of the teeth is essential. (See following pages.)

Horses eat slowly as a rule, partly because the upper jaw is larger than the lower, and they can chew on only one side at a time. Chewing up a pound of hay can take from fifteen to twenty minutes, while a pound of grain is devoured in about half that time. Horses who bolt their food should be discouraged.

The chewed food, aided by saliva, quickly passes through the pharynx, aided by the automatic blocking action of the soft palate, which prevents the food from entering the windpipe or nasal passages, or from returning to the mouth. This built-in safety valve also prevents a horse from breathing through his mouth. From the pharynx, food passes by a wavelike contraction through the four-to-five-foot esophagus, a muscular tube on the left side of the horse's neck, into the stomach—a one-way action that accounts for a horse's inability to vomit. The stomach is guarded by a powerful and involuntary ringlike muscle. When food becomes lodged in the esophagus, a horse will choke but won't be able to regurgitate.

The stomach is so small that it can handle only eight to seventeen quarts of food at a time—the reason for small feedings—and it has a peculiar way of arranging food in layers, the most recently digested food on the bottom and the fully digested food on the top. The enzymes in the stomach wall help to break down proteins and fatty acids for later digestion. Excess food or partially digested food passes on to the small intestine by contracting and expanding of the muscles in the stomach walls. Emptying the stomach is a continuous process during digestion, since it takes twenty-four hours for all food to leave the stomach.

After the food has mixed with the various gastric juices, it passes into the small intestine—a misleading description of an organ seventy feet long and three to four inches wide with a forty-eight-quart capacity. Food passes through this tortuous route and is broken down further. The partially digested matter then mixes with more enzyme secretions. Considering the length and narrowness of the small intestine, it isn't surprising that many digestive problems occur during this process—a twisted or telescoped intestine being among the most common.

Next stop on the digestive route is the four-compartment large intestine, where the most important digestive actions occur. Here fatty acids are absorbed, amino acids and B vitamins are synthesized, and carbohydrates like starch and sugar are melded into energy-yielding, volatile fatty acids. Because of the pressure of the food on the funnel-like compartments of the large intestine, impactions can occur here.

All water is reabsorbed before entering the rectum, to unite with the waste of indigestible and undigested food and residue cells cast off the intestinal walls.

Healthy horses void anywhere from five to twelve pounds of feces daily or thirty-three to fifty pounds a week, depending on how active they are—something to think about if you're contemplating putting up a stable in a suburban area. That's a lot of fertilizer.

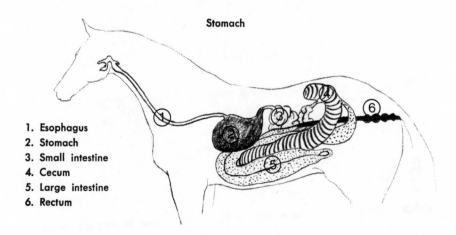

Stomach

1. Esophagus
2. Stomach
3. Small intestine
4. Cecum
5. Large intestine
6. Rectum

So if a horse eats the wrong things or too much of the right things, he's susceptible to a number of digestive disorders, one of which is a painful stomach ailment called colic (*see* chapter 8).

In order to keep a horse healthy and up to proper weight, he must be fed *little* and *often,* one of nine rules to remember about feeding horses.

1) Feed little and often
2) Feed plenty of bulk feed
3) Feed according to work done
4) Water before feeding
5) Feed only clean and good quality food
6) Never make sudden changes in types and amounts of food
7) Avoid sudden changes in feeding time
8) Never work a horse immediately after a full meal
9) Have your horse wormed and his teeth checked regularly

All of these rules have a reason. *Feeding little and often* is an effort to imitate nature. At Saratoga and other racetracks, stable managers go all out to imitate nature, feeding racing Thoroughbreds and Standardbreds six to eight times a day in small quantities. Frequent feedings enable a horse to get the most out of his food, particularly a high-strung, hardworking horse.

Obviously as an average horse owner you can't keep up with this kind of schedule and shouldn't try. Done correctly, feedings can be safely limited to two times a day. The only time you might want to give your horse the racing-Thoroughbred treatment is when he needs fattening up, something I'll discuss farther on.

Feed plenty of bulk feed because a horse's digestive system won't function properly without it. Bulk feed means grass or hay, which a horse should have access to at all times when grass isn't available.

Among the horsey adages that make sense is "feeling one's oats." Oats and other grains are high-energy foods; so are pellet concentrates. When a horse is worked hard, he needs a larger ration of energy foods. But if he's just loafing around the pasture, a working ration could make him sick and will certainly fill him with a lot of unexpendable energy. Lacking a constructive outlet, he'll work off the food by kicking, snorting, cribbing, weaving, and doing other obnoxious things. One mare I know, when fortified with a few extra oats, just stands in her stall and bucks. A few quarts of grain go a long way with some horses—often too far with a pony. (Ponies can frequently subsist on hay alone, depending on their size.)

That's why it's important to *feed according to the work done*. On days when your horse doesn't get a workout, his grain should be decreased and his bulk ration increased. There will also be times of the year when you won't be working your horse at all and he'll need less energy food, a subject I'll go into later.

To make sure food stays in your horse's stomach long enough for the nutrients to be fully absorbed, always *water before feeding*. If you feed grain, hay, and then water, the food will be washed through the system and much of the vitamin and mineral content lost.

A horse should be watered first, then given his hay, followed by grain. Water, by the way, must be clean and fresh. Dirty water buckets attract viruses and bacteria. And you'll find that many horses are as finicky as cats about what they drink. Some of them won't go near the water pail if there are a few wisps of hay drifting around on top.

Which brings us to rule five: *feed only clean and good quality food*. Where grain is concerned, this usually means good oats in the summer and a balanced blend of grains, corn, and meal in the winter to give him the right amount of protein, carbohydrates, fats, vitamins, and minerals to keep him in condition and his energy up. Food quality is covered later in this chapter. If a food is good quality, it will be very palatable, with a high proportion of digestible nutrients.

Your horse can only get out of his feed what's in it. Thus it's more economical in the long run to feed clean, good food because there will be less waste and you won't run the chance of making your horse sick.

A *regular feeding schedule* is very important if your horse is to keep his weight up and stay in "bloom," a phrase used to describe a horse's glossy coat and vigorous appearance.

One pupil of mine, who used to feed her horse whenever she got around to it (sometimes at 8:00 A.M., sometimes at noon), complained constantly about how thin the mare was. Although I had tried tactfully to suggest why a number of times, the message didn't sink in until the summer the girl went on vacation and sent her horse to a boarding stable for a month. At good stables, feeding is done in a businesslike way, at precisely the same time every day. After only thirty days of regular feeding, the mare returned home plump and healthy looking. She hadn't been getting any more grain or hay than she got at home, but she was fed on time. If a horse is accustomed to being fed at 8:00 A.M. and 6:00 P.M. daily, his digestive juices begin to flow at those hours and he is physically and psychologically prepared to utilize his food. He's relaxed and *ready* to eat.

This is why it's important to *avoid sudden changes in feeding time*. Begin a routine and stick to it, not varying by more than fifteen minutes from day to day. Horses that are underweight and nervous must be fed on time if you want to keep them in any kind of condition.

The same rule about changes in feeding time also applies to the type and amount of food your horse gets. Seasonal adjustments should be made gradually, extended over a period of several weeks. Even a one-quart overnight increase in grain could cause colic in some sensitive horses if there is no corresponding increase in work. On the other hand, if a horse is standing idle for several days after very hard work, his grain must be dropped by a half or full quart. In this instance don't be afraid to cut back suddenly on the food to avoid Monday morning sickness or founder (*see* chapter 8).

Obviously you should use the same grain measure at all times. A one- or two-pound coffee can, while not elegant, is an accurate and durable measure. Remember, by the way, when changing over from one grain to another that a can of mixed feed will be heavier than a can of oats. Weigh them out to get the right equivalent.

Never work a horse immediately after a full meal for the same reason that a person shouldn't swim after a heavy dinner. The blood supply is concentrated in the digestive system. But during exercise, it is diverted to the lungs and muscles and a recently fed horse may get cramps.

Likewise, you should never feed a horse immediately after working him. Cool him off by "walking him out" for a half hour or so before serving him dinner. If your horse isn't properly cooled down after being worked, eating could bring on colic or founder.

To get the most nourishment from his food and keep his weight up, *it's essential that your horse be wormed and have his teeth checked regularly.* There are several types of stomach parasites, all of them bad (*see* chapter 8), and almost all horses have them. They are unavoidable when one or several animals are kept in a small area where they

Walking him out

contaminate each other and the pasture. These parasites, which can cause severe damage to internal tissues, can and must be controlled. To be done properly a stool sample should be checked by your vet early in the spring and late in the fall. The theory here is that the first frost will kill any worms in the pasture, so that the horse won't reinfect himself during the winter.

Worms can run down a horse in record time. One winter, a second-term boarder of mine returned from his summer at home looking terrible. The pasturage at the farm had been ample, and his owner assured me that he'd been fed enough grain. So we had the vet check his stool, and he turned out to be wormy. Two weeks after a dose of worming medicine, he looked like a different horse—with a glossy coat and weight back to normal.

There are commercial worming medicines that you can give your horse. But you may find that he won't eat medicated food. And you run the risk of making him seriously ill by overdosing or giving him medicine when he doesn't have worms. If the vet finds worms in the droppings, one efficient method of getting rid of them is by "tubing."

This procedure, which must always be done by a vet, consists of passing a plastic or rubber tube down the esophagus and pumping the liquid worming medicine directly to the stomach. This ensures that the horse gets exactly the right amount of medication.

The syringe method, which my vet jokingly calls dial-a-worm, uses a worming paste in a small plastic tube in which the dose can be adjusted to the horse's weight. Some vets administer the paste in a large plastic tube, called a gun, with a trigger mechanism instead of a syringe.

If you have your own place it's a good idea to worm your horse by one of these methods quarterly. Before turnout in spring pasture, summer, early fall, and the tubing in January to get rid of the bots. This will ensure that your horse will be in prime condition all year.

During the warm months, particularly if a horse is grazing a small area, use a package wormer, varying the types and flavors so your horse won't catch on to the medicinal coverup and so the worms don't build up an immunity to the particular medication. The latest wormers come in a variety of flavors, from apple to corn. While you can use molasses, horses tend to catch on to this disguise quickly, figuring rightly that any meal with molasses in it has something less palatable as well.

If your horse is the clever type, who doesn't like even well-disguised package wormers, try giving him half of his regular feed the night before and half of his normal grain ration with wormer in the morning. Don't give him hay until he's cleaned the dish. This usually works. If not, you'll have to use a syringe-type wormer with varying medication each time.

Whether your horse is young or old, his teeth must be checked regu-

1 Nose Clamp (Humane Twitch) in place. Device puts pressure on horse's upper
   lip, allows vet to work unaided
2 Vet inserts tube into larynx, blowing to ensure correct internal position

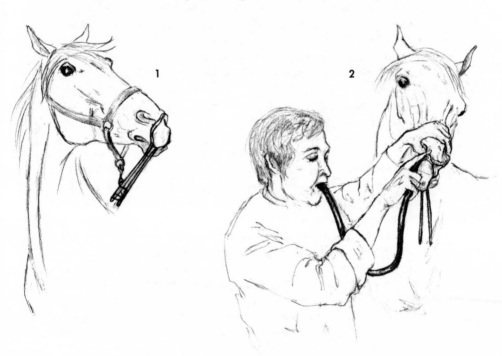

larly. When horses chew, their top back teeth grind laterally against the bottom ones, creating sharp points that can cause damage to the tongue and cheek, as well as being painful. Pointed teeth are obviously not efficient grinding instruments, and the horse that has them will eat food slowly and waste a lot. If the hay or grain isn't ground up enough when it reaches the stomach, a lot of nutritive value will be lost because the digestive juices can't act unless the surfaces of food particles are broken.

A horse with bad teeth won't gain weight no matter how much you feed him. And he may have trouble eating or possibly not want to eat at all. If your horse salivates a lot, drops large portions of his grain as

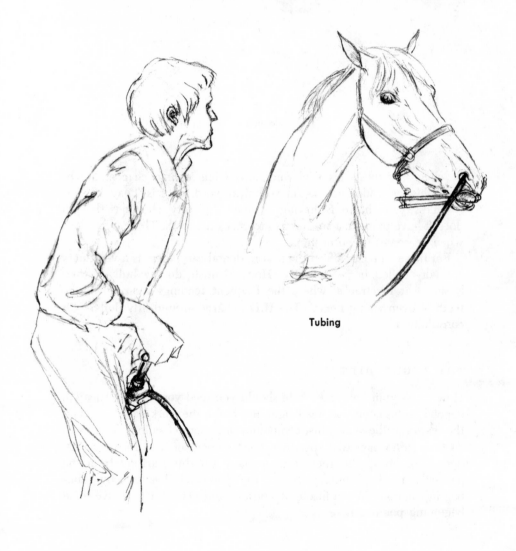

Tubing

Floating

he chews, or twists his neck and head while eating, chances are he needs his teeth filed down. The technical word for it is "floated."

Unless your horse is having obvious difficulty chewing, the vet doesn't have to make a special trip to check his teeth. This can be done when he comes to worm him.

For those who can afford the best in dental care, there is a veterinary specialty called horse dentistry. Horse dentists do the bulk of their business at racetracks, where the frequent feedings wear down the teeth of even young horses. The H.D.s charge around fifty dollars per consultation.

THE RIGHT DIET

How much grain or concentrate should you feed your horse? This will depend on his condition, his height and build, the work he's doing, and the season of the year. Most companies print some feeding instructions on their grain bags that specify a given amount of food for every 100 pounds of horse. But there are so many variables, arising from the particular needs of different horses, that you can't always go by grain-bag instructions. When in doubt, consult your vet. I'll try to give some beginning pointers here.

At some times of year when your horse isn't working a lot, you may want to give him more hay than grain. If you have high-quality hay or excellent pasture, you might not want to give much grain at all. But when your horse is working hard, he needs grain for energy and nutritive content. And some people feel that a hardworking horse should have very little hay or bulk. When fed in small amounts, hay should be of such excellent quality that it is almost the nutritive equivalent of grain. (Most ponies can and should get along on good-quality hay alone.)

Too much hay will give a horse the equine equivalent of a beer belly (in this case called a hay belly). Although they may look superficially robust, hay bellies burn off very fast. And it's possible to have all that weight down in the belly while the ribs are showing up above.

A hay belly

Hay bellies aren't to be confused with the full barrel of a mare in foal. I mention this because I've heard of five cases in a single year where knowledgeable people have confused the two conditions. A few months after putting their horses on a crash diet, they walked into the stall one morning to hear the pitter-patter of little hoofs. It can happen to the best of us. One owner was an obstetrician, another a nurse, a third a horse dealer. And in one case, it happened to the puzzled trainer of a two-year-old racing Thoroughbred, who couldn't figure out why his filly wasn't making better time on the track. He stumbled over the newborn foal on a morning the mother was scheduled to race. Many horses have a husky conformation that disguises pregnancy well.

If you're in doubt about the two conditions, there are some telling signs of pregnancy. Near the final part of the gestation period the udder drops down and the bag fills up. But in some horses this doesn't occur until the day before foaling. So it's best to have a vet check out any mare before you buy her. An unexpected foal is a pleasant surprise—two for the price of one, as it were. But if you're unprepared, it could be detrimental to the health of the newborn. I knew of a foal who died probably because the expectant mare had been fed limited amounts of high carbohydrate food—mostly corn—throughout the winter.

When a horse is in good condition, his build will determine the amount he is to be fed. Two horses of the same height may require widely different amounts of grain, depending on their conformation and their weight.

Some horses are "easy keepers." This term usually refers to compactly built animals that need relatively little grain for their size. An angular, high-strung horse of the same height might need twice as much grain to be "in good flesh."

It's wise to learn for yourself what a horse looks like when he's in good condition and how to tell when he's losing or gaining weight. That way you can get into the habit of looking critically at him, and any sudden weight change can be corrected before it gets out of hand. Horses can lose a hundred pounds before it becomes noticeable to the untrained eye. And by the time you can see a horse's ribs, he has lost so much that it will take a year or more to bring him back to condition. In the case of an older horse with a digestive system "set in its ways," this kind of weight loss is literally irretrievable. It's practically impossible to put significant weight on horses over fifteen years old.

The illustrations in this chapter of what horses look like in various conditions point out trouble spots to watch for if you think your horse is dropping weight.

If your horse is in poor condition, his diet should be adjusted accordingly. If he's overweight, you'll want to put him on a gradual diet, reducing his hay and grain ration by small percentages. When a heavy horse has stablemates who aren't on diets, he can get very put out watching them still eating while his dinner dish is bare. To keep him happy, you can add diet foods like carrots, turnips, or other snacks to his grain.

Overfeeding is never a good idea. A horse is supposed to be athletic, lean, and hard, rather than fat and soft. Fat horses are obviously not very agile. They're also prone to founder and Monday morning sickness. The extra weight puts a strain on the muscles and skeletal system. And in the case of broodmares and stallions, excess weight lowers fertility.

If your horse is too thin, you'll gradually increase his feed, along with the number of feedings. But before putting any horse on a diet of any kind, be sure to check with your vet. An animal that looks too fat to you might be just right for his particular build. And a thin horse may not need more food but medication to cure a low-grade infection that is sapping his strength.

Horses, like people, need more energy when they're working hard. Exercise burns more calories and more food is needed to keep weight up.

A horse's work can vary from two hours in the ring to a four-hour hunt to eight hours on the trail; and his food must vary accordingly—based on the number of hours and type of exercise. Again, it's hard to set up precise rules for this because horses vary so much in their needs. I have a sixteen-hand fourteen hundred-pound hunter who gets eleven quarts a day when idle and sixteen quarts when working hard. But a fine-boned Thoroughbred of the same height, weighing one thousand pounds, gets six quarts daily when worked lightly. When she's hunted, I up it to ten.

Young horses have special feeding needs. Because they reach one-half of their mature weight by the age of one and continue growing for another four to six years, colts have to be fed larger rations with more protein during this period. Bone formation isn't completed until

In good condition

In poor condition

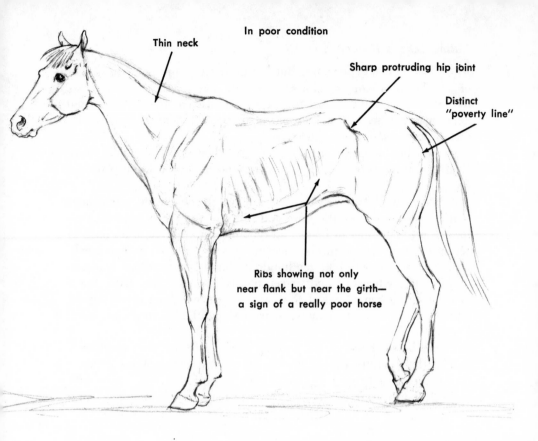

Thin neck

Sharp protruding hip joint

Distinct
"poverty line"

Ribs showing not only
near flank but near the girth—
a sign of a really poor horse

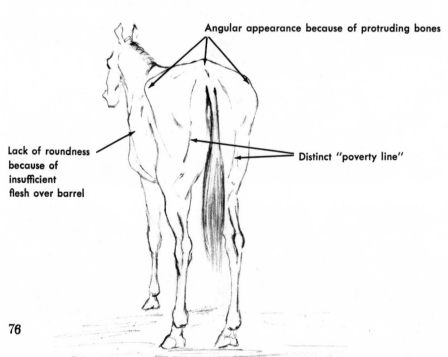

Angular appearance because of protruding bones

Lack of roundness
because of
insufficient
flesh over barrel

Distinct "poverty line"

the fifth or sixth year in most horses, when the pelvic bone finally os-
sifies completely. One three-year-old of mine, who finally stopped
growing at seventeen hands, was getting twenty quarts of grain a day
for more than a year.

Older horses present special feeding problems, too. After fifteen, as
mentioned, weight maintenance is extremely important. Many horses
develop problems with their teeth with advanced age and may need
an easily chewed hay substitute like beet pulp, or perhaps a very fine
second cutting of hay, which is shorter and more tender. Again, your
vet can advise you on the proper food.

TURNING HIM OUT

When spring comes and the grass turns a luscious shade of green,
there's a great temptation to throw open the barn doors and let your
horse out to graze until sundown. *Don't do it.* Remember the rule about
not making sudden changes in feeding. Your horse has been on a hay
and grain diet all winter and the spring grass is far richer. It also has
a much higher water content than dry hay. For the first few weeks of
spring, introduce him to the pasture for a few hours at a time, no
more than thirty minutes the first day, increasing this by about half an
hour a day for the next two weeks. If you absolutely must leave him
out for longer periods, fill him up with plenty of hay beforehand to
reduce his appetite.

Even when a horse is carefully reintroduced to the pasture, the high
water content of the grass may have a laxative effect for a few days.
But this is normal and nothing to worry about if he seems all right
otherwise.

By around the middle of August in the northern states, the pasture
will be dried out and scuffed up, and your horse will need a hay supplement to get enough nourishment. If you have a small pasture, he
may need it earlier. It's easy to tell by looking at the grass whether
there is enough food to keep him well nourished.

But remember that most horses refuse to eat where they urinate or
defecate. So what looks like a lush green pasture to you may be off
limits to them. Mowing or dragging a pasture on a regular basis helps
to control weeds, and horses are apt to be less finicky when droppings
are neatly distributed.

For those lucky enough to have the space, authorities advise allotting
two separately fenced acres a summer to each horse, rotating them
every four weeks. While one acre is in use, the other can be clipped
and dragged and allowed to go back to a lush state. A pleasure horse

on good pasture doesn't need grain or hay or nutrients—only a free choice of mineral supplements in his salt block. But beware. Very few are blessed with a good lush pasture that can sustain a horse. So don't kid yourself into thinking that any sweeping expanse of green can do the job.

You'll be able to tell if a pasture is adequate by a horse's condition. If you can't see the ribs but can run your hand over his barrel and feel them, the horse's condition is adequate. If you have to dig for the ribs—a hand test that is generally reliable—the horse is too fat.

The best pasture is the one that grows in your area the best, depending on climate and soil. Bluegrass, for instance, is one of the prettiest but matures too quickly in many areas, losing its nutritional value. And it can't stand drought. Your county extension service will give free advice on what grasses to plant where.

Around mid-October in the north, later of course if you live south, the grass will become sparse and you should start a regular regimen of hay and grain, that is, at least twice a day. By the end of the month, a horse's menu should be changed from his summer ration of oats to his winter diet—a mixed, heating, or high energy, feed; and by the middle of November, he should be entirely on his winter ration. In the spring, this procedure is reversed. If you're fortunate to live far enough south, the change may not be necessary.

In the best of all possible pastures, water should be available to horses at all times so they can take short drinks while grazing. Horses consume a lot of water every day, and the amount increases in the summer. Watering infrequently is dangerous because a horse tends to gulp large amounts of cold fluid at one time—a shock to the system and an invitation to colic. For this reason a horse that is being cooled off after hard work should be given numerous short sips of water—no more than a quarter pail at a time, then walked for four or five minutes before watering again.

If you're lucky enough to have a stream or stream-fed pond in your pasture, you won't have to worry about watering before feeding. There are also some expensive automatic watering devices available to assure a constant water supply, but a large tub accessible by hose is a practical solution in warm months.

Water should be fresh and preferably not icy cold. The containers should be clean at all times. This means cleaning them by hand with disinfectant each week. Carelessness can be lethal. Several years ago at a large breeding farm, where the horses drank continually out of the same container, one valuable animal was totally blinded by a virus and several others had their eyesight seriously damaged. The water

became stagnant and was invaded by the virus. With proper cleaning, this wouldn't have happened.

In the winter, snow is definitely *not* an acceptable substitute for water. Most horses will lick snow from time to time without harm. But if their water supply runs out, they may be tempted to gulp large quantities—with disastrous consequences. One morning when my stream froze over, a horse ate snow to quench his thirst and came down with laminitis, or founder, and a temperature of 106 degrees.

Salt should be available to horses at all times because it helps the body retain water. Obviously more salt is needed in the summer when a horse is sweating. Salt is available in plain white bricks, as well as

Salt lick in pasture

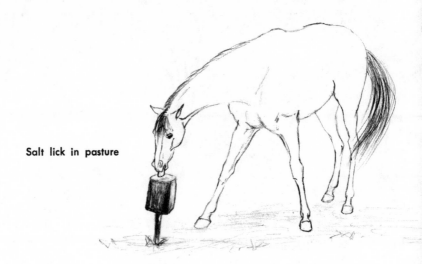

red, blue, and gold. The colored varieties contain different types of minerals and vitamins, all of them a good supplement to the regular diet.

In summer, it's convenient to buy the large fifty-pound blocks of salt and leave them in a sheltered spot where rain won't erode them. There are also small four-pound bars that are handy for hanging in the stall. Most feed shops and tack shops stock all kinds of sizes. You might want to buy one of the special salt dispensers available. Some of them have a separate container for minerals and vitamin powders on the other side.

ALL ABOUT HAY

There are a lot of kindly old farmers around waiting for an opportunity to get rid of last year's moldy hay on an unsuspecting neophyte. To avoid getting stuck, it's wise to learn how to tell the good hay from the bad. It's also vital to the health of your horse. Ninety percent of a horse's food problems could be solved if good hay were available.

There are several grasses that make good hay, depending on the area of the United States you live in.

In the Northeast, the most common hay grasses are rye, timothy,

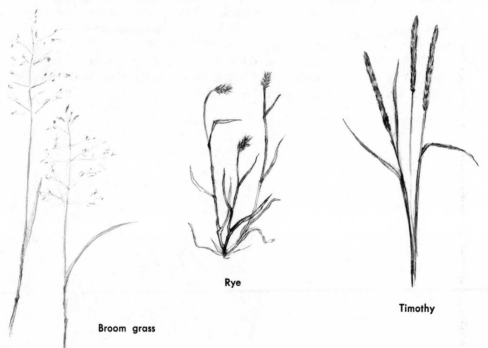

Rye

Timothy

Broom grass

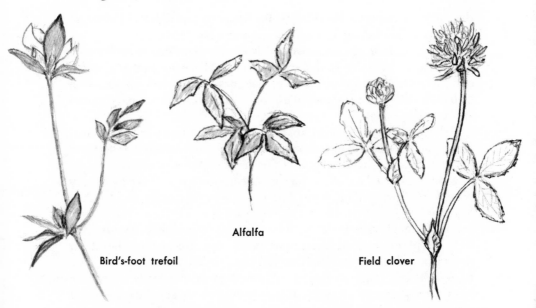

Bird's-foot trefoil

Alfalfa

Field clover

blue grass, broom grass, and orchard grass. All of these are best when mixed with a **legume,** a leafy, succulent grass like alfalfa, trefoil, or clover. The best hay combination for my money is timothy and one of the legumes.

Apart from being a valuable addition to the pasture because they release nitrogen into the soil, legumes have a high protein, vitamin, and mineral content that helps correct nutritional imbalances in grain. This provides a well-balanced diet that is particularly important for young horses and broodmares. Legumes are also rich in Vitamin A (carotin), and those that have been field cured have a high percentage of the sunshine Vitamin D. Some dealers cure their hay in the barn, which reduces the D content—a point worth checking out before buying. The legume highest in protein is alfalfa.

In all stages, **alfalfa** is by far the better hay nutritionally. It increases the utilization of protein, an effect that alarms some owners and trainers because it makes a horse urinate more frequently (the same effect a high-protein diet produces in humans). The cost may be too much for tight budgets, with bales generally running higher than the $1.25 to $2.50 for hay. The standard hay is **timothy.** To tap its highest nutritional value, timothy should be cut when the head is just beginning to peek through the blades. But because there's less tonnage at this early stage of growth, farmers often let it grow until the nutritional value is reduced or gone.

Because legume hay is so rich, never feed your horse an exclusive

diet of it. At most, it should take up between one-third and one-half
of the daily hay ration. Too much can have a laxative effect.

Clover, while it has only two-thirds of the digestible protein value
of **alfalfa,** surpasses it in net energy value. The main thing to watch
out for in clover and alfalfa hay is moldiness. It has more moisture in
it than the other grasses and unless cured until fully dry it molds more
easily.

Different types of legumes are best for different types of soil. Alfalfa,
for instance, grows well in very damp, rich soils. **Trefoil** is hardier,
doing well in dry, acid soil; and it doesn't need to be reseeded as often.
A good growth of trefoil, if fertilized, can last for as long as twenty
years without reseeding. Some farmers allow one cutting to sit in the
field and go to seed to make a thicker growth.

The main characteristic of all good hay is leafiness—because the
leaves contain most of the nourishment—and greenness. The stems
should be soft and pliable; it should be a faded green in color, free
from dust, and fragrant. Hay should smell sweet and fresh. When hay
has no fragrance at all, it is either overmature or sun bleached—and
worthless.

Hay should be free of foreign matter like weeds, stubble, and other
refuse. On occasion I've opened up bales to find old candy wrappers,
crushed tin cans, and, in one instance, a dead mouse. These things *can*
happen to otherwise good hay. But if you find surprises in every other
bale, find another dealer.

Hay has no value unless it is cut at the proper stage of maturity,
when it is highest in protein, digestibility, and mineral and vitamin
content. Cut past its prime, it goes to seed. And if hay has been lying
in the field more than a few days, exposed to sun, rain, or both, it
quickly bleaches out and loses most if not all of its nutritive value.

Sometimes even the most experienced farmers can't bring in a good
crop of hay if the weather isn't right. There's a period of about a week
when hay should be cut and harvested. After mowing, it must be picked
up within three or four days—a period that should be dry and preferably breezy.

In a wet spring a crop may sit in the fields getting drenched until it's
worthless for anything but mulch. Springs like this usually mean
higher hay prices the following winter—unless your dealer is large
enough to own special hay dryers for his barn and special hay machines
that crush the moisture out of the stems.

With equipment like this, a farmer can often get a field cut and
baled in a day. And in a good year in the Northeast, large farms often
harvest as many as four hay crops. But in a bad year, they may not
get two good cuttings, and prices will soar as high as $125 to $150 a

ton in midwinter. That's if you can find any hay to buy. Finding and keeping a good source of hay is a little like discovering buried treasure —a secret you may become reluctant to share.

Good hay is never cheap, even in the summer. It's always economical to buy the best because there is almost no waste, and you can save on grain. Although prices vary from $1.25 to $2.50 a bale in rural areas of the northeast, depending on seasonal scarcity, in the near-city countryside, I've heard of people getting as much as $7 a bale! Ideally, try to order for the whole winter in advance. Summer hay prices are cheaper, and you'll have a wider choice available.

In rural areas, farmers will often give you a break on prices if you come into the fields at haying time with your own truck and load the bales. Bales vary in weight from twenty-five to eighty pounds and are tied with either string or wire. When you open one, it falls apart into numerous thick slices or sections, which *must* be shaken out to get rid of accumulated dust before you feed it to your horse.

The amount of hay a horse gets depends on his size and the quality of the hay. An average horse of about fifteen hands, weighing nine hundred pounds, normally gets around twenty to twenty-five pounds of hay a day. Depending on how much the bale weighs, this could be an entire bale or several sections.

To see your horse through from November to March, you'll certainly be investing in two tons of hay, possibly more.

Be sure to open up a few bales at the dealer's to see that the hay is fresh and green inside as well as out. And when it's delivered, you may want to weigh a few of the bales to make sure you're getting what you paid for.

Because of the rising price of hay, the use of pellets and cubes has

increased. It's easier to store, and you don't have to stockpile in advance. But the use of pellets alone does have drawbacks (see following pages).

GRAIN AND OTHER FEEDS

Unless you have a very small pony who can get along on hay alone, you'll also be making a substantial yearly investment in grain and/or mixed feeds. In the summer, the best food for a horse is **oats**. These are high in protein and low in heating carbohydrates. Also, the bulk supplied by the oat hulls creates a loose mass in the horse's digestive tract. Heavier foods like corn and barley tend to pack down.

Oats can be cracked, flaked, crimped, or rolled as well as whole, processes that improve digestibility by opening the hulls and making less chewing necessary. The more involved the process, the more expensive. Crimped oats cost around $5.00 a 50-pound bag, while regular whole oats go for $8.50 for 100 pounds. Triple-cleaned racehorse whole oats (they're more desirable because they're dust-free) sell for about $10.00 a 96-pound bag. Processed oats are of the greatest benefit to horses that have difficulty or who gulp their food. Many racehorse trainers believe processing gleans greater nutritional value. But ground grains do tend to pack down. Whole oats are best, being the least dusty and providing the greatest bulk. But a lot of horses won't chew whole oats properly, and some feed suppliers don't carry them. The next best are crimped oats, which have been run through a machine to crush the hulls. Crushed oats are broken down still further. Some companies mix crimped oats with barley and molasses, which is a good food for fussy eaters. All oats should smell sweet and fresh, be plump in appearance, a mellow yellow in color, and free of excessive dust.

Sometimes, when hay is scarce or you have storage problems (or if you have a horse who is allergic to hay or grain, which occasionally happens) you may want to give **pellet concentrates** as an entire ration. Concentrates have all the ingredients of the best legumes and grain, along with a wide assortment of vitamins and minerals, all rolled into tiny, easy-to-chew pellets.

Among the exotic ingredients in one variety are hominy and cornmeal, cane molasses, oat hulls, ground limestone, vitamin B_{12}, niacin, and vitamin E—to name a few.

Pellet concentrates have a lot going for them. When a horse eats them, he's getting a balanced diet with all the nutrients in it, and he can't eliminate things he doesn't like (some horses don't like barley, for instance). So pellets eliminate waste, which can comprise 20 percent of the food of a horse with sloppy eating habits. Most horses waste about 10 percent. And in general pellets tend to keep a horse trimmer.

Pellets assure a high-quality hay content, along with the most palatable feeds. They also incorporate those feeds that might be too dusty in their regular form. Obviously they require less storage space than hay, and they cost less because the delivery charge isn't as high.

It's hard to judge the quality of pellets because the ingredients are ground up before compression. Make sure you're buying from a reputable firm, and be suspicious if the cost is too low. The roughage in pellets can be any combination of beet pulp, soybean meal, or alfalfa. Protein levels are ofen raised by adding supplements—and these may vary from day to day, depending on what's available to a manufacturer at the lowest cost. Even green pellet alfalfa meal may not have compressed alfalfa as its main source of protein. Some manufacturers add a protein supplement and put green dye in the formula.

There is a variety of pelleted foods. One is the complete ration mentioned above. But there is another available as a supplement, and still another as a grain and supplement mix. There are even pure alfalfa pellets.

But pellets as a complete diet do have their disadvantages. Because they're so high in protein, some horses can become absolutely unmanageable on this kind of diet. Also, they lack the roughage so desirable in hay.

Because they are grazing animals, horses are happiest when they have something to chew on. When fed pellets, many horses will get bored and chew anything in sight—trees, fences, hay cribs, and windowsills. I know a few stables where concentrates are used exclusively, and you can tell which ones they are when you walk in the door. If you do use pellets, there are sprays available to cut down cribbing, or chewing on the stall, but a horse will probably find another way to express his boredom.

In the winter, in temperate climates, your horse will switch from oats to one of the mixed **heating foods** available at all feed supply houses. These are higher in carbohydrates, fats, and oils, giving a higher energy content per unit of weight and keeping the horse warmer. Some mixed feeds are more suitable for colts; others are specifically prepared for broodmares. Those normally given have dozens of different vitamins and minerals in them, along with nourishing additives like hominy, soybeans, sesame oil, and wheat hulls. Mixed feed, depending on the brand, varies from nine to eleven dollars for a 100-pound bag.

A horse can only get out of his food what there is in it, i.e., the Total Digestible Nutrients (TDN) present in grain, concentrates, and hay. Corn, for instance, has the highest TDN of all feeds—80 percent. Yet corn, as mentioned, has less protein than oats (70 percent TDN) and legume hay (52 percent). To help you understand what a balanced equine diet is, follow the chart showing TDN, protein, and vitamin content of various foods.

Composition of Some Common Feeds for Horses [a]

Feed	Dry matter	TDN [b]	Digestible protein	Calcium	Phosphorus	Carotene
	%	%	%	%	%	mg/lb
Roughages						
Alfalfa hay						
All Analyses	88	50	11.0	1.47	0.26	27.7
Early bloom	90	51	12.1	1.25	0.26	57.7
Full bloom	88	48	10.0	1.28	0.30	16.8
Past bloom	91	44	9.9	1.34	0.35	12.2
Clover hay (all analyses)	90	46	10.0	1.41	0.29	24.9
Mixed hay (less than 30% legumes)	89	48	4.8	0.90	0.19	8.0
Oat hay (Dough stage)	90	46	5.3	0.33	0.17	14.6
Timothy hay						
All analyses	88	45	3.1	0.37	0.19	6.2
Early bloom	88	47	4.2	0.60	0.26	9.2
Full bloom	87	43	3.4	0.41	0.19	4.4
Past bloom	87	37	2.9	0.35	0.21	2.8
Concentrates						
Beet pulp	92	70	6.0	0.56	0.08	—
Corn, yellow #2	89	80	6.7	0.02	0.27	5.5
Linseed meal	91	71	29.5	0.40	0.83	—
Oats	90	70	9.4	0.09	0.33	—
Soybean meal	89	77	38.2	0.32	0.32	—
Wheat bran	89	63	13.0	0.14	1.17	—

[a] Taken from NRC publications 585, 659 and 1137.

[b] As determined with ruminants. Values for roughages when fed to horses would be 5–8% lower because the horse does not digest crude fiber as well as ruminants.

Bran is the coarse outer coating of wheat. Served cold, straight from the bag, it is bulky and palatable and acts as a mild laxative.

In the summer, some people mix bran with oats in a 3–1 ratio for bulk and as a general conditioner. But others are against it because the combination is higher in phosphates than calcium, and they feel it interferes with bone building. Bran should be used sparingly with young horses for this reason.

Barley by itself tends to pack down too much in a horse's stomach, much as corn does, and could cause colic. Also, most horses find an exclusive barley diet unpalatable. This grain is usually present in mixed feed and pellets and has approximately the same TDN as oats.

Milo is a cereal grain, one of four varieties of sorghum, common to the Southwest. It is highly drought resistant and can be grown on soil too thin for corn. Sweet sorghum, another variety, is ground to make molasses. Some twenty million acres of sorghums are grown in the United States. Grassy varieties are ground for silage or used for hay.

Soybean meal is high in TDN (77 percent), with the highest digestible protein (38.2 percent) of all feeds. This can be used successfully with bran as a mixed feed; bran provides the bulk, soybean meal the nourishment.

Molasses has 80 percent of the nutrient value of corn. Though most economical in the South where it's made, it can be used anywhere to make grain more palatable, to stick pellets together, and to keep dust down. (Though mineral oil and water can also be used for the latter purpose, it's not as nutritional.)

A lot of horse owners like to cut corners by feeding things like stale bread, corncobs mixed with beet pulp, and whole corn on the cob. The less said about bread the better. It just won't do.

As for whole **corn,** I don't recommend it except as an occasional hors d'oeuvre before dinner. A friend of mine recently spent a dismal evening with the vet trying to push a corncob down the throat of her miserable horse who had swallowed it whole. There are, of course, a lot of people who feed nothing but whole corn and get away with it, but I'd never take the risk.

Cracked or rolled corn can be added to mixed feed, but whole corn should be fed only sparingly, like an apple. And if your horse tends to gobble his food, *never* give him corn on the cob. If he's prone to colic, never give him corn at all.

Some horsemen feel that **shelled cracked corn** isn't as safe as an exclusive diet, claiming that it forms a doughy mass in a horse's stomach. Other equine nutritionists sing its praises, saying it's an excellent feed, even for racehorses, if they are fed carefully.

Shelled cracked corn costs about half as much as oats, so you can cut grain costs by a quarter by switching to corn and halving the ration. Corn becomes heating only if the horse is eating more energy food than he needs. Take care to cut back on it in the summer when he won't need as much heating food.

And be sure to remember, if you plan to switch to corn from another feed, that food is measured by weight, not volume. Given the same ration of corn as oats, a horse could founder. The coffee-can measure has been the undoing of many a horse.

PROTEIN SUPPLEMENTS

Peanut oil, cottonseed, and linseed meals: Of the three, cottonseed is closest to soybean meal in digestible protein. All have high energy value. But never overdo feeding any of these supplements. They're not only expensive but can cause digestive upsets if given in too great amounts too frequently. You will want to use them with young horses, lactating mares, or mares in foal.

HOT MEALS FOR HORSES

The British, known for lavishing attention on their horses, spend a lot of time thinking up new and tantalizing hot menus. And they've found that a hot meal a few times a week pays off by keeping a horse in top condition.

Cooked grain is more easily digested than raw grain, and it's particularly good for old horses or horses with problems of the teeth or of the digestive system. But remember that boiled feed has a relatively low-energy value and shouldn't be fed to hardworking horses more than once a week.

What should you cook? Oats, whole or crimped, barley, linseed, and bran lend themselves to cooking. And each grain has a special nutritive effect. All boiled feeds, bran in particular, have helpful laxative properties—useful when a horse has been stabled for long periods. Cooking also swells feed and makes a meal go further. It helps finicky eaters regain their appetite and maintains a horse's body temperature on cold days.

Whole Oats are the least expensive to cook and take the longest—up to four hours simmering time before the husk cracks, exposing the grayish kernel. Costlier crimped oats take only about three-quarters of an hour to cook. Steamed oats don't stretch as far as the boiled, but they have a great aroma and are an excellent feed for horses in training.

Linseed is poisonous unless thoroughly cooked. (Linseed meal, oil, and cakes don't need cooking.) When done, the husk cracks open, exposing a yellow kernel, and the liquid thickens into a gray, jellylike gruel. This grain also expands to about two-and-a-half times its normal volume. Linseed of course is a supplement, not a whole food, and should be added to regular feed or mixed with dry bran.

Bran Mash is an excellent feed for a horse who's had a hard day hunting or showing. For sick or tired horses, a hot bran mash is the equine equivalent of a nourishing milk toast. Try to serve it twice a week in the fall and winter as a conditioner and laxative. Because of its laxative effect, your horse shouldn't be worked hard the day following his bran mash meal.

Barley: Cooked barley is an excellent way to put weight on a horse without heating him up. It's even good for show horses during the summer. But it shouldn't be fed more than three times a week. And as a steady diet, it will make a fit horse fat and thickwinded. Only *whole* barley should be used for cooking. Flakes turn into an unappetizing mush. Like oats, barley should be cooked until the husk cracks. It expands to about two-and-a-half times its original volume. (See the Appendix for recipes on hot horse meals.)

ALLERGENIC FOODS

Any horse with respiratory or allergic problems needs a scientifically balanced diet to replace the hay or grain that his system can't tolerate. Respond is one of the several feeds you can buy for a wheezy or "heavy" horse, and it's excellent—if you can afford it. A 50-pound bag costs about five dollars, and five bags a week would be the average amount consumed by a 1,500-pound horse.

If this is too much of a strain on your budget, consult your vet. One Cornell grad pupil of mine worked out an alternative to this expensive fare consisting of three parts beet pulp, two parts sweet feed, one part alfalfa pellets, and eight ounces of Calf Manna twice daily. Respond, its commercial equivalents, or this inexpensive substitute, is also good for horses recuperating from a respiratory illness that involves a temporary cough.

Coughs and wheezes may also appear in dry weather when the pasture has dried up and the hay in the barn has become dusty. In either case—after an illness or in dry weather—you should treat a horse as though he were chronically heavy, by changing him to an allergenic feed. If you don't, you may cause damage to the respiratory system, and the temporary condition may become permanent. Allergenic feeds usually clear up these temporary problems within a few weeks. Dryness irritates this problem too, so be sure to wet down the feed during a particularly dry spell. I've done this every summer with one dust-sensitive horse, and the regime has kept him cough-free.

Beet Pulp, the leftover result of sugar-beet processing, has an 8 percent protein content and is a fiber substitute, especially for horses with allergic or respiratory problems and for old horses. It comes in two forms: loose dried bulk, which is chopped and bagged, or in pellets. Both types must be mixed with water—an equal ratio of water for the loose type and three parts water to one part of the pellet variety.

I've known horses that have had chronic allergies to hay, causing them to cough shortly after they eat it. They've been on continual diets of beet pulp, wet feed, and supplements and have done extremely well, staying in top condition for all types of strenuous competition.

Beet pulp is often misused by those who think it's an economical shortcut and use it as a grain substitute during lean winter months. A horse wintered on this type of feed program will lose tremendous amounts of weight and come into the spring looking wan and haggard, without the energy that grain would have provided and unable to get back into condition quickly.

I use beet pulp as a supplement when hay is in short supply or of bad quality. But with school horses or those who are working hard, I make sure to drop off the pulp when they start working.

If your horse requires a sole diet of grain and pulp, be sure to increase the grain when he's working. For a large horse, a supplementary lunch is a must to compensate for the lack of hay in his diet. Also, it keeps him from gnawing everything in sight.

FOOD AND VITAMIN SUPPLEMENTS

Most horses who are well fed don't need supplements. Those obviously run-down, underweight, undernourished, and unable to gain weight despite regular worming and adequate food will benefit from one of the variety of supplements now on the market. Supplements are also indicated for young horses that need help in reinforcing their diet in order to develop to their full potential and for those horses who have chemical imbalances that prevent them from utilizing food properly.

Getting the most out of the feed at hand is the main purpose of supplements, which can take the form of syrups, liquids, powders, and pellets. These enable the horse to get maximum benefit from what he eats, so in the long run you'll end up feeding him less. But supplements are expensive (a 24-pound bag of Drive averages over thirty dollars), and they're not intended as magic potions. Some people expect overnight miracles from these additives.

Though many vitamins—B12, for instance—are contained in many food supplements, they're of no value. B12 is used only for anemic horses. In a normal horse, this vitamin has no effect on the blood count, nor will it increase the flow of oxygen to the veins and aid performance—as some have claimed.

Horses grazing on lush pasture get all the A, D, and E vitamins they need, and extras are completely unnecessary. The average horse needs 2,000 to 5,000 units of vitamin A daily, 200 to 500 units of vitamin D, and 20 to 50 units of vitamin E. When a horse is stabled, these vitamins can be added to grain. But before rushing off to the nearest tack shop to buy them, check out feed stores, where you can usually find the equivalent for a quarter of the cost. Calf Manna, for instance, gives the same nutritional boost to colts and fillies.

Many supplements include coat conditioners in the formula. Others are conditioners only. If your horse's coat is scruffy and dull, there's an inexpensive way to make it glossy: corn oil, which is just as good as commercial coat conditioner, which costs more because the liquid has to be processed to powder form. Liquid fat is commonly used on the track to make yearlings sleek before they're put up for auction. I recently used corn oil with great success on a middle-aged school horse named Moose. He looked positively glamorous after two weeks of one tablespoon added twice daily to his feed.

If your horse is run-down and anemic and really does need vitamin B, brewer's yeast is the least expensive source for this vitamin. Sometimes, if a horse is in really poor shape, supplements help to get him in condition. I recommend giving Drive for at least two months (supplements fed for any shorter period won't have the desired effect). The manufacturers of this supplement invite you to make your own test, putting two horses on identical feed programs for sixty days, with one of them getting Drive and the other getting a brand X conditioner. They offer a money-back guarantee that your horse's coat will be glossier, his hoofs better textured, and his energy, strength, and disposition improved. As mentioned before, it's an expensive proposition, but one that will pay off by saving you money on feed bills in the long run.

But please remember not to give vitamins unnecessarily. I know of one overzealous woman who gave her new foal one of everything available in vitamins. He ended up with a skin condition—the result of oversupplementation. And vitamin D, given in excess to any horse, can be dangerous, causing calcification in the soft tissue. So don't be impressed by a long list of ingredients in food supplements. Just because a product has thirty-five additives in it doesn't mean your horse needs them!

Hoof Gro is another supplement I've used with great success on a horse that was generally sound but had cracked hoofs, which grew outward in an odd platterlike manner. He also had dry skin and a dull coat. I gave him Hoof Gro and a vitamin supplement, augmenting this with daily vigorous grooming and good feed. Within a few months, this scrawny, outwardly unappealing animal made a Cinderellalike transformation into a beautiful show horse who was sold for four times his original price.

Hoof Gro works from within, closing cracks from the coronet downward and from the proliferating tissue outward, to build strong hoofs. Among its many ingredients are dried egg yolks. Other nutrients are related to the substance of the hoof itself. Horses with shelly or rough or ridged hoofs seem to respond particularly well to this supplement.

Clovite is a hormonal supplement that helps regulate the fertility cycle. One boarder of mine used it on a mare who wouldn't come into season despite a summer-long series of shots by the vet. She was started on Clovite in the fall and came into season right on schedule the following spring, conceiving on her first visit to the stud farm.

STABLE MANNERS

Horses, like people, have different eating habits. Some bolt their food. Others pick away at it. When a horse bolts his food, he isn't chewing it properly and he won't get enough nourishment. One indication of a bolter is finding substantial quantities of whole grain and corn in his manure (this could also mean that his teeth need floating). Watch your horse as he feeds. If he seems to be consuming the food in record time, sort of like a vacuum cleaner, you should take steps to slow him down. A few companies manufacture special feeding dishes. A less expensive cure is to put large, fist-sized rocks into his dish which forces the horse to slow down as he works around them. Often, feeding pellets or chopped up hay **chaff** as a supplement can accomplish the same thing.

There are also finicky eaters. They play with their grain like a child toying with a bowl of spinach and sometimes don't even finish the entire ration at one feeding. Or else it may take them a couple of hours to get it down between sips of water and nibbles of hay. If you have several horses, this can be infuriating—particularly if they're being fed in the pasture or an open shed. The nibbler will just stand by and watch his stablemates gobble his grain.

Finicky eaters are usually those horses that can't afford to lose weight in the first place. They may be high-strung horses under a lot of strain or in poor health from a previously bad diet or lack of exercise. So it's important to take measures to whet their appetites. Often this can be done with a change of menu—certain foods are less palatable than others. Or you can add some molasses, sugar, or honey to make the feed more enticing (no more than 5 percent of the total ration, however). In extreme cases, medicine is used to increase the appetite.

Sometimes temporary gastronomic traumas will turn formerly finicky eaters into gluttons. A Thoroughbred filly boarded at my stable for a while after a brief career on the racetrack, where she'd been under a great deal of tension. I had tried all sorts of gimmicks to get her to eat—chopped-up carrots, and molasses, neither of which she liked. Although she gained a little, she still wasn't up to top form.

A few weeks later the filly had an injury that forced her to be confined to her stall for several weeks. During her convalescence she had to be kept as quiet as possible; consequently I was forced to cut down on her grain. This upset me because I had worked so hard to build her up. But when she recovered and went back on full rations that period of semistarvation paid off in an increased appetite, verging on gluttony. Ever since she's cleaned her dish out in record time.

Fasting to achieve a *bon appétit* has recently been endorsed by the experts. When horses have to be fed a lot—because of age, size, or work

load, it helps to keep their appetite sharp by putting them on a one-day semi-fast a few times a month. Many breeders and trainers are doing this, to fend off the culinary blahs and keep the equine appetite keen.

Snacks are an excellent way to lure finicky eaters to the feed dish as well as add bulk to the ration of a dieting horse. Snacks are also very nutritious as an appetizer for a healthy horse and useful as a reward for good behavior. A product called Horse Treats is now on the market—sort of an equine answer to dog biscuits. All contain vitamins and minerals and come in apple, carrot, and sweet corn flavors. Feed them like carrots or apples, one or two at a time, as a reward or an after-work tidbit.

Carrots are particularly good for horses. One pound of fresh carrots contains forty-eight milligrams of carotin, enough to meet the daily requirements of a thousand-pound horse. In contrast, a pound of field-cured timothy contains 2.1 milligrams. Carrots are also high in calcium and phosphate. In the winter, when there is no green feed available and horses are stabled a lot, one to two pounds of carrots daily will stimulate appetite, increase growth, add to bloom, and even increase fertility. They should be fed sliced in small strips and mixed with grain.

Other root vegetables, as long as they are cut up fine, are also nutritious. These include turnips, parsnips, and sugar beets. Among the fruits and vegetables horses like (and those safe for them) are peaches, pears, and plums (with all stones removed) and pumpkins, melons, and squash—all cut up and in small quantities. Apples should not be fed more than two a day.

One track official, entrusted with the care and feeding of some finicky horses slated to run in the Washington, D.C., International, says: "To satisfy the palates of our equine guests, we've had to shop not only for carrots and apples but also lettuce, leeks, powdered milk, honey, eggs and stout"—the last item, you may have guessed, was for an Irish horse.

GETTING A FODDER COMPLEX

As the price of feed continues to climb, many horse owners are tempted to take money-saving shortcuts. After all, you may reason, it's wasteful to throw things away. Why not spread that slightly soiled hay or grain out for a horse to pick through?

Don't do it. You can't assume that a horse will pick out only the good food. A naive young horse or a wise old glutton may gulp it all.

Always make sure that food is clean and unspoiled, that the containers it's kept in and the dishes it's fed in are scrubbed out regularly.

Smell the feed yourself before dishing it out. Bad feed has a sour smell and is guaranteed to make a horse sick. Handle the feed and *look* at it. Don't use grain that's stuck together in a wad or feels wet. Examine all feed for traces of mildew. And if you buy a sack of feed that's below standard in any respect, don't hesitate to take it back—or throw it out. But don't feed it to your horse.

Carelessness with feed is often fatal. A few summers ago, a large feed store near my home was selling off the last of its stock before reordering—bags that had been stored in the back of the shed for months. I was the recipient of some of this backlog, and every feed bag I opened had clumps of mold in the grain. I took the bags back and got them replaced, but another stable in the area, where the feeding methods were haphazard and the help inexperienced, used the feed as it was. The result: a young horse died.

Hay and grain can also be affected by bacteria and fungus while they're growing—something that all farmers know but which some may disregard. It was once common practice to send horses into the field to eat the unharvested cornstalks and the "seconds" not fit for cutting. One hopes that the high fatality rate resulting from this "shortcut" has discouraged the practice.

Certain grains can be infected by parasites, rusts, and blights. Botulism can be caused by the spore from a dead animal lying undetected in hay or silage. Botulism is often odorless and usually has no effect on taste or appearance. Whenever animal remains are found in a bale of hay or a batch of silage, don't hesitate. Throw the whole thing out.

Good food is cheap compared to the replacement costs of a horse—and the realization that he has been killed by negligence.

5

housing
your
horse

> Now . . . Augeas's [stable] yard and sheep-
> folds had not been cleared away for many
> years, and though its noisome stench did
> not affect the beasts themselves, it spread
> a pestilence across the whole Peloponnese.
> Moreover the valley pastures were so deep
> in dung that they could no longer be
> ploughed for grain. Hercules hailed Augeas
> from afar and undertook to cleanse the yard
> before nightfall. . . . Augeas laughed in-
> credulously. GREEK MYTHS, VOL. II
>
> —ROBERT GRAVES
> TRANSLATING THE FIFTH LABOR OF HERCULES
> IN WHICH HE HAD TO DIVERT TWO RIVERS
> TO CLEAN KING AUGEAS'S INCREDIBLY DIRTY
> YARDS AND STABLES—A CHORE HE WOULDN'T
> HAVE FACED IF THE KING HAD PRACTICED
> PROPER STABLE MANAGEMENT.

Sooner or later, if your horse has any kind of imagination, you'll open
up the stable one morning and find him waiting to greet you at the
outside door. Twelve hours earlier, he was neatly tucked away in his
stall, with everything in apple-pie order. Now the stall door is hanging askew on one bent hinge. Your new saddle, stirrups amputated, is
lying upside down in a pool of molasses. And everything else is
smothered in a sea of hay. Ambling around happily in the midst of it
all, molasses all over his muzzle and dripping from his mane, is your
#$%&!"# horse.

Depending on how you keep your stable, these experiences will
range from the merely hilarious (in retrospect) to the extremely dan-

gerous. Unless your feedbox or area is horseproofed, for instance, he has probably gorged himself on oats or something else and will need immediate treatment to prevent colic.

If your tools haven't been properly put away, your horse may have punctured his foot on a pitchfork or become tangled in some old strands of baling string or wire. The disaster potential is almost unlimited, as you'll learn the hard way if you fail to run a well-kept stable.

Stables are, or ought to be, thought of as akin to ships. They have a limited amount of space that must be utilized efficiently, with a place for everything and everything in its place.

Ideally, your feed and tack should be kept in a separate, locked room. Tools and grooming equipment should be hung neatly on the wall, and medicines and molasses kept in an enclosed container, preferably a wall cabinet. (Horses adore molasses. I've seen them eat through plastic and stomp through metal to get at it.)

Hay should be stored in a separate room when possible or kept overhead, always making sure that the storage space is dry and well ventilated. Hay molds easily from dampness, and it is highly combustible.

If you're building a stable from scratch, all these things can be provided for. If you're converting an old building, there are ways of

improvising. If you choose the third alternative—housing your horse in an open shed—you must make arrangements to store food, hay, and equipment in a separate building.

FIELD KEEPING

Horses are naturally outdoor animals, and a lot of them prefer to remain outside most of the time. Most are hardy enough to need shelter only during severe storms—like hailstorms or thundershowers. And in the summer, they need a place to escape the heat and flies.

On the theory that pasturing is better for a horse's health (it aids circulation, develops muscles, and strengthens legs and feet), more and more people, including many horse breeders, are using large open sheds to house horses, individually and in groups. Sheds also keep building costs down and less stable help is needed to maintain them.

One of my horses would rather stay out in almost any weather. Freezing rain and extreme heat are the only conditions that will keep him inside. I've seen him standing in howling blizzards, a foot of snow piled on his back and icicles hanging from his nostrils. He's the healthiest horse I've ever had and a very easy keeper.

"You never have unexpected vet's bills when horses are field kept," says one horse breeder in my area, who uses large, sloping, three-sided sheds, open to the south. He advises building sheds on the highest point in the paddock, with a southern exposure to minimize wind and drifting snow, allowing at least 12 × 12 feet of space for each horse. The ceiling slopes from at least twelve feet in front to nine or ten at the rear—high enough so a horse can't hit his head when he throws it back. The roofing is aluminum, and the structure is built of 1 × 16 green oak planks lined with smooth plywood. The planks are the same size the breeder uses on his fencing.

The sheds are built with a natural dirt floor that is cleaned thoroughly of manure twice a year and disinfected. In the summer, a sixteen-foot wooden board overhang across the front entrance provides shade, which keeps down flies.

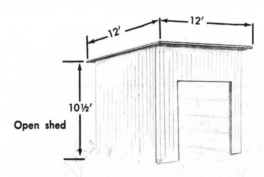

Open shed

The most durable, easily maintained (and expensive) sheds are of concrete-block construction. Allow 12 × 12 feet of space per house, with the roof sloping up from ten-and-a-half feet at the lower end to twelve-and-a-half feet at the entrance. These vertical measurements, which also apply to wooden sheds, should allow for six to eight inches of bedding.

Each horse in your stable should have at least two acres of good pasture. Otherwise, he'll need a hay supplement in the summer. Five acres of grazing land per horse is ideal, but beyond the economic reach of most backyard horseowners. The larger the pasture, the more room available for rotation of grazing areas. Field-kept horses should have a shed in each area.

The building you'll use in a shed varies according to what's available. In Kentucky, for instance, some large horse farms use tobacco stems, which are very absorbent and heavy enough not to be blown around by the wind. This type of bedding should be eight inches thick, and the top must be cleaned off and replaced at least every ten days. Because of its absorbency and easy handling, Stae Dri is another good shed-bedding choice, with wood shavings running a close third.

If you have the space, fat, aggressive horses should obviously be kept in one shed area, where they'll eat less, while skinny, timid horses need a separate niche, in which they can eat more without constant harassment. Each group should have a separate shed.

Try putting a hay crib or net inside in a corner of your shed. Trough-shaped hay cribs built in a field are also a good idea. Although it is often done, feeding hay on the ground is a very bad idea. Horses tend to walk through the hay and soil it, and there is a great deal of waste. Furthermore, in a small pasture, soiled hay is likely to be a repository for parasites in different stages.

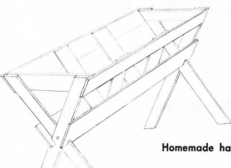

Homemade hay crib for a single horse

When building an outside shed, make ample provisions for hay storage in another building. Two tons of hay for instance take up approximately a thousand cubic feet. Before buying some and sticking it away in an old chicken coop, make sure the floor is dry and the roof doesn't leak. One end of a garage or tool shed can be used for keeping feed, stored in plastic or galvanized pails with clamp-on lids that are rodent proof and horse proof. The first place a horse will head when he escapes from the stall or the pasture is to the feedbox. They have an uncanny ability to find it. Unopened feed is no insurance. Horses bite right through bags and drag them around.

Garage walls can also be used to hang grooming equipment and racks for bridles, halters, and saddles. You'll also need the stable-cleaning equipment listed in the following pages to keep your shed in good order, and the tools necessary to maintain it.

Although sheds are the most economical way to house your horse, they still cost at least four hundred dollars for a one-horse enclosure, if you don't do it yourself.

I have one friend who went all out for her three horses, converting a lovely three-room guest cottage into a three-stall barn, complete with a view and indoor plumbing. Extra overnight guests now have to put up with a sofa bed in the den.

CONSTRUCTION TIPS

With the cost of seasoned lumber running so high (34 cents a board foot for fir 2 × 4's and 2 × 8's), you might want to buy green lumber and season it yourself—a process that takes at least six months, but which can save you approximately half the cost of finished wood. Hemlock is an inexpensive rough lumber—a hardwood that is less expensive than oak. It seasons to a soft gray in color. Just be sure, when you put it aside for seasoning, it's laid straight and is in a dry place where it won't warp or swell.

Some people use unseasoned rough lumber for the outside of sheds, overlapping boards with batten so the shrinking lumber won't leave gaps. But many breeders won't use it because the protruding batten makes a tempting target for horses that like to chew. Hemlock is supposed to be less appetizing than other woods, but I think it's better to use seasoned wood and not take a chance.

THE PERMANENT STABLE

Of course not all horses can put up with the outdoor life. Some are too highly bred and literally thin skinned to tolerate prolonged exposure.

Riding horse barn

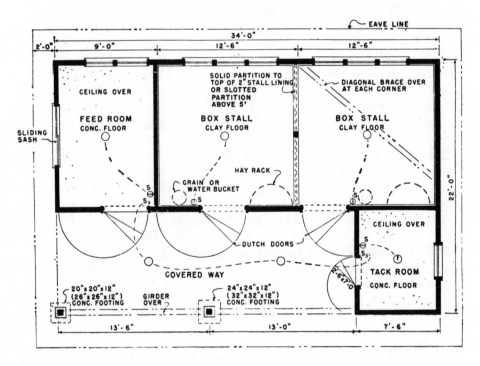

They may not grow a sufficiently thick coat in the winter, or they may be especially sensitive to flies and need to be stabled during summer days. If you have doubts about your horse's ability to rough it, be sure to check with your vet.

Those of you who have the financial resources may want to build your own permanent stable. There are a number of firms that sell prefabricated stables, for which you must have a foundation built. Or a choice of building plans are available from several private companies that advertise in leading horse publications. (*See* Appendix for low-cost plans.)

Before starting to build, be sure to check your local zoning ordinances. Make sure that stables, and horses, for that matter, are allowed in your community and know what distance they must be from property lines.

The one-horse owner willing to go to the expense of building a stable might as well provide for the possibility of a second horse. It seems to happen this way, and it is not that much more expensive. Otherwise, build so you can add on later. Or build tack and feed areas to stall dimensions so they can be quickly converted. But let's assume here that you're building a two-horse stable.

Stalls

The box stalls should be as roomy as possible—10 × 10 feet is adequate, 12 × 12 feet is ideal, and 12 × 14 or 14 feet square is even better. I suppose a small pony could get by in a 9 × 9 enclosure, but it's best to plan for the future when your child outgrows his pony.

Straight stalls (5 × 8 feet) or tie stalls are not recommended at all. If you have one in an existing stable, use it for storage of hay and bedding or as temporary quarters until you get a large stall built. If you put your horse in a tie or straight stall, temporarily, make sure that the tie ring and manger are at the proper height (three and a half feet from the floor) and that your lead rope is tied long enough to allow the horse to lie down but not long enough to get his legs caught in. When tying, use only a slip knot that can be easily released in an emergency —by you and not the horse. If you have a horse who is a genius with knots as well as latches, he shouldn't be in a straight stall.

The width of the stable entrance should be at least five feet to allow horse and owner to pass through abreast if necessary. It should be ten feet high, so the horse won't hit his head accidentally.

Straight stall

Storage Space

A separate area or an overhead storage space should be provided for hay and bedding. Figuring on two tons of hay per horse per winter (from November to March in the Northeast) and a ton and a half of bedding, you'll need at least 1,750 cubic feet of storage space for each animal. This varies, of course, according to the size of the animal and the size of the stall to be bedded.

If at all possible, keep your feed cans inside a metal-lined feedbox to keep it off bounds for horses and rodents. When the cold weather sets in, your stable will be mecca for all kinds of creatures—mice, moles, voles, and worst of all, rats. Feed sacks and plastic containers can be chewed through in no time by rodents; and they can easily climb into uncovered feed cans, where they are likely to bite you on the hand as you measure out the oats.

Tack should be kept neatly in a corner, way out of horse nibbling distance. I once hung an expensive borrowed whip too close to a stall, and by morning a bored horse had make it look like a piece of limp spaghetti. Racks should be provided for hanging up bridles, halters, lead ropes, and saddles. Saddle brackets and racks start at about ten dollars. Bridle racks start at about four dollars. An inexpensive alternative for a round bridle rack is a painted tuna fish can nailed to the wall.

Your stable should have a special corner or wall where stable-cleaning equipment is stored and a *toolbox*. It's essential to have a few common tools on hand for the simple repairs that always come up around a stable or pasture—a loose board, sagging fence, broken latch, or torn screen. You'll need a:

- large hammer
- screwdriver
- pair of pliers
- pair of scissors (for string bales)
- pair of wire cutters (for wire bales and fences)
- box of assorted screws
- box of assorted nails
- roll of picture-hanging wire (for mending screens)
- roll of 10-gauge wire for fence repairs
- box of extra insulators
- sledgehammer ⎫
- crowbar ⎭ for sinking fence posts

Try to get in the habit of returning everything to the toolbox after use—a pair of pliers can be as elusive as a needle when you're groping through a haystack. And, ladies, try your best to learn how to use these tools. For the same reason that women ought to be able to change a tire, they should know how to hold a hammer properly and drive a straight nail. There will be plenty of times when your husband isn't around and there is no handyman available when you'll be stuck with a loose horse and a broken fence.

Every stable should have an old burlap sack hanging in a corner or an extra garbage pail to hold old baling wire, string, and other refuse that could injure you or your horse if left around.

If the stable floor is cement, asphalt, or creosoted wood, provide a peg or hook to hold a length of hose for swabbing down in the summer.

Always provide a well-lit, roomy aisleway where a horse can be crosstied for grooming, shoeing, and visits from the vet.

STABLE CONSTRUCTION

The location of a stable is important. And the adjoining paddock area —the stableyard—should face south toward the sun and be sheltered from the north winds. It should be insulated, if possible, and well ventilated, with windows at each end. The more light inside the better.

Wood should be the only acceptable material for stable walls and stall divisions, and wood means oak. When horses start kicking out, they can go right through a thin pine wall and make plywood partitions look like matchsticks. Cinderblock could injure your horse if he kicks out. Your exterior wall should be two-layers-of-wood thick, so a horse can't kick through it. One economy here is to buy green oak and season it yourself. (See following pages.)

Doors and Windows

The doors of the stall should be able to withstand the weight of a horse leaning against them. Thus the hinges must be extra heavy and the latches strong. Stall doors should be at least four feet, six inches high. That extra six inches prevents horses from reaching out and pushing over the doors to spar with their stablemates as they pass through the aisles. When the door is at this height, they can't put their maximum weight against it. Doors should be wide enough to allow a horse to pass through easily without scraping his hips. The height of the opening should be the same as the stable entrance, or a minimum of ten feet.

If you don't want to build your own stall door, there are heavy screen gates available. These are very sturdy and have the advantage of allowing your horse to look through. They come in two different styles —one has an opening for your horse's neck—and three different sizes, from 54 × 37 inches to 52 × 63 inches. Prices range from about sixty dollars and up—about what you'd spend on an oak door.

It's convenient and pleasant for your horse to have a dutch door opening directly out into a paddock through which he can come and go at will. A paddock can be a relatively small area, as little as fifty feet square, either separate from or connected to the pasture by a gate. It's a place where your horse can be turned out on bad days.

Every stall should have a minimum of one window, opening outward to provide ventilation. Windows should be at least four feet off the floor. If made of glass, they should be protected by wire mesh on the *inside*. If you have no door opening to the paddock, try to make the window large enough to allow your horse to put his head out and look around. Horses are happiest when they can see what's going on around them. So the paddock door or the window should have a hinged screen or door, and always remember to hook it open so it doesn't swing shut on your horse's nose when the wind blows. Sliding windows are best because they stay open without hooks.

Latches are extremely important for stable security. If you want to prevent the sort of fiasco described earlier in the chapter, ask your hardware dealer for the most horse-proof latches he has on hand. Saddlery supply houses sell special ones. It's wise to put a latch on both the bottom and top of the stall door.

There will always be some Houdinis of the horse world with dextrous teeth and muzzles that can undo the most complex latches. I know because I own one. One of my horses has managed to figure out the combinations of the sturdiest devices on the market, even when a snap clip was added for extra protection. A neighbor of mine has an equally adept and democratic horse who, after making his escape, lets all his stablemates out too.

About the only way a horse like this can be foiled is to put in an overhead door so he can't get his head over the bottom one and fiddle around. It's somewhat like solitary confinement, though, and it makes my horse very unhappy.

Stall Guards

Stall guards are interwoven strips of heavy canvas with three clips on each side, set up at chest level so the horse can see what's going on, while being kept in his stall. They're used in warm weather when you want the door open for maximum air circulation. I've also used them to close off the top of the door for temperamental horses who value their privacy. One touchy mare with a foal, who objected to even a passing glance from stablemates, was mollified by the addition of a door-top stall guard. They are also useful if you have an open-top stall near your crossties with an inmate that likes to grab at the ties or nip at stablemates attached to them.

But note a few precautions: If you use a stall guard to close off the top of a door, be sure the bottom of the guard is flush with the door so your horse can't get his head caught between them. When used as a door substitute, make sure the guard is set high enough to prevent a horse from catching a pawing hoof in the canvas strips.

Although I find stall guards invaluable in the summer, contributing to cooler stables and dryer stalls, I won't leave horses alone behind them for long periods of time because of the possibility of injury. And I'm leery of using these devices at all with my more accident-prone horses. One horse of mine managed to get two front feet through a hay net hanging seven feet off the ground from a tree. I shudder to think what he'd do with a stall guard.

I also hesitate to use these devices with aggressive horses who are apt to lunge out at passersby—or with colts that might get tangled up in them out of curiosity.

Stall screens for the summer are also available and cost about sixty dollars each.

Skylights

Skylights in the stable look pretty, but they're better suited to greenhouses. They make stables hot in summer and get covered with snow and leak around the edges in the winter. An alternative is fiber-glass paneling between the top of the roof and the stall wall, which lets light in without excess heat. Were I building from scratch, this would be my choice.

When installing **light fixtures,** put in heavy-duty devices with push-button switches and hardware that is moistureproof and waterproof.

Partitions

Partitions or stall dividers can be built all the way to the ceiling. I prefer to let light in between by building them six or six and a half feet high, then topping with metal flashing to prevent chewing, and separating them from the ceiling by heavy hardware cloth nailed down with brads. This keeps horses from sparring between stalls. An alternative stall topping is grillwork made of three-quarter-inch iron pipe, allowing two and a quarter inches of space between stalls and three and a quarter inches on the aisles.

Flooring

Stable floors can be made of oak, asphalt, cement, clay, just plain dirt, or a combination of woods. Any one of these materials is acceptable as long as the floor is strong enough to hold your horse and is easily drained.

The only type of wood strong enough for flooring is oak. Though the tack room and feed areas where a horse isn't traveling may be made of something cheaper than oak, always bear in mind that your horse could take an unauthorized stroll into these areas when a careless stable assistant leaves a door unlatched. I used oak floors in my stalls and aisles and hemlock, a hardwood much cheaper than oak, in the tack and feed areas. When I converted my stable, the floors were the major areas of reconstruction in the two-story building, which was previously occupied by chickens. The oak and hemlock planks were reinforced with 4 × 8 studding and supported by several hydraulic jacks to handle the weight of the new tenants. The flooring materials you use will depend on whether you're converting a building or starting from scratch, whether you have a breeding or a riding stable, and the area in which you live. To preserve the wood, planks should be soaked or painted with creosote before being laid down. Underneath you'll want to put a solid framework of 2 × 4's, making sure to provide for drainage in the foundation. When the floor is in place, drill holes through the wood so urine can drain out and the floor can be hosed down occasionally.

These holes should be cleared regularly with a dowel or screwdriver; otherwise they quickly become clogged and you won't be able to find them. Some people dislike wood floors because they retain odors and get slippery when wet. I use them, but if we were building a new stable, my preference would be asphalt or Diamond Tex.

I can't overstress the importance of sound flooring, having recently seen a valuable horse go through the pine floor of an old building and hang, terrorized, with legs suspended into the basement below, as her owners worked frantically to extricate her. It took them more than two hours to pile hay bales beneath her feet to give her enough leverage to get out. The injuries she received in the accident have resulted in permanent blemishes. Fortunately, she survived.

Asphalt is very desirable as a flooring because it gives with the horse's feet; it's strong enough to withstand pawing and stomping, and it drains well. It can also be comparatively easy to install. When you're building, the stable foundation can be filled in to a depth of about eighteen inches with gravel ("ones and twos" in the jargon of the gravel company). If you have a problem with drainage, you may want to bury a network of interconnected Orangeburg piping (plastic pipe with holes in it) under the gravel, with a drain leading out into the stable and slanting slightly downhill.

Many large stables use asphalt, but it needs a regular, daily cleaning to maintain the porousness that makes it so desirable. If manure piles up, the pores in the asphalt clog up, causing it to lose its resilience and preventing fast drainage. For this reason, peat moss or sawdust can't be used as bedding over asphalt. When swept and cleaned, asphalt can be hosed down and sprayed with disinfectant.

In heavily trafficked areas, asphalt compresses or corrodes, and some stables use solid rubber mats to prevent this. Asphalt is also difficult to repair, tending to break in on the sides. And after two or three years, the porous holes tend to seal up by themselves. Some professionals don't like it for this reason. Others object that the slight angle at which it's laid is bad for the feet and legs of horses. Still others swear by it and wouldn't use anything else. Because of the rough, abrasive surface of this flooring, bedding should be at least eight inches thick, and straw is probably the best choice. Cost of graveling and asphalting a 12 × 12 space is approximately one hundred dollars.

It's sometimes difficult to get hot asphalt delivered in the small quantities you'll need for a floor. A less expensive, do-it-yourself alternative is something called **cold patch**, the stuff road crews use to make temporary repairs on macadam. Cold patch has the consistency of sandy cement. It can be shoveled on top of the gravel, then rolled down with a large lawn roller and left to set for two or three days. This kind of floor is porous, and urine seeps into the gravel base and through the drains below, making it easy to hose down.

Stone Dust, the fine screenings left over after rock crushing, is a good flooring surface when underlaid by coarser rock. It's very absorbent, but easily dug up.

Diamond Tex, a rather exotic flooring used by one noted horseman, is the same clay and sand mixture found on the skinned part of baseball infields. It's very absorbent, and any parts that get dug up can be raked out, mixed with hay bedding and more Diamond Tex and spread out to be tamped down by the natural action of horses walking on it. D-Tex is cleaned by sprinkling with disinfectant. Just make sure, if you decide to order some, that all the fine stone is removed before delivery. Otherwise, the flooring doesn't set evenly.

Tartan is used by some of the largest and most elegant stables in the country. The expense is exorbitant, but it's nice if you can afford it. This flooring is applied and spread over existing concrete floors laid at a slight incline leading to a drain. After spreading, a chemical catalyst is added to bond it together, and strips of solid tartan are laid around drains. The slightly porous, rough surface has to be vacuumed rather than swept. Its main advantages are easy drainability and sound-absorbency. The rough surface resists friction, muffling the sound of clomping hooves. Recommended beddings are straw and shavings.

Concrete is all right, I suppose, if you're careful to make an extra deep bedding for your horse. Its disadvantage is that it doesn't give with the horse's feet and can cause hoof problems if the bedding isn't thick enough. Concrete can also be slippery and slow to dry unless provision is made for drainage.

Believe it or not, some stables are now experimenting with **indoor-outdoor carpeting,** laid down over well-drained concrete flooring. It sounds ridiculous, but apparently is being used with great success in a number of dairy farms, and stables are starting to try it. The carpet is soft under the hoofs and can be hosed down without rotting.

Clay used to be the traditional flooring for horses because it is easy

on the feet. But it doesn't have much else going for it. Clay tends to get dug up, creating an uneven surface that forces your horse to assume awkward postures. To keep it level, you have to get new clay brought in every year and tamped down—an expensive process.

Dirt floors are inefficient for the same reason. But people do use them, and they can be safe if heavily bedded down and well drained, with a generous subflooring of cinder and gravel. But the larvae of some parasites will burrow in dirt, and to be hygienic, you should get ten inches of the floor replaced every year, which is a nuisance.

Water Facilities

In the stable, providing water for your horse can be as simple as a hook to hang a bucket on, making sure the bucket hangs low enough for easy drinking—at least three and a half feet from the floor. Putting buckets on the floor isn't a good idea, because they are easily kicked over in the night and stepped on.

If you live south of the Mason-Dixon line and don't have to worry too much about freezing weather, you might want to invest in an automatic watering system for your barn. Automatic fountains, which fill when your horse presses his nose against them, start at around twenty-five dollars and run as high as fifty-five dollars. Of course the main expense there would be running the pipe from your water supply to the barn.

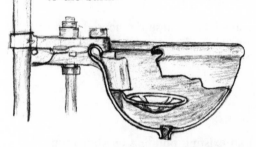

Automatic water fountain cut away to show interior

In colder climates, this gets quite involved, because the pipe has to be sunk three feet below the frost line, or else swathed with a heating cord, sort of a large extension cord plugged into house current, to keep it from freezing. The only trouble with a heating cord is that it doesn't work when the electricity fails. This happens almost as often in the country as it does in the city these days. And when the mercury is at ten below, it doesn't take long for a water pipe to freeze—and burst. After getting soaked a few times, you may find it easier to carry your water out from the house.

Once, in the course of an extraordinarily hectic week in midwinter, quite suddenly the electric heating cord to the barn failed. My husband and I had to remove about twelve feet of cord and insulation and thaw out that entire length of pipe with a small gas torch—a job that took more than three hours. During that period I had eight horses in the barn. It was days before we found the trouble spot, during which I carted about sixteen pails of water a day more than two hundred feet from the house to their stalls.

To guard against this kind of crisis, you can get a cord with a thermostat. When the light in this special thermostat goes out, you know the cord has too. It's worth it.

Of course if you can afford to sink several hundred feet of pipe four feet under, automatic watering fountains are marvelously convenient. If your barn is close to your house it might not be prohibitively expensive, however, and it's worth checking with a plumber for an estimate. Heated fountains go for around one hundred dollars. And if you really want to get fancy about it, you can get field-watering fountains—which run considerably higher. Should you decide to invest in a system like this, be sure to place the fountains very close to or between fences, so that the horse doesn't put his foot in them or foul them.

Several friends who have automatic water fountains still have their problems in winter. Unless the barn is kept closed in the daytime when the horses are out, the automatic fountains will freeze and must be thawed quickly to prevent pipes from bursting. (When horses are stabled and the building is tight, their body heat keeps the stable quite snug.)

Hydrantlike frost-free pumps are available. These are housed below the frostline, only drawing water up when the spigot is turned, with water draining out of the pipe after each use. These run about fifty dollars.

CONVERTING AN OUTBUILDING

Some of you may want to remodel an existing building on your property for a stable. I've seen everything used, from an old chicken coop to the back of a large truck. Garages are the most common converts. All of these things are fine, as long as you keep in mind the points already mentioned, paying special attention to the height of doorways and ceilings and the condition of the floor. If the floor isn't sturdy enough to withstand nine to fifteen hundred pounds, it has to be reinforced or rebuilt with sturdy wood framing and planks. If it's dirt, you should dig it up and underlay it with cinder or gravel for drainage. Make sure there is enough space for a box stall—at least 12 × 12 feet. Don't ever build a tie stall if you can possibly find space for a box.

If you can arrange it, build a six-foot overhang on the outside of the stable as a shady spot where horses can be tied in the summer.

KEEPING HOUSE

Once your stable is built and occupied, you'll be faced with the daily chore of maintaining it, i.e., keeping the tack and feed rooms tidy, the stalls clean, and the bedding fresh. For cleaning, mucking out stalls, and replacing bedding, you'll need the following tools:

- Five- to ten-pronged manure fork (not to be confused or interchanged with your three-pronged hayfork. If you want to spend more money, there are fancy manure scoops available for around twenty dollars). Incidentally, the four- or five-prong fork is better for straw bedding, while six to ten prongs is better for looser bedding, like shavings, sawdust, and Stae Dri, since it allows them to sift through as you take the manure out.
- Metal or wooden fan rake (optional)
- Long-handled flat shovel
- Wheelbarrow (size depending on you and number of horses) and/or
- Manure basket. Though optional for a small stable, this can be a very handy piece of equipment anywhere. It's good for quick pickups and for taking with you to shows.
- Broom
- Hydrated lime (for wood and clay floors, with dispenser)
- Liquid disinfectant for asphalt and cement floors
- Bedding of your choice

Assuming that you will be short of time, the fastest way to clean your horse's stall will be to work around him as he eats. I know many authorities advise putting a horse in crossties while you muck out. But

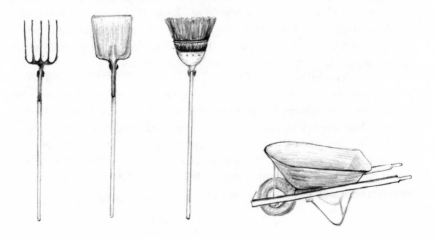

there is no reason why a well-mannered horse won't let you work close to him—as long as you handle the manure fork with care. Naturally you don't want to force the issue if it looks as if you'll be kicked or nipped. In cases like that, feed your horse his grain in the stall and then put him outside with hay and water while you clean. But if he won't let you work around him, your horse has a behavior problem that should be overcome in the interest of an enduring relationship.

The first step in cleaning a box stall is to pick up all the wet bedding and droppings with the manure fork and load them into a wheelbarrow. In the winter, when the manure is frozen, it might be more convenient to shovel the droppings into a manure basket and carry them to the pile. Try to save as much bedding as possible, banking it up around the sides of the stall to dry. By nightfall, it should be ready to reuse unless the weather is particularly cold or damp. You will see how some beddings dry more easily, making them more economical than others in the long run.

When you get down to the bottom of the bedding, you'll probably need a shovel to get the stall really clean. If an accumulation of moisture remains on the floor after the droppings are cleared away, you might sprinkle some chaff from hay or straw around to absorb it, then shovel it up. The final step, for wood, dirt, or clay floors, is to sprinkle on hydrated lime and let the surface dry out during the day. In the case of asphalt or cement floors, use a disinfectant during the summer after hosing down. Don't use liquids on asphalt or cement in the winter. They might freeze. At night, before letting your horse back in, push the banked-up bedding back into the center and add to it if necessary.

When a horse is stabled continually, droppings really ought to be picked up three or four times a day.

If your horse is in a tie stall, which I hope he isn't, it will be simpler to clean because there won't be as much bedding. In the morning, bank the damp bedding against each side of the stall and toward the front. At night, make sure it's pushed far enough forward to give your horse a soft place to rest his knees as he lies down. *Note:* Remember, never leave stable-cleaning tools in the stall with the horse, even for a minute. It's an invitation to injury.

If you're around all the time and want to do a super cleaning job, there are practically no limits as to how fastidious you can be. Horsekeepers, like housekeepers, have their eccentricities, and some are almost compulsively neat. Of course any really large stable has grooms to do the work. They do a major mucking out early in the morning and then systematically pick up during the day so that a visitor seldom sees a soiled stall.

Every once in a while I run into someone who tells me that he leaves all the manure in the stalls during the winter because it heats the stable as it rots. While I don't want to offend anyone who is sold on this theory, it's a potentially dangerous old wives' tale. A horse left to stand in wet manure can develop thrush and a variety of other unpleasant skin irritations, like scratches. Manure is also infested with parasites (in various stages), many of which survive over the winter. While it seems like an easy way out of an unpleasant job at the time, you will be facing a herculean task of stable cleaning when spring rolls around. It's healthier, more economical, and in the long run *easier* to clean your stalls daily.

FIREPROOFING

Millions of dollars and hundreds of valuable animals are lost annually in stable fires, 90 percent of them the result of human carelessness. The fault could lie in heaters, bad wiring, hot plates, a discarded cigarette, children playing with matches—and arson. Only 5 percent are the result of lightning or the spontaneous combustion of hay.

Early detection is the key to preventing total loss. But to make sure it never reaches that point, construct and organize your barn to *prevent* fire. And always have a plan of action ready should an accidental fire occur.

Large stables can afford sprinkler systems and smoke detectors, which are priced out of reach of the average backyard horseowner. But the big businesses that have suffered fire losses have some tips about fire prevention that can be incorporated into everyone's building plans:

- Try to build with concrete block exteriors.
- Treat stall partitions with noncombustible liquids available through your local lumber suppliers.
- Use fiber-glass windows that don't explode under high heat (as does glass), and therefore help contain fires.
- If you can afford it, construct stables with *fireguard*, a specially treated noncombustible lumber. The cost is high because it's treated under pressure, and therefore it isn't recommended for small stables.
- Wiring should be threaded through metal conduit pipes so rodents can't chew through. This is a *must*.
- Have wiring inspected periodically by an electrician or other qualified professional who can spot any potential problems.
- Install lightning rods on your stable roof. The most reliable kind should bear the label of Underwriters Lab, Inc. This ensures that

rods and ground conductors have been made and installed to specifications.

- The roof of your stable should be in good condition so it won't collapse in a windstorm—an invitation to fire and potentially lethal to your horse.
- All doors should be properly hung so that they open quickly.

All of the points on the above list are factors that insurance companies take a close look at before writing your policy, and they affect the rates.

And you could have trouble getting insurance unless you follow these general rules:

- Keep debris that burns easily—loose hay, scrap lumber, and oily rags—away from the stable yard.
- Store hay and bedding away from the stable area, with only the minimum of bales needed kept in the barn itself.
- Hang at least two fire extinguishers in an easily accessible place. These are only good for containing surface fires, however, and would be useless for deep fires in hay, which need a complete soaking to be put out.
- "No Smoking" signs should be posted on the door and at several points in the stable.
- The bulbs in electrically lighted stalls should be protected with heavy wire cages to keep them from breaking.
- Farm vehicles and any gas-powered equipment should never be housed in the barn. The inevitable leakage of gas, oil, or grease is a fire hazard.
- Make sure hay is well cured so it won't spontaneously ignite or combust—it can happen in only a few hundred pounds of hay. Fresh-cut hay should be cured on the field or in the haymow before baling. And be sure to watch all shipments of hay carefully for about six weeks for any signs of heating. Dampness on the surface and a fruity odor to the hay are the first signs of trouble. The National Fire Prevention Association suggests that when there's any doubt about a load of hay, you should stick a pipe several feet down into the bales and then drop into the pipe a thermometer tied to a string. If the temperature is 160 degrees F. or more, you have cause for alarm. Get on the phone to your fire department for immediate advice.
- Remove the manure pile regularly. Keep it well away from barn. Manure piles can heat up and invite spontaneous combustion.
- Keep grass around the barn mowed closely, particularly during

the dry season, to cut down on the possibility of a spreading brush or grass fire.

Should the worst occur and fire break out in your stable, be ready for it. If you're in the house, call the fire department or quickly dial the operator and have her report the fire. If you're in the stable, you'll want to evacuate the horses first rather than take time for a phone call. A horse in a burning stall must be out of there in less than half a minute.

This leads to the age-old problem of whether or not to halter a horse when he's stabled. In emergencies, it's certainly better to have a halter on. If you prefer not to halter (or can't because of a skin irritation) have a place near the door to hang a halter on so it's quickly accessible. And you might practice putting halters on in quick-time, getting a friend with a stopwatch to time you.

Because most horses panic when they see fire or smell smoke, keep a ready supply of towels or burlap bags around so that you can cover their heads as you lead them out of the barn.

Keep the most high-strung horses near the door (some stables keep the most valuable horses there). But any horse that puts up a fight about going out should be left until last. You don't want to waste precious minutes struggling with a temperamental horse when more docile animals would make a fast exit.

Always lead a horse *away* from the direction of the fire. Ideally, every stable should have two exit doors, and if you're planning a stable from scratch, make this a must.

And if the fire seems to be spreading rapidly, don't worry about getting horses to a fenced area. Just lead them to the door and let them loose.

Because even the most docile horses become nervous when they smell smoke, stable owners in western areas where grass fires are common evacuate their stock early—before the fire even comes close to the barn. If you have a fire in your area and the smoke drifts your way, take your horses out to the paddock or pasture. It will be easier on their nerves and save wear and tear on the stable.

BOOBY TRAPS

One vet who has sewed up many horses after stall accidents feels a lot of problems could be solved if owners would put themselves in their horse's place. Stand in the middle of a stall and consider your horse's natural habits. Think about the quick movements he makes and look for things he could get hung up on—like nails, loose water pails, unprotected light bulbs. And check for loose wires, broken glass, broken rails or boards, protruding latches, hinges, or bolts. And that's not all.

- Make sure that any stall or shed is flush with or sunk into the ground so a horse can't get his foot caught beneath it. Stall doors should have a bottom latch for this same reason. Without one, a horse lying down could shove the door open at the bottom and get his foot trapped beneath it.
- In the pasture, make sure that the ends of each board on the fence meet flush at the post. Overlapping boards leave a protruding edge where a horse could snag himself.
- Wooden fences are always an invitation to chewing or cribbing. A coating of creosote will discourage this as well as add years to the life of your fence. Anti-crib paint can also be used, but it's a more expensive and less long-lived solution.
- Aluminum gates, which look nice and are lightweight for easy handling, must be hung with the small slats at the bottom so horses can't get their feet through. No bolts or sharp edges should protrude, and the opened gate should lie flush with the fence or building. Latches should be of the chain and snap types, which fall out of the way when the gate is open. When setting a gate, use carriage bolts with round heads.
- Junk or farming equipment shouldn't be kept where horses are stabled or pastured. I recently heard of a terrible accident where a horse caught his halter on a manure spreader left in a pasture, ripping the side of his face open in the struggle to get free. The smaller the area, the more care should be given to potential booby traps. Corrugated metal, for instance, often used for construction, should be checked for sharp edges or projections. And if your pasture is within an arm's throw of a well-traveled road, check frequently for beer cans, bottles, and trash. Litter bugs seem to find pastures an inviting place to dump.
- Buckets should be fastened securely. And if you use an open hook to hang the bucket on, make sure the hook side faces the wall. I learned about this the hard way after a horse of mine ripped open her nostril on a bucket hook; it took five stitches to repair the damage. Since then, I've used snap fasteners on both ends.
- Check your automatic water fountains to make sure a halter can't get caught on any of the hardware.
- Make sure Dutch doors are fastened back securely. Should a top door swing shut, it may tempt the horse to go under. When you use a stall guard, clip it to side when leading a horse out. Likewise, clip ropes at back of straight stalls so horse won't get tangled in passing.

- Never tie a horse to a potentially moveable object—like a wheelbarrow or a mailbox, or anything he could pull from its moorings. Should he start pulling, the bouncing object behind him will frighten him into moving faster to try to escape it. And the faster he goes, the more panicked he'll become.
- Tie horses only to fence posts, never boards or rails. And make sure the tie is of proper length, with a slip knot for easy removal.
- Be careful about turning a new horse out with other horses. (See following pages.)
- Make sure that guy wires from telephone poles and power lines don't protrude into the pasture. They're difficult for a running horse to see. Ideally, your fence should be built around them. If this isn't possible, tie strips of sheeting to the wires.

BEDDING DOWN

A horse has to be bedded down in the interest of comfort and safety. Without anything to absorb moisture in the stall, the floors would become slippery. And a wet stall full of manure is obviously not a healthy place for a horse to lie down at night. Or to stand in for that matter. Probably most people are aware of the necessity of bedding, but I mention it here because occasionally I run into someone who believes in saving money by not using it.

Bedding must be deep enough to allow a horse to lie down comfortably. A bedding of Stae Dri, for example, should be about four to six inches deep. Straw should be twice as deep. When first bedding down a stall in straw, I usually open up a whole sixty-pound bale (for a 12 × 12 stall). It's more economical to begin with too much than too little. A small amount of bedding will quickly get soiled and wet.

When a horse is left standing in a stall all day, most of the bedding will be banked to the side, but some must be left under him to absorb waste. Otherwise it will be a mess when you come back at night. In the evening, the soiled bedding can be shoveled up and discarded and dry straw or other material forked around him. This is the least expensive way to do it. If you want to be elegant, keep him knee deep in bedding all day and pick up the droppings three or four times.

The three most commonly used types of bedding are straw, Stae Dri, and wood shavings. I personally prefer straw because it offers good drainage, it's clean and fresh looking and dries most easily of all beddings.

There are a few exceptions. I had one horse that was impossible to bed down because he was completely omnivorous. He even ate wood shavings. Eventually I ended up keeping him outside all the time—so he wouldn't get colic. Not too many horses are that undiscriminating, but a lot of them will eat straw. You'll just have to try out different beddings to find out.

Because it dries so well, much of the **straw** you use will be reusable, making it the most economical of the three. I also happen to like the general appearance of straw—there's something luxurious about it, and it is the traditional bedding.

Good straw is made from the stem of wheat, oats, or rye. It comes in bales that vary from forty to sixty pounds, and it should be yellow, crisp, and completely free of weeds and grass.

Depending on how neat your horse is—some will consistently leave their droppings in the same place—you will probably use between three and four sixty-pound bales per horse per week in a 12 x 12 stall. In some areas, this is a major expense. Where I live, a sixty-pound bale of straw runs between $2.20 and $3.00, according to the time of year.

One disadvantage of straw is the problem of how to get rid of the manure. Many people don't like to use straw mulch on their gardens because it's too bulky, and it also creates a much larger manure pile than other beddings.

Stae Dri is made of chopped sugarcane. It is highly absorbent and tightly baled, so that it expands a lot and increases in bulk as the horse moves around in it. While it does absorb more moisture, it doesn't dry out as well as straw, and the wet bedding usually can't be reused unless you happen to have a succession of warm, breezy days. If you have a fairly clean horse, you'll use at least one bale of Stae Dri each week, and it costs over $6.00 per bale, the price depending on your area. Since it is imported, however, it's sometimes not available.

Wood shavings and **sawdust** are sometimes available from sawmills free if you live in a lumbering area. I used to go pick them up in burlap bags, a tedious job that took half a day but saved me several hundred dollars a year. Now, shavings are sold by the bag, and occasionally they come baled. They are very suitable bedding if they are properly kiln dried. The cheapest way to buy them is in quantity.

Shavings and sawdust (and Stae Dri, too) tend to be dusty beddings and shouldn't be used if your horse has allergic tendencies. Shavings aren't very absorbent and are not generally reusable. They are also a storage problem because it takes a lot to make a soft bed, and in the stall they quickly mat down.

There are a few other beddings preferred by some horse owners:

Peanut hulls are reasonably good for bedding, even though they don't sound like something you'd like to lie down on. Like shavings, they are fairly inexpensive but even less absorbent, and they can't be reused at all. It takes a lot of peanut shells to bed down a horse comfortably, and it's no fun to pick them up. You use a shovel instead of a manure fork. Also some horses will eat peanut shells. One of mine even likes peat moss. Unless you live near a peanut farm, you'll probably prefer another bedding.

Peat moss is the crème de la crème of beddings. It is used in some of the most exclusive stables in the country and is priced out of reach of the average horse owner. But even if money were no object, I'd still prefer straw.

Peat moss is very easy to shovel up. But because it's so dark, it's hard to separate the bedding from the manure. And when a light-colored horse lies down in peat moss, he comes up dusty.

The big thing going for peat moss, as far as I'm concerned, is something that most people who can afford it don't care about: it makes your manure pile an asset—as you will see below—instead of a liability.

For those faced with the job of cleaning out stalls every day, the manure pile is a subject there is literally no getting around. It gets to be one of the big headaches of horse ownership—particularly when you live in a suburban area. Unless your neighbors also own horses, you'll discover sooner than later that they are less than entranced with the sight and smell of that mushrooming mound of steaming straw behind your stable.

Consequently, the site of your manure pile should be given careful consideration. Ideally, you should have a covered pit, not a pile, built over concrete for easy cleaning. But because this kind of arrangement is prohibitively costly for most, I'll go on with the pile. It has to be close enough to the barn to be easily reached by a wheelbarrow, accessible by truck, far enough away so it doesn't attract flies to the stalls or your house, and located out of sight and downwind of neighbors.

If you own only one or two acres, this will be a difficult feat. Yet there are a lot of people who keep horses and neighbors happy in suburban surroundings with small pastures of less than an acre. If you're one of them, you may have discovered that the cost of peat-moss bedding is offset by its public relations value. Most suburbanites are avid gardeners, and the very best all-around mulch-fertilizer combination they could buy would be peat moss and manure (aged for a year), sweetened with the lime you use on the stable floor. (It helps to throw a little lime on the manure pile, too, from time to time.) Come springtime, when the wind shifts, get on the phone and invite everyone in a quarter-mile radius to come over with his wheelbarrow. If you still have some left over, you will probably be able to sell it to a local landscaper. If he won't buy it, he'll certainly come over to cart it away free.

Stae Dri, sawdust, peanut hulls, and wood shavings also make good garden mulches, but nothing like peat moss. Straw manure is a very bulky mulch for gardens, only desirable in places where the soil needs lightening. However, mushroom farms use only straw and Stae Dri manure, so they're a possible outlet; and you might try a landscaper here, too. If the pile is easily reached by truck, you probably won't have much of a problem. If all else fails, you'll have to invest in a two-wheeled cart that pulls behind your car and take the manure to the dump yourself. Manure piles should be cleaned up monthly or more often if possible in the warm months of the year. (Again, the ideal is daily or weekly, but for most people this is just impossible.)

FENCING AROUND

With the arrival of summer, come the phone calls—from irate neighbors. "Those damn horses of yours just trampled my tomatoes, and now they're in the marigolds," is a typical opener followed by, "If you don't get them out of here right now, I'll shoot."

I usually ask for a description because it's usually impossible to tell whether it's my horses or not. Even so, a black horse usually turns out to be the one that went by the fastest. Regardless, I always run out to the pasture and count noses, just to make sure they're not mine. Of course, occasionally they are.

Large, elegant stables and breeding farms never seem to have problems like this, probably because they have acres of rolling pastures and can afford the best kind of security available, like Man-o'-War fencing (named for the winner of nineteen out of twenty stakes starts and famous sire). This is a sturdy fence with four horizontal poles supported by posts at eight-foot intervals. Often these fences are electrified along the top for extra security. They are available in sections for about fifteen dollars for eight feet, and if you don't mind the expense, it's well worth the investment.

Looks usually have very little to do with a fence's durability. The two main requirements are that it be safe and strong.

Man o' War fencing

Posts and rails are the most popular fencing and are very pretty. They are also extremely expensive. One ten-foot-long section of a typical three-rail fence, which should be at least four feet high if it is to hold a hunter, is fifteen to twenty dollars or more, about $200 for 100 feet of fence. A disadvantage is that both posts and rails tend to split when a horse leans against them. Also, the rails can be worked loose from the posts and must be reinforced with nails. Unless you have an exceptionally docile horse, to keep a split-rail fence intact you should run a strand of electric wire around the top.

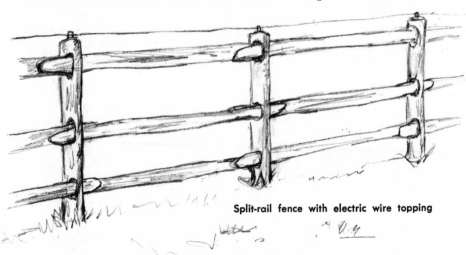

Split-rail fence with electric wire topping

Electric fencing is the cheapest and most reliable, even though its looks leave something to be desired. The electric wire can be attached either to wooden posts sunk solidly in the ground—after being soaked in creosote—or metal posts, which are more expensive but more easily driven in because they are sharper and smaller.

Each post must have a plastic or ceramic insulator nailed to the wood

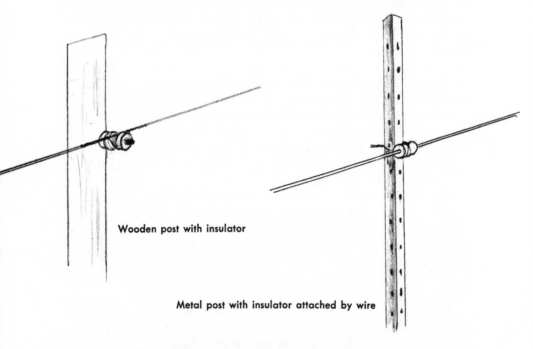

Wooden post with insulator

Metal post with insulator attached by wire

or wired on the steel post with a wire thread. When attaching the electric wire to the insulators, it's best not to wrap the strand around, because the wire, for some unfathomable reason, will periodically need tightening. You want to be able to pull the fence tight in one operation instead of having to unwind it all. Unless you have a small pony, one strand of electric wire won't be enough protection. Use two, the top one about three and a half feet off the ground and the bottom one two and a half feet. If you have a lot of land to fence, a special wire-tightening tool is available.

Once it's up, the thing to remember about electric fencing is that the wire can't touch any objects, including tall weeds, grass, nails, trees, or posts. If it touches anything except the insulator, the fence will be grounded and lose its charge.

All wire connections should be very secure. Otherwise the current will "arc" or jump the faulty point of wire, causing a short. This also can happen with rusty wire, in which case it should be sanded down so that the connections are clean.

This is important for social as well as security reasons. Shorts on your wire will cause static in neighbors' TV sets, car radios, and house radios within about a two-hundred-yard radius. This once happened to my fence when I was on vacation. I returned to hear that everyone in the immediate neighborhood had phoned the electric company to complain of faulty TV and radio reception. Now whenever Channel 2 starts blipping out, I get phone calls. Shorts also cause sparking which could start a fire.

Try to avoid patching a fence with small strands of wire. It dilutes the current and encourages the circuit to arc or short out. So aim for a single strand of wire, limiting patches to two or three per fence.

Every year, those pieces of wire wrapped around the insulators on posts should be checked for rust. In the dry season, shorting out can cause fires. (For the same reason, don't drop the electric gate on the ground when you're opening it. If the handle is rusty, it could short out and ignite the dry grass.)

If you have a short in the fence, check the wires thoroughly, first for any grass or sticks that might be touching them. Then take a close look at the transformer. I once did a microscopic examination of my fence after a storm and failed to find the short. My two-hour search ended at the transformer, which in desperation I took for an appraisal, and it turned out to be the culprit. A simple five-minute replacement of the part restored the power.

If you are using a transformer, you will hear a clicking sound as the electricity is generated into the line. The current is not steady but pulsating at regular intervals. But just because the transformer is clicking doesn't mean your fence is working. It could still be grounded. So invest in a dollar tester and check out the line several times a week, especially in the summer, because of interference from thundershowers and overgrowth of plants.

Your electric fence can be powered either by battery transformers that can be left outside or by an electric transformer that plugs into your house current. Battery transformers have limited lives that shorten in proportion to the size of the pasture, and the batteries cost over ten dollars each. If you can do it easily, it's cheaper to connect the fencing to your house current. Be sure, however, to install a metal ground rod attached to the transformer and buried in the ground to a depth of three or four feet.

When a battery-type transformer stops clicking, it's dead. Always check this type of transformer after a storm, because any short in the fence will drain the life out of the battery.

The cost of electric fencing will depend on the area to be enclosed. Metal posts, which should be spaced about eight feet apart, cost around three dollars each. Wooden posts are about $1.50 for a seven-footer or eight-footer. These are usually made of cedar, sometimes locust, which runs higher.

Wire for an electric fence is cheap. It usually has to be bought by the "rod," a sixteen-and-a-half-foot length, but don't worry about having some left over; it always comes in handy. Ten- or twelve-gauge wire is the handiest for this purpose. Remember, you'll want at least two strands.

Although it sounds cruel, when you put a horse inside an electric fence, be sure to lead him up to it and let his nose touch the wire—just to make sure he gets the idea. Also, unless you want to give your neighbors' children a jolt, buy a few warning signs at the feed store. The voltage is 115.

Above all, remember to check the fence regularly. A grounded or shorted electric fence is useless, a social nuisance, and can be as dangerous as barbed wire.

Some horses are extraordinarily intuitive about electric fences. I'm convinced it's not the clicking sound because my battery is too remote from the area where my horses are pastured to be audible. Yet the minute it stops working my four-year-old colt will amble through it.

While equine escapees are often good for a lot of laughs, I can't overstress how dangerous it is for your horses to get loose on the road. Recently two horses were killed during one twenty-four-hour period in different sections of my neighborhood when they got loose and ran onto the highway. You must always think of fencing as a basically protective device. And you, as owner, are responsible for keeping that protective device in good order.

Barbed wire is a horseman's nightmare. I know it is used almost exclusively out west where it's the only practical way to fence hundreds

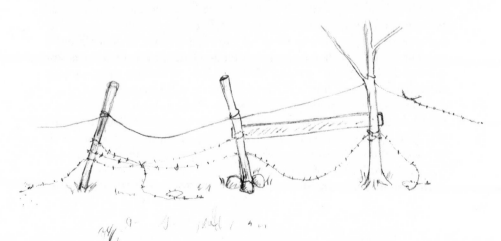

of acres, and many horses there bear scars. One tip here: If barbed wire is already there and in good shape, and you want to risk it, make sure the bottom strand is thirty inches from the ground so the horse can't snag his leg. You may want to remove the bottom strand (or clip it off) to get the fence to a safe height. I hope you won't have to have a horse badly mangled by barbs to become convinced that it's a bad fencing choice. A horse that has his legs caught in barbed wire and panics can literally tear himself apart.

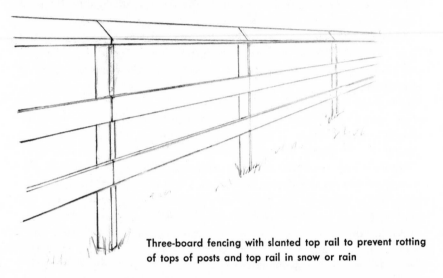

Three-board fencing with slanted top rail to prevent rotting of tops of posts and top rail in snow or rain

Board fencing, reinforced with electric wiring, is a good-looking compromise for the suburban horse owner. If you want to cut a few corners, put up a two-board fence in places where it will be seen, running your electric wiring around those parts of the pasture that are hidden from view. The cost will depend on the thickness of the boards —lumber is always expensive—and you can count on even a small pasture running into several hundred dollars.

Resist the temptation to leave off the electric wire. It looks prettier without it, but it will stay up much longer with it. Horses lean across unelectrified fences to graze, and if they see something they want on the other side, they are capable of going right through it.

Board fencing should be painted or stained with whitewash or shingle stain as a preservative. The ends of the posts should be soaked in a tub of creosote overnight before sinking them in the ground. This is a messy job—creosote is sticky and has a strong smell—but it will add years to the life of your fence.

Use eight-foot posts, if possible, with the idea of sinking them two to three feet below the ground for maximum strength. The boards come in twelve-foot sections, so it makes sense to set the posts six feet apart rather than cut off valuable wood. If you can find boards in fourteen-foot lengths, set your poles seven feet apart. Be sure to use thick wooden posts (4 × 4 inches or thereabouts in circumference) for board fencing. Lighter ones, which can be used for electric fences, won't take the nails without splitting.

A three-board fence is most satisfactory, with the top board between four and a half feet to five feet off the ground. Boards should be three-quarter inch to one inch thick and six inches wide. Hemlock is good because it's stronger than pine. And for a longer-lived fence, it's worth the time (and mess) to paint the whole thing in creosote. (If you do, make sure to wear heavy gloves and a long-sleeved shirt to protect against burns.)

Digging post holes is a tedious task unless you have a gas-driven post-hole digger. You may find that the saving in your time merits the expense of renting such a machine—or hiring a post-hole digger. Remember that the holes must be dug straight down. Any angles will create lots of problems when you put in the posts.

Rocks encountered en route are removed with a hand trowel or a crowbar, both essential pieces of equipment in this venture. The trowel is also handy for removing loose dirt as you dig the hole.

Before putting the pole in, use small stones mixed with dirt at the bottom to give the pole a firm foundation. As you refill the hole, pack dirt and pebbles down with a trowel, using lemon-sized stones to wedge the post in.

Gates can be as simple as two bars across an entrance of double posts with cross boards. But bars are awkward to open when you're leading a horse with one hand. Also, in a small pasture where the inmates become bored, they are easily worked open. To make them escape proof you'll have to run your electric fence across the bars and fasten it with a rubber-handled hook that can be opened and closed.

Wooden gates are fairly easy to construct. Even better are the aluminum gates you can buy at most feed-supply stores for about thirty dollars and up.

The only sure way to find out whether your fence is adequate is to put your horse inside and see if he stays there. If you see him walking down the road a few hours later, you'll know you've failed. Even if you don't see him make his exit, your neighbors will be sure to keep you informed of his progress. Don't be discouraged. Check out your fences to see where he escaped and how, and try again.

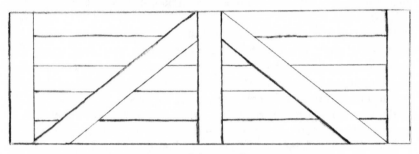

A type of homemade gate

GREEN PASTURES

Ideally, each horse should have a minimum of an acre and a half to graze on. The pastures should be broken up into three separately fenced areas so that you can keep rotating your horse from one to the other when a field becomes grazed down. In early spring, for instance, you won't want your horse to graze on ground that he'll be pastured on later in the summer—he'll turn it into a mudhole. It's helpful to build a small paddock to turn him out in during the sloppy months when the pastures are growing. Because of the danger of contracting parasites in a small area like this, many experts are now advising people not to try to grow grass at all in the paddock area but to put down cinders or fine gravel instead.

One family that had less than a quarter-acre paddock in a suburban neighborhood kept it green year round by stabling their two horses in the wet spring and fall, as well as at night. And they kept the paddock picked up regularly—twice a week; it's possible, if you're willing to put in the effort.

When you have large fields, your soil should be tested yearly and limed if necessary. Liming should be done very early in the spring, even on top of the snow, which carries it into the ground effectively as it melts. Reseeding can also be done on the snow.

Obviously none of this will do any good unless your horse is kept off the new seedlings. A new pasture will have to be left ungrazed for a year to become firmly established.

Manure must be picked up regularly from all pastures, an annoying job but an absolutely necessary one. If left to stand, manure kills grass, spreads worms, and looks awful. Fresh manure should never be spread for fertilizer the year the pasture will be grazed. It should either be plowed under or the pasture given a year's rest to kill the parasites.

If you have an old pasture that needs a new lease on life or a new one that needs sowing, your county agricultural agent will be able to tell you what grasses grow best in your area. You should also have your soil tested by the agent to see if liming is necessary.

Remember always to have a ready water supply in your pasture. If your horses are kept close to the house—it's always nice to have a pasture where you can see it and enjoy your horse visually—it's usually practical to run a hose out to a large galvanized pail or plastic tub. Old bathtubs are very useful for this purpose because of the drain in the bottom—if you don't mind looking at an old bathtub.

Always remember to keep these watering troughs clean. Algae accumulate rapidly in hot weather, along with harmful bacteria.

Where there is a pond or stream in a pasture, it's wise to have it tested for purity by your agricultural agent. If this is the only water

supply you have, be sure to recheck it often during hot and dry months in case it suddenly dries up or becomes stagnant. Horses drink more water in the summer because they perspire more. As mentioned in the chapter on feeding, 50 percent of a horse's weight is water. Leaving a horse without water for long periods causes serious dehydration problems.

Now that your horse is properly housed, pastured, and fed, we can go on to some of the finer points of horse care—like how he looks and what you can do to make him look and feel fit.

6

the
well-manicured
mount

In the era of the horse and buggy, grooming was something that grooms did. Times have changed. The average modern equestrian, beset by car payments and mortgage installments, can barely afford a horse, let alone a groom. He has to do the hard, dirty work himself.

Appearance is not the sole reason for grooming your horse. A daily once-over is essential to the animal's health during the riding season. I've already mentioned that it keeps pores open, helps circulation, and maintains muscle tone. Grooming also assures cleanliness and gives you a daily opportunity to check your horse over for cuts, scratches or other irritations. Obviously a thorough grooming also improves appearance and when you go to a show or a hunt, there are a few extra things that can be done to make your mount look glamorous.

133

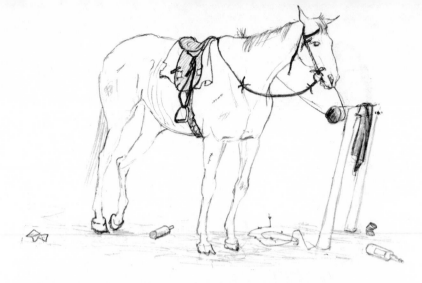

A horse should be well groomed before working and lightly groomed afterward. Some horsemen do it the other way around, because after work a horse's pores are opened and his circulation is going. But either is a good general rule to follow. If your horse is stabled at night or throughout the winter, he should also be groomed every other day or so. There is a difference of opinion about field-kept horses. Some feel that accumulated dirt acts as insulation. Others, myself included, believe that an occasional grooming will keep the coat in better condition.

Grooming is a time-consuming job that puts a decided strain on the arms and back. If you're not tired after grooming your horse, you haven't done a very good job. When I finish working on two or three horses, I usually don't feel very much like riding. But it has to be done.

A word of caution: while your horse may express his delight by arching his back as you curry him or curling his lip into a classic horse laugh as you brush a favorite spot, always be wary of sensitive grooming areas that might irritate him. One Thoroughbred I used to own was too thin skinned to be curried at all. It was easy to tell the way she felt about it by the set of her ears, which she pinned flat back, and her glare of displeasure at the sight of the currycomb. All Thoroughbreds —in fact most purebreds—should be groomed with caution until you learn how sensitive they are. When the mud is two inches thick it may be hard to restrain yourself, but your new horse will trust you more if you begin by handling him with care.

HOW TO HANDLE HIM

To groom a horse properly, you have to be able to work comfortably with him in close quarters. He should respond to your spoken commands, and be easily haltered, tied, and led around.

134

Let's assume that you've just bought a horse, and don't know how he responds to grooming on a day-to-day basis. (Naturally, first you picked up his feet, led him around, and rode him.) When you enter his stall for the first time, keep your hands at your sides and speak in a reassuring, firm tone of voice. Since the equine vocabulary is limited, it's not what you say but how you say it that counts. Don't shout or speak sharply to your horse unless he has misbehaved. If you yell at him all the time, he'll eventually tune you out entirely and become completely unresponsive to spoken command. Just converse easily with your horse as you work to let him know where you are and where you're going next. One young pupil of mine, not the most casual of talkers, walked into the stall and announced: "How do you do. My name is Brian and my father owns a bakery. We live on Cherry Hill Drive."

When you want your horse to move over in the stall, put your hand against his shoulder or his rump and firmly say "over." If you want him to back up, stand in front of him with one hand against his chest and the other on the bridge of his nose or under the halter and say "back."

When you walk behind him, keep your hand on his rump and pass *close* to him. That way, if he should ever get startled and kick out, he won't have the leverage to hurt you. If the worst happens, you will only get bumped with his hock.

If your horse seems nervous when you work next to him, call his name in a friendly voice and say "easy" or "steady."

Any well-mannered horse should respond to these simple word commands. If he doesn't, he'll learn.

When approaching your horse from the front, walk slowly and don't wave your arms around or jump up and down, or do other strange things. When walking up on your horse from behind in a straight stall, remember that his rear vision is limited. When he faces straight ahead, he can't see all the way back. Although they do have more rear vision than people, horses, too, have a blind spot behind. So it's essential to speak to him first, letting him know you're there. Come up close, and give him a light pat on the rump.

A nine-year-old student of mine who thought talking to a horse behind his back was silly, walked unannounced into the stall of the most docile, child-loving mare I own and got kicked in the stomach for the oversight. The mare, who was probably half-dozing at the time, was so startled that she acted reflexively, lashing out with a hind hoof in self-defense and knocking the girl to the floor. I don't know who was more shaken by the experience—the horse was obviously as surprised as the student. But this is a dangerous way to learn a simple lesson.

Always stay as calm as possible. If you appear nervous, jumpy, or frightened, your horse will sense it and react to it. Most horses are

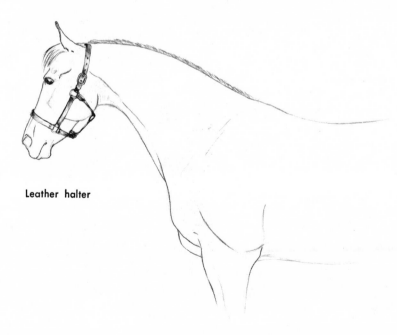

Leather halter

reasonable and like human company. If handled properly, they will be obedient and affectionate.

Any talk about working around a horse is pointless unless you know how to lead and tie him correctly. Everyone I've ever taught has just assumed that all horses take naturally to being led and tied. They don't. Like everything else, this is a matter of training.

A halter and lead rope are obviously necessities if your horse is to be led and tied. Halters come in various materials, colors, and sizes. The sizes progress from pony, colt, and cob to standard and large horse. (The cob is for horses with small heads or ponies with large heads.) Standard materials are leather, rope, nylon, and a newer material called polyprophelene, which is softer than nylon.

I personally prefer halters that have buckles on the crown and a clip under the chin for easy fastening. Nylon halters that open only on the top are a real nuisance—awkward and time-consuming to fasten and dangerous because they won't break in an emergency.

I also find it convenient to get a different color halter and matching lead rope for each horse. Most horseowners find it convenient to have an everyday halter of rope or nylon and a leather halter for show, which gets the same care and maintenance as tack.

Halters can cost as little as $4 and as much as $43 (for those of the finest craftsmanship with brass fittings). Western horse halters have contrasting stitching, and those designed for saddle horses have patent leather pieces. Others are even decorated with hearts, flowers, and Indian motifs.

Should your horse get rubbed from a halter, you can get pieces of Equi-Fleece tubing, which looks like sheepskin but is machine washable, to fit over the cheekpieces and across the crown and noseband. Horses with very sensitive skin may need these on their bridles too (not in the show ring, of course).

The least expensive lead ropes are made of rope or cotton and cost from $2.50 up. Leather lead shanks—straps with chain—run as high as $18. You can also buy nylon shanks with chains to match the color of your halter.

I recommend shanks for people with strong horses who try to lead them; for young, obstreperous horses; and for small people with large horses. Shank leads allow sure control over your horse if you slip the chain through the near side ring of the halter cheekpiece, run it under the horse's chin, and clip it to the offside ring. When the chain is attached this way, a little jerk will punish the horse under the jaw— a sure means of disciplining a horse that wants to pull you around and a method that isn't as brutal as putting the chain over the nose, which often makes a horse pull back or rear.

Don't, however, use the shank lead straps for tying; they don't slip out easily enough. Use the shank for leading only, and carry another rope lead with you for tying.

If you have an aisle in your stable, you may find it most convenient to crosstie your horse when he is being groomed, or you can put rings in a box stall for crosstying. Crosstie chains can be purchased for as little as $6 or $7 or up to $10 for the new elastic kind. Rings should be set about five feet from the floor on each side of the aisle. Lead ropes can cost about $3 each; just make sure they have a sturdy snap. Avoid homemade ones.

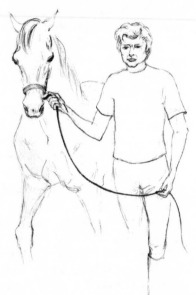

The proper way to lead a horse

To lead a horse properly, stand beside his shoulder, on the near side, facing forward. Try not to turn and look at your horse as you walk; this confuses him, and he may stop. Stand far enough from his side so that your arm is almost straight as you walk, allowing you to stay in your path and he in his. Walking in front of a horse is a good way to get stepped on; he'll normally do everything he can to avoid you, but he can't help it if you're directly in his path.

Remember to stay by his shoulder as you both walk forward. By walking ahead, you pull on his head, causing him to draw back and refuse. Done often enough, this kind of pulling will make your horse impossibly balky and unleadable. As you walk, hold the lead rope in your right hand, about four to six inches beneath the snap. The slack rope should be gathered in your left hand, so that you or the horse can't trip over it.

The incorrect way to lead a horse

In 4-H Fitting and Showmanship classes a child is judged on whether he leads his horse correctly. When leading, your right leg should move forward simultaneously with the horse's near forefoot. If you do it the other way around, the chances are good that your toes will be stepped on by his front foot.

Never lead by the halter alone, which will result in tugging on your horse's head, causing him to pull back. Also, it's easy for a halter-led horse to get away. Once he's done it a few times, he'll realize he has the edge on strength.

Encourage your horse to step along at a brisk pace, one that is comfortable for you. If he goes too fast, say "easy" in a firm voice, restraining him and repeating the command until the pace is comfortable.

Should your horse start to bolt or shy when being led, resist the impulse to let go of the rope. Say "easy" or "steady" and try to keep a hand on the rope, staying next to his shoulder. If allowed to pull back so that you're facing him, he could rear up. And if he starts backing when you're in front of him, all you can do is try to hold him or back up with him. Either way, you'll be on the losing end. So try not to get excited or angry and work on slowly regaining your position by his shoulder where he cannot get you into this unfortunate predicament. If all else fails, get someone else to stand a safe distance behind him, and then say "walk." It's important to stick with situations like this, and even if it takes a half hour to correct the problem, you will have kept a bad habit from forming.

One high-strung filly I used to exercise was very neurotic about many things, including being led. When I led her out of her barn, which had a very narrow doorway, she always went through the same routine. Because of the narrowness I had to pass in front of her in order to get through the doorway without being crushed between her and the doorjamb. As soon as I'd pass in front of her to go through, she'd stop dead, nearly pulling my arm out of the socket. Two things finally improved the predicament: when leading her, I now always allow plenty of slack in the lead rope, and a cooperative stablemate in a box stall close to the door reached out over his stall door one day (during one of my filly's sieges) and bit her on the rump.

In leading your horse through a narrow opening, walk ahead of him, giving him a little slack rope and keep the same pace. Don't pull the rope taut, or he'll stop and throw his head up. A lot of loading problems start when the rope is pulled too tight on the way into the van.

When you stop, a trained horse should stop with you. If he doesn't, say "whoa" or "ho" emphatically and restrain him. Restraint doesn't mean pulling, tugging, or jerking on the lead. One should never pull against a horse; rather, you behave like an immovable object, not *allowing* him to move forward.

Several things must be avoided when you lead your horse. Don't ever yank him around by the nose, or he'll respond the same way he does to heavy hands on his mouth—ignoring or fighting you. Nothing is more irritating than having a horse pull you around the paddock. A properly trained horse has been taught from early youth never to lean on a rope and he consequently never gets to know his own strength.

If you have a horse that flunks out in this schooling lesson, life in the stable will be difficult. One summer I boarded a mammoth sixteen-hand horse that weighed at least fifteen hundred pounds and appeared, in the working ring, to be a real sweetheart. After our first schooling session, I began to lead him into the stable and his new stall. As we approached the stall door I applied my customary restraint, but the boarder didn't get the message. He kept right on going, traversing the entire length of the stable, stopping only when his nose touched the far wall—and there we stood until I put the lead shank (combination chain and leather lead) around his nose and got him in hand. This is what happens when a young horse is allowed to find out that he can lead his owner around.

Just as you can't assume a horse leads, you can't assume he ties. Never tie your horse by the bridle rein to a fence or hitching post. It's a sure way to break both. As mentioned earlier, your horse will panic and pull back until something gives—usually the reins. Western horses, of course, are taught to ground tie, but that's another subject. If you're planning a trail ride or are in a riding situation where you will want to dismount and tie your horse, take along a halter and lead rope that you can slip over the bridle.

Some English horses will only tie with a halter (some won't tie at all

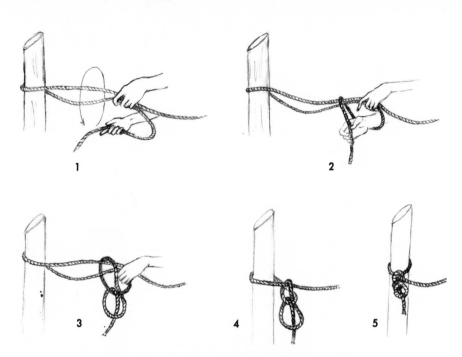

Tying a halter hitch knot to secure a horse to a post

except with crossties). But they should never be tied by the neck. Some Western horses necktie with a special knot—a bowline—that won't slip no matter how hard he pulls. But if you tried this approach with an English horse, he would probably panic. A friend of mine who rides Western once innocently necktied one of my horses, and the horse pulled back so hard that he would have strangled himself if we hadn't cut the rope.

When tying the end of the lead around a post or on a ring, be sure to make a slipknot that can be easily pulled loose in an emergency. Leave about two feet of rope, enough for your horse to move his head, but not enough to allow him to catch his legs.

Even a horse trained to tie can become a problem if you're sloppy about the procedure. Rope that is too old or tied too loosely will encourage him to fool around and possibly break the lead. Once this happens a few times, he'll get the idea and become a chronic rope breaker—a real drag.

I've stressed tying, leading, and working around your horse because these are such basically important things, particularly if you live in a relatively isolated rural area or have no help. It's no fun when you have to spend half the day getting your horse into or out of his stable. And you won't be able to start grooming until you're able to manage your mount.

141

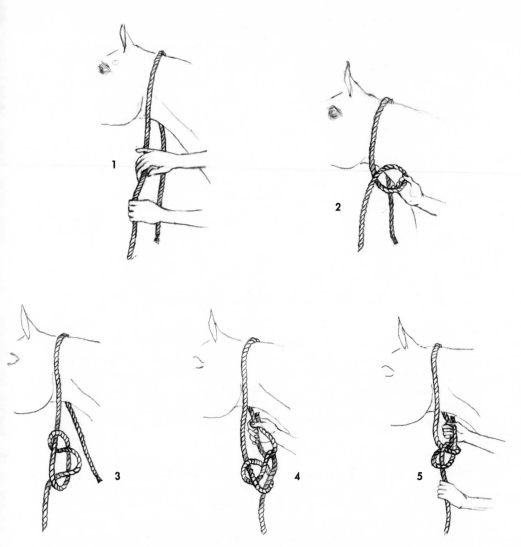

Tying a bowline knot for a horse trained to tie by the neck

BASIC GROOMING

It's convenient to crosstie your horse in an aisleway in the barn or tie him in the stall itself for grooming. An aisle, however, is lighter and roomier. But if you're without an aisle, tie him to a ring in his box stall, or crosstie him, and work there. On nice warm days, most horses

Crosstied in an aisleway

can be tied to a post outside. Some horses, however, are too high-strung to be secured in this manner and must be crosstied.

If you're wearing riding clothes, be sure to wear a grooming apron (an old smock or a large sheet will do) and women should wear a scarf. Or, you can put on old clothes and change afterward. The point is that you're going to get dirty if you do a good job.

Grooming tools can be kept in a shoe bag or box, on a shelf or on hooks close to the grooming area—someplace where it's easy to get at them and where they can be replaced after using. Special grooming kits with collapsible legs that make a convenient stand are available at tack and saddlery supply houses. But a shoe bag is just as good and a lot cheaper. If you don't have an organized spot to keep your tools, children will leave them all over the place and they'll get buried under the feed or mangled underfoot.

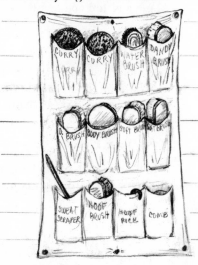

You'll need the following grooming equipment:

Necessary Tools (all prices approximate)

Hoofpick. 75 cents.

Rubber currycomb. $1.25–$2.00. Metal ones are too hard.

Stiff dandy brush, wood-backed. $2.00–$3.50. Choose one made of quill or rice-root bristle.

Soft dandy brush. $2.00–$3.00 (wood-backed, white fiber bristle).

Body brush. $4.95 and up (for leather-backed one) to $14.95.

Cactus cloth (optional). $4.95.

Stable rubber or cloth toweling. If you use old, *clean* towels, this won't cost anything. If you want to be fancy you can buy stable towels made of Irish linen and even raw silk.

Water brush. $7.50.

Shedding blade. $3.00–$3.95.

Sweat scraper. 50–75 cents.

Small wash bucket.

Sponges (plastic). $.75–$1.00 for small ones. You'll need two. $1.25–$1.75 for the large size.

Sponges (natural). Better than the above but expensive, costing about $6.00 for a large sponge and $3.00–$3.50 for a small one.

Fly repellent and hoof dressing. Price depends on size.

Occasional Tools

Fetlock shears. $3.95.

Fetlock hand clippers. $7.00–$9.00, but a waste of money because they're inefficient.

Fetlock electric trimming clippers. $10–$20, a lot more expensive but quicker, and they do a much better job.

Body clippers. $60–$95. Try to borrow or buy these secondhand.

Mane and tail comb. $.60–$1.25.

Very Occasional Tools

Grooming vacuum cleaner: hand model, $70–$75; floor model, $125–$350 (for the stable that has everything, but which does as good a job as you can do by hand.)

Take Your Pick

Begin grooming by picking out your horse's feet—so you won't forget to do it afterward. This is really the most important part of grooming,

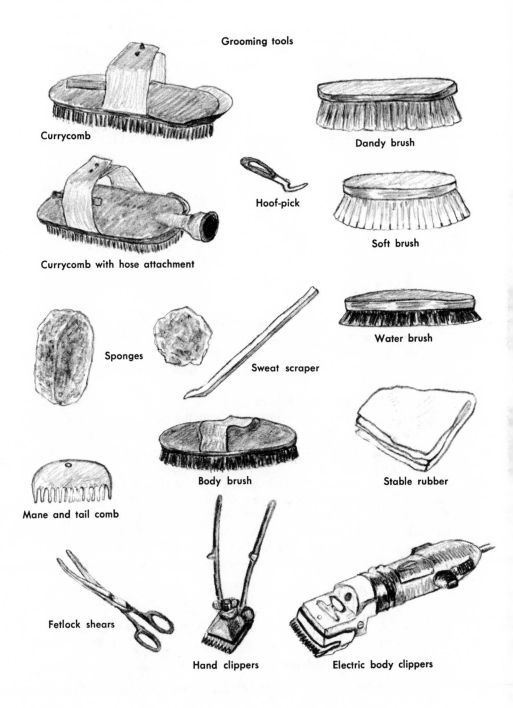

Grooming tools

Currycomb

Dandy brush

Currycomb with hose attachment

Hoof-pick

Soft brush

Sponges

Sweat scraper

Water brush

Mane and tail comb

Body brush

Stable rubber

Fetlock shears

Hand clippers

Electric body clippers

because something caught in a hoof will make your horse lame and unridable. I've found all sorts of strange things jammed into my horse's hoofs—pieces of wire, old chunks of concrete, even a high heel from a woman's shoe. If a horse walked on any of them for any time, his foot could be badly bruised by the constant pressure, and he would go lame.

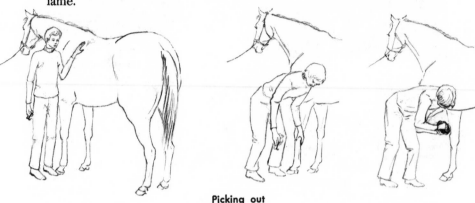

Picking out

To pick out, start with the near forefoot—the left front foot. Facing your horse, lean your shoulder against his, pushing away from you. Then slide your hand down his leg and pick up the hoof. The force of your weight against his shoulder, not your hand, is what makes him lift his foot.

Lift his foot above the height of your knee and support it well with one hand as you pick out with the other. If the hoof is held too low, your horse will be tempted to put his foot down again. Once your horse has been taught to pick up his feet, you need only touch his foot to make him lift it.

Use the pick going away from you along the side of the frog (*see* chapter 7), digging out all the manure and other foreign matter until the entire sole becomes visible. Also, clean along the cleft of the frog. If the hoof smells bad and you find that the sole is flaking off, your horse probably has thrush which should be treated immediately.

Use the pick going away from you along the side of the frog.

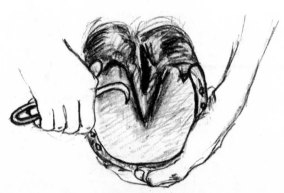

How to pick up the hind leg

Step 1

Step 2

Step 3

147

Next, move down and do the hind leg on the near side, standing with your shoulder against your horse's rump but still facing his rear. As you lean against him, run your hand down his leg and pick up the hoof. You'll find that this is harder work with the rear hoofs.

Pick up the hoof with your right hand, then reach over and grasp it underneath with your left, supporting the hoof on the left knee as you work. Repeat the entire procedure on the offside.

When grooming for a show, finish off the feet by taking a stiff scrub brush and wash the hoofs thoroughly, leaving them to dry while you groom the rest of your horse. At the end, paint on hoof dressing—or, if you like the effect, black shoe polish.

Sponge Baths

If your horse has large manure or grass stains on his coat, start his grooming by scrubbing down the area with the big body sponge. Use the washing pail, filled with warm water. Rub the sponge with a mild soap, and do a little bit of your horse at a time. On light-colored horses it may help to sprinkle a little bran on the stains; it acts as a cleansing agent. Light-colored horses also get grass stains on their coats, which is a real nuisance. You just have to keep working at them with mild soap until they disappear. After rinsing off the sponged areas, let the coat dry while you groom the rest of him.

Shedding Blades

In the spring, when your horse's coat starts to come off, you'll need the shedding blade before currying to get the loose hair off. There are one-

Applying the two-handled shedding blade

and two-handled shedding blades. One model has two handles that convert to one by tucking one under a strap. Go very easy with this tool on the sensitive underbelly and on the flank and don't use it on the face and below the knees or hocks.

The Currycomb

The most efficient and professional way to work with the curry is to hold it in your right hand and the dandy brush in your left, cleaning the comb against the brush as you work. Begin currying from the poll or top of the neck on the near side, working toward the back. Curry in a circular, counterclockwise motion against the hair—i.e., rub the hair the wrong way. This works the dirt to the surface. When the curry gets dirty, which happens dozens of times in the course of a grooming, rub the comb against the dandy brush so that they're both cleaned out at the same time. The currycomb is excellent for removing dried mud and caked sweat.

Do *not* use the curry on the face, on the legs below the knee, or the rear belly. Be sure, however, to curry between the front legs. And use it carefully under the girth and along the flanks. Some horses are ticklish. You'll quickly learn whether yours is one of them if he pins his ears back, makes a threatening biting expression, or tries to cowkick at you. When a horse tries to bite or kick, always punish him with a sharp "no" and a hard slap on the nearest area—usually the neck or shoulder. But respect his wishes—and protect yourself—by being more considerate in the future.

If your horse is particularly thin skinned, he may not tolerate a curry at all, as in the earlier example. Again, he will be quick to let you know about it. If your horse is pasture kept, this can be very inconvenient. You'll have to improvise with a stiff dandy brush and a sponge. It's really difficult, though, to remove caked mud or dried sweat with anything but a curry.

Never use a metal currycomb. These are much too harsh for even a thick-skinned horse, and if he has a scab or a scar under his coat, you run the risk of opening it up and causing infection.

As you've probably realized by now, a good currying job takes a lot of elbow grease.

The Stiff Dandy Brush

This is used to brush mud and dirt from the hocks, fetlocks, pasterns, and hind legs—the places you couldn't curry—and for drawing out the dirt raised by the currycomb. You also use it to brush out the mane and tail and to train the mane to the offside. Do *not* use the stiff dandy on the face. As you brush, hold the currycomb in your left hand and clean the dandy against it.

After brushing the mud and dirt from the uncurried areas, begin again at the near poll and brush with a vigorous downward motion, this time going with the hair. This draws out the dirt and is good for a horse's circulation. Be sure and keep the dandy free of dirt by frequent cleanings with the curry.

The Soft Dandy Brush

This is the next grooming tool to use. I prefer to work with two soft white dandy brushes, one in each hand. Start out by gently brushing your horse's face and around his ears. Then smooth down the mane and the tail. Starting at the near poll again, do the body with alternate, swift downward strokes. This will pull out any remaining dust and dirt and really put a gleam in your horse's coat. Use less vigor around his flanks and belly area. The brushes can be cleaned against each other as you work. Follow this by a thorough, energetic wipe with a clean towel (or stable rubber) which squeezes the oil out of the glands of the skin and makes the coat shiny.

Body Brushes

These are sometimes used in lieu of the soft dandies. It's really a matter of personal choice. I prefer the two dandies.

Stable Rubber

This is the English term used for linen towels that are used to bring out a high gloss on a horse's coat—the final grooming touch.

Cactus Cloth

If you have one, use it next in the grooming. Its ancestor is the English wisp, a handmade straw grooming tool used as a massage to harden muscles, stimulate skin, and to put extra polish on a horse's coat. It's also supposed to be a good muscle conditioner, helpful for rubbing down a horse after using a sweat scraper. The cactus cloth should be dampened and brought down with a hard motion on the horse's coat.

Small Sponges

Some people prefer to use these first in a grooming. I think it's better to wait until the end to pick up any dust that may have settled on your horse's soft parts. Use one sponge to gently wipe debris away from his eyes and nostrils. This is especially important in the summer when the secretions around his eyes and nose attract flies—not only annoying but a source of parasitic infection. With the other sponge, clean the dock area beneath the tail. When cleaning a gelding, be sure periodically to wash the sheath and penis. If not done regularly, urine and scale will accumulate which can cause swelling and soreness, and in extreme cases, the urinary tract can become blocked. If the genital area is cleansed carefully with warm water and mild or antibacterial soap, most horses won't object.

Hoof Dressing

This can be used once or twice a week on both the wall of the hoof and the frog and sole, not only to improve appearance but to keep the hoof flexible, to improve the pliability of the frog, and keep the heels from cracking. Hoof dressings should be used up around the coronet band. They're usually applied with a brush to a *clean* hoof. Some dressings can be sprayed on, others have an ointmentlike consistency and can be purchased in quart or gallon sizes. Do not use it more often, however, or it will have the opposite effect and seal moisture out.

When you think you're through grooming, be sure to check between your horse's front legs, inside his hind legs, and under the girth area to make sure you've done a thorough job. There's a lot to a horse, and it's easy to overlook some of it.

One small nine-year-old girl in my stable management class consistently forgot to groom behind the ears—because she couldn't see that high. You'll find that 4-H and Pony Club Fitting and Showmanship classes are very thorough about forgotten areas like this. They always check behind the ears and under the dock and belly. It's important because a horse can get bridle sores from a buildup of mud behind the ears and saddle sores from accumulated mud in the girth area.

At this point, if you were in the English cavalry, an inspecting officer would run his white-gloved hand over your horse's coat. At horse shows, judges in grooming classes run a hand through the horses' manes. Both glove and hand had better remain clean!

During the fly season, finish up the grooming by wiping or spraying on—if your horse will tolerate spray cans—a fly repellent. Never spray around the face, and be careful when applying the repellent with a rag not to get the chemical in the eyes or nose.

Some repellents are diluted with water; others can be applied directly from the can and have an oil base. Make sure you read the directions and know what kind you have. An application of undiluted concentrate could cause serious skin problems.

The advantage of the diluted kind is that you can vary the strength, depending on the sensitivity of your horse's skin. Special fly-stick applicators are available for the face areas, or you can wipe the well-diluted liquid repellent on with a rag and then cover the whole face thoroughly.

I've found that a lot of repellent gets wasted when you use sprayers. Kids tend to get carried away and end up spraying everything but the horse. My solution is to keep a repellent-soaked rag in a plastic bag or covered coffee can in the tack room.

During the summer, horses should be thoroughly covered with repellent before going out to pasture. Special attention should be paid to the stomach, chest, ears, and other areas where flies can cause irritating sores.

Some horsemen claim that the addition of vinegar to the horse's water reduces the flies because it changes the composition of the horse's sweat. As yet this has not been thoroughly tested.

These grooming procedures should be done on a daily basis when you're riding regularly. Other grooming chores must be done periodically, and this is where the occasional grooming tools mentioned earlier come in.

MANES AND TAILS

Many horse people prefer to let manes and tails grow full on the theory that it's more natural looking that way. Provided you brush them daily,

this is okay—if you don't mind undertaking the job of braiding them for a show. It's almost impossible to get a mane like this to look neat in braids. Braiding is covered later in this chapter.

If a tail is allowed to grow out full, it must be kept clean. Otherwise you'll find that your horse will rub it against fence posts or trees—which can also be a sign of worms—until the ends break off and it sticks out awkwardly on top. When this happens you have to wait for the broken ends to grow out—which takes a long time.

Some horses have truly unmanageable manes that always want to lie on the wrong side. If you have an English horse whose mane tends naturally toward the near side, you'll have to wet it and brush it over to the offside whenever you groom. (Use your water brush rather than wrecking your dandy brushes.)

If you have a real problem mane, wet and braid it, put elastic bands on the ends, and leave it overnight. Sometimes just wetting will do the trick. Occasionally, if your horse has to be stabled several days for

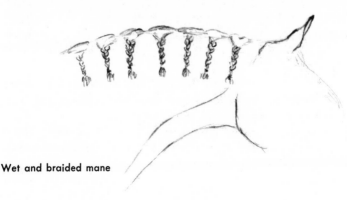

Wet and braided mane

153

some reason, you can leave a mane in pigtails for several days until it lies over properly.

One of a horseman's biggest headaches is burdocks. When they get stuck in a horse's mane or tail, you're faced with what my daughter calls the "frizzy blues." A horse can go out to pasture looking clean and lovely and come in looking as if he's been to a hairdresser who forgot to take the curlers out. Everything is sticking up and out in all directions. Getting rid of burdocks is an awful job, and one that gets worse the longer you let it go. Sometimes the only solution is to cut them out. If you catch them immediately, however, they can be painstakingly removed by separating the hairs around them, a job that may take several hours.

When you're through you might as well vent your accumulated wrath on the burdock bushes in your pasture. They should be removed for two reasons: your horse's appearance, and because the large leaves shade and kill the grass beneath them. Left unattended, the burdocks reseed themselves every fall.

The best time to pull burdocks is early spring, when the ground is soft. You can recognize the plants by the pretty little prickly purple flowers that grow up and turn into ugly burrs. Make sure you pull the whole plant up; burdocks have very long taproots. The bushes also pull out easily in the winter when the tops have died down. In summer, however, they'll resist everything but clippers or choppers. You'll have to cut them down even with the ground and sprinkle rock salt on top to kill them. Don't ever use rock salt in a pasture that is being grazed. It's toxic.

The Mane and Tail Comb

This tool is really misnamed, because it's not used for combing but for "pulling" hairs, a procedure similar to what hairdressers call teasing, except that you end up by pulling the remaining long hairs out. Pulling is done to thin and shorten the mane and tail and to make them lie flat. The procedure is used with both English and Western horses. Some Western horses have their whole tails pulled so that the top looks clipped and the bottom hairs hang naturally at the height of the hock. This is done to keep the tail clean and free of burrs and free also of the rope.

English hunters have their tails "banged" or pulled until perfectly even with the hocks. It's considered bad form to cut them this way; pulled tails look much more natural.

A horse's mane should never be cut with shears. The only place it is trimmed is over the poll, where the bridle goes, and three or four inches by the withers on some horses. Occasionally, if the mane is in

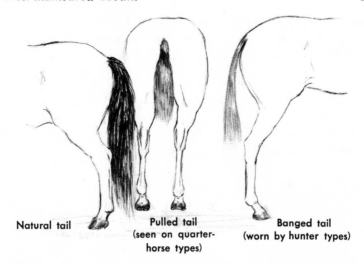

Natural tail

Pulled tail
(seen on quarter-
horse types)

Banged tail
(worn by hunter types)

terrible shape, it's better to just start all over again and roach it. A three-gaited American saddle bred is always shown with a fully roached mane. Quarter horses' manes are frequently roached except for a spot on the withers, called a "handhold," and the forelock—a practical procedure with roping horses, where the rope might get tangled in a long mane.

When pulling a mane, take small quantities of hair and push it back with the comb until it's frizzy. Then pull out three or four hairs at a time—the horse won't tolerate more—until the mane is four to six inches long and looks neat. You're both shortening and thinning at the same

Full tail, broken and set
(as seen on a five-gaited
American saddle bred)

Natural tail
(as seen on Arab types)

Docked tail, broken and set
(now seen only on Hackneys)

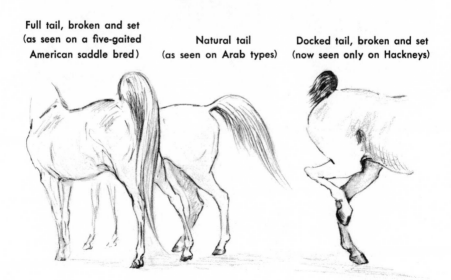

time, and this can be a tedious process if the mane has been growing out all winter. It is also hard on the hands, and gloves are recommended.

How to shorten a mane

How not to shorten a mane

1. Natural full mane and fore-lock (as seen on an Arab type).
2. Roached mane (worn by three-gaited American saddle bred).
3. Pulled mane (as seen on hunter type and some quarter horses).
4. Roached mane with pulled forelock and handhold (worn by some quarter horses).
5. Braided mane and forelock (for hunter types).

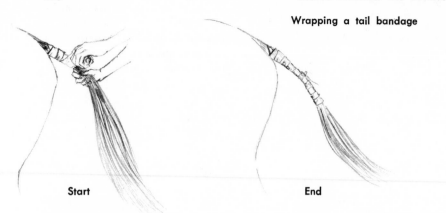

Wrapping a tail bandage

Start   End

Tail Bandages

These are a good idea if you've just pulled the top of a horse's tail and want it to lie flat, if you've braided it and don't want it to get mussed, or if your horse is being vanned and you want to protect the tail. Use a plain Ace bandage (*not* a velcro-lined leg bandage). Wet the tail down first above the end of the bone. Then lift it with one hand, winding the bandage around close to the top and overlapping it once as far up as possible to hold it secure before starting down. Keep winding until you reach a point slightly above the end of the tailbone and secure with a pin or ties toward the outside. All bandages are machine washable and should be cleaned and dried after use, rewound, starting with strings or velcro, always making sure that the fasteners are on the inside. Or if you prefer wraps without either one, just use masking tape to secure the bandages on the horse's leg. If your horse has a fat tail (thick tailbone) that resists holding a bandage, you can secure it by flipping a few strands of hair upward in the course of wrapping. Do this three or four times with the top half of the tail, making sure to hide the hairs with succeeding overlaps. It's a sure way to make the bandage stay put. I prefer to use elastic ace bandages— the only kind, in my experience, that will stay on a fat-tailed horse.

The USET Rx for unruly tails is a wool bandage with three ties attached by a crupperlike strap to a surcingle on the horse's blanket. It' an elaborate prescription, but many horse tails won't stay flat for anything else.

Trimming

All horses need to be trimmed occasionally. In the spring they will retain the shaggy fetlocks or "feathers" that protect their legs when they are standing in mud and snow. As soon as the weather warms up, you'll want to trim these off, along with two or three inches of mane on the withers and a bridle track up by the poll. Trimming the whiskers and the inside of the ears completes the basic job.

If you're showing a horse, the Pony Club will mark it against you if you shave the inside of the ears. They feel the hair is there for protection against flies. A slight trim to make the hair look neater is allowable by the PC.

In 4-H shows, a close ear trim is optional. I wouldn't opt for it because a horse's ears really suffer from flies. The only place ear shaving is absolutely required is in a model class, where you'll be marked down if you don't do it.

Pony Club will also mark you down for clipping feelers and muzzle whiskers, feeling that they are also there to serve a natural protective function. But 4-H will mark you down for *not* trimming them.

When trimming your horse, particularly if he tends to be shy, it's best to crosstie him or have someone hold him if that doesn't work out. Rubber crossties are really handy in this kind of situation.

A small pair of electric clippers do a much better job than hand clippers or fetlock shears. The clippers should always be sharp and clean. When running them, keep a small container of kerosene nearby, dipping the clippers in it after each clip to clean the cut hair off the head. You do this by holding the head in the solution, then turning

Where to clip: 1. 3 to 4 inches at withers 2. 3 to 4 inches at poll (for bridle and halter) 3. ears 4. feelers above and below eyes 5. whiskers the clippers off and wiping the head dry. This assures a good cut and continually clean blade as well as helping to keep the clippers cool. Also, the horse is less aware of them because they will do a smoother job. Some horses are shy about clipping. If yours is, make a point of keeping the clippers running near him, without using them, on a few successive days until he becomes accustomed to the sight and sound.

Starting around the hoof, trim against the hair around the coronet and up along the fetlocks and back of the pastern. Never press down hard, and be sure to keep overlapping as you trim. The clip should appear smooth and even, leaving no excess hair on the legs. Even if you do a terrific job, it will still take a few days before it looks completely natural.

If you have a horse that wears a roached mane, do this next, first clipping one side, then the other, and finally going up the middle. When trimming the ears, turn them inside out and shave very gently. This gives your horse a neater, more alert-looking appearance. It also improves looks to trim away excess whiskers on the jaw—some horses are hairier here than others. The long feelers around the eyes, which are not to be confused with eyelashes, can be trimmed by hand.

Body Clipping

For this, you'll definitely need large electric clippers. One cheap way out is to find a stable nearby where you can take your horse to be clipped in the fall. Clips (hunter or trace) run between twenty and thirty dollars. Or perhaps you could get together with several fellow horse owners and buy a common pair.

The **hunter clip** is a trim over the entire body, leaving the legs long and a patch under the saddle. This body trim often is given to field and show hunters in the fall to prevent these hardworking horses from catching cold standing around in long, wet hair. (It also gives a sleeker appearance in the show ring.) With a trimmed coat, he cools and dries out much faster. Some people clip their horses early in October and then give an additional trim in December. The leg hair is always left long to protect the horse from the brush and stubble he'll encounter in open country. The disadvantage of a hunter clip is that horses must be blanketed—in both barn and pasture—when not worked. Usually a double blanket is worn inside and a single one outside.

If you do your own body clip, try to use the best quality large clippers you can get so that they won't heat up rapidly. This is a big job, and you can plan on spending two to four hours at it, depending on how efficient you are and how well your horse will stand for it.

Make the saddle patch first, taking a regular saddle pad and clipping around it. This affords double protection for the horse's back on a long ride. In the show ring, the pad is sometimes left off for a neater appearance. You then clip everything else—including the cheeks—excepting the patch area and the legs. You can also leave long a triangular point over the tail for a more polished look.

Try to keep an even pressure on the clippers so that you don't end up with "railroad tracks" all over the body. Work over your horse sys-

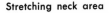
Stretching neck area

tematically, starting at a point on the near side and working back so that you know where you've been. When you come to loose flesh, like that under the neck, try to stretch the area taut and make sure your horse is standing still, so that you don't nick him. Anyone who shaves knows the routine.

When the clippers get hot, turn them off until cool; otherwise they will irritate your horse in sensitive areas. Be careful when coming up the neck along the side of the mane not to trim the mane by accident; if you do, it will grow out all stubbly.

Western riders don't give body clips, although occasionally they trim the entire horse in the spring rather than bother with shedding blades.

Trace clipping is an easy way out for people who want to hunt but don't want to spend hours with the clippers or have to bother with blankets in the winter. This kind of clip is given only under the neck, under the chest and belly, across the arm and stifle and up along the buttock beside the dock. Trace clipping is not good looking, but it's very functional because it takes care of the places where your horse sweats the most, yet it gives him enough upper body protection so he won't need a blanket in the stable or pasture. This clip is preferred by many people who have to care for several horses themselves. It's also recommended for those who work their horses a great deal in the

Trace clip

fall, even if they don't hunt. And ponies, who tend to develop extra-shaggy winter coats, also benefit from a trace clip.

Mud Tail

Brush the tail out. Then, beginning at the base of the bone, braid it as a woman would her hair. When eight inches from the bottom, stop and divide the remaining hair into two sections or "strings." Fold the braid in half, below the bone. Take the two "strings," or sections, behind the tailbone and push them *through* the unbraided hair around

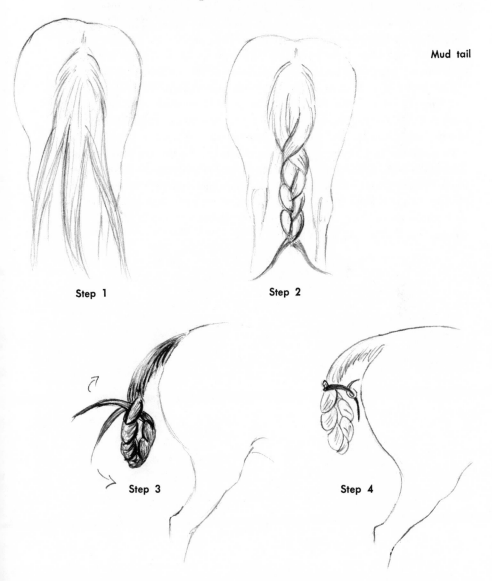

Mud tail

Step 1   Step 2

Step 3   Step 4

the bone. Cross over and go back through again to the back and tie in a single running knot. Then you can put on an elastic band, tucking the remaining ends anywhere in back where they can be conveniently hidden. In sloppy weather at hunts or shows, this is a good way to save yourself work. It isn't supposed to look good, but like the trace clip, it's functional.

Braiding

When you want your horse to look extra special, either for a show or at certain hunts like the opening meet, you'll want to braid his mane and tail. Always do both, never just one or the other. They do have special horse hairpieces—braids that you can match to a horse's hair color and just slip on to save you the trouble of braiding—but they really aren't worth the investment unless you show or hunt a great deal.

The looks of a horse's neck and head are definitely improved by braiding. A lot of little tiny braids will make a short, fat neck look longer. Conversely, a horse with a long skinny neck looks better with fewer, fatter braids. The forelock, by the way, is always braided too.

In England and in some parts of the United States, tradition rather than looks dictates the number of braids. In Britain you aren't supposed to have more than eleven braids on a mane, and there are other schools of riding that believe geldings should have an even number of braids and mares an odd number. Conforming to these rules is all right, of course, but I prefer to go by looks.

Braiding a mane

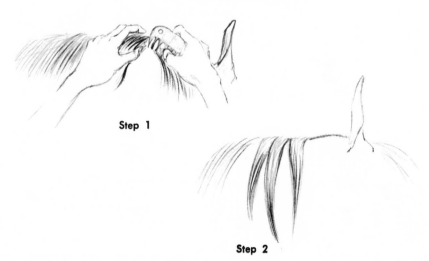

Step 1

Step 2

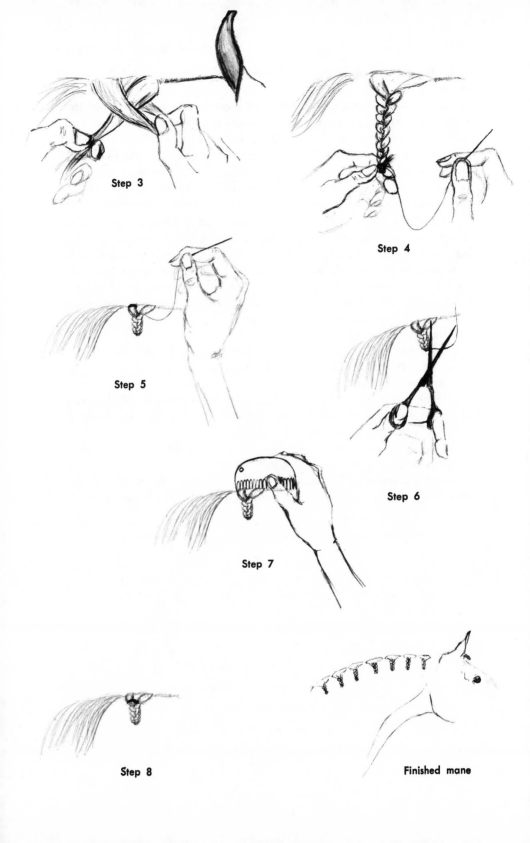

Step 3

Step 4

Step 5

Step 6

Step 7

Step 8

Finished mane

To braid a mane, part it with the comb and be sure to start each strand of braid in the same direction. Have water at hand to wet each strand as you go along. And when you get to the bottom, wrap the pigtail with thread, turn it under, and sew it down with a needle and thread. It can be secured with elastic bands, but this doesn't look as neat. For sewing, buy a large upholstery needle and coarse thread the same color as your horse's mane. When you're through sewing a braid, slipknot it at the end. With sewing, you're sure to get all the little ends tucked in.

To braid a tail, you reverse the direction of a human pigtail. The strands go under instead of over. When finished, it looks like a raised braid going down the tail. To do this, take a few pieces of hair with the comb to begin with, adding to it on the way down. At the end, usually just before the tip of the bone, you'll have a long braid of hair left that you can either tuck under and sew or roll. Sewing looks neater here too. If you sew it, put a slipknot at the end that can be easily undone without cutting the tail hairs.

Horses that are ample in the aft look more refined with longer, smaller tail braids. Those with small rumps benefit in appearance from larger, shorter braids.

All tail and mane braids should be as tight as possible. If they are at all loose, they won't hold. After finishing the tail, wet and wrap it with a tail bandage until you get to the show.

Braiding is made easier these days by using little bandettes that tack stores carry in a variety of horse colors.

Another method of braiding, used a lot by those who show hunters, and which holds well, is the addition of one strand of yarn to each

Starting a braid   Completing a braid

Tucked under

Rolled

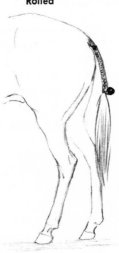

Short braid for a light horse

Longer braid for a heavy horse

braid about halfway down. On a wet mane, it makes the braid very tight. When you come to the end of the braid, tie a knot in the yarn, double it back under the braid, and tie another knot. The yarn, of course, should match your horse's mane color. It's faster than sewing and holds better than elastics.

You can make a pull-through out of bailing wire or a hanger (it looks like a large needle with wire wound down it). The eye is filled with yarn—a quick and efficient tool.

Andalusian or Viennese Braids

These are seen in many old paintings and are believed to have originated with the Lippizans at the Spanish Riding School. Their ancient
origins and elegant appearance belie the real purpose of these braids:
practicality. In an age when horses are valued as much for versatility
as breeding, the Andalusian braid allows the long, flowing manes of
Arabians and Morgans to be decoratively pinned up for stadium jumping and hunting equitation class. Long tresses are an obvious hazard
when hunting or competing in a cross-country event, and they don't
have the workmanlike appearance required in hunter equitation
classes. In dressage, where turnout is next to godliness, this braid helps
make long locks look tidy.

This is not an easy braid to master. After having my first attempt at
an Andalusian braid fall out in the middle of a dressage class before
a particularly distinguished judge, I've learned some tricks the hard
way. And I recommend several practice sessions before taking the
braid into the ring. But it's definitely worth doing. A traditional hunter
braid on a foot-long mane looks like a row of hanging sausages. Those
who want to try an Andalusian braid should first master the French tail
braid (see following pages).

Before starting the Andalusian braid, check the mane to make sure
it's of an even length and thickness. If too thick, it becomes unwieldy.
And if it's unevenly thick, the finished braid will look lumpy.

Begin by brushing the mane out thoroughly, removing all tangles.
Then wet the mane down—but don't use Show Sheen on the mane or
conditioners if you're planning this type of braid. It makes the hair
slippery and hard to handle. Wait until the braid is finished before you
spray on a conditioner.

Starting at the top of the mane, pick up a section one inch wide or a
little larger, depending on the mane's thickness. Divide this into three
pieces, then cross the right strand over the middle, followed by the
left. Pick up another piece and add it to the middle strand. Then cross
the right section, then the left section, over the middle again, picking up
another piece to add to the center. Continue down the mane in this
fashion, always keeping three strands in your hand and pulling them
tight as you go along.

Make sure the braid never gets ahead of the piece of hair you're
braiding in or you'll end up with a sag. The finished braid should slant
down gradually, starting about an inch from the crest of the neck to
five inches near the withers. You can finish off the end with a rubber
band or by sewing it up, selecting colors that match the mane. By
using a piece of matching yarn to weave into the braid, you get a
tighter product.

Andalusian braid

The end of the braid can be decorated with pompons the same color as the horse's mane—or, in dressage competition, with a contrasting color, or in your stable colors.

Blanketing

There are several pros and cons to blanketing. If you want to keep your horse's coat down in the winter, put a blanket on in early autumn. He'll naturally grow a little coat anyway, but this will keep it smoother and sleeker.

Those who show their horses late in the fall and early in the spring start blanketing horses at night as soon as the weather gets cool. Some even use a hood, which keeps the neck sleek too. After showing stops, the blankets come off and the coats come up. In the spring, to force the coat to shed early, blanketing is started again in early March (in the north). By the end of the month, the blanketed horse's coat is way ahead. An alternative is to clip off the coat in the spring, but clipped coats don't look as shiny and natural as those that are naturally shed.

Palominos and chestnuts can become sun bleached in the pasture. To keep their color, they can be blanketed in light cotton or kept in their stalls during the day. Blanketing in the pasture also helps keep light horses clean prior to a show. (*See* chapter 9 for types of blankets.)

Shaving Botfly Eggs

In the summer, this is an absolutely necessary part of every grooming job. With a razor (a single- or double-edged holder with blade) dipped in kerosene, shave off the areas where the eggs have been deposited. The bots lay one egg on each hair, and an accumulation of them looks rather like pollen. They usually appear around the front legs and parts of the body. It's very important to keep up with this on a daily basis. Otherwise the horse will lick them, encouraging them to hatch in his mouth. (*See* Internal Parasites in chapter 8.)

Sponging

When you come in from a ride in the fall or spring, you'll find that your horse is perspiring under the saddle and girth and between the legs. He should be sponged off with lukewarm water to remove all the sweat from the coat, so that when it dries it will be shiny again. The sponging is also important to restore circulation under the saddle area. Always sponge the wet areas well, scraping excess water off with the sweat scraper, going with the coat. Then rub dry with a clean towel so the horse doesn't pick up dirt. A little astringent added to the sponging water acts like a skin bracer and makes a horse smell wonderful when he dries.

Endurance riders have found that a little salt in the sponging water will toughen the sensitive areas.

I find it handy to keep a large bucket filled with clean water in a sunny spot in the stableyard. It's available at the correct temperature during the day and needs only a rinse out and refill for the next use. At shows, it's handy to take along a washbucket, filling it as soon as you arrive and putting it in a sunny spot where it will stay warm for quick, between-act touchups.

When your horse is especially worked up, scrape him down well with the sweat scraper on the body—carefully on the soft parts—*before* sponging. Pay special attention to the inside of his legs, his belly, and dock. When you wipe around his head, squeeze the sponge out well before you start.

After the sponge bath, lead him around for a while to graze while he dries out completely. If you let him out to pasture immediately, the first thing he'll do is roll, and you'll have a double grooming job the next day.

It really pays to do a thorough sponging job. Dried sweat is not only very difficult to get out of a coat, but it attracts flies. And it takes the sheen out of the coat.

In the early spring and late fall you obviously can't bathe a horse this way or he'll catch cold. At these times of year, rub him down with straw or clean towels and walk him around as he dries, then groom him lightly. If it's cold and your horse is still slightly damp, put his blanket on and push wads of straw up underneath it so that the straw is between him and the blanket. The air thus circulates under the blanket and your horse avoids getting a chill from standing under a damp blanket. An anti-sweat sheet, or Aeroborn sheet, is a handy addition to your horse's wardrobe. It keeps flies off in the summer and can be placed under a blanket or cooler to keep air circulating when you're walking your horse out in chilly weather.

Bathing

In late spring, when the weather gets warm, it's good to give your horse an occasional bath. The first bath of the year is important to clean off the winter's accumulation of dirt and all that spring mud. Be sure to pick a warm day, when his coat will dry quickly. Before starting his bath, of course, you will have securely crosstied or tied him and made sure that your water supply is ample. The mane should be scrubbed well, pushing it over to the wrong side, being very careful not to get soap in your horse's eyes.

Wash the tail by sticking it in a bucket and scrubbing it—like a head of hair—digging way into the roots to get out the dirt. Brush through it with a clean dandy brush to get it really clean. It will probably take three to four pails of water to rinse it off. To get knots out of the mane or tail, pull the hairs apart by hand before you wash it. Don't use the comb.

In bathing the body, you may find it helpful to use the currycomb with water attachment. If your horse seems shy of it, use it around him for a few days before his bath until he becomes accustomed to it. The attachment saves a lot of rinsing time.

Start bathing his body on the near side by the poll, just as you would begin a grooming. It's a good idea to divide the horse mentally into sections, soaping and rinsing one at a time. Otherwise the soaped area will start to dry while you're working on the offside.

Using the body sponge, really work the coat up into a lather. Then rinse, making sure all the soap is out. When the entire bath is finished, rinse him down all over again and then scrape off the excess water with a sweat scraper. Walking until dry is essential, or he'll go out and roll and need another bath.

How often should you wash your horse? This really depends on his color and how clean he keeps himself. Some horses are naturally sloppy and always seem to have grass and manure stains on their coats.

Try not to bathe your horse the day before a show because it tends to take the oil out of his coat. Allow at least three days, preferably a week after a bath, for his coat to regain its natural sheen. Special horse shampoos are designed to condition a coat, leaving the gloss in, but it's still going to look better if you wait a few days.

A bath will take a few hours, and be sure to dress for the occasion. You might take the opportunity here to give your grooming tools a good scrubbing at the same time; you won't want to groom a clean horse with a dirty curry any more than you would use a soiled brush on freshly washed hair.

Catching the Judge's Eye

Many years of showing have taught me a lot of lessons about getting ready for the big event—precautions you can take to make sure your horse will enter the ring looking glamorous, and that you'll be calm and contented instead of near nervous collapse.

Although dark horses can be bathed several days before the show and blanketed at night with a very lightweight cotton sheet to keep them clean in the interim, light-colored horses are almost impossible to keep clean for more than a day. These pale, pristine beauties will have to be bathed the morning or afternoon before you take them into the ring. While this won't give their coats time to recapture their natural sheen, you can spray or rub on a coat conditioner like Sho Sheen or Dazzle while the coat is drying. These products make the coat shiny and soft and—perhaps more important—repel dirt and make it easier to wipe off stains and grime.

As the owner of a light palomino horse, I can assure you that there are any number of ways this kind of horse can and will get messed up during a night (or even a few minutes) in the stall. There are a few precautions you can take, however. For example, after he's had his bath, you can braid him while his mane is wet or leave it until the day of the show. And don't leave him alone for a minute until you've covered him up with a light cotton sheet and wrapped his tail with a mud bandage, braiding up the bottom like a mud knot, covering that with a plastic bag—with another bandage over that for sure protection. Don't leave a single hair exposed. If you do, it's sure to be stained with manure or grass when you arrive, dressed to the nines, to lead him out of the stall. I once put my horse back in the stall in the morning after his final grooming while I made a quick phone call. Five minutes later, I returned to find him lying down, his cotton sheet scrunched up beneath him, with manure stains covering his derriere—a good reason to keep stalls picked up at all times.

So, despite all precautions, plan on taking a half hour before loading your pale horse to do patch cleaning jobs. In really desperate cases, when you're on a tight schedule and have to braid that white mane the night before, you can put a lightweight fishnet hood over his entire head, with a halter over that to prevent the hood from slipping over his eyes. Then pick out his stall carefully before going to bed, and pray.

A sheet, tail bag, and face hood is the next best thing to putting him in a plastic bag. I usually leave my horse's tail in the bag until we reach the show grounds. And I have my helper (anyone with a light-colored horse needs one) carry along a towel for instant use. The kids call him the green hornet with his green hood and blanket.

Horses of any color should have their hooves scrubbed and washed off the night before. In the morning, brush or wipe them off again and pick them out. When the hooves are completely dry, brush on any one of the liquid hoof dressings available. They come in black, brown and clear and are guaranteed to make the dullest hoof shine. (Some people economize by using baby oil.) Apply the dressing evenly and carefully to the entire hoof, including the heels. Make sure all hooves are dry before you return your horse to his stall, lead him to the yard, or apply leg wraps for traveling. Wet hoof dressing picks up dust and dirt and sticks to bandages. But it's worth the extra trouble because it definitely makes a horse look spiffier.

The night before the show is the time to organize and set out your show grooming kit, along with clean tack, riding clothes, two buckets (one for drinking, one for washing), and a hay net.

If the budget allows—and you do enough showing—it's convenient to have a separate set of grooming tools kept in a special box. In it, you put:

- Hoof pick
- Curry comb
- Dandy brush
- Two soft brushes or a soft body brush
- Mane and tail comb
- Two sponges, one for body, one for face

- Three or four all-purpose towels, good for everything from rubbing a horse down to wiping boots and tack
- Fly repellent and applicator (during fly season)
- Sweatscraper
- Small plastic bottle of shampoo (a must for light-colored horses)
- Saddlesoap and sponge for quick tack jobs
- Modified first-aid kit containing wound dressing and bandages
- Extra elastics, thread, needles, yarn, and other braiding materials for last-minute mane and tail repairs—and safety pins for your own.

7

it's all riding on the hoof

Now I submit that the first thing a man who owns a horse should obtain is knowledge of the foot and the best method of protecting it; because it is the foot and the condition of it on which depends the value of the animal, whether he be kept for pleasure or profit. . . . A horse without sound feet is no horse at all.

—W. H. H. MURRAY,
The Perfect Horse, 1873

Back in the days when mustangs had hoofs instead of engines, village smithies stood under spreading chestnut trees forging, among other things, horseshoes. Smithies have since become almost as scarce as American chestnuts. Reliable farriers (the proper name for blacksmiths that specialize in horseshoeing) are as hard to track down nowadays as good carpenters, plumbers, hairdressers, or anyone else in great demand.

How do you tell a good blacksmith from a poor one? His experience or lack of it is a basic yardstick of performance. Be skeptical of farriers who have graduated from school a few months before and who boast of their prowess with corrective shoeing. This chapter will help you to recognize a good smith.

When you do manage to find a good smith, go out of your way to ensure his continued services. Feed him if he looks hungry, offer him a beer or Coke when he's thirsty, talk to him if he seems lonely. In return, try to extract a promise that he'll return every month or six weeks.

WHY SHOE?

Shoeing is basically an unnatural procedure made essential by man's domestication of the horse. The nails of a shoe weaken—actually damage—the horn of the hoof, already weakened by a heavy artificial grain diet and the enforced idleness of the stall.

In their natural state, horses grazed over soft, clean ground, on the nutrient-rich grass of the plains. The calcium and minerals in the grass grew good horn. And as the horses walked over large, flat areas, hoofs were worn down gradually and evenly.

But the mustangs of the Great Plains didn't have to carry several hundred pounds on their backs every day, nor were they worked on hard, uneven surfaces. Under these unnatural conditions, imposed by man, hoofs must be shod and trimmed regularly to protect them.

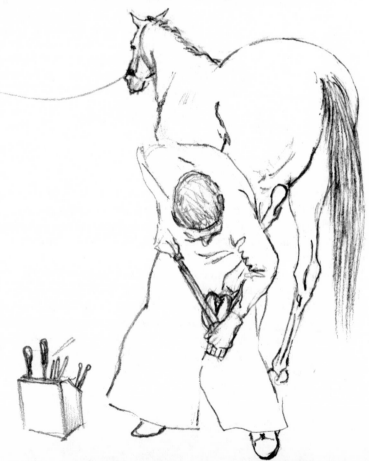

Basically, a shoe protects the hoof wall from excessive wear on hard surfaces. It also provides a better grip for a horse in more difficult going—on hard roads, in mud, and on ice.

Shoes can be used to help cure diseases or conformation defects. They can relieve the pain of deep cracks, corns, bruised soles, or pulled tendons; and they can help change gaits or action and compensate for faults.

Shoes affect the length of the stride by minimizing it or extending it. To achieve the long, low, reaching stride desirable on a Standardbred trotter, for instance, a smith will put more weight on the toe of the shoe. With a Western horse that does practically no trotting, he'll trim the hoof close all around and shoe it lightly to produce a short stride that is close to the ground and more suitable to a lope. Light shoes improve the performance of racing Thoroughbreds and Standardbreds, while weighted shoes, sometimes added behind the toe to make some horses reach out farther and on the heel to make the hoof "fold" or curl under, accentuate the unnatural flashy action of park-type saddle horses like saddle breds, Tennessee Walkers, and Hackneys. This way of moving must be there to begin with, however. Shoeing only accentuates it. It doesn't create it. Saddle breds carry twenty-two ounces or more of shoe per hoof, Tennessee Walkers about thirty.

Short toe—as on a quarter horse

Long toe—as on a three- or five-gaited American saddle bred

Some ponies do not need shoes. Because most pony breeds evolved in rocky terrain, their feet are extremely hard, and as long as their feet are trimmed properly, these animals can be ridden barefoot all the time.

Trimmed feet enable a horse to stand square and upright. Uneven hoofs, on the other hand, can strain tendons and cause deformative action and unsoundness. Because horn grows as much as half an inch

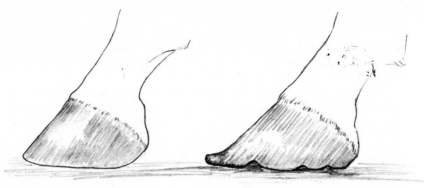

Trimmed foot—standing square   Untrimmed foot showing irregular wear

a month, it must be trimmed regularly to keep the wall from breaking off, chipping, or wearing irregularly. If allowed to wear away on either the heel or toe, the angle of the foot will change, putting an unnatural stress on the legs.

PARTS OF THE FOOT AND HOW THEY WORK

A healthy hoof should be full and round and open in the heel. The form of the foot is important because it affects a horse's stride. The shape and symmetry determine the point at which the leg breaks over. If the inner or outer quarter is higher, which happens when a horse toes in or out, the stride will be awkward.

Hoofs should be proportionate to size. Very large feet are usually a sign of poor breeding. They not only look clumsy but result in an awkward stride. Small feet, while they may look cute and delicate, are also inefficient—for obvious reasons. A large horse with tiny feet will have an oversized share of foot problems.

More rounded front foot   More oval hind foot

HEEL

QUARTER

Bulbs
Central cleft
Angle of wall
Bars
Lateral cleft
White line
Apex of frog
Wall
Sole

TOE

Horses should stand squarely on all four feet. Although they often shift their back legs, healthy horses never lift the front feet in like manner. When a horse is standing, his two front feet should be squarely on the ground. The equine center of gravity is located just behind the withers, consequently a horse takes about 10 percent more of his weight on the front feet.

A normal, properly cared-for hoof should be centered under the leg, so that when it's viewed from the front, a straight line could be drawn down from the middle of the knee dividing the hoof into equal parts. Seen from the side, the hoof position should match the natural angle of the pastern and cannon, with the foot centered under the leg.

Assuming that your horse has no conformation faults in his limbs, balancing his feet is simply a matter of correct trimming to maintain the normal angle of the pastern bones and create a continuous line from ankle to toe (see following pages). A horse with too much heel will have a pastern that buckles forward, putting a strain on tendons and ligaments. On a horse with too little heel or too much toe, the bones in the foot will buckle backward, causing strained flexor tendons—the large, important tendons in the horse's legs—and making the animal forge (see following pages). Stumbling would be a result of either of these foot problems.

Step back and take a look at your horse from the side. If the inside wall of his hoof is too high, the ankle will buckle outward. Too much foot on the outside makes ankles buckle in. If either of these conditions are neglected, a horse could end up with strained tendons and ligaments, contracted heels, and faulty gaits, like paddling or interfering.

Once a hoof is out of line, the imbalance reinforces itself with every step taken. The horse's weight has been redistributed and will rapidly wear away that area of the hoof carrying the burden and take its toll in the entire leg (like a run-down heel on a human's shoe distorts and strains the spine).

Another problem occurs with horses that have a conformation defect in their ankles, knees, hocks, or stifles. This can result in an abnormal stress on one area of the hoof, causing it to wear away. In this case, worn hoofs are not the cause but the symptom. But the result is always the same: uneven distribution of weight. The important difference is that a normal hoof can be corrected with trimming. A hoof worn through conformation fault can only be trimmed to look presentable; the fault will remain uncorrected.

Whether the problem is in hoof or in conformation, the remedy is the same: restore the natural balance and angle. Most so-called "corrective shoeing" is done in the *trimming*, not the shoeing.

The **wall** of the hoof is the horny outer shell that protects the sensi-

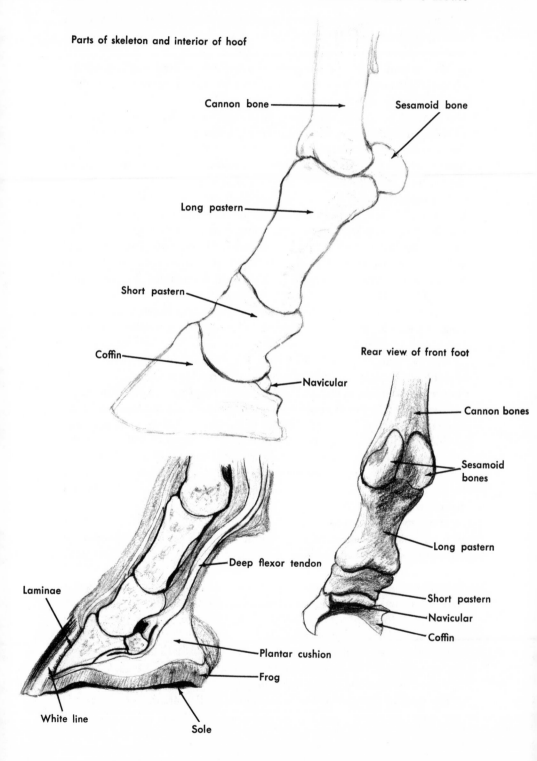

Parts of skeleton and interior of hoof

Cannon bone

Sesamoid bone

Long pastern

Short pastern

Coffin

Navicular

Rear view of front foot

Cannon bones

Sesamoid bones

Long pastern

Short pastern

Navicular

Coffin

Laminae

Deep flexor tendon

Plantar cushion

Frog

White line

Sole

tive inner tissue. It has a give to it under the full impact of the horse's weight. In order to maintain this important quality of expansion and flexibility, the hoof cannot be allowed to dry out.

The **white line** is the thin boundary line between the wall and the sole. It's actually a continuation of the laminae on the inside of the hoof. The **bars** give additional strength to the outer wall and protect the heels from extreme wear.

The **frog** acts as an elastic cushion that reduces the concussion when the hoof strikes the ground, protecting the legs from the full shock of impact. The frog should always be in contact with the ground when a horse is standing. If allowed to dry out, it shrinks and loses contact, causing contracted heels. If it is too wet, on the other hand—which happens when a horse stands on muddy ground or in manure for long periods—the frog can become rotted (*see* thrush in this chapter). Some idle horses shed their frogs several times a year. In an animal that is receiving the right amount of exercise, the process should be so gradual as to be barely noticeable.

The **sole** is a horny substance that protects the inner tissues of the foot. It is slightly concave, which helps to support the hoof, and it is soft enough to maintain a flexible wall that will give when a horse puts down his foot.

There is another, almost invisible, part of the hoof called the **paripole.** This begins at the junction of the hoof and hairline and extends down over the entire outside wall as a thin natural varnish that coats the hoof and prevents moisture from escaping. When a blacksmith is shoeing, he is (or should be) careful not to rasp away large portions of the paripole.

The **plantar cushion,** which can't be seen from the outside, is a fiibrous, fatty mass, located inside the hoof above the frog. This is the real cushion of the foot that the frog acts on. It pushes outward when pressure is greatest on the frog, and it contains glands that keep the frog supplied with moisture to assure its elasticity.

The **coffin bone** forms the internal bony foundation of the hoof. When a horse is foundered, the coffin bone tips down, causing the sole to drop and separate from the wall—a condition called "seedy toe."

The **lateral cartilage** attaches to the upper rear edge of the coffin bone above the coronet. It is an important aid to the expansion and flexion of the hoof on impact.

HOOF TROUBLES

There are several hoof problems and diseases that you should watch out for. Some will require the attention of a vet.

Bruised soles can be caused by stepping on a sharp object, by getting a stone lodged in the crevice of the frog, or by an ill-fitting shoe. The foot will be tender to the touch and may have a reddish mark on it.

Corns look similar to bruises, and they are caused by the same things. A corn is a bruised, discolored area in the sole, usually between the bar and the wall.

Dry corns are bruised areas in the sensitive tissue, manifested by red staining—the result of dried blood inside the sole. A moist corn is more serious because of the seeping fluid beneath the sole. If allowed to become infected and abscessed, this condition can be very dangerous, causing permanent damage to sensitive inner tissues.

Horses with flat feet are prone to stone bruises and should be protected with leather or plastic pads.

Cocked ankles are a condition common among young horses that haven't had enough exercise, a proper diet, or regular trimming. It distorts the horse's way of standing.

With **contracted heels,** because the cushion of the sole is drawn up and the frog loses contact with the ground, the outer wall is left to bear the weight of impact. This is a severe strain on the leg. The condition is the result of a chronic lameness, like navicular disease.

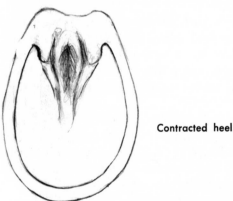

Contracted heel

Dry hoofs, as mentioned above, cause contracted heels along with a number of other problems. Often the walls can crack so badly that the horse goes lame. And brittle hoofs are very difficult to shoe. This is usually only a problem in the dry summer months. To prevent and treat it, stand your horse in wet clay or mud for an hour or so every day. In the stall, you can wrap his hoofs tightly in water-soaked burlap bags for a few hours. If drying out is a regular problem, you may want to invest in some felt swabs, available through mail-order catalogues. After soaking the feet, allow them to dry to the touch and apply hoof dressing. Linseed oil or neat's-foot oil will do. Never put hoof dressing on more than twice weekly, however, or it will have the opposite effect from that you intended—acting to keep moisture out. For this reason, always be sure to remove any hoof dressing before soaking the feet.

Navicular disease is a degeneration of the navicular bone. Navicular disease is similar to arthritis. This very small bone inside the hoof acts as a pulley to change the direction of the tendons that come down the back of the leg. This is usually caused by too much fast work on hard surfaces or by intense work after a long period of rest, and it is incurable. Sometimes navicular disease is a secondary ailment caused by contracted heels. It can also result from severe conformation faults that put an unnatural stress on the bone. One symptom, mentioned before, is a tendency for the horse to "point" the affected front foot. The vet can diagnose suspected cases through X rays, nerve-block histories, and the use of hoof testers.

Ringbone is an arthritic condition occurring on the bottom or top of the pastern joint, caused either by hard work or old age. In some cases, it is believed to be hereditary.

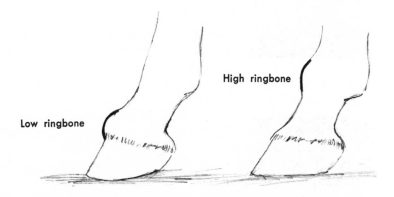

Low ringbone

High ringbone

Sidebones are a hardening of the cartilage on the inside of the hoof. This can be caused by serious conformation defects. The condition also occurs in racehorses that have been worked too hard too early, resulting in permanent lameness. There are a few instances where sidebones, like ringbone, have been inherited.

Quarter cracks are vertical cracks on either side of the hoof or toe, in which case they're called toe cracks, caused by drying out. When the cracks extend to the hairline, dirt and sand may work their way up into the coronet, fester, and cause lameness. Some horses seem to be more prone to cracked hoofs than others—perhaps because of a deficiency of the paripole. In any case, the remedy is the same as for dry

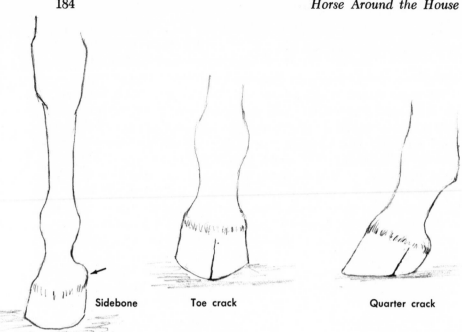

Sidebone   Toe crack   Quarter crack

hoofs. Some blacksmiths advise shoeing to keep the crack from widening. Plastic is sometimes used to fill in very wide cracks, and special trimming to take the stress off the cracked area is usually effective. This may not be as serious as it looks. A lot of horses continue to function well with severely cracked hoofs.

Quittor is a fistulous sore which forms on the coronet. It can be caused by a blow from a horse's own foot or from pus working up from some other injury in the hoof, such as a corn or a nail he might have stepped on. Or it could be the result of a piece of sand working its way up a crack in his hoof, becoming embedded under the hairline and festering. A quittor is painful and usually causes lameness. The vet should be called and he will probably recommend a poultice.

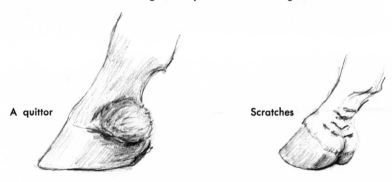

A quittor   Scratches

Thrush is a rotting of the tissue around the frog, causing it to darken and soften. It usually begins in the cleft of the frog and extends into the bars and sole. Severe cases are caused by damp, dirty conditions in the stall or paddock. But mild cases are common in the spring and other extended periods of wet weather. Thrush is easily detected by the foul smell it gives to the hoof. A thrushy sole also flakes away easily when picked out. Mild cases can be successfully treated with a daily sprinkling of lime on the frog area. Other remedies are available through the vet or your local tack shop.

Scratches, or cracked heels, are a scabby condition of the back of the pastern below the fetlock, usually occurring after a horse has cut or scratched the area and then been made to stand in damp, muddy areas or in manure. Horses left for long periods in dirty stalls or very wet grassy pastures often contract it without prior injury. It's somewhat like chapped skin. Symptoms are scabby, pustulous spots on the pastern. Unless treated, the discharge keeps spreading the disease. It is important to keep infected areas dry and cleaned out with antibacterial soap.

Some horses are more prone to this affliction than others. My horse, like many others, will get scratches if his legs are left wet after a bath or after a cold or hot water treatment for an injury. So I must always be sure to rub the heel, fetlock, and pastern area dry before putting him back in the stall. When you are hosing the leg of a horse who has scratches, apply carbolated vaseline to the heel on the fetlock and to the back of the pastern to protect it. Some vets recommend an application of vaseline before pasturing. Some horsemen I know use Desitin, some use Bag Balm Corona Wool Fat.

THE BLACKSMITH

Blacksmiths are professionals, and they like to work with professionals. So you'll be much more likely to engage the services of a competent farrier if you understand what his job is all about and call him on a regular basis.

Those who call up once or twice a year, usually a few days before going to a show or hunt, are a blacksmith's bane. It has nothing to do with money—good farriers always have more work than they can handle. Rather, a regular shoeing schedule ensures a smith of a sound hoof on which he can best display his craft. When a horse is shod only a few times a year, a lot of hoof has to be trimmed off at once. This isn't good for a horse. It changes the way he moves and can cause lameness.

Also, farriers know that infrequently shod horses often present behavior problems. My blacksmith told me about one nightmare of a horse he worked on, who would only submit to shoeing when tied and thrown on his side, with the owner sitting on his head to hold him down.

If your horse gives the blacksmith a hard time, you can expect him to use appropriate disciplinary methods to make your horse stand and hold his feet up properly. With a real problem horse, he may have you use a twitch—a device that puts pressure on a horse's upper lip. It is cruel, but it works. Remember that the physical safety of the farrier is more important than your horse's feelings.

Problems like this illustrate why it's so important to handle a horse's feet from early infancy. I've known horses that were the most lovable animals in the world except for the unfortunate quirk of hating black-smiths.

A young foal should have his feet handled almost from the day of birth to educate him to stand for hoof trimming and the blacksmith. His feet must be trimmed regularly by the time he is weaned and con-tinued at regular intervals to assure proper wear and correct balance. And they should be picked out daily by his owner.

Depending on individual problems and how much your horse is used, four to six weeks is the maximum time to allow between shoeings; unshod hoofs should be trimmed equally often. Young horses, under the age of five, need a trim every three weeks.

Hoofs should be cleaned daily and kept from drying out. A horse is only as good as his worst foot is an old saw, and none will be very good without regular care.

Whenever I judge 4-H horse shows that have fitting and showman-ship classes, I always ask the child to pick up the feet, not just to see whether they're clean but to discover whether he or she does it prop-erly and, from the reaction of the horse, whether he's accustomed to having it done regularly. If your horse gives you or the farrier a hard time about picking up his feet, you should begin this essential training all over again. Work on it every day, giving a carrot or some other treat for every foot your horse picks up without a hassle.

It's up to you to tell when new shoes are needed. Remember how busy blacksmiths are. They don't have the time to keep schedules for their clients.

If you're unsure of whether a horse needs to be shod or trimmed, how can you tell? There are several things to look and listen for:

The clinking or loss of shoes—an extreme I hope hasn't been reached. It means your horse hasn't been shod for several months. And when a horse's shoe is as loose as this, it can shift on the foot and cause bruised soles or corns.

A missing shoe. A horse that has lost a shoe should not be ridden heavily, especially if the shoe has been thrown in front. The unshod hoof will wear down and chip, and the blacksmith may have a problem getting a new shoe on it if you let it go too long. Never jump a horse with a shoe missing in front. The difference in weight and height between the feet throws his balance way off.

Angle of the hoof. Untrimmed hoofs will distort the angle, which should be the same as the pastern, or around 45 degrees. An uneven

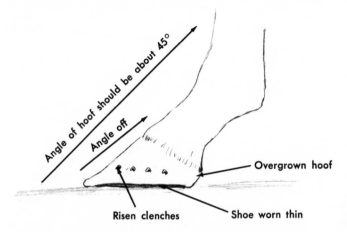

wearing away of the heel or toe will put a strain on a horse's tendons and joints and show up in an awkward stance.

Risen clenches. The clench is the turned-over end of the nail used in shoeing. If these stick up a quarter of an inch above the hoof, reshoeing is a must.

Stumbling. I've had several horses who would remind me when they needed to be shod by their gait. If your horse is normally surefooted and starts to stumble, check the calendar. His toes may be overgrown.

Thin spot on shoe. Worn down spots on toes or quarters or heels of a shoe are signs of the need for reshoeing. These shoes cannot be reused.

You'll find that if you want the blacksmith this week, you should have called him last week. Unless you have a sizable stable, a farrier can't be expected to show up without a reminder. So it's useful to mark the dates he'll be needed on a calendar in the stable or above the kitchen phone.

WHAT TO DO WHEN THE BLACKSMITH COMES

By the time your blacksmith arrives, you should have crosstied or tied your horse in a light, roomy area on a flat, dry surface where work can be done efficiently. The farrier begins by removing the shoes, cutting the clenches so they won't damage the hoof wall when the nails are taken out. Using pincers, he pries out the nails and pulls the shoes. Sometimes shoes can be reused if they haven't been badly worn.

1. Trimming away old
   sole with drawing knife

2. Cutting away excess
   hoof with hoof cutters

3. Rasping heel of hoof

To prepare a hoof for shoeing, the excess wall is clipped back to its correct length. Then the old sole and frog are cut away with a drawing knife and a rasp is used to flatten the bearing surface of the wall—the part that rests on the ground.

When a horse is just getting a trim, the smith finishes the job at this point by rounding off the rim of the wall. If he is making the hoof

4. Trying on shoes to find
   the largest

5. Nailing shoe

6. Cutting nail ends with
   claw hammer

ready for the shoe, he flattens it. The hoof is then measured and the largest shoe selected that is closest to it in size.

Perhaps the heels of a shoe will be too narrow, or too wide, in which case the farrier shapes the shoe with an anvil and hammer. Shoes should always be made to fit the hoof—not the hoof rasped away to fit a shoe.

The nails are driven in lightly at first until the farrier finds the right spot. He then hammers the nails in, making sure the angle is right so that the nail doesn't come out too near the edge or too high up.

If too close to the edge, a horse can pull off the shoe and split his hoof. If too high, a nail can pinch and put pressure on the laminae, causing the horse to go lame. Inexperienced farriers will often place nails too low rather than risk this.

7. Filing nail groove

8. Seating nail head in nail groove

9. Clenching nail with hammer

The farrier's final job is to cut off the protruding nail point with a claw hammer, using the clenching bar to bend the end down into a clench that secures the nail and keeps it from slipping back through. Before bending it, he rasps a small area below the nail to bend the clench in so it lies smooth. As a finishing touch, the clenches are rasped off and the edge of the hoof filed flush with the shoe to keep it from splitting off.

In the old days, shoes were always forged at a smith's shop and put on the hoof still sizzling. Many farriers and horsemen believe that hot shoeing makes the shoe adhere better. Nail holes are made while the shoe is still hot, just after measuring the foot.

Some smiths still do hot shoeing, but it is standard practice today to have the farrier bring a variety of shoes of different sizes to your stable. He shapes these with a hammer and anvil—a process known conversely as cold shoeing.

The weight of the average-size keg or ready-made horseshoe is about sixteen ounces. Handmade shoes vary from six ounces for an aluminum racing shoe to thirty ounces or more for weighted shoes used on horses like saddle breds and Tennessee Walkers.

Those who can afford it use handmade shoes that give a better fit and are generally lighter. Light shoes are particularly desirable in a young horse, where you don't want to interfere with the natural stride.

A new shoe has just been developed that curves with the wall of the foot. These are said to wear well and to be as natural as any shoe can be.

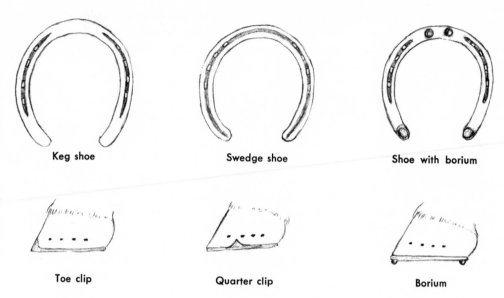

Keg shoe   Swedge shoe   Shoe with borium

Toe clip   Quarter clip   Borium

There are a few useful shoe accessories in the blacksmith's trade that you should know about:

Borium is the name given to small knobs of metal, made up of hard bits of carbide set in steel. It gives an excellent bite on ice, not wearing as fast as steel calks. When borium is used on the heel and toe, combined with a convex leather pad, it makes an excellent winter shoe that prevents slipping and keeps snow from balling up in the foot. One thing against borium is that the knobs raise the hoof off the ground, lessening pressure on the frog and reducing heel expansion. But under certain conditions, they're indispensable.

Snow balling up in the hoofs is awkward and dangerous. Years ago, according to a Danish horseman I know, farmers using horses in winter would clean the hoofs out well with alcohol and then cover the sole and frog area with heavy grease. One western farrier, who uses borium shoes without pads as they do in the east, sprays liquid plastic Varath on the hoof to produce a slick, semi-hard surface that snow can't stick to. For the plastic to stick properly, the hoof must be cleaned thoroughly with alcohol and allowed to dry before the Varath is applied. After the application, the hoof must dry on a flat hard surface. If done properly, he claims this treatment will last three days.

Calks fit on either the heel or toe and give a better grip on the road or when a horse is jumping, hunting, barrel racing, pole bending, or carrying weighted shoes. They can be turned over from the steel of the shoe itself or screwed or welded. Some of these have a larger metal center that doesn't wear away as fast. In the old days, farmers used to have the calk points on their draft horses' shoes sharpened in the winter to keep them from slipping.

Rubber pads are mostly for horses ridden frequently on the road, notably driving horses. They keep the hoof from slipping and absorb some of the impact of the foot on hard surfaces as well as keeping the heels from getting sore.

The rubber pads have a convex bubble that sticks out. I prefer to use these in the winter because the snow can't pack up inside the pad; it just pops out. This is an important difference if you're a serious winter rider. Considering the high cost of winter shoes, you might as well pay a few dollars more for the most snow-worthy pads.

Leather pads are often used on Hackneys, saddle breds, and other park-type horses with long toes; they build up the hoof and keep pressure on the frog. Some pads cover the entire sole; others, in small pieces used in conjunction with the larger pad, build up the heel. Pads are helpful on flat-footed or tenderfooted horses who are doing a lot of fast hard work or on those recovering from lameness.

Plastic pads are used for the same purpose as leather pads. I've tried both, and they tend to wear equally well. The plastic type are available in colors—if you're that color conscious.

Swedge shoes have a small crevice running around the middle of the shoe to give it more bite. These are relatively light, used frequently on trotters and often on hunters, reining horses, and barrel racers, sometimes with calks added.

Most horsemen believe that hoofs should be given a rest once a year, a period of several months when they are left unshod. Your horse's hoof vacation will probably depend somewhat on the climate. In northern regions, winter is obviously the most convenient time, for those who don't plan to ride frequently. An occasional ride on the snow in bare feet won't damage a horse's hoofs. But if you will be riding on the road, or where it is icy, your horse should be shod throughout the winter with borium.

A rest period allows hoofs to expand as well as restoring the frog and foot to their healthy, natural state. Regular trimming during this period is still essential, however.

Working cowhands generally don't shoe their horses unless they will be doing a lot of riding on the road or other hard surfaces. The hoofs of the native cow ponies are naturally hard and stay much healthier when left unshod. The cowboys are, however, scrupulous about regular trimming of the feet.

Because of the long toes certain park horses must grow for show, it's impossible to give such horses a rest. It takes months for their toes to grow out to the desired length of six to eight inches. And without shoes, the end of the hoof would quickly chip off.

Some horses have exceptionally thin walls to their feet, making it difficult for them to keep shoes on. Often these horses will lose a shoe before four weeks are up and go lame as soon as it happens. In these cases, frequent shoeing, as often as every three weeks, is advisable. If you let it go longer, when the horse is reshod the pinching of the nails in the wall against the sensitive laminae can cause a short stride or result in general tenderness and lameness—like someone wearing a tight shoe.

The approximate cost for trimming a horse's feet is twelve dollars to fifteen dollars. Complete shoeing work, depending on type of shoes, runs twenty-four dollars to thirty-six dollars for the average keg shoe. Of course, if the blacksmith is a great distance from you, it will certainly cost you more.

FAULTS OF GAIT AND CONFORMATION

Pigeon toes and **splay feet** are usually conformation faults of the front feet that strain tendons, joints, and ligaments in the forehand. Often, however, a slight tendency to toe in or out is aggravated by improper and/or infrequent trimming of a young horse's feet. These conditions can't be corrected in older horses, but they can be compensated for by trimming the hoofs so that the horse's weight is properly distributed on the front feet. In some cases, special corrective shoes are helpful. But usually shoes of this sort only add more lateral motion—like winging, dishing, or paddling, which toeing-in or -out can cause, too. These look very much as they sound. If not too severe, a horse can learn how to compensate for many of these difficulties and to balance himself through proper training.

Speedy cutting, or **cross-firing,** happens when a horse cuts the inside of his knee with the shoe of the opposite hind foot. This can be helped by special trimming and shoeing and by protective boots. Trotting horses most commonly have this fault.

Brushing often occurs with splayfooted horses, which are likely to brush the inside of their ankles (fetlocks) when the hind legs reach through.

Overreaching, or **forging,** is just what it sounds like, a fault of horses who literally overreach in their stride. When this happens, the toe of the hind foot reaches out and hits the toe of the front foot. Young horses will sometimes do this when they're uncollected, a problem that

Forging—hind toe striking front toe

can be corrected with training. Shoeing also helps, and in some situations quarter boots are the answer.

Trimming and shoeing can help most mild conformation problems, and there are special boots available to protect a horse's legs from injuries caused by faulty gaits. **Brushing boots** buckle on the outside of the leg and protect the inside of the ankle. **Quarter boots** or **bell boots,** protect the heels from overreaching, faulty gaits, and conformation defects or condition. Many different kinds and sizes of brushing or galloping boots are on the market. They're made of felt or different qualities of leather and have various means of attachment.

Brushing or galloping boots also come in different lengths. If your horse has a problem only with ankle brushing, you'd want to use a shorter boot when on the trail, hunting, or schooling him.

Some leather boots are very expensive and, of course, the length will up the price. When on, galloping boots should fit the leg contour and should buckle toward the back. The fit should be snug, but not so tight that the boot itself causes rubbing or chafing of the skin. Felt boots with velcro fastenings are available, but I don't advise them. They stretch when wet, keep coming unfastened, and don't last as long. Leather boots, given good care, should last for years, with only occasional replacing of elastic. Good care means keeping them clean (brushing off dried mud) and treating them with oil and saddle soap. Otherwise they dry out and crack, while any mud residue on the inside can cause skin sores.

I've found that sometimes, when a horse isn't in good flesh or muscle tone, he has a tendency to brush his heels or ankles together behind. Galloping boots should be used while working this type of horse until he gets into better physical condition. Once he becomes better balanced through training and his weight increases, he will be less likely to brush himself. I've seen many cases where galloping boots can be removed when a horse's physical condition and training have improved.

When schooling young horses over jumps, it is a good idea to protect both the front and back legs with boots—especially if it's a young or green horse.

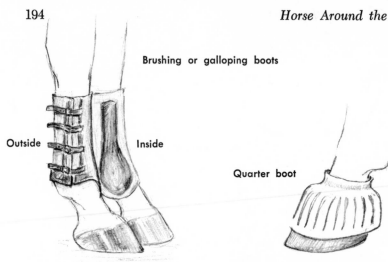

Brushing or galloping boots

Outside   Inside

Quarter boot

Exercise bandages (see Chapter 8) serve the same purpose as galloping boots, although they tend to slip off behind when a horse is really moving out.

Quarter boots or **bell boots** are used to protect the heels of the front legs from overreaching. These rubber boots come in many different types, fastening either with leather hooks, leather buckles, or Velcro. Other types slip over the foot, and I recommend these for cross-country riding, where you want to be sure to keep them on. I've seen the buckle variety lost by the wayside in almost every cross-country event I've attended. One problem: if the going is muddy or wet, they can chafe and rub the pastern raw, causing more problems than they prevent. An alternative: use self-adhesive elastic bandages in muddy weather or when schooling, putting the bandage on in a figure-eight pattern.

Young or rambunctious horses should be booted when pastured to keep them from self-destruction.

Shoe-boil boots are used when the horse develops a lump on the elbow of a front leg, caused by the foot's rubbing against it when lying down.

Remember that blacksmiths are not magicians. Good ones are able to compensate only partially for conformation and gait faults by special trimming and shoeing. These conditions can't be permanently "corrected," and be wary of any farrier who says they can.

Some people do their own shoeing, like out west, where blacksmiths are few and far between and it's often necessary. But the homemade jobs I've seen were all inadequate. This is one area where you should not cut corners by doing it yourself.

8

healthy as a horse

He will rarely consult his own interest who, not having had the advantage of a veterinarian education, undertakes the treatment of any of the serious diseases of the horse.

The Horse, PUBLISHED UNDER THE SUPERINTENDENCE OF THE SOCIETY FOR THE DIFFUSION OF USEFUL KNOWLEDGE, LONDON 1831.

Getting to know your horse well is important, both in the interest of a happy relationship and for the sake of the animal's health. Uncharacteristic behavior is often the first sign of illness; so if you keep a strict schedule of stable management, you'll be able to tell quickly when your horse varies from the norm. Odd behavior, on the other hand, might just be an individual quirk and no cause for alarm. It's a good idea to know which is which before rushing off to phone the vet.

Many horses have strange habits that could be taken for signs of illness by owners who don't know them well. Some horses like to take morning naps in the stall right after breakfast, for instance. Others snore raucously as they sleep. One palomino I know takes sunbaths in

195

the pasture at high noon, even in midsummer, looking to all outward appearances stone dead.

When these things happen all the time, it's normal. But if your horse lies down at an unexpected time or place, it may be a sign of illness. Likewise, finicky eaters are normally finicky eaters. But when a horse who usually eats voraciously suddenly loses interest in his food, he should be watched carefully. Or, if your horse customarily greets you at the stall door with a bright eye and friendly nicker, you have reason to suspect something is wrong on that morning when he fails to appear. If he is standing in his stall with his ears at half-mast looking miserable, something is definitely wrong.

Some symptoms will always call for your attention and further observation. Any two together will require an immediate call to the vet. Never try playing vet yourself. It takes a tremendous amount of experience to know what these signs of illness mean. The following are the most **common symptoms:**

- Increased pulse rate
- Runny nose or eyes
- Swelling or bruises
- Cuts
- Listlessness
- Lack of interest in food
- Heat in legs or feet
- Bare spots on skin
- Unusual lumps
- Dull coat
- Persistent coughing
- Temperature

Any one of these can be serious. In combination, they are reason for alarm. In all cases, you should take your horse's temperature before calling the vet.

Special horse thermometers are available, but a regular rectal thermometer with a string tied to the end will do. Make sure your horse is securely tied or crosstied. After shaking down the thermometer, rub Vaseline on the nub end of the thermometer and insert it gently into the anus. Stand close to and slightly to the side of the horse's rump in case he kicks out. Leave the thermometer in for two to three minutes.

A normal temperature for a horse is 99.5–100.5 degrees. This may go up to 101 in the afternoon or following hard work. Any reading over 101 merits a call to the vet.

If a horse is allowed to run a high temperature for prolonged periods, it can cause chronic founder. Temperatures over 106 are usually fatal. Vets know several methods of bringing a high temperature down quickly, so the sooner you get a vet to the feverish horse the better.

The pulse is taken on the artery under and inside of the jawbone. The normal pulse for a horse is forty-four beats—give or take a few—per minute but it can range anywhere from twenty-three beats per minute to seventy beats per minute if he's excited or afraid, has a fever, a stomach disturbance, or an infection. A strong pounding pulse in the feet may mean that a horse has foundered (laminitis).

Pulses are often taken during endurance rides and at some combined events. As it does in humans, the recovery rate of the pulse indicates a horse's general condition.

To get a normal pulse rate, pick a time when your horse is relaxed, then take the pulse several times a day over a two- or three-day period when he's at his leisure. That way you'll get a normal average to compare against the abnormal.

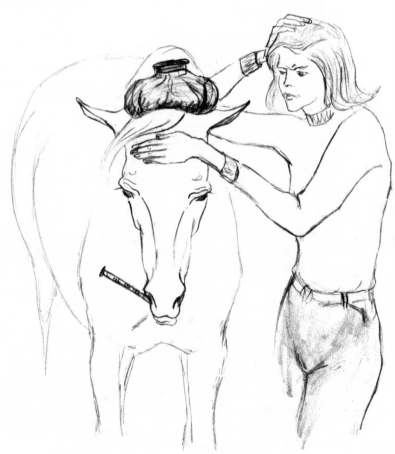

Some ailments you will be able to treat yourself under the vet's instruction. For simple first-aid treatment, your stable **medicine chest** should include:

- Thermometer
- Scissors
- Roll of gauze bandage
- Cotton in a roll
- Disinfectant
- Bacterial or disinfectant soap
- Boric acid powder (for washing eyes)
- Colic medicine (prescribed by vet)
- Dose syringe (to give liquid medicine with)
- Liniment for swollen or sore legs
- Salve for aiding hair growth after scrapes
- Scarlet oil (available through vet, for minor cuts)
- Vaseline
- Hoof dressing
- Clean towels
- Large roll of cotton

Be sure to use only those medicines the vet recommends and follow his instructions carefully. Even simple medicines improperly used can cause severe problems. Absorbine, for instance, can blister the skin if used too long.

With time, you'll accumulate a number of prescribed ointments, powders, liniments, and lotions that the vet will have told you how to use. All these should be kept on high shelves or in a locked chest. In the winter they must be brought inside where they won't freeze.

WHAT AILS HIM

It's important for you to know the most common horse ailments so that you can take the proper precautions. But by no means should you become your own diagnostician.

Digestive Disorders

Azoturia (or Monday morning sickness). This used to be a common disorder among farming horses that were worked very hard during the week and then stabled over the weekend on the same working food ration. On Monday mornings, soon after starting work, the horse would break out in a cold sweat and his back legs would stiffen and buckle. The same thing can happen if a horse is worked too hard *after* being stabled (and/or overfed) for an extended period. Azoturia affects the muscles, particularly those of the loins and quarters.

To alleviate the symptoms, stop working your horse immediately and keep him warm and quiet. The way to prevent the disease is to make sure your horse gets exercise when not working and that he is fed according to the work done. And when starting work after a period of idleness, always warm him up slowly.

Colic. Because of a horse's peculiar one-way digestive system he's particularly prone to digestive disorders. One of the most common, and therefore the most important to learn to recognize, is colic. Some horses are more susceptible to it than others. I used to know an old Tennessee Walker who would just look at clover in the spring and get laid up with a chronic case of colic that lasted for more than a week.

Colic can be caused by any number of poor feeding practices. It can be quite mild, like a stomachache, or extremely serious and sometimes lethal—as two families in my area sadly experienced. It can easily be avoided through proper care and safety measures. The symptoms of colic are restlessness, biting or kicking at the flank, turning the head toward the stomach, tossing the head, and a recurring desire to lie down and roll. Suspect colic when a horse is off his feed, is listless, and has a high pulse rate. The temperature and respiration rate may increase. The stomach distends, and the color of the mucous membranes turns dark. Failure to defecate within a twenty-four-hour period implies a blockage. But horses with simple flagellant colic usually respond to a mild analgesic and light walking. Veterinary assistance is indicated when stomach pain is moderate to severe. You'll notice it by the compulsion to lie down and subsequent extreme restlessness.

Colic kills more mature horses than any other ailment. It's a clinical sign of pain that is caused by the stretching of the abdominal wall, which puts pressure on the sensitive nerve endings in the intestinal wall. Colic accompanies many conditions. In fact, it's difficult to find a symptom that could have so many different causes.

The different types of colic:

- *Gastric.* An overloading of the stomach with fine indigestible material, creating sudden and intense pain.
- *Spasmodic.* This type is characterized by loud bubbling, popping, gurgling noises in the stomach. It's most frequently caused by sudden changes in food, by long, cold drinks of water, or by an unusual strain of work and fatigue.
- *Impaction.* An acute obstruction (either partial or complete) of the intestines. The pain is mild and persistent, and a horse so afflicted will act dull and depressed.
- *Obstructive.* This is the most severe type of colic and is usually caused by strongyle worms (see following pages). The blood supply of the stomach is supplied by only one artery, and when para-

sites damage the wall of this artery, the blood flow is cut off, causing permanent damage that eventually leads to gangrene and death.

- *Recurrent colic.* This can be the result of parasite infections, of impactions, of irregular feeding, or of overfeeding.

The vet will tell you to walk your horse and perhaps prescribe a dose of milk of magnesia or other colic medicine before he gets there. After giving the medicine, walk your horse for no more than an hour. Then give him a rest, watching him closely, and begin to walk him again. You don't want to tire him to exhaustion. On the other hand you don't want to give him a chance to roll and possibly twist his long intestine. Also, a rolling horse will throw his head around and against any proximal object—like mangers, feed dishes, and buckets. The colic-prone Tennessee Walker above had to have everything removed from his stall when an attack came on.

The best treatment for colic is early detection and care. When you describe your horse's symptoms to your vet, be sure to tell him how long the horse has appeared ill, the exact changes he's gone through physically and any changes in his disposition. Any variations in feeding routines or any medication you are currently giving the horse should be included in this description.

Be familiar with your horse's physiological signs. Know his normal pulse rate, temperature, and respiration (the latter being twelve to fourteen breaths a minute for a normal horse). Also take note of the normal color of mucous membranes around the eyes, nose, and mouth. These reveal the amount of oxygen in the blood and the rate of the blood flow. Gums should be pinkish with a slight yellow tinge. If you press the gum with your finger, it should turn white or light in color, returning to normal within one to one-and-a-half seconds. Gums that are very pale, dark red, or bluish are abnormal, as are those that take more than three seconds to recolor.

Unfortunately, the serious colics that may need surgery begin the same way as the mild types, not showing their severity for hours. Once these signs do occur, the only solution is immediate surgery. Time is of the essence. It's helpful if a horseowner knows beforehand the location of the nearest clinic that can handle this type of emergency.

But, as for all ailments, the best solution to colic is prevention. Pay careful attention to your feeding program and make sure horses are wormed regularly for strongyles, roundworms, and bots. Depending on the size of your paddock and pasture, you might find it necessary to worm your horse every eight weeks. It's hard to believe, but alas true, that a worm measuring less than an inch in length and weighing a fraction of an ounce can cause the death of a fifteen-hundred-pound horse.

Laminitis, or **Founder.** Acute cases of this disease are usually caused by excessive feeding, fast work on a hard surface, or drinking large quantities of cold water after working hard. Founder causes an inflammation of the sensitive laminae on one or more feet, usually the front. The horse will be very lame and in pain, and his feet will be hot and sensitive to the touch because the expanding laminae, pressing against the wall and sole, cause extreme discomfort. His temperature might go as high as 106°, causing him to sweat profusely. In chronic cases, the hoofs can become so distorted that the sole separates entirely from the wall, the hoof dishes inward, the toe curls up, and the sole drops down. A horse that has foundered badly has very clearly defined markings on his hoofs. Normally any rings on the hoof will parallel the coronet. But founder rings tend to cluster up around the coronet and drop down toward the heel in back. Fever and changes in nutrition will also create rings, but of the type that parallel the coronet lower down.

In acute cases of founder, apply wet cold packs to the feet or stand your horse in wet clay or a cold stream until the vet arrives. In chronic cases, special trimming and shoes are required after the temperature has been stabilized, and the horse is on the mend. Horses that founder badly will probably never be completely sound again. Sometimes founder develops as a complication following other diseases.

Founder

Laminitis is considered chronic when the coffin bone rotates, a situation that occurs when the tissue (laminae) connecting the coffin bone to the hoof wall weakens and actually breaks down. This is caused by toxins, especially histamine, which changes the permeability of blood vessels in the laminae. This could happen three to five days to a few weeks after the onset of founder. The catalyst is probably too much carbohydrate in the system, caused by too much grain, lush pasture, etc.

Veterinarians consider laminitis an elusive, little-understood disease. Many questions about it remain to be answered. Early detection is the key, so if you even suspect founder, consider it an emergency and don't hesitate to call the vet. It could make the difference between a healthy and a permanently unsound horse.

Should you feel in your horse's foot and suspect laminitis, some vets recommend soaking the hoof in epsom salts to help remove those toxins that caused the inflammation. Others will tell you to walk your horse out twice a day to restore circulation. Find out what your vet advises and for the best results follow his advice to the letter. Most vets will begin therapy with a shot, which aims to quell the disease from the inside out.

Infectious Diseases

Colds. Horses get them too, and the symptoms are similar to the human varieties. Colds can begin with a nasal discharge, a persistent cough, temperature, general listlessness, and disinterest in food. Of course the vet should be called. To prevent colds, don't allow your horse to be put away hot; always cool him out thoroughly after work. Don't let him stand in drafts, and keep his resistance up by proper feeding. If he gets overtired or chilled, you're inviting a cold. Also be careful to keep the drinking water clean.

Equine encephalitis. This disease, which is almost always fatal, has three common forms: Eastern, Western, and Venezuelan (VEE). All are carried by mosquitoes or other bloodsucking insects, which pick up the infection from birds. Whereas the Eastern and Western forms can only be transmitted individually by carrier insects, VEE, endemic in the United States since 1971, is contagious—to humans as well as to horses. Vaccinations for all forms are strongly recommended. VEE vaccination is mandatory if your horse will be raced, shown at state events, or will be traveling interstate. Inoculations should be given in the winter if you live in the north; elsewhere, when your horse is not working. Symptoms are fever, impaired vision, lack of coordination, irregular gait, yawning and drowsiness, followed by difficulty in swallowing, and, finally, paralysis and death.

Flu. Horses are susceptible to a type of influenza caused by a virus closely related to the human type. Though rarely fatal, the infected horse must have extended rest while the fever and cough that accompany the flu subside. My vet recommends vaccinating for influenza a month before a horse is to be shown or worked in company. There are initially two injections given two weeks or a month apart. Every year after that, a booster is sufficient.

Infectious anemia (swamp fever). Within the past decade, this has become the most written-about disease of the horse, an incurable, usually fatal illness for those horses acutely afflicted, and one that, at this writing, is still controversial.

Horses with acute swamp fever die within three to five days, suffering through an interim period of sweating and stiffness and weakness in the hindquarters, with temperatures often rising to 108 degrees.

Early symptoms include anemia, jaundiced mucous membrane, edema and swelling in the legs and lower body, loss of weight, and failing condition. Horses with swamp fever are dejected and off their feed, often refusing even to drink water.

Some horses may seem to recover from equine infectious anemia (EIA). Others show a progressive debilitation, which results in death after two to four weeks. It's not uncommon for a horse to have a chronic case of infectious anemia, with intermittent attacks of fever combined with one or more of the above symptoms.

To the best of current knowledge, EIA is caused by a hardy virus—so hardy that it can withstand enormous variations in temperature and survive over long periods of time. EIA or swamp fever is transmitted from horse to horse by bloodsucking insects (the vectors are mosquitoes and flies), and horses pastured near swamps or stagnant ponds are its easiest victims—hence the name.

EIA can also be transferred via hypodermic needle from one horse to another. But whatever the source of the disease, once a horse is infected, he carries its antibodies for life.

Since 1973, it has been mandatory for all horses suspected of carrying EIA to take a Coggins test to detect the swamp fever antibodies. Most states still require that any horse that has been recently sold or transported across state lines must have a Coggins. And at least one state—New Hampshire—requires the test of any horse that is ridden, driven, or otherwise transported off the owner's property. Those horses that react positively to the test are, in most states, either destroyed or compelled to stay in a screened isolated area for the rest of their lives.

The controversy over swamp fever has arisen because many outwardly healthy horses are carriers of the antibodies (Typhoid Marys of the equine world), and it has yet to be determined absolutely whether those carriers are the health menace that many believe them to be.

The big questions are whether test-positive victims with no clinical signs of the disease can infect other horses and whether carriers with no previous signs of the disease can become acutely ill.

If the answers are yes, then all horses are a potential threat, and testing is the only way to identify and eliminate the menace. If the answers to both questions are negative, then only acutely ill horses are a cause for concern; they, of course, must be destroyed.

The debate over these questions has become more heated since a prominent veterinarian experimented with an entire herd of test-positive horses that were outwardly healthy and found that none of them developed the disease. Her conclusion: "Although ten fly bites would be enough to transmit swamp fever from an acutely ill to a healthy horse, the bites of one hundred flies couldn't transmit it from a carrier to a healthy horse."

The problem, of course, is that many otherwise healthy carrier horses have been destroyed as a result of the Coggins testing program. And while the test has made a substantial difference in the incidence of the disease, bringing it under control in many states, owners of the carrier animals are understandably upset to see their valuable investments destroyed.

Legislative ears have not been deaf to the swamp fever furor, and many of the first states to institute mandatory Coggins testing have become the first to repeal it, no longer requiring the test of horses sold, transported, or entering competition. One of the biggest lobbyists for such repeal is an organization called Concerned Horsemen Against Test and Slaughter (CHATS), which has chapters throughout the country.

New Hampshire allows owners of test-positive horses to resubmit the animal for testing at state expense. If the second test proves positive, the horse is marked with a lip tattoo. But only horses who show clinical symptoms of the disease are quarantined. Nevertheless, no positives are allowed to leave the state.

CHAT believes that many healthy horses have been unnecessarily destroyed in states where EIA is not a problem, and they argue that Coggins testing has not controlled the disease in the Missisippi delta areas, where it's endemic.

Strangles (also called **Distemper** or **Shipping Fever**). The symptoms may vary, but this disease is caused by a single bacteria: streptococcus equi. It's an upper respiratory infection that begins with a high temperature, fast breathing, and general listlessness, usually followed by a nasal discharge and swelling of the lymph nodes under the jaw, which frequently abscess. Call the vet immediately when any of these symptoms appear, because this is a highly contagious disease.

The vet will treat the bacteria, usually with antibiotics, and will tell you how to treat the abscesses. A horse recuperating from strangles should have complete rest and fresh drinking water at all times. He should be fed light feed like bran mashes, and be kept warm and out of drafts.

Strangles is often called shipping fever because it affects horses transported long distances; their resistance is lowered through fatigue and nervousness. If you buy a horse from a stable or a dealer, there is a good possibility that he has contracted shipping fever or is carrying it, which is equally bad. Hopefully, the vet you take along will spot it. If you have other horses, keep new arrivals separate in a different building and pasture for at least three weeks until the danger period is past.

Respiratory Diseases

Heaves. This is an asthmatic condition resulting in overexpansion of the air cells of the lungs, which causes a horse to take in extra air and then use his stomach muscles to force it out. Heaves are usually provoked by something extraneous—often bad feed or musty hay. Or a bad bronchitis might develop into chronic heaves. If not too advanced, the disease can be arrested with proper attention. The vet may tell you to eliminate hay temporarily or possibly permanently and substitute special feeds, such as a pellet concentrate. Even a slight cough should be checked out by the vet and treated. A horse with heaves destroys air sacs every time he coughs, just as a human with emphysema does. The lungs have lost their normal elasticity, and the affected horse breathes in and out with two distinct movements. This strain on the lungs causes barrel chests and an enlargement of the stomach muscles, called a **heave line.** A heavey horse may tire easily and have difficulty breathing during even moderate exercise; his breaths will be hurried and his nostrils dilated.

Symptoms are a deep, barking, persistent cough. In severe cases the nostrils become extremely distended, even when the horse is idle.

Some ailments (like sinusitis, pneumonia, and anemia) are separate diseases that may appear in addition to heaves as a result of the horse's weakened respiratory system, but they are not part of the same disease.

Roaring and whistling are two different stages of the same disorder, resulting from a paralysis of the nerves that power the vocal-cord muscles. In mild cases, the horse makes a whistling sound when he inhales. In severe cases, there is a loud wheeze known as roaring. This shouldn't be confused with the normal, snorting sound a horse makes when excited; roaring occurs only during inhalation. Sometimes the disorder will follow a case of strangles. The majority of cases occur in very large horses; ponies rarely suffer from roaring or whistling—why no one knows.

Lameness

If your horse goes lame when you're riding, you will usually detect it by his uneven stride or an unnatural bobbing of his head. Dismount immediately and check his feet for a lodged stone in his shoe. It's a good idea to carry a hoof-pick with you on hunts and trail rides for this purpose. If there is no obvious reason for his lameness, jog him out on a level or uphill stretch. His head will nod each time the sound leg hits the ground in front. If the lameness is behind, instead of nodding he will put most of his weight on the sound leg. To find the right spot, run your hands simultaneously down two legs and try to notice differences. You will want to compare for heat, bumps, swellings, or obvious signs of sensitivity. Sometimes several of these symptoms will be present; in rare cases, none. Always call the vet, and your horse will have to rest until he is cured. You will probably be instructed to soak the affected area in epsom salts, or pack it with ice, or stand him in running water or hose the leg.

Sprains. When a sprain occurs, a horse is usually quite lame, and the injury may look very serious. Within a few hours, it will begin to heat up and swell. Sprains can result from a sudden movement, a fall, or a quick turn on muddy ground. Overgrown toes can also put more stress on tendons and ligaments to cause a sprain. Jog your horse out to find out which limb is affected and call the vet, who may recommend an overnight poultice or a hosing down.

Leg Problems

Several of the following conditions are similar to bursitis and arthritis in humans. Some are considered serious unsoundness, others are blemishes that don't interfere with a horse's way of going. Remember to check each with your vet.

Capped hock is a swelling caused by an injured bursa (one of the fluid sacs that surround various joints, tendons, and ligaments) at the point of the hock, causing it to secrete an abnormal amount of fluid. It's like "water on the knee" in humans (except in this case it's water on the hock).

Curbs are inflammation of the plantar ligament on the back of the hock. It is seen mostly in Standardbreds, sometimes in Thoroughbreds, and is usually due to poor conformation (like sickle hocks or cow hocks).

Bog spavin is caused by inflamed bursa in the joint capsule at the

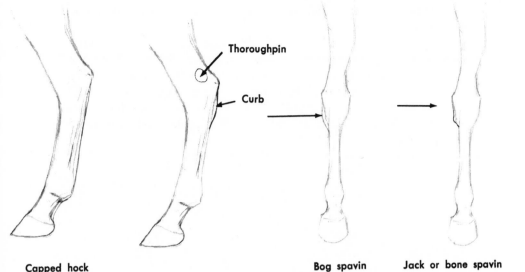

Thoroughpin

Curb

Capped hock   Bog spavin   Jack or bone spavin

front end and sides of the hock. This usually doesn't make a horse lame. The condition is often caused by conformation faults like straight hocks.

Bone spavin (or **jack spavin**) is more serious than the above and usually considered an unsoundness. This is a little like arthritis of the hock, usually resulting from putting a heavy strain on a horse—like working him a long time in very heavy going.

Sickle-hocked or cow-hocked horses are more susceptible to this disorder because the faults put an abnormal stress on the hock. To detect jack spavin, hold your horse's hind leg and fold it under for a few minutes, then trot him out. Any stiffness will be apparent in his gait immediately.

Thoroughpin is a swelling in the lubricating sheath that surrounds the tendons on the sides and back of the hock. It is soft and spongy to the touch and not usually serious enough to cause lameness. The cause is overexertion.

Splint ⎯⎯⎯⎯⎯⎯⎯➤

Splints are inflammations of the ligaments that hold the splint bone to the cannon bone. The condition is fairly common and can be caused by simple accidents like bumping a rail when jumping. After the initial period of swelling, calcification usually occurs. When the heat is down, it won't interfere with a horse's way of going—if not involved with or close to a joint or tendon.

Stocking up. Many horses left standing idle for long periods after hard work will get edema in the legs. This is usually caused by poor circulation, which can be caused in turn by conformation faults. To keep legs from filling up with fluid, be sure to walk your horse out well after working. Support bandages, sort of like Supp-hose for horses (called Equihose), help this condition. (See stable bandage later on in this chapter.)

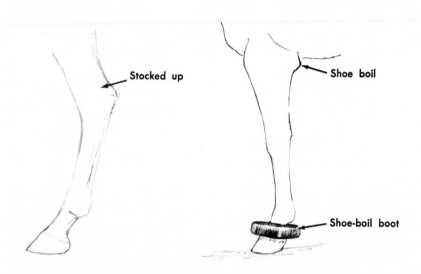

Shoe boils, the growths or lumps on the elbow of the front legs which develop after a horse has repeatedly rubbed the elbow with his front hoof against the area when lying down, can be alleviated by the shoe-boil boot, a round tube of canvas that fits over the lower pastern and protects the elbow.

Bandaging

There are special leg bandages for horses, with ties or velcro to hold them firmly in place. These are used over cotton batting or cotton wrap and give real protection to the leg.

Before starting to bandage, put your horse in crossties. Don't park yourself on the floor where he might kick you if he moves suddenly; crouch down so that you can easily get out of the way.

Begin by putting the cotton batting over the cannon bone. Have your bandage rolled and ready to go, with the velcro or ties on the inside of the roll. Begin in the middle of the leg, wrap down to the top of the fetlock and then back up again. Bandages should be firm but not tight.

It's helpful to wrap the cotton batting in gauze, taped on the outside, to protect the material for reuse. Be sure when you do this to keep the tape on the outside of your horse's leg as you bandage.

Trucking bandage and **stable bandage.** This is used for protection in trucking or vanning a horse, or to keep him from stocking up when he will be stabled for an extended period. Wrap the cotton from a point below the knee right down to the coronet, making sure it covers your horse's heels to protect them from injury in shipping. Beginning at the

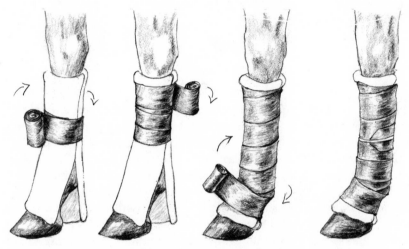

Stable and transportation bandage

middle of the cannon, work down to the fetlock and back up. You may have to use two bandages to cover the entire lower leg. Be sure to keep it from getting too tight, or the bandage will leave a mark on his leg if he fills up at all. Bandages should tie or fasten on the inside or outside of the leg, never on the front or back.

Exercise bandage. These are used occasionally to give support to a leg (to reinforce weak tendons) when riding, as decoration for a parade or to protect it from brambles or thorns. Only the area from below the knee to the top of the fetlock is covered. The bandage should be applied quite firmly, making sure not to cover the joint.

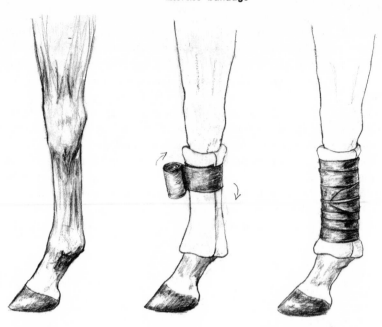

Poultice bandage. You would use this if your horse got a puncture wound on his foot and it became infected. The bag part is useful for moistening feet. After putting the medicine (recommended by the vet) on the sole of his foot, get a plastic bag and put it over the hoof. Then cut an L-shaped bandage out of a burlap bag or a feed bag and wrap it as shown.

Spider bandage. This is an excellent solution used for a wound at the joint. The bandage is cut from a burlap bag. The sections of burlap are then loop-tied down the leg, holding the underlying batting firmly in place.

Cold water bandages. These are used to cool hot or strained muscles and to reduce swelling. It's best to use a quilted padding because cotton dissolves quickly. (You could, for instance, cut up an old mattress cover for wraps and put a regular stable bandage over it.) Wrap the leg as you would for an exercise bandage, but make it a little looser—and include the ankle. (You want to be able to hose water down into the bandage, hence the looseness.) You can also soak cotton pads in ice water before wrapping. It's very important to keep this bandage soaked in cold water, otherwise it defeats its own purpose by heating up. Your vet may also prescribe white lotion, which you should pour down the bandage at frequent intervals to keep the leg cool.

An alternative bandage, which is better than hosing with cold water,

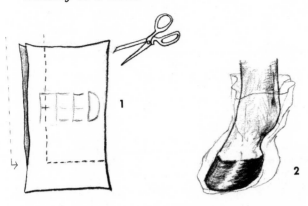

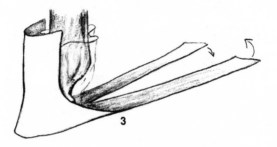

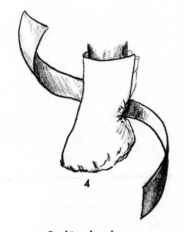

Poultice bandage
1. Cut along dotted lines. Use clean feed bag
2. Apply poultice to sole or infected area. Cover with plastic bag
3. Place bandage cut from bag over both hoof and plastic bag
4. Cross long tails of bandage in back of pastern and bring to front of pastern
5. Secure in front with bow or slipknot. Cut off or tuck in long tails of bandage

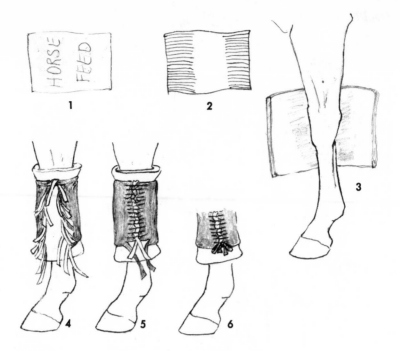

Spider bandage
1. Feed bag
2. Cut strips on sides about 1 inch wide
3. Wrap cotton or gauze around leg
4. Fold ties over one another . . .
5. . . . covering ends as you descend
6. Tie in bow at end, cutting off all remaining ends

is an ice-filled rubber wrap. I've made these myself by cutting off about three feet of tire tubing. This is slipped around the horse's leg, wrapped with a cotton leg bandage at the bottom, and filled with cracked ice all around. Or it can be tied at the bottom under the hoofs with bailing twine (if the strain is lower down), so your horse can stand in it. A commercial five-pound bag of ice will last in the tubing for several hours.

The bandage works wonders, quickly reducing swelling and getting rid of inflammation and heat. Always check with your vet first, of course, but I found it most effective with any of my horses that has a badly pulled tendon. They often recover in three to four days with this ice treatment.

Hot water bandages. This is identical to a cold water bandage except for the temperature. Wraps are soaked first in hot water, with a dry outer bandage over that and medications like Ichthamol used to draw out an abscess or infection. Hot water bandages don't have to be re-soaked, but they must be changed frequently so that pads will remain hot.

Water therapy. Some exclusive stables use mirrored and tiled Holly-wood-style whirlpool baths to keep horses clean and cool after work-outs. The horse is generally led down a sloping side into the pool and handled from the deck by a pole attached to his halter. Many big racing stables find water therapy so beneficial that they have installed swim-ming pools for horses. These are fantastic for keeping a racehorse fit when he is recovering from an injury, because they allow the leg to heal and keep the muscles and lungs in condition without putting any strain on the affected leg. Whirlpool baths are out of my price range, but when I once had a horse that needed that kind of therapy, I im-provised by putting the injured leg in a large bucket, then running the hose of the vacuum cleaner, in reverse, to circulate the water. It's a very noisy process, and not too many horses would put up with it, but in his case it worked.

Tetanus (lockjaw)

The bacteria that cause this disease can only flourish in an airless (anaerobic) environment. Puncture wounds that quickly close up are an ideal breeding ground. The incubation period for tetanus varies from a week to a few months, and the disease is almost always fatal. Because the bacteria are so common, all animals should have a yearly tetanus vaccination. If your horse is not protected, he must get an injection of antiserum within seventy-two hours after injury. In its acute stage, tetanus causes spasms of the neck and back muscles that distend the head and neck, making it difficult for the animal to breathe and impossible for him to eat or drink. Nowadays a horse has an initial tetanus shot at three to six months of age, with a second shot following a month later. Thereafter he has a booster every two to three years.

Cuts

With a clean cut or a tear, the immediate danger is excessive bleeding. If the blood is spurting out and bright red, an artery has been severed and the flow must be stopped with a tourniquet immediately, before you phone the vet. Use a torn sheet, twisting a stick in the knot to bring pressure to bear above the wound.

Less serious wounds need to be cleaned out immediately to reduce the chance of infection. All the hair around the wound should be removed first with a razor. Then clean out the area with lukewarm water, squeezing a clean wet rag gently over the wound. Never rub, or you may rub the dirt in. It's helpful in this kind of emergency to have a syringe to squirt the water over the wound. After cleaning, spray or dab on a disinfectant solution or antiseptic powder you could get from the vet. If your horse is afraid of the spray, put the disinfectant on a cloth and dab it on. Some wounds can be bandaged, but wait until the vet gets there before you proceed.

A puncture wound usually produces swelling and soreness. Sometimes the wound itself is invisible.

Swellings should be soaked in epsom salts or packed with ice, depending on what kind of injury your horse has. Sometimes running a cold hose on the swelling or standing him in a running stream is effective. If swelling persists for more than twenty-four hours the vet should be called.

With any of these wounds the vet should be called immediately if there's any doubt as to whether or not the horse has had his annual tetanus shot.

Saddle Sores and Galls

These are usually a result of ill-fitting equipment, or they will appear on an out-of-condition horse that has been ridden particularly hard. The girth of the saddle may pinch or rub the skin, making a raw spot. Or if the saddle doesn't fit properly, or the pad is too small or improperly placed, it may cause a sore or bruise. Most saddle sores are caused by pressure on a small area where the tree has borne down on the withers. This leaves a welt that gradually reduces in size and eventually becomes concave, as the pressure is removed. The hair around this type of sore will turn white. Another easily irritated area is underneath the cantle. Saddle sores here are usually caused by riders who sit too far back and don't balance themselves correctly, bouncing around rather than redistributing weight to their thighs. Horses' backs take the beating for poor horsemanship .(To protect the horse in such cases, the U.S. Army many years ago developed the uncomfortable Mc-Clellan saddle, which distributes weight evenly down a horse's back and protects him from the bouncing derrieres of green cavalry troops.) When allowed to go unattended, these sores can become very nasty and hard-to-heal. The usual treatment, which you can do yourself, is to give the area a rest and apply some sort of drying medication recommended by a vet. If swollen and not open, the area can be soaked, or it may respond to an ice pack. Your vet may have other suggestions, like a warm-water-and-salt bath. If you absolutely have to use a horse with a saddle sore (at least let it partially heal), a hole can be cut in a thick saddle pad to relieve the pressure on the sore. But complete rest is far preferable.

Curb-chain gall can occur because of a twisted curb chain or strap that is too tight.

Sunburn

This is most common to albinos, palominos, cremes, or tiabinos (pintos). Horses with light-colored skin can get burned and their coats can be faded by the sun. Light-colored show horses with coats that fade under the sun are blanketed with a light cotton sheet when not worked, and care should be taken to work them either in the morning or in the late afternoon.

Sunburn is indicated when skin gets red and swollen. This can be a direct cause of the sun's rays or a secondary reaction to light, triggered by an allergy to certain foods like buckwheat and St. Johnswort (see Appendix). Several other grasses can cause this two-step reaction, and some high grasses and weeds, when wet, will irritate the skin. Because any number of other things could cause them, any red or swollen areas should be looked at by the vet.

Parasites

With some 150 varieties of parasite to choose from, the odds are good that your horse will have one or several of them. There are external parasites—flies, lice, and ticks—and the internal ones—stomach worms, bots, and bloodworms. Each of these species has a subspecies, and the whole thing can get very complicated. Bloodworms, for instance, come in forty different varieties.

The important thing to remember is that all parasites are harmful and you should try to keep your horse as free of them as possible with regular wormings and good barn and pasture hygiene. (A horse can be permanently damaged if not regularly wormed when fighting parasites.) Prevention of parasites should be of paramount concern for every horse owner. Although treatment of a severely infected animal is obviously necessary, most of the damage has already been done when that point is reached.

To reduce the number and variety of parasites around your stable, try to follow these recommendations by the U.S. Department of Agriculture's Horse Science Program:

- Keep grain in covered containers, so that flies, birds, and rodents —all carriers—can't get into them.

- Never feed grain or hay on the floor. It is likely to become contaminated by wormy manure.
- Keep stalls clean and rebed them frequently to reduce chances of fecal material getting on food.
- If the stall has a dirt floor, ten inches of soil should be removed and replaced each year. Many larvae will burrow into it.
- Try to remove manure as regularly as possible. (Ideally, it should be removed from the pile daily and spread on a field that is not being grazed; but this is out of the question for most busy horse owners.)
- Don't let your horse drink from accumulated puddles in the barnyard or from water holes contaminated by manure drainage.
- Spread gravel or fine shale on corrals and paddocks when possible so that your horse doesn't eat infested grass.
- Prevent flies from breeding by keeping stables and surrounding areas free from manure, soiled bedding, and wasted food. To break the life cycle of parasites, rotate pastures as often as possible. Horses shouldn't graze continually in one area.

Internal parasites can enter a horse's system in a number of devious ways—as eggs, larvae, or adults, carried on the heads of face flies, on the blades of grass, or on birds and rodents.

Worms are dreadful things that can kill a horse if uncontrolled. In sufficient quantity, they can be a severe physical strain, causing a horse to work less efficiently, preventing proper utilization of food and causing colic, periodic lameness, chronic coughs, or bronchitis. Bloodworms can affect circulation and, in extreme cases, cause death from blood clots. Other worms produce toxins that destroy red blood cells and create anemia. Immature worms migrating through the body tissues open the way for bacteria and fungus to enter the system and cause other diseases. Sometimes they can damage tissue irreparably.

There are a number of telltale signs indicating that your horse is wormy:

- Dull coat
- Frequent rubbing of the tail
- Listlessness
- Loss of weight with no decrease in diet
- Possible sores on the skin
- Lameness
- Frequent colic

Only one worm can be seen with the naked eye—the pinworm. It's very important, therefore, to have a manure sample checked under the microscope by your vet at least twice a year, in the early spring and late fall. If your pasture area is small, even if you rotate systematically, it's wise to have even more frequent checkups.

There are commercial worming medicines that you can administer yourself, but I don't advise it. While most horses have worms, there are exceptions, and all medicines used for worming are highly toxic when they have nothing to act on. So it is imperative to have a vet check first; and it's advisable to let him do the worming to assure that your horse gets all the medicine in the right place and in the proper quantity.

There are five major types of internal parasites: **The botfly,** which looks like a bee as it darts around a horse's legs, hovering and waiting to lay eggs on the hair. The eggs are deposited along the forelegs, belly, flanks, mane, and occasionally the shoulder.

When a horse licks the area where the eggs have been deposited it warms them and stimulates hatching. The larvae then migrate to the mouth where they either burrow into the tongue or work down into the stomach. Bot larvae attach themselves to the stomach walls and migrate through the surrounding tissues, spending eleven months in-

Botfly

side the host horse until they reach maturity. Then they pass out through the manure, the fly develops, lays more eggs, and the cycle, unless interrupted by medicine and hygiene, goes on.

Bloodworms or **strongyles** are the most devastating of all internal parasites. These are the species that come in forty different kinds, and all of them attach themselves to various organs of the body, where they suck blood. After leaving the body of a horse through his manure, the eggs become attached to the tips of pasture grass and are ingested by grazing horses. Bloodworms on artery walls can cause certain kinds of lameness and sometimes death when they restrict the flow of blood.

Pinworms are about two to three inches long and easily spotted in manure. They mature in the large intestine and pass out through the rectum, irritating the dock area and causing the horse to rub his tail. Most pinworm eggs develop in manure and are picked up by a horse when he's grazing.

Intestinal worms, or ascarids, deposit their eggs in the small intestine. The small intestine is seventy feet long, so they have a lot of territory to settle. The eggs penetrate the wall of the gut, entering the bloodstream where they travel into the heart and lungs. The larvae then leave the lungs and migrate up the trachea to the throat, where they are swallowed again, going back to the small intestine to develop through maturity. Again, these worms are chiefly picked up through grazing or unclean pasture. Ascarids are a particular threat to a young horse. In extreme cases of infestation, they cause blood clots.

Stomach worms come in ten varieties. Four of them cause lesions of the stomach wall. Others are thought to be responsible for a skin disease known as summer sores. The eggs are laid in the horse's stomach by adult worms. They pass out with the manure, where they are picked up by maggots—the larval form of the stable fly. When the flies mature, the worms hatch on their heads, leaving them when the flies feed on the moisture around the horse's lips.

External Parasites are abundant:

Horse lice live on the hair of a horse, biting, sucking blood, causing bare spots, and making him itch, rub, and bite. This parasite is usually spread by direct contact with an infested animal or by dirty tack and grooming tools. There are shampoos that will kill lice. But be sure to have your vet check a suspected case first.

Mites are not always visible to the naked eye. These are bloodsuckers, which lay eggs in furrows of the skin, causing irritation and inflammation and making a horse itch. If scaly-looking skin develops and your horse is scratching, mites should be suspected. Call the vet.

Ringworm is a fungus that shows up like raised circles on bare skin. Itching of the infected area causes lesions that become covered with a grayish crust. Itching also spreads the ringworm to other areas. This should be treated immediately by your vet because it is highly contagious, not only to other horses but to people.

Ticks can be a real problem in some parts of the country. They are bloodsucking insects that can spread other serious diseases. There is a medicine that your vet can prescribe, which is swabbed on each tick to suffocate it.

Flies have developed in numerous shapes and sizes, all of them a constant irritation and some of them potentially dangerous. There are horn flies, blowflies, deerflies, horseflies, and stable flies. All of them either bite or suck blood. The biting varieties carry diseases like sleeping sickness. Blowflies, common to some areas of the country, lay eggs in wounds. One fly in its larval form is the screw worm, which feeds on live tissues and can be fatal. House, stable, and horn flies usually lay eggs on any moist material available—rotting vegetation, manure, or spilled grain. Face flies lay eggs on fresh manure (and, as mentioned, carry worms on their heads). Deer- and horseflies leave their eggs near water, either in swamps, high grass, or salt marshes, which is why they always seem to be around when you go swimming.

To control flies, keep manure and other likely breeding materials away from the stable. When practical, use screens. In the Northeast, horseflies run as large as three inches in length. They dive-bomb their targets, and four or five of them can literally drive a horse up—and over—a wall. (Once they've landed, however, they're very easy to kill.) On hot days horses bothered by flies can lose a lot of weight as they race around and work themselves into a lather trying to avoid them, risking injury as they flee. I've seen horses throw themselves in thick bramble bushes just to scrape the flies off. Flies are one of the biggest nuisances in any stable. Keeping them off your horse and under control requires time, ingenuity and the right fly spray. It's exasperating to spray a horse and watch the flies start to land before you put the cap on the bottle. Every serious horseman I know pays careful attention to getting the right kind of spray—one that will last and that his horse's skin will tolerate. Flies seem to build up an immunity to sprays as they do to certain kinds of wormers. For this reason, a spray that works wonders this summer may not be effective next July.

Some fly-prevention hints:

- Clean and groom your horse before every workout and wash him afterward, paying particular attention to removing dried sweat.
- Keep the stable clean, cool, and dark in the hot months.
- Keep stalls disinfected and clean your feed and water buckets every day.
- Keep the manure pile as far from the barn as possible.
- Keep pastures dragged and paddocks picked up. When dirty, these are the breeding grounds for flies, and they attract other insects.
- In the summer stable horses in the morning and turn them out in the late afternoon. This keeps them relatively relaxed and fly-free.
- Cover each horse with spray before turning him out.

Some horses have extremely sensitive skins and will become allergic to sprays as well as to flies. Signs of such allergies are large hivelike welts where sprays have been applied.

Some horses are afraid of sprays, and they should have the solution wiped on with a rag or be trained to get used to the spray. Do this by holding them on a lead (never spray a horse of this type in crossties). Start away from the horse and spray into the air so he gets used to the sound. Start with the leg and work your way slowly up the body. On the head use a mild solution and wipe it on—or use a deodorant stick-type, wiping it around the face area and under the jaw. Pay special attention to the undersides of stomachs and to the sheaths of geldings and teats of mares. And keep these clean.

If you're experimental, I've heard of one Thoroughbred breeder who uses a sheep-dip bath in lieu of fly spray; he claims it keeps horses fly-free for three or four days without any allergic reactions.

Some fly sprays are oil-based and last longer than the water-soluble variety, but they also attract dirt. There are also **fly traps,** which you can place in your barn, and portable or electric **fogging machines** (before using foggers take all horses out of the barn and cover all feed and water dishes). Spray the interior manually with solutions such as Baytex and Cygon. Take care to thoroughly spray ceilings, walls, and all around doors and windows. One gallon of the solution covers five hundred square feet of surface.

Horses that are field-kept all the time should have their manes and tails left long during the summer months for fly protection. And it helps to turn a horse out with a friend, so they can protect one another with their switching tails. And some vets suggest keeping whiskers long to protect against face flies. One reason why sheds are recommended for winter and summer is so horses can escape to a shady, relatively fly-free haven.

When riding in fly weather, try to pick a good time of day—early in the morning or late afternoon—in a pleasant spot, preferably on high, shady ground, away from swamp or marshy areas. You can get net bonnets that fit over the horse's ears to give him fly protection, and it is helpful to carry a fly switch (or pick a leafy branch) to ward off deer flies, the little brown ones that are the worst culprits.

Some horses become neurotic about flies, tossing their heads even when there isn't a fly in sight. This habit usually disappears with the passing of the fly season. Several friends of mine own horses with a seasonal fly neurosis that they have had to learn to live with. One sent her horse to Cornell for treatment because it was so bad.

Teeth

As I explained in the chapter on feeding, the condition of a horse's teeth is vital to his well-being. All horses wear down their teeth through chewing, creating sharp points that can be painful and are inefficient for grinding food. An animal with bad teeth may lose food as he eats; but most important, the portion that is swallowed won't be properly masticated and therefore will pass through the digestive system without giving full nutritive benefit to the horse.

Some teeth wear better than others, depending on how hard or soft they are and on the construction of the jaws. If the upper jaw is larger than the lower, the grinding action causes points to form on the outer edges of the upper molars and on the inner edges of the lower molars. The upper points can create sores on the inside of the cheek. It depends on the conformation of a horse's jaws. (Like people, some horses could use an orthodontist; but horse dentists have yet to invent any horse braces.) In any case, the vet should check out your horse's teeth twice a year and "float" or file them if necessary.

A male horse has forty permanent teeth, a mare thirty-six. Sometimes a horse will acquire two extra teeth called "wolf teeth" which grow in next to the lower rear molars. These sometimes cause difficulties with chewing; more often, they will rub against the bit and annoy or pain the horse. So the vet should remove them—a surprisingly simple and relatively painless procedure.

KEEPING THE VET HAPPY

If you have to call the vet, try not to get hysterical. Give the symptoms as calmly and objectively as you can over the phone. When he arrives, if there's nothing you can do, stay out of his way until the examination is completed. The vet can't listen to you and your horse's stomach and respiration at the same time. At the end of the exam, he'll probably have all the answers to the questions you wanted to ask anyway.

When asked to hold your horse, do so, trying to keep him as quiet as possible. Some horses are terrified of vets. If yours is one of them, warn the doctor about it and then be as reassuring to your horse as you can. Speak to him in soothing tones, scratch him on his favorite spot. It may help.

If your horse has a severe vet complex, it may be necessary to use more aggressive ways, such as a twitch, to make him stand for examination and treatment. While it may seem cruel, remember that your horse's health, possibly his life, is at stake. The more thorough the examination, the more accurate the diagnosis. And remember that the doctor's physical safety, like the blacksmith's, may depend on your learning how to hold a twitch properly. The vet is there to do his job. If you haven't done yours, which is to manage and train your horse properly, you'll have to suffer the consequences.

My vet once apologized for being rough with our brutish, seventeen-hand colt (there were three of us holding him at the time); actually I was delighted with his handling because one of the colt's problems—in this kind of situation—has always been that no one has been strong enough to force him to behave.

The nose clamp or the Humane Twitch, which can be ordered through saddlery supply houses for under fifteen dollars, enables one person to restrain and handle the animal at the same time.

It's important when applying a twitch to approach your horse calmly. Gently pat his nose, then grasp a large portion of his muzzle (the top lip, between the nostrils) firmly in your hand. Avoid grasping the nostrils themselves, which will interfere with his breathing and cause him to panic. With your other hand, slide the nose clamp over the muzzle and secure it by winding the cord around the ends and clipping the snap to the nearest dee ring on your horse's halter. This should be enough to keep any horse quiet.

Prevention of disease is obviously preferable to waiting until a horse gets sick. Apart from the economic benefits, effective prevention means that you don't lose time nursing and taking care of a sick horse—also losing the use of him during his convalescence.

The best prevention is to feed your horse properly, meaning a balanced diet, along with providing clean and sanitary facilities for him, controlling parasites, and keeping him outdoors as much as possible

with room to exercise. He should also be worked enough to keep physically fit and groomed regularly.

Remember that you alone are responsible for your horse's well-being, so try to anticipate possible difficulties before they occur. Seventy-five percent of all calls to the vet, my own included, are the result of some carelessness on the part of the owner. With more foresight, they could have been avoided.

The cost of a horse call will vary from twelve to twenty-five dollars, depending on how far away from the vet you live and the part of the country you live in. This basic price won't include shots and other medications he prescribes—which also vary widely.

9

talking
tack

The gemmy bridle glittered free
Like to some branch of stars we see
Hung in the golden galaxy
The bridle bells rang merrily
  As he rode down to Camelot
And from his blazon'd baldric slung
A mighty silver bugle hung,
And as he rode, his armour rung,
Beside remote Shalott

      —ALFRED LORD TENNYSON
      "The Lady of Shalott"

Medieval war saddlery, the direct ancestor of modern Western tack, was the most elegant and impressive in the history of horsemanship. And for all its bulk and glitter it was highly functional. The heavily armored knights needed the deep seat, curved pommel, and high cantle to support their ungainly weight and to keep them from being unseated by a lance blow from an opponent. And their long stirrups balanced them during a charge.

The force of the ponderous battle horse, combined with all that heavy armor, all focused on the point of a lance, made a secure seat of the utmost importance. The impact was about equal to that of two speeding cars crashing head on.

224

Medieval warriors used a curb bridle to control their spirited stallions (geldings were sometimes used, but they were a less prestigious mount). The horse responded to an ancient version of the neck rein, the reins being held in one hand, leaving the other free for the sword or lance.

Nosebands, now worn to help keep a horse's mouth closed over the bit, may have had their origins in the muzzles worn by these war-horses off the battlefield to keep them from biting. The horses were trained to fight along with the knights, biting and striking at opponents with their front legs. In fact, many of the elaborate exercises performed by the famous Austrian Lippizans today originated in battle, where they were designed to terrify the foot soldiers.

To control these spirited animals with a single hand, weighted down by armor and with a heavy lance tucked under one arm, took a high degree of horsemanship. Knights have been unfairly depicted in much popular fiction as deadweights in the saddle, moving like robots. In fact, considering their handicaps, they were surprisingly dextrous.

But the Moors who invaded Spain in the eighth century, with their small fast horses, light saddles, and style of riding, had a tactical advantage over the Spanish knights. The invaders rode with short stirrups and were perched lightly on their saddles, often dropping the reins over their horses' necks when they used their bows and arrows.

During the Moors' seven centuries' occupation, much of the Moorish culture was adopted by the Spanish, including their finely carved leatherwork which was widely used on saddles and bridles.

When the Spanish invaded the Americas in the fifteenth century, they rode in these elaborately carved war saddles, with long stirrups, using the traditional neck rein. The few noblemen who could afford it brought along their best-trained horses. The other conquistadores, most of whom were men of modest means seeking their fortunes in the New World, rode common horses of Arabian and Barb ancestry.

THE MODERN WESTERN SADDLE

The war saddle that gave security to the knights has, in modern form, done the same thing for the cowboy. Wranglers need a deep seat and long stirrups to brace themselves against the weight of a dropped steer. Equally important, the seat and wide **swells** are comfortable, allowing the saddle to serve as a rider's chair for days at a stretch.

The rest of the modern Western saddle is equally functional. The **horn,** with the opening at the fork, is designed to hold the lariat. After a steer has been downed, the cowboy wraps the rope around the **pommel** to create tension, against which the horse is trained to pull—

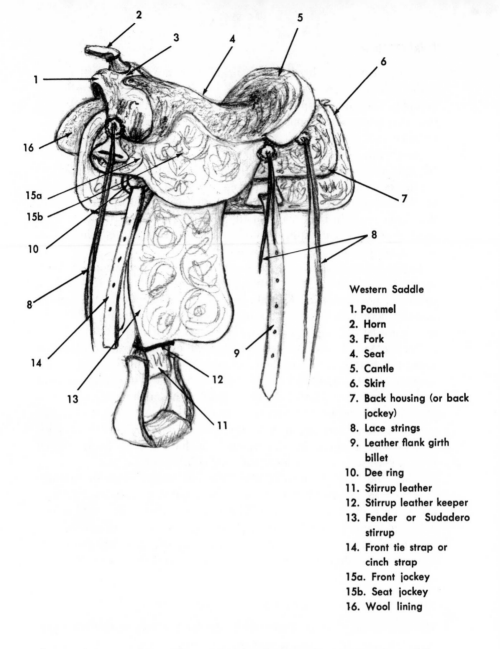

Western Saddle

1. Pommel
2. Horn
3. Fork
4. Seat
5. Cantle
6. Skirt
7. Back housing (or back jockey)
8. Lace strings
9. Leather flank girth billet
10. Dee ring
11. Stirrup leather
12. Stirrup leather keeper
13. Fender or Sudadero stirrup
14. Front tie strap or cinch strap
15a. Front jockey
15b. Seat jockey
16. Wool lining

playing the steer almost like a fish. The **flank girth** prevents the saddle from flipping up in back with the impact of the dropped animal.

Wooden stirrups, carved out of light wood, were traditionally accompanied in the Old West by **tapaderos**, or hoods, which protected a cowboy's feet from brush and thorns and kept them warm and dry. The **fenders** protect a rider's legs from the horse's sweat, which is substantial during a day of working cattle. **Rawhide strings** fastened to the saddle can hold all the gear a cowboy might need on a long drive—slicker, bedroll, saddlebags, food, utensils, and rifle scabbard.

Because the condition of a horse's back is vital on a long ride, a cowboy is careful to protect it. In addition to the lining of the saddle, a thick **Navajo blanket** is customarily used as a saddle pad—an article of trade common in the Old West and still made for this purpose today on reservations.

In parts of the West and Midwest where cattle are still worked from horseback, the cowboy's tack is as functional as ever. Although to eastern eyes, wranglers appear to be sloppy about some aspects of horse care, cowboys are very concerned about how their saddles are made and how they fit the horse—often having them custom-made.

Rodeo riders prefer a more decorative saddle, while a roping contestant might prefer a variation on the stock saddle with narrower pommel and more sloping swells for quicker dismounting. One old bronc-riding saddle found in Nebraska has swells eight inches high and twenty-four inches wide.

The utility stock saddle shouldn't be confused with the overdecorated creations worn in parades. These silver and sequin monstrosities rival medieval battle garb. They often weigh as much as three hundred pounds, not including the breastplate, the jeweled bridle—or the rider. A small Western horse that can still prance along under all those entrapments should be pitied as well as admired.

Reflecting the trend away from work on horseback and toward more pleasure riding, another type of saddle has been created with a flat seat very much like that of an English saddle. Named after its creator, it is known as the Monte Foreman Balanced Ride; and it puts the rider in the center of the horse rather than back on the cantle as traditional Western stock saddles do. This new saddle type have become very popular with Western-style riders in the East; and it is working its way across the country. Without special trim or fancy carving these saddles cost around $500 to $600. Other saddlemakers are coming out with similar designs.

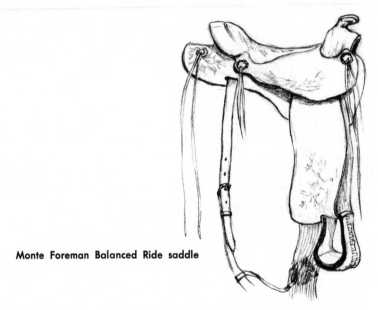

Monte Foreman Balanced Ride saddle

An average stock saddle, which weighs around thirty pounds, starts at $250 undecorated and then averages around $600 to $1,500, depending on the intricate workmanship. Western saddles average in size around fifteen inches for the average adult rider.

The most widely used Western blanket is a protective pad made of two layers of pile. This washable blanket is ideal for everyday and show riding, coming in all colors, even with your initials added. The plain ones begin at twenty dollars. Some riders still prefer the double woolen Navajo, which begins at twenty-four dollars. One of the more recent additions to the Western saddle pad family is a Flo-Form pad, which enables the horse's back to breathe as well as relieving pressure points. For eighty dollars and up, you can purchase one of these blankets, which fits the contour of your horse's back.

Western saddles come complete with all fittings except cinches. These are available in washable mohair and cord, preferable to leather because there is less chance of girth sores. The price depends on whether or not they have buckles. Without a buckle these usually run around seven dollars; with a buckle, around ten dollars.

Mohair cinches

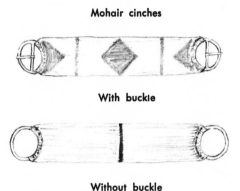

With buckle

Without buckle

THE ENGLISH SADDLE

The precise origin of the English and northern European saddle is hard to pin down to a single source. During the Middle Ages, light saddles with low cantles and narrow to nonexistent pommels were widely used for sport and pleasure riding. Wealthy knights owned three horses and three saddles: one for battle, one for hunting, and one for everyday use. Even the knight who could afford only one horse owned a change of tack.

In the jousting arena, knights would choose their saddles along with their weapons. The cantles in these sporting events were always low, the object being to unseat rather than kill. Consequently a well-placed lance blow would send an opponent sailing over his horse's croup.

The height of the pommel depended on the weapons used and the nerve of the knight. It was less secure, and therefore more sporting, to ride with a low pommel. But it provided more room to maneuver one's sword.

In the fifteenth century, the Hungarian cavalry, which was unarmored and used bows and arrows, rode with a light, elegantly crafted saddle that had a pommel but no cantle. The saddle was flat with a slight depression for the rider's seat. During the same period, saddles with lower pommels and cantles were used for hunting throughout Europe and the British Isles.

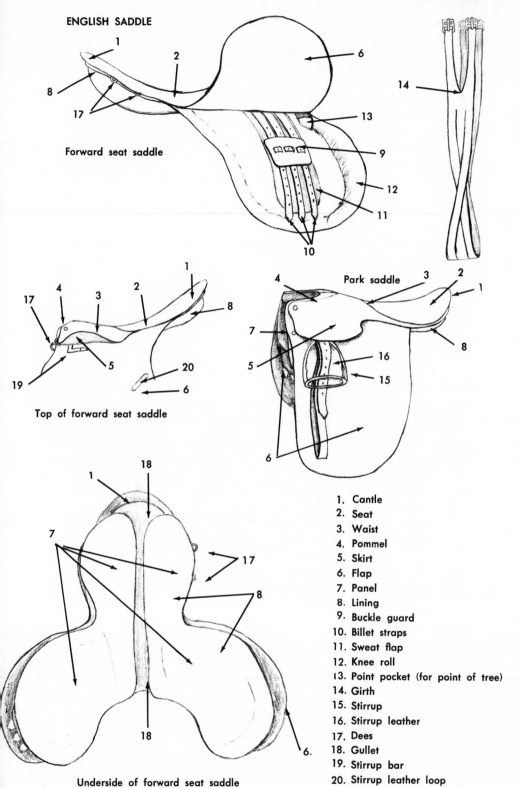

Chafless fitted girth

ENGLISH SADDLE

Forward seat saddle

Top of forward seat saddle

Park saddle

Underside of forward seat saddle

1. Cantle
2. Seat
3. Waist
4. Pommel
5. Skirt
6. Flap
7. Panel
8. Lining
9. Buckle guard
10. Billet straps
11. Sweat flap
12. Knee roll
13. Point pocket (for point of tree)
14. Girth
15. Stirrup
16. Stirrup leather
17. Dees
18. Gullet
19. Stirrup bar
20. Stirrup leather loop

The modern English and European saddles with low pommels are probably a fairly recent development—within the past two hundred years—as a piece of sports equipment that put maximum demands on the skills of the rider.

Today there are three major types of English saddle: the forward seat or jumping saddle, with knee rolls; the park saddle for saddle-seat riding, with the center of the seat placed close to the cantle; and the all-purpose model used for the balance seat—employed in dressage and cross-country riding. Some of these saddles also have a thigh roll, which anchors the rider's legs between the knee and thigh roll, helping him to maintain his position. There are many interpretations of these basic types on the market made all over Europe, Britain, Ireland, India, South America, and, in the last few years, Japan. Certain makes fit some riders and horses of different breeds and conformations better than others.

It's important to know how you are going to use the saddle you are buying. If you are buying a saddle for jumping, are you going to be jumping in the show-ring or for pleasure or eventing? Your answer will decide the type of saddle you buy.

The **forward seat saddle** has the deepest part of the seat in the center, just behind the pommel, with suede knee rolls to keep the knees in place during jumping. Some riders prefer these suede rolls, which lock with the suede patches on riding breeches for more support. But suede isn't at all practical in wet weather; if you plan to do a lot of cross-country riding, I don't advise using it. The current trend is toward a lightweight saddle with a minimum of leather between horse and rider to allow closer contact and a better feel of your horse.

For show-jumping, a rider would prefer a very lightweight saddle. For quality leather, these range in price from $500 to $900.

The **park saddle** is customary for saddle-seat riders. This is an ordinary English saddle, minus knee rolls, cut straight from the pommel down. There is a special cutback saddle of park type, used mostly for showing, in which the pommel is cut back in front to allow for the horse's high neck carriage. In both of these, the center of the seat is closer to the cantle, allowing the rider to interfere as little as possible with the action of his horse. When a rider posts in a park saddle, he stays behind the motion of the horse.

These saddles are also made of very thin leather, bringing the rider's legs extremely close to the horse. Park saddles are great for the show-ring but give the rider very little support on the trail. They cost between $300 and $360.

All-purpose saddles are designed for the rider who wishes to do a combination of dressage, show, or cross-country jumping. Because it's a heavier saddle, it is particularly good for cross-country work. One difference between the all-purpose forward seat and show-jumping saddles is the lack of a thigh roll on the all-purpose. Also, the smooth flap allows the rider to use a long leg in a dressage balance seat, while he is also able to shorten the stirrups and use the knee rolls for cross-country riding.

All-purpose saddles can be bought from any leading saddle manufacturer and range in price from $400 to $600.

If you are buying your first saddle and don't plan to start off immediately in big competition, try to buy a secondhand saddle of good make rather than a new inferior one. Fine secondhand German, Italian, and French saddles are often advertised in saddle shops and circulars; you might be able to pick up an especially expensive model for half its original price. Often the person selling a good saddle is only letting it go to buy another kind; and the tack is consequently well cared for. Before buying, however, always make sure that the stitching is sound and that the tree isn't broken.

The quality and workmanship in any saddle will vary according to price. Craftsmanship and workmanship on a fine saddle will cost more; but good leather, properly cared for, will last a lot longer. While it takes some time to break in a new saddle, once the leather is supple, it will fit you like your favorite chair.

Leather is tanned through two different processes, each of which gives it a particular color. **Bark curing** (or tanning), which leaves leather with a brownish color, takes cleaning and oiling well, and absorbs the grease better than the **chrome** method of curing, which is characterized by a greenish color. Different parts of the hide are used for saddles, the most preferred taken from the hindquarter, which has little stretch and is most durable.

Saddlemakers grade leather according to the country it comes from and the curing methods employed there. Of the five grades of leather, the poorest quality is Indian leather, which is tanned in clay vats, comes out very dry, and is unable to absorb additional grease, making it prone to cracking and further drying. Fourth-grade Japanese leather has poor strength, and the fibers separate, tear, and stretch easily. South American and Southern European leather is considered third grade because it is hard, often has grub holes in it, and needs a lot of work to make it pliable. The best quality leather, both first and second grade, comes from England, Germany, and the United States, where tanning processes create an unblemished soft and pliable product. Unfortunately, the consumer has no way of knowing what kind of leather he is getting. No government-regulated mandatory grading exists.

An important consideration in buying a new saddle is the **tallow,** a process in which the leather is greased with mutton lard to keep it from drying out or cracking and to make it easier to work with. Tallow is the whitish substance often seen on new saddles, and it is an essential part of the leather-treating process.

Some saddles are constructed from as many as five types of skins from three different animals. One manufacturer uses well-stretched pigskin in the seat and thick cowhide for the skirts, with a pliable horsehide panel on the underside. Horsehide is used because it wears longer and doesn't crack from the horse's sweat.

Aside from the quality of its leather, the frame or the **tree** of the saddle is its second most important part and has the most to do with the price you pay. The cheapest frame is laminated plywood without any steel reinforcement, the type used on many Argentinian saddles and the reason they open up with wear (a condition called treespread). Some Argentine saddle trees are reinforced with fragile barrel-hoop wire.

One of the best types of wooden tree is made of hickory and birch and reinforced with flexible spring steel. But the most desirable and comfortable (and very expensive) saddles have leather trees. Made by the Smith-Worthington Company, most experts believe these are the best in the country.

Nowadays some trees are fabricated from fiber glass. They're durable, but I find them to be very hard on a rider's seat; and the screws used in parts of the saddle can lose their thread if they wrench out, and they can't be rescrewed.

Cheap saddles have little or no **underpadding.** The quality of materials used and the amount and type of padding improves with the quality (and, naturally, the higher price) of the saddle.

Good saddles have Irish linen **webbing** with several layers of canvas and often a foam-rubber pad under the seat, so the rider is spared the hard frame of the saddle.

Used Tack: How to Tell What Shape It's In

It's impossible to return the tallow to dried-out tack. The drying out process begins with cracking, and you should check for this by bending back the skirts, billets, and stirrup straps. Billets are very expensive to replace, and leather that is cracked on this part of the saddle isn't worth restoring to its original condition.

Good saddles should have a variety of lengths of **stitching.** Areas that take strain are usually sewn with a long stitch that takes fewer holes, while spots that bear less strain have more stitches. Any ornamentation on a saddle should be closely stitched. The thickness of leather is no indication of its quality. Thin leather is frequently superior. The tallow and the part of the animal from which the piece is cut are the most important factors.

Fitting the English Saddle

The way a saddle, Western or English, fits your horse is more important than the way it fits you. A saddle that doesn't fit a horse properly will cause him pain and eventually lead to bruises and saddle sores or girth galls. It often takes a long time for these to heal, and they can leave marks and permanent tender areas.

Saddles should fit your horse's back so that weight is evenly distributed along the fleshy muscles on the back and side; where it lies across the withers and spine, make sure that it is free of pressure. When you stand up with your full weight on the stirrups there, should be room to insert two fingers between the pommel of the saddle and the withers.

On a high-withered horse, you should be able to fit three fingers between the withers and the underside of the saddle, making sure first that the horse's back and the saddle are absolutely clean.

Always try the saddle on the horse you intend to buy it for. Just because a saddle feels good to you doesn't mean it will fit your horse. A reputable tack shop should let you take it home and try it out. If not, don't buy it. Remember that you're investing anywhere from $150 (for a second-hand saddle or an inexpensive Argentine one) to $900 for a deluxe show-jumping saddle made of bridle leather, and you'll be throwing away your money if it doesn't fit.

A saddle that is too narrow on your horse won't settle down properly, and it will slip around. You'll never feel secure or comfortable in it. If it's too wide, the tree will press down on the tender spots on his back. A long-backed horse would be better off with a long saddle, because the weight is distributed over a larger area. Some trainers feel that, in hunting, eventing, or endurance riding, where the horse is making quick changes, a **breastplate** should be used to keep the saddle from slipping around.

Make sure the seat is in the center of the saddle if it's a forward seat. If it's too far to the rear, it will throw you back and you'll feel that you are traveling behind the motion of your horse. A comfortable saddle should enable you to keep your seat in balance at all gaits.

Some saddles are designed especially for wide-backed horses, like Morgans, or for short, narrower-backed horses, like Arabs. Others, like Argentinian saddles, are more suited to narrow-backed horses but are generally too narrow for hunters.

English saddles vary from sixteen inches for a child's saddle to nineteen inches for a large man. They should be measured straight across the top from the nailhead at the side of the pommel to the center of the cantle. Different makes run slightly different in size—one's seventeen-inch might be equal to another's seventeen-and-one-half-inch —another reason for trying out a saddle.

Fittings

Most new English saddles are sold without fittings, meaning without stirrups, stirrup pads, stirrup leathers, and girths.

Stirrups are available in never-rust stainless steel and in nickel. I prefer stainless steel because it is the hardest and most rust-resistant.

Stirrups—fit and types

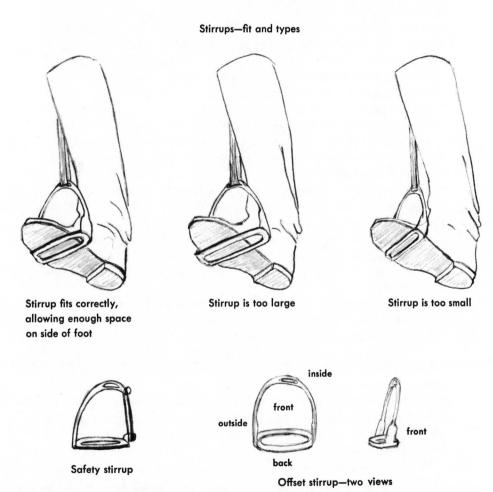

Stirrup fits correctly, allowing enough space on side of foot

Stirrup is too large

Stirrup is too small

Safety stirrup

inside

front

outside

back

front

Offset stirrup—two views

When trying a stirrup on for size, make sure it is large enough so that the widest part of your foot can fit in with an inch to spare on each side. Children's stirrups should not be so large that their feet will slide all over or through it. If the stirrup is too small, on the other hand, a foot could become wedged in it.

Safety stirrups with a thick elastic on the outside are an alternative. The idea is that if you fall, the elastic will come undone and the foot will easily come free of the stirrup. I've found, however, that the elastic is a nuisance, tending to break in nonemergency situations. Even so, safety stirrups should always be used on bareback pads, where they are hooked to metal dees, rather than the usual safety bars. There are also offset stirrups used by some hunter seat equitation riders. These are tilted to help the heels stay down. However, they can't replace a relaxed ankle.

Stirrups vary in price from ten to fifty dollars or more, depending on size and the quality of metal. The rage in English stirrups is a Fillis, an expensive, heavy model with a sharp, thin edge that holds the foot well. These are particularly nice because they stay down and don't slide around. But they start at twenty dollars.

Stirrup pads are handy for cross-country riding or any conditions where your soles might get slippery. Also, in cold weather they act as a separation between the cold metal and your boot. Foot warmers that fit over the stirrup are also available for around eighteen dollars, lined with Equi-Fleece.

Stirrup leathers can be purchased in short sizes and narrow widths of less than an inch for a child or up to sixty inches long and one and three-eighths inches wide for an adult. Extension leathers are available for a large horse you have trouble mounting. Leathers are attached to the saddle on metal strips, with safety bars at the end. These bars should always be left down so the stirrup can slide off easily in case of accident.

Girths are made of several different materials. The simplest leather girths are folded with the open side toward the rear of the horse. Others are shaped and cut away at the horse's elbow to prevent girth sores. These are sometimes called "chafeless girths." You can also get an Equi-Fleece tube to slide over a regular leather girth as a protective device.

Leather girths start at around fifteen dollars. There is a really excellent chafeless, leather contour girth with sturdy elastic ends that gives a good fit to hunters, jumpers, and horses large around the barrel, which costs around thirty to forty dollars.

Webbed girths are usually used on park-type horses, and they are made of canvas. I've never liked them after seeing one split down the middle when a horse was jumping. These are really only suitable for show. In any other kind of riding, an additional narrow girth should be worn over them.

Mohair and cord girths are my favorites, because they allow air to circulate and are least likely to give saddle sores. These also are relatively inexpensive and can be washed. If possible, buy two girths, a leather and a mohair, using the latter for muddy and very hot weather.

Nylon is all right, although I've found that it tends to stretch a little and curl, so that one part ends up wider than the other. It is washable, however, and prevents chafing.

Some girths work better with different horses. With very thin-skinned Thoroughbreds, I'd use a fitted, tapered leather girth. Remember, keeping a horse physically fit by daily exercise can be a great prevention against girth and saddle sores. Also, keep the girth clean.

SADDLE PADS

Saddle pads are essential, no matter what type of saddle you use—both for the sake of your horse's back and the long life of the saddle, which can be damaged by sweat. In the show-ring some English riders prefer not to use a saddle pad because it doesn't look as neat; but their saddles are always cleaned thoroughly immediately after showing and the horse is carefully groomed and rubbed down. Even in shows, hunters and jumpers should have pads. When a horse jumps, his spine curves and it may make contact with the saddle.

When you put the saddle pad on, you should be able to fit a few fingers between the withers and the pad to make sure it isn't pressing down on the horse's back. If the pad becomes wrinkled or bunched up while you are riding, you should immediately dismount and fix it. If you don't, you are inviting severe saddle sores.

For everyday use, the best buy is Equi-Fleece, which looks like sheepskin from a distance but can be thrown in the washing machine. It's also moth- and mildew-proof. Real sheepskin is a nuisance because it has to be powdered, dried, and brushed out before reusing.

There are several other types of pads: hand-washable felt; machine-washable quilted flannel; and an all-wool, hand-washable variety. Horses with extremely sensitive backs should have a double-faced, Equi-Fleece pad.

Saddle pads come in different styles and colors to fit every type of horse and saddle. When a single Equi-Fleece pad doesn't fit exactly, cut it to shape with a scissors. At least an inch of saddle pad should show, so that it doesn't bunch underneath and allow the saddle to touch your horse. All English pads have "keepers" on them that slip over the billet straps for this purpose. Sometimes the pad slips around, even when these keepers are on. If so, you can now buy a new type of pad, which is cut to fit four kinds of English saddle and has a side pocket into which the saddle panel can be slipped. It's advertised as a pad that will always stay in place.

A clean **saddle pad** is of equal importance. Endurance riders, competitive riders, and polo players like a genuine Navajo, because it is washable, easy to keep clean, and doesn't become hard and crusty. Foam rubber is good for horses with sensitive backs, but it must be kept from direct contact with the back or it will cause a heat buildup that could lead to saddle sores. Place foam rubber between the saddle and the pad to avoid this.

Sheepskin pads, Equi-Fleece, and any other synthetic pad fabrics must be kept clean to do the right job. When dirty, they become matted and stiff. After washing, these pads must be brushed out before each use. It's helpful to get several pads, so you have a clean one in the barn at all times and can rotate them for washing.

BITS AND BRIDLES

In the Middle Ages, when blacksmiths were concerned more with appearances than humaneness, horses were fitted out with a variety of torturous but decorative mouthpieces. Forged out of gold and ingeniously carved in the shape of monsters, dragons, and flowers, the beauty of the bits masked the terrible toll they took on a horse's mouth. The characteristics of these harsh bits can still be seen in some modern Western bridles.

A basic bridle is made up of a bit, reins, and headstall. The latter is comprised of two cheek straps, a crownpiece (sometimes called a headpiece), throatlatch, headband, and cavesson (on an English bridle) or noseband (on a Western bridle). The crownpiece and throatlatch (one piece on an English bridle) fasten to the cheek straps, which are attached to the bit. This fits over the horse's head behind his ears, held in place by the headband in front and the throatlatch, fastened loosely under the horse's throat.

The cavesson, one piece with a strap going up over the horse's head and a piece that goes around the nose, slips through the sides of the headband and is worn under the above pieces.

The reins attach to the bit and provide the rider with a direct means of communicating with the horse's mouth.

Bridles vary greatly, as do bits, depending on what the rider is using the horse for and the education of both horse and rider.

Anatomical bar (within boxed area)

Basically, a bit acts either on the tongue, the cheeks, or a part of the mouth, called the *bar,* between the incisors and molars, or on a combination of these. The bar is a barren spot on the jawbone, thinly covered with flesh and very sensitive. Continuous pulling on this area of a horse's mouth is what causes it to become numb, or a "hard mouth." A severe or ill-fitting bit will put undesirable pressure on the palate or other parts of the mouth.

English Bits

Snaffle

The mildest type of bit is a **jointed** (or **broken**) **snaffle.** It acts on the cheeks and bars, with a slight pinching action on the tongue. For a young horse with a sensitive mouth or for an inexperienced rider who hasn't developed a light touch with his hands, a broken snaffle is the best choice. Combined with a dropped noseband (a corrective bridle accessory), a snaffle can control almost any horse. In addition to keeping a horse in check, it has a lifting action on the head.

Snaffles today come in all shapes and sizes. Some apply more emphasis on the cheeks, others on the bars and tongue. The thicker the mouthpiece, the milder the snaffle. A smooth mouthpiece is milder than a twisted one. Some very mild snaffles have a straight bar of soft rubber, hard rubber, or metal. The rubber ones are used primarily on horses with very sensitive mouths or on those recovering from a mouth injury. Copper bits are used because they encourage a horse to chew the bit and help to create and maintain a soft mouth.

The most severe snaffle is a twisted wire mouthpiece. This type of bit should be used only in the hands of an experienced rider. Full cheeks and half cheeks prevent the rings of the bit from sliding through a horse's mouth, as well as keeping the rings from rubbing and applying pressure to the sides of the cheeks.

Egg butts and **dees,** types of snaffle bits, are terms denoting the shape of the ring. A dee bit is quite frequently used on racehorses. It's important to fit a snaffle so that it isn't too wide for the mouth. Other-

English bridles with bits (All Pelhams and curb bits are used with curb chains and lip straps and kimberwicks are used with curb chains alone)

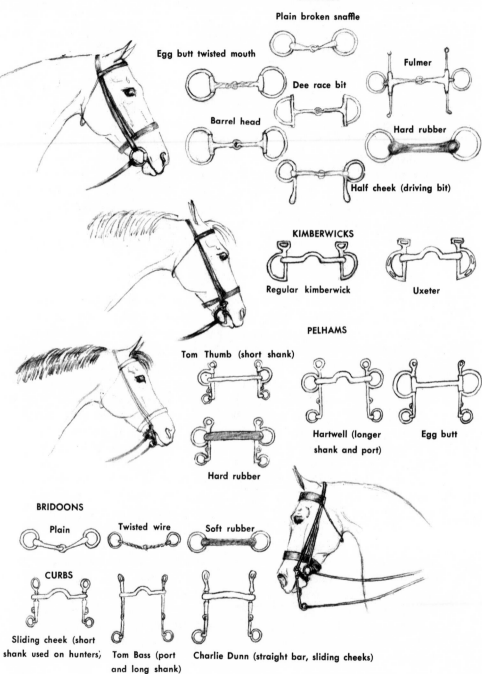

SNAFFLES

Plain broken snaffle

Egg butt twisted mouth

Fulmer

Dee race bit

Barrel head

Hard rubber

Half cheek (driving bit)

KIMBERWICKS

Regular kimberwick

Uxeter

PELHAMS

Tom Thumb (short shank)

Hartwell (longer shank and port)

Egg butt

Hard rubber

BRIDOONS

Plain

Twisted wire

Soft rubber

CURBS

Sliding cheek (short shank used on hunters)

Tom Bass (port and long shank)

Charlie Dunn (straight bar, sliding cheeks)

wise the joint will hit the roof of the mouth. If too narrow, it will pinch the cheeks and cause sores.

We now come to the **bridoon,** which is a snaffle used in combination with a curb bit. This is known as a **full bridle, double bridle,** or as a **Weymouth.** Of the number of different English bridles designed to go with different bits, it is the most complex.

Curb Bits

The **curb** can be most severe of bits if improperly used. In experienced hands, however, the combination with a bridoon will enable a rider to get the most advanced kind of performance from a horse. In English riding, by the way, the curb is never used alone.

The mouthpiece of the bar (and **port,** if there is one) of the curb acts on the anatomical bars and the tongue. As with the snaffle, the degree of severity depends on the curb's shape. The wider and more shallow the mouthpiece, the milder it will be. The narrower and steeper the port, the harsher it will be.

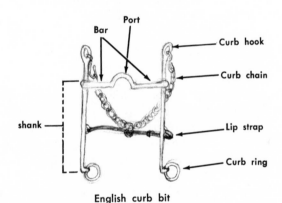

English curb bit

Curbs draw in the horse's chin and make him flex at the poll. The shank, when used with a curb chain, acts like a fulcrum, putting pressure on the bars and tongue. The longer the shank, the more pressure it puts on a horse's mouth.

Remember that a thick curb chain, which is always used with a double bit, shouldn't be so tight that it cuts into the horse's chin. It should fit comfortably in the curb groove, located under the chin. When too taut, the chain can cause curb galls. For horses with sensitive skin you can get a curb-chain guard made of leather or rubber.

In a full bridle, the bridoon goes on the top and the curb goes on the bottom. Each bridle has its own crownpiece, and the throatlatch is attached to the curb. A lip strap is usually added to keep the curb chain and bit in place.

Pelham Bits

The **Pelham** is sort of a cross between a snaffle and a curb. It tries to act a little like both and ends up less effective than either. Yet some horses will go better in a Pelham than a snaffle, so this type of bit has become a necessary evil. Pelhams come with long or short shanks, with mouthpieces of varying thicknesses and curves. Some horses that do well in the schooling ring on a snaffle with dropped noseband are ridden in Pelhams on the trail or hunted and jumped in them because this bit gives greater control. However, the double reins used on a Pelham tend to be difficult for children to handle. An inexperienced rider or child may, for this reason, want to use a converter—a leather loop between the snaffle and curb rings, allowing control by a single rein. Although it does simplify control, the converter, by this loss of versatility downgrades the bit even more.

Kimberwick Bits

Kimberwicks are being used more and more frequently, which is bad. The exaggerated port on the mouthpiece (varying in severity) combined with the curb chain tends to make a horse in inexperienced hands overflex or pull, drawing his chin in too far. Nor does it help a horse's mouth. While some horses do well in Kimberwicks, usually they'll do just as well in a snaffle after a little work. But, like the Pelham, the Kimberwick bit does give greater control, especially for riding in the open.

Fitting the Bit

When you buy your first bit, either English or Western, ask your riding instructor to help you select it. A horse should be ridden in the lightest bit he will take. And his mouth can be ruined by a mouthpiece that is too harsh or doesn't fit properly.

When a snaffle bit is in place in your horse's mouth, it should cause a single wrinkle at the corners of the mouth. If too narrow, the rings will pinch the corners and cause sores; if too wide, the joint will hit the roof. Neither should it hang too low or your horse will fiddle with it. A Pelham, curb, or Kimberwick should not wrinkle the corners of the mouth.

If your horse is dissatisfied with the bit, he'll throw his head around and generally act uncomfortable, never letting you sit quietly on him. He may also salivate excessively, tossing his head and pulling at the bit as if trying to get more rein. If you feel your horse needs a new bit, be sure to consult a professional rather than experiment. There could be other factors involved—a green mouth, for instance, or an inexperienced rider using too long or too short a rein. You may also find that the bit is aggravating an old mouth injury or that your horse has a wolf tooth.

Before buying a new bit, I advise my pupils to try a few of mine out to see whether the horse goes well in it. Bits are expensive—as much as twenty dollars or more—and it's foolish to buy one without knowing whether it will be suitable. To measure a bit so that it is the correct size for your horse's mouth, refer to the previous illustration under "Curb Bits," though this applies to any type of bit. Measure the bar from the inside of the shank or ring (you will get a figure somewhere between four and a half and five and a half inches).

English Bridle

A complete English bridle without bit varies in price according to quality and workmanship. An average schooling bridle that will last reasonably well costs around thirty to forty dollars. Fine, rounded bridles that accent the elegant look of a nice head go for about eighty-five dollars, depending on the leather quality.

English bridles come in a variety of sizes: pony size, cob size for large ponies or small horses, regular horse size, and oversized models for hunter types with large heads. All come in different widths. For a big horse, a wider headstall will look better, while a fine-boned horse should have a thin one. Widths of leather range from three-eighths of an inch to an inch, depending on whether the bridle is for a hunter or a saddle horse.

Saddle horses are shown with decorative, colored headbands and cavessons. The hunter is always shown in a plain leather headband and cavesson.

English Reins

A snaffle bit calls for a single rein, buckled at the center rather than sewn. This is to allow the rein to be slipped through the rings of a run-

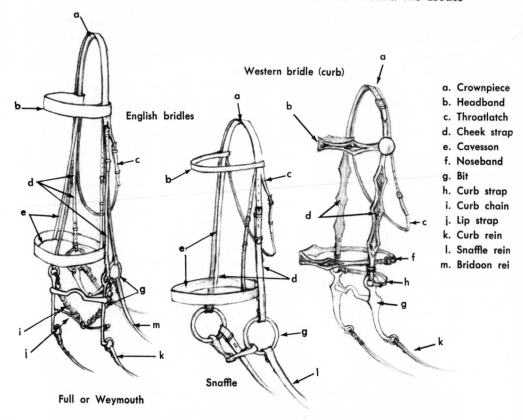

English bridles

Western bridle (curb)

a. Crownpiece
b. Headband
c. Throatlatch
d. Cheek strap
e. Cavesson
f. Noseband
g. Bit
h. Curb strap
i. Curb chain
j. Lip strap
k. Curb rein
l. Snaffle rein
m. Bridoon rei

Full or Weymouth

Snaffle

ning martingale. Many people prefer to buy plaited, or braided, reins because they give a better grip. For a woman's hand, a narrow three-quarter-inch rein is a good size. For a child, a slightly smaller one is better. Thick reins are difficult for young riders to hold properly.

In a full bridle and on a Pelham, two reins are used: a snaffle (or bridoon) and a curb. A narrow rein, sewn at the center, is buckled to the curb. The curb rein is usually an eighth of an inch thinner than the snaffle (or bridoon) rein, which attaches either to the snaffle or bridoon bit and buckles in the center. The width of the snaffle or bridoon rein varies, depending on the rider and the situation.

Often, on a hunter or jumper, when a Pelham or full bridle is used a braided or laced rein is employed on the snaffle bit for easier handling.

While most bridle reins buckle on, it is more elegant looking and much stronger if the cheek pieces and the reins are sewn on. In certain show classes, like Corinthian Hunter, it is required in the appointments that cheekpieces and reins be sewn onto the bit.

If you want a better grip on a jumper's reins, purchase those in cotton webbing or with rubber handgrips. However, these are not permitted in hunter classes.

Western Bits

Grazing Bit

There are as many fads in Western as there are in English bits. I don't think much of the grazing bit, which has a broken mouthpiece with shanks that bend back when a horse puts his head down to graze. It encourages a bad habit.

Roping Bit

Roping bits have two shanks that curve down and meet together with a ring below the chin. This keeps the rope from getting caught in the shanks when working cattle. Most cowboys today use steel bits with a medium port and a medium-long shank.

Spade Bit

The spade bit is a severe device that looks as harsh as it must feel in a horse's mouth when in the hands of an inexperienced rider. Used properly, a horse can be trained not to fight it, but in the hands of a beginner it could be disastrous. Derived from the Spanish bit, this type is very popular in California.

Hackamore Bit

The hackamore bit with a straight mouthpiece is sometimes used on working cow horses and often on contest-roping horses; with sudden stops, the mouth doesn't receive the full brunt of the rider's pressure on the reins. Like English bits, the longer and straighter the shank, combined with the curb chain, the more severe the bit. And the more narrow and steep the port, the harsher it is.

Western Bridle

The **bosal** (pronounced boh-zahl') is used as a training device on most Western horses. It is a braided rawhide band that attaches to a head-stall and goes around the nose. The reins are tied to the bosal with a special knot called a *fiador*. This knot determines the amount of pres-

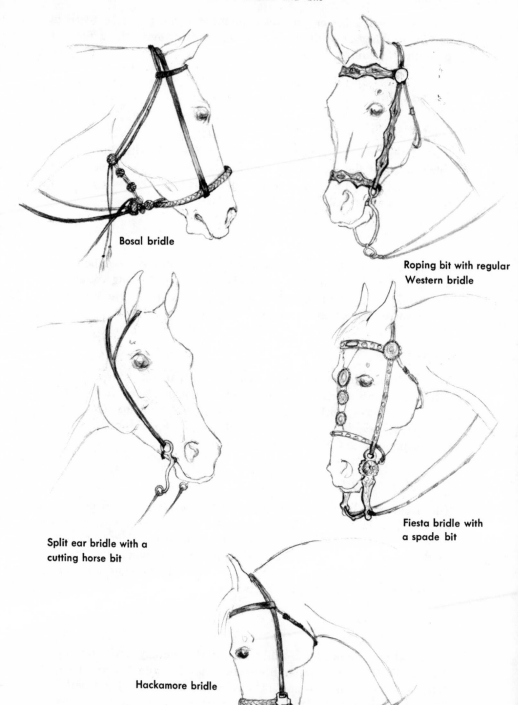

Bosal bridle

Roping bit with regular
Western bridle

Split ear bridle with a
cutting horse bit

Fiesta bridle with
a spade bit

Hackamore bridle

246

sure a horse receives on the rear of the jaw and behind the poll. A lot of people prefer the bosal to a hackamore because it doesn't squeeze the nose. A horse can be trained to neck-rein nicely with a bosal. When a young horse is being taught to stop with this device, the rider doesn't pull but uses an alternating action with each rein. Pulling on the nose will have the same undesirable effect as pulling on the mouth.

The **hackamore** puts a squeezing action on the nose. It has a piece that goes across the nose, along with a curb strap and shanks. Some cutting horses have to be schooled in tight hackamores to train them not to bite the calves they're cutting. These horses get so involved in their work that they get angry at errant cattle and give them a nip, behavior that counts against the horse in competition.

The simplest kind of Western bridle is the **split-eared** type—a simple headstall with no throatlatch. Most Western horses are shown or worked in the split-ear bridle because it is more workmanlike and neat in appearance. It is easy to put on, and in an emergency if a ground-tied horse has become frightened and is stepping on the reins, the bridle would slip off easily instead of breaking.

Some riders use a bridle that is similar to the English one, that is, it includes a noseband and a throatlatch. These bridles generally are elaborate, with carving and studs decorating the wide leather pieces.

Western Reins

The Western rider has both narrow and wide reins to choose from to suit the "feel" in his hand. Reins are made of leather, rope (as with the bosal), and horsehair (for decorative purposes).

Western reins usually are long and split in the middle, except the reins on a roping bridle. These are a short, continuous loop to accommodate the rider who is leaning forward over his horse's neck and who may drop his reins while roping and wish to recover them quickly.

CORRECTIVE SADDLE AND BRIDLE ACCESSORIES

Dropped Noseband

This comes down over the nose and buckles behind the chin over a snaffle bit on an English bridle. It keeps the horse's mouth closed over the bit. The noseband also prevents a horse from sliding his jaw sideways and getting his tongue over the bit. It's important to keep the front strap above the nostrils so that it doesn't interfere with breathing. It is an extremely effective device and excellent for schooling young or green horses. Dropped nosebands aren't allowed in hunter or equitation

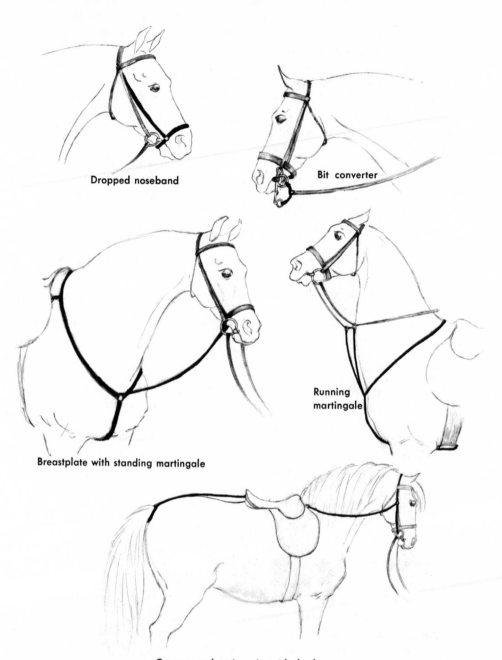

Dropped noseband

Bit converter

Breastplate with standing martingale

Running martingale

Crupper and antigrazing sidecheck

classes, but they are accepted in dressage competition and eventing. When used for eventing (in the cross-country and stadium-jumping phases) a figure-eight noseband that won't interfere with the horse's breathing is required.

Breastplates

These are used on horses with very heavy or undefined withers to keep the saddle from sliding back. Hooked to dees on the front of the saddle, they are often used to help keep saddles in place in strenuous cross-country work—like hunting and horse trials. Western horses with heavy or undefined withers also use a breastplate for doing quick turns or maneuvers, as in barrel racing or cutting.

Two types of breastplate are used for English riding: the hunting type, which is less cumbersome and doesn't interfere with the horse's shoulder movement (and, when adjusted correctly, doesn't cause friction or irritation to the skin), and the breast collar, which is used by many riders in eventing. The latter type of breastplate has no straps running between the horse's legs, and the piece that encircles the chest can be fitted with Equi-Fleece tubing to prevent chafing.

Martingales and Tie-downs

These aid in keeping a horse's head down. These artificial aids should be adjusted to allow the horse the natural freedom of his head, and they help to keep the horse on the bit. The **standing martingale** loop is slipped on to the back of the cavesson. Any horse with a ewe-neck will probably need one. Its Western equivalent is a **tie-down**, which attaches to the noseband of the Western bridle. A tie-down is particularly effective in keeping a horse's nose down when he stops quickly. The advantage of the standing martingale is that it acts directly on the horse's nose rather than putting pressure on his mouth to keep his head down. Horses are not permitted in certain show classes with them.

The **running martingale** has two rings instead of the single piece of leather used in the standing martingale. The snaffle reins are unbuckled, slipped through the rings, and buckled again. Because it is connected directly with the horse's mouth, this type of martingale should only be used by experienced riders. It's best to get expert advice before using it. They are sometimes used to train park horses to set their heads properly. And they are used in open jumping when necessary, where any interference with head and neck movement is undesirable. Again, rules don't permit these in certain classes. Either martingales or tie-downs can be used with breastplates, in which case they may be purchased as a combination.

If you're showing, be aware that martingales are not permitted at all in some classes (horsemanship on the flat, for instance, and pleasure classes like road hack). In hunter classes, standing martingales only are allowed, but in jumping classes, where Federation Equestrian Internationale (FEI) rules are in effect, only running martingales are permitted. The same is true in eventing in both the stadium and cross-country phases.

Cruppers (for ponies only)

These hook to a dee on the cantle of the saddle and loop under the pony's tail to keep the saddle from sliding forward. Cruppers are normally used on a narrow-shouldered pony, or on those whose lack of form in the shoulder, withers, or barrel has to be compensated for.

Antigrazing Sidecheck

Usually used on hungry ponies who like to stop unexpectedly and graze, it attaches to the bit and prevents the pony from suddenly lowering his head. They cost from sixteen to twenty dollars new, but I've had success using a checkrein from an old driving harness, attached to a regular bit and set loosely. The sidecheck comes halfway up the cheeks and back to hook to the dees on the saddle. This allows normal head carriage but prevents the pony's head from dropping below his chest.

Other Artificial Aids

Crops

Among English riders a crop is also referred to as a "stick," "bat," or "whip." Western equivalents are the "quirt" (a piece of braided leather with more flexibility than an English crop, which is carried on the saddle when not in use) and the "romal," a special type of quirt that attaches to roping reins (a requirement in some Western classes).

There are different types of English crops to accompany different riding styles. Saddle-seat riders, for instance, carry a long whip. Likewise, the hunt crop has a special function, discussed more fully in Chapter 11.

English riders should always carry a crop. I don't see how a horse can be schooled without one. Even the most hot-blooded mount will have lazy moments; and if a horse is not immediately responsive to normal aids, he must be punished with a firm smack behind the saddle. (A crop is never used on the horse's neck or around his head.) Also, for hot horses, a short, light, racing bat about sixteen inches long is often used on hunters. They are inconspicuous, but the sound and the accompanying slap are difficult for a temperamental horse to ignore.

While it is an invaluable part of any rider's equipment, the crop must never be used as a substitute for correct seat and leg aids. Nor should it be expected to make up for inadequate training. Remember always to use your crop with discretion. If your horse is frightened of an obstacle, for instance, give him time to look it over before employing this aid.

Everyday English riding crops should be easy to carry and should feel comfortable in your hand. An experienced rider can handle a crop with either hand, which of course takes practice. Should a horse shy to the left or acquire some other habit that needs correction on that side, an alert rider will be prepared for it.

Dressage whips, though not allowed in the ring during tests, are extremely helpful in schooling or warming up a horse. I have also found them useful in schooling hunters and pleasure horses to get them to move from behind. Dressage whips run from forty to fifty-four inches in length. They allow the rider to keep a rein in each hand, while tapping the horse behind the leg with a flick of the wrist if the horse is being lazy. Getting a balanced whip is important. Too much weight at the top will make the whip unwieldy. A good whip should be springy to be effective.

Driving whips, which run $7.50 and up, are about five and a half feet long with a lash four to eight inches or longer. The whip is held toward the top of the stock near the ferrule. The whip is not used on the horse's back or the hindquarters, but is used behind the backpad and on the sides, approximately where a rider's leg would fall. Driving whips are safety devices, not offensive weapons, and they should be carried and used effectively.

Nor is a whip just a decorative accessory. A trained driver uses it for giving signals. Slapping the horse with the reins and yelling "Yo!" is acceptable only in Hollywood westerns. Off the set, it's a good way to get a kick in the buckboard.

Care of whips. Whips with short lashes can be hung on broom-type wall brackets, handle up and lash down. Never stand lunge (see Chapter 10) or driving whips in a corner; they'll get bent out of shape. Long-lashed whips are best stored flat or in a whip bracket that has a spool for the lash. (It's possible to use a tuna or cat food can as a spool, letting the lash hang down around the perimeter.)

Spurs

Spurs are an advanced piece of equipment, comparable to a full bridle, and don't belong on the feet of a beginner or novice rider. Used improperly, spurs can degenerate into a substitute for the training of either horse or rider and will numb a mount to correct leg aids. One beginning student showed up for a lesson on his young Morgan filly sporting Western spurs and a long, saddle-seat whip! Used with care, however, spurs are helpful for keeping a horse up on the bit and, for some, are essential for jumping.

Most English spurs have blunt ends, and some have very tiny rowels. The most sensible are dressage and offside schooling spurs, on which the projection is slightly to the inside of the rider's heel rather than at the center.

Western spurs have larger rowels than the English type and are usually made of aluminum.

TACKING UP

Preparation

Whether Western or English, the saddle is usually put on first. It allows the horse to get used to the weight and to depuff. (Some horses will blow out or fill up with air when the girth is first buckled and it takes a while to return to normal size.) The first step in saddling is to have your horse secure. Either tie him or put him in crossties.

If you have a martingale or tie-down, this goes on before the saddle, fitting the girth or cinch through the loop of the strap. When removing tack, reverse the procedure, with the martingale or tie-down coming off last.

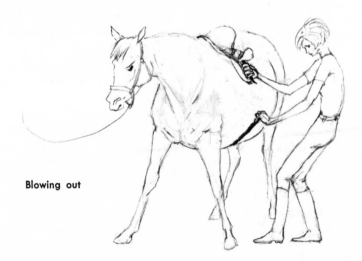

Blowing out

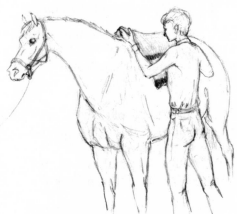

1. Putting on the blanket or pad

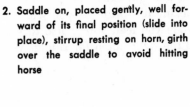

2. Saddle on, placed gently, well forward of its final position (slide into place), stirrup resting on horn, girth over the saddle to avoid hitting horse

3. Bringing cinch under horse's girth

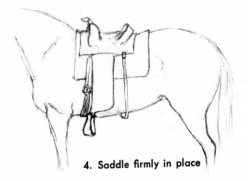

4. Saddle firmly in place

253

The next step is to slide the saddle pad into place, beginning in front of the withers and sliding toward the horse's rump until the pad is correctly in place. Make sure it is lying smooth and straight on both sides. On an English saddle, fasten the saddle pad to the billet straps at this point.

Before putting on the saddle, attach the girth to the offside. It's more convenient. Pick up the saddle with the pommel in your left hand and the cantle in your right. If the saddle has been properly put away, the girth will be folded up over the seat; with an English saddle the stirrups will also be run up. On a Western saddle, you can hook the offside stirrups over the horn.

Ready for the Saddle

The saddle should be put down gently and well forward so that you can slide it into position without ruffing the horse's coat the wrong way. If you see that it is too far back, lift it up and replace it. Moving to the offside, drop the girth down (and the stirrup if it's a Western saddle) and then return to the near shoulder to pull it under. Hook it up only one notch to begin with. Now, circling round the front, go to the offside again to make sure the saddle pad isn't bunched under and that the girth is lying flat. With a husky horse that has wrinkled skin around the girth area, you may want to lift one front leg to stretch it out and minimize the possibility of chafing. After the final stage of tacking up—bridling—you will tighten up the girth another notch, and when you lead your horse to where you will mount him, cinch it up to the right notch for riding. With an English saddle, always leave a

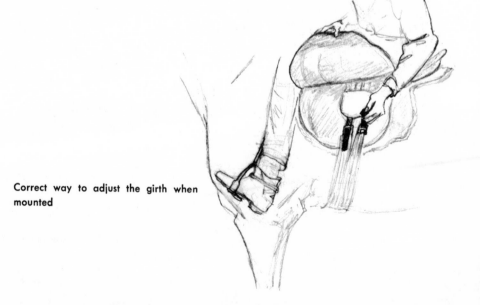

Correct way to adjust the girth when mounted

couple of holes on the girth strap on each side, or it may break. Should your horse acquire a few extra inches around the middle during the winter, you can buy elastic girth extenders for five to six dollars.

The girth may still need adjustment after you mount. Some horses puff up farther and for a longer time than others. Just remember not to attempt to get the girth as high as it will go on the first try. Your horse may react by cow-kicking, biting, or—in extreme cases—developing a "cold back," in which case, when the saddle goes on, he shoots straight legged into the air—something like a bronc. A young horse that has had a saddle slapped suddenly on his back and pulled up tight may react just this way. In either situation, your horse will probably forewarn you by pinning back his ears and looking annoyed. Mounting or riding with a loose girth is obviously dangerous, so the solution is to think of your horse and take up the girth in stages.

How to Put on a Bridle

If your horse is tied by a lead rope, unsnap it; or unsnap the crosstie chains. Then put the reins of the bridle over his head before removing

Correct way to put on a bridle

the halter. This way, if he decides to leave, you'll have something to hold him with.

Face forward, with your right shoulder by the near side of his head. Holding the crownpiece of the bridle in your right hand, slip your right arm under the throatlatch so your horse's head is looking over your right shoulder and the bridle is under his nose. Take the bit across your left palm, the thumb and index finger supporting it at each end. As you bring it up toward the horse's mouth, balance the bit on your palm with your index finger and stick your thumb in the near side of his mouth on the bottom bar, which causes him to open it. As soon as he separates his teeth, slip the bit *gently* into his mouth—jam-

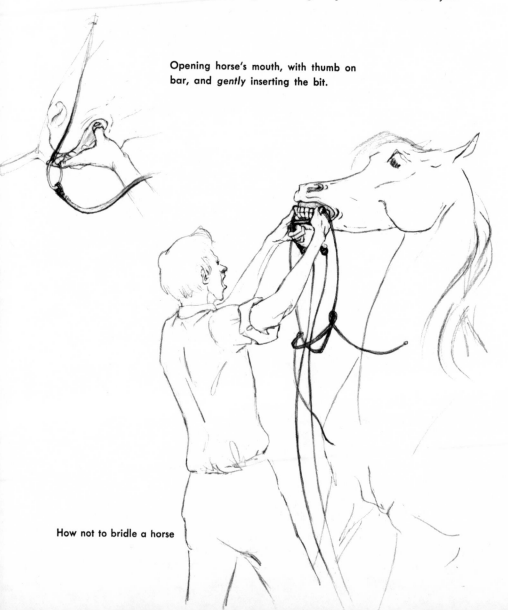

Opening horse's mouth, with thumb on bar, and *gently* inserting the bit.

How not to bridle a horse

Sliding the crownpiece over his right ear by feel

ming it against his teeth is a sure way to make him want to avoid the bit—and slide the crownpiece over his ears, gently, one at a time, beginning with the right ear, by feel. Some horses are extraordinarily well disposed to bridling. Yours may even lower his head and open his mouth for the bit. Or he may throw his head back to avoid it—undoubtedly because of a bad experience.

If you have a Pelham or curb bit, fasten the lip strap next; then the curb chain, or strap, if it's a Western bridle. Make sure this is flattened out and lying smooth before hooking or buckling it, adjusting it so that the strap or chain is not too tight and the bit operates correctly. Adjust the cavesson the same way, remembering to put the straps on the *inside* of the cheekpieces. Allow space for two fingers between the back of the noseband and the horse's jaw. If you have a standing martingale or a tie-down, it will be attached to the cavesson or noseband now.

Next, hook up the throatlatch, taking care that all the leather is flat, with no twists. The throatlatch should be loose enough to allow a hand to slide palm down between it and the horse's throat. If too tight, the throatlatch could interfere with his breathing. Going around to the front of the horse, smooth out the forelock and make sure everything is sitting straight. The browband, for instance, shouldn't be drooping over one eye.

If your horse is impatient about bridling, it's worth a few weeks' time and patience—and bribes of carrots, grain, or molasses offered with the bit.

After your horse is tacked up, you may want to leave him in his stall for a few minutes before setting off for a ride. If so, put a halter over the bridle to keep the ends of the reins from catching on anything in the stall. Then run up the stirrups and put the reins under them. Otherwise the reins may drop down on his neck where he could step on them. English riders, by the way, should always make a habit of keeping the stirrups run up when not riding so they don't get caught on objects.

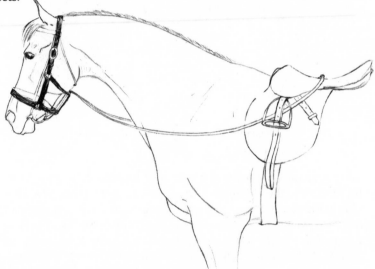

How to leave a horse in a stall with bridle and saddle on and the halter over the bridle

UNTACKING

On return from a ride, when you are dismounting, loosen the girth a bit before walking your horse out to let the circulation return to his back. Some horsemen feel so strongly about the bad effects of removing a saddle suddenly that they will leave it on for an hour or more after working a horse. In the Vermont one-hundred-mile ride a few conscientious souls leave the saddles on for three hours, loosening the girth a hole at a time.

After dismounting, immediately run up your stirrups before moving your horse a step. I've seen a dangling stirrup catch on the strangest objects, and one horse banged his nose with them while trying to bite a fly. Start by bringing the reins over your horse's head and hold on to them as you fix the stirrups on the offside. Then loosen the girth and lead him to wherever he will be tied. Remove the bridle, leaving the reins over his neck until the halter is on. Undo the curb chain first, then the cavesson and the throatlatch. The bridle should be hung on a bracket, which you can get for $3.50 or so, or any semicircular device that will keep its shape—painted one-pound coffee can, large tuna fish can, etc., nailed to the wall. When secured, the bridle should be high enough for the reins to hang down straight. If not, loop the reins over the bridle rack and fasten the throatlatch in a figure eight around the cavesson and headpiece. Or fasten the cavesson around the reins, hook the curb chain in front, and catch the reins in the throatlatch. This is one correct way to "put up" an English bridle. The Western bridle is hung up as is, with reins looped over the bracket.

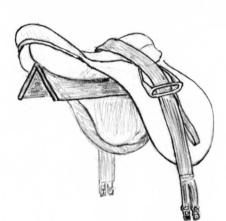

Bridle bracket

Saddle and bridle put up correctly

When he is tied by the halter, remove the saddle. If the girth is covered with mud, throw it across the withers to be wiped off as soon as you get inside. A muddy girth could scratch the leather. (A wet saddle pad or girth should be hung up to dry.) If clean, slide the girth up through the stirrup on the offside, over the seat, and down through the near stirrup; then take the saddle off. Don't just throw the saddle down on the barn floor or the ground; the front is vulnerable and easily scratched. If your saddle rack isn't handy, try resting the

Saddle rack

saddle on something or lean it against the wall, with the pommel resting on the girth. Then when you've finished with your horse you can put the saddle on the saddle rack. The best kind is open at the bottom so that the air can dry the underside and the lining. Racks are sold for between ten and fifteen dollars. The pommel should be toward the wall. Cover the saddle with a saddle cover (they range from ten to thirty dollars) or a clean towel. See Appendix for making your own saddle cover.

Your horse should now be tied or put in crossties and given a rub-down—or a sponge bath, whichever is appropriate for the weather—then untied and walked until he's dry, and returned to his stall.

BLANKETS

Every horse should have blankets, whether or not they are used regularly. For northern climates you may want two blankets—a heavy waterproof one with canvas lining outside and wool inside and a "sheet" or cotton blanket. In warm climates a sheet is adequate, and is

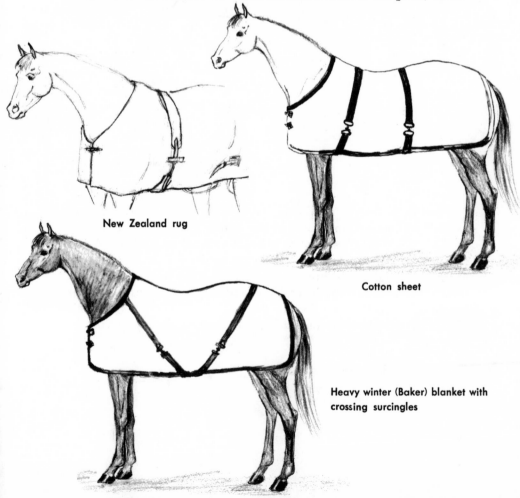

New Zealand rug

Cotton sheet

Heavy winter (Baker) blanket with crossing surcingles

handy for flies, vanning, or when your horse gets overheated on a cool day.

Consider, before buying, that heavy blankets are not necessarily the best. It's the layering of the material, not the weight, that counts. This is why many people prefer a wool liner under a cotton duck blanket. Many clipped hunters wear a lightweight duck blanket with a heavier blanket over the top. Two types of blankets are water repellent (not waterproof), and these are designed for outdoor use: the **New Zealand rug** and the **Levenham.** The New Zealand rug is difficult to keep clean (launderability is something to consider before you purchase a blanket). If you dry-clean it, it loses its water repellency; it must be washed and scrubbed by hand; and in a downpour or snowstorm, water will seep through it. The New Zealand rug has a canvas top with a thin wool liner and clips that go under a horse's leg.

The Levenham rug, which originated in Ireland, is quilted on the outside and has brushed tricot inside. While not quite as durable as its down-under counterpart, the Levenham is more washable. Most horsemen I know use a New Zealand or Levenham when blanketing a clipped horse outside in winter, changing to a regular blanket in the barn.

Horses that must maintain a short showcoat (see Chapter 6) throughout the winter can be kept cozy with the **Congress blanket,** a quilted nylon fiber-filled covering with an inner fleece lining (it originated at the Quarterhorse Congress in 1971). It's cozy but costly ($500). These blankets come in a variety of colors and in embossed designs, with a matching lined hood to prevent your horse from growing a furry winter head of hair to contrast with his sleek body. These blankets are usually contoured and fitted to a horse's body. They're washable, tough, and some of them are water repellent.

Inexpensive **duck blankets** are usually lined with wool or nylon combinations. Some are water repellent. But the wool lining makes them harder to wash than a plain duck sheet, and because of their inexpensive construction, they often wear out in a season.

For the summer, you can buy cotton duck **fly sheets** and **rain covers.** Fly sheets, which are made of mesh, have always seemed impractical to me because they easily catch on things going in and out of the trailer or barn, and snag. A lightweight cotton duck sheet is a very practical thing to have around when you're showing, because it keeps a horse clean after grooming. And for those who show or enter other types of competition, a rain sheet is a handy addition to the equine wardrobe. Rain sheets are only to keep the horse and saddle dry and clean. They're not for warmth. The sheets fit loosely, like a cooler, and it's easy to make one yourself from thin layered nylon covered with polyurethane. (See Appendix for how to make your own cooler.)

A cooler

The **anti-sweat sheet,** or Aeroborn sheet, which looks like thermal underwear, is made of washable synthetic fabric. It traps body heat and permits sweat to evaporate. This is the blanket I wouldn't be without. It serves as a fly sheet in summer and as an underliner to heavier blankets (in lieu of straw). They're easy to wash, too.

Wool coolers, which cover a horse from the poll to the tail, are used in cooler weather when a horse is being cooled out. Coolers must be treated like a good wool sweater—washed by hand and blocked to preserve their shape. Because this is such a time-consuming venture, some well-known horsewomen have improvised by making elegant coolers from king- and queen-size wool polyester bed blankets. They buy them during sales and attach cotton web fastening to the head and the tail. This cheap, attractive alternative to the wool cooler can be washed and dried by machine.

Care of blankets

Heavy-duty washing machines are best for washing horse blankets, although your local laundromat may not appreciate the business. One friend of mine (who sneaks into the laundromat late at night loaded down with blankets) puts her extra-dirty blankets through a rinse cycle, adding a bit of ammonia. Then she washes them in soap and warm water with a final cold-water rinse to hold the color. The best way to dry blankets is on a double clothesline, which allows the air to circulate evenly. Another alternative is to spread them flat on the lawn, turning them frequently to let the blanket dry equally on both sides. Dryers shrink blankets.

Fitting the blanket

To get a proper fit, measure from the center of your horse's chest and back along the side to the point of the rump. Take these measurements with you when you go shopping, rather than making a rough estimate of your horse's size when you're there at the store. A hairy horse blanket can't be returned.

Always buy sheets and coolers a size or two larger than your horse, to allow for accidental shrinkage and also to provide a fuller fit. This way you can make sure the blanket closes completely around the chest and that it covers the entire rump.

Some blankets are cut back at the neck for horses with braided manes, and some have matching hoods.

Surcingles should be fastened snugly—not too tight, but tight enough so that the blanket doesn't slip around. Take your horse's eccentricities into consideration when you select your blanket. I have one horse who takes to leg straps on New Zealand rugs as though they were bucking straps—and reacts accordingly, going on a bucking spree. So know your horse's temperament before investing in an expensive blanket.

HARNESSES

As more and more people are learning to enjoy greater use of their horse through driving, harnesses are once again an important part of the tack scene. Here are some tips on selecting, fitting, and caring for your harness.

When buying one secondhand, check it out as you would a used saddle, making sure the leather is not too dry or cracked, that all the hardware is there and that the stitching is secure.

Inexpensive new, and very serviceable, harnesses can be bought in the Amish areas of Pennsylvania, Ohio, and Illinois for around eighty dollars. Since the Amish travel only by horse-drawn vehicles, you know that their harnesses are safe and utilitarian.

Some friends of mine have bought very good harnesses at auctions. Sometimes they select them for the rare hardware alone and then have the harness rebuilt by a reliable craftsman—more and more masters of this craft are appearing throughout the country as driving increases in popularity. A good craftsman should be able to copy any style of harness. Those who prefer a more elaborate harness could spend up to $1,500 for a custom-made job.

Harnesses, of course, can also be purchased from any leading tack distributors in the United States.

Whether it's new or secondhand (make sure the leather is pliable and that the fittings and hardware are in top condition), a harness has to be fitted properly to your horse. Every piece of this elaborate equipment has a reason. An ill-fitting harness won't do the proper job, and it can cause sores, discomfort, and pain, any of which could sour a horse from driving forever.

The type of carriage you're driving will determine the type of harness you select. The thickness and width of harness pieces will vary according to the type of work being done. For instance, a two-wheeled wire cart—a jog cart or a pleasure cart—used close to the ground in a show-ring needs only a thin, one-inch breast collar harness. But a four-wheel or one- to two-seat buckboard would take a breast collar harness of heavier and thicker dimensions. A Stanhope gig or any other formal, heavy vehicle takes a harness with a collar.

Fitting the harness

Depending on the type of harness you select, the **collar** or **breast collar** is put on first, overlaid by the Hames—a brass fitting that encircles the collar—to which the traces are attached. The collar is placed over the horse's head upside down, with the traces still attached but crossed over the horse's neck so they don't get stepped on. The collar is then turned over at the top part of the horse's neck and slid down into position.

I can't overstress how important it is to get a proper fit on the collar— the reason why breast collars are recommended for novice drivers who often start with used harnesses. If it isn't fitted properly to the horse's neck, the collar could press on the horse's windpipe or pinch his skin, situations that occur when it's either too short or too narrow. A collar should lie flat and comfortably on your horse's shoulders and be roomy enough at the bottom to allow a hand to slip between the collar and the horse's neck. You may find that a collar that fits your horse early in the season when he's not in top condition will be too tight in July when his muscles have developed and he's filled out.

Breast collars are placed over the head and fitted so that they lie above the point of the shoulder. If it is too low, the collar will rub, if too high, it will interfere with the horse's breathing. Both breast and neck collars must be immaculate on the inside. Dirty collars cause sores.

After fitting the collar, place the **saddle pad** on the horse's back, leaving it unfastened until the tail is placed through the **crupper.** If your horse is new to driving, take care to place the crupper on lightly and have someone standing near the horse's head in case he acts up. Unlike riding saddles, the harness saddle should be placed a good four to five inches behind the elbow. The **girth** is then tightened.

The strap between the saddle and the crupper must not be too tight or it will put stress on the dock of the horse's tail, causing chafing or even kicking. This is also a reason why careful attention must be paid to the crupper's cleanliness and pliability.

Breeching is seldom used in the show-ring or on light carts or show buggies that will be rolling on flat ground, where it isn't really necessary. But with heavier vehicles—especially in hilly country—and with traditional harnesses, breeching is needed to hold back the carriage. Breeching is next connected over the horse's rump and through the **backstrap,** and then the horse is bridled in the usual manner. The type of bit you use will depend on your horse's mouth and the type of driving you'll be doing. Among the bits commonly used are **half-cheek, straight-bar, snaffle, Liverpool** or **Buxton.** The latter two can be adjusted at several points and are traditionally used because they allow the driver maximum control.

Parts of a harness

1. Blinker	14. Belly band
2. Blinker stay	15. Girth
3. Rosette	16. Shaft loop
4. Terret ring	17. False martingale
5. Rein	18. Hames
6. Liverpool bit	19. Bottom hame strap or chain
7. Backpad	20. Wrap strap
8. Back strap	21. Shaft
9. Crupper	22. Collar
10. Loin strap	23. Bearing rein or checkrein
11. Breeching	24. Bearing rein drop
12. Breeching strap	25. Bearing rein hook
13. Trace	

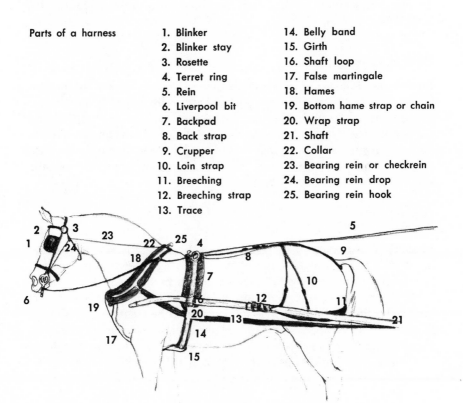

Finally, the reins are threaded through the terrets and attached to the bit and bridle in that order. Use the reverse procedure in unhooking the harness.

Now comes the **cart.** To make sure you don't end up with the cart before the horse, it is easier and safer to have two people attach the vehicle to the harness—especially when the horse or driver is inexperienced. It's helpful to have another person standing at the horse's head to hold him.

Pull the cart slowly up behind the horse, shafts raised in position to run through the loops or **tugs** (on the saddle pad) on both sides of the horse. Always attach both shafts at once, to avoid an accident should your horse become restless and move forward. Each set of straps is done up before the next is started: **traces, breeching,** and **tug wraps,** if harness has them. Uncross the traces and run them through the loops on the shafts if there are any, then hook the traces to the trees in back so that they are practically taut when the shaft tip is at the point of the shoulders. After both traces are attached, the breeching is secured by slipping it through a metal eye or leather loop and then wrapping it around the shaft, encircling the traces three times and buckling it to itself. The breeching adjustment will be correct if you push the cart forward about four inches, until the breeching presses against the horse's hindquarters.

Care of Harness

In cleaning, follow the same procedures as you would for the rest of your tack (see end of chapter). Special harness hooks can be purchased at auctions and farms, or they can be homemade. It is essential to keep the harness clean and dry. The backpad, collar, and attachments should be hung in such a manner that they don't lose their shape. In the last century, when carriages were the main form of transport, elegant stables stored harnesses in glass cases to protect them.

Blinkers

Blinkers are necessary to keep the horse from being distracted by passing events, to keep him from seeing the moving wheels, which create the illusion of overtaking the horse when in motion, and to keep his mind on the driver—especially on a busy road. The eyes should be centered inside the blinker. The blinker should be centered and should face ahead, so the horse can't see above, below, or around it. But it should not press on his eyes or eyelashes, which would cause irritation. The cheek-strap buckle above the bit adjusts the position of the bit in the horse's mouth. The blinkers shouldn't flap and must not be too tight. Improper adjustments can be disastrous. One very experienced driving horse saw the cart through flapping blinkers and took off in terror. He smashed his leg and had to be destroyed.

The **checkrein** is an optional piece of equipment, the use of which depends on the type of driving you'll be doing. It is required if you are entering a driving class and at all breed shows run by ASHA rules. Many driving advocates believe that the horse should not depend on a checkrein, but be properly balanced and able to carry himself without one (like any properly schooled riding horse). The choice of whether you use this device for normal everyday driving and in local ADS American Driving Society) sponsored competitions is up to you.

SELECTING A CART

Before the advent of the internal-combustion engine, hundreds of types of buggies, carts, and sleighs were manufactured. Every carriage maker had his own style of building and his own names for his vehicles. Consequently many similar carriages have different names, even though they're nearly identical in construction and purpose.

The Spartan show buggies often seen in fine harness classes are mere skeletons when seen alongside the elegant Victorias, Landaus, and Phaetons that used to travel American highways. Some carriages had names later adopted by auto makers, like station wagons and coupés.

Pleasure drivers can choose nearly any type of vehicle they fancy. But those who intend to show should read rule books carefully before selecting a cart or buggy. Each breed has different regulations requiring different harnesses and vehicles.

The most rugged, durable, and inexpensive cart for pleasure-driving is the high wooden-wheeled type that usually has hard rubber tires and is variously known as a jogging cart, road cart, breaking cart, or cross-country cart. Another type of vehicle often used by beginners on flat ground only is a one-seated light jogging cart with bicyclelike wheels, which is available at most established tack shops. Two-wheeled carts are considered safer for beginning horses than are four-wheeled buggies; they're more maneuverable.

Any cart should be well sprung, so that it's comfortable for the passengers and evenly balanced for the horse. It should fit your horse in size, with shafts level and correctly balanced when the horse is hitched. If the wheels have no rubber, you'll probably want to have rubber fitted to them. Because of the growing interest in driving, wheelmaking is reviving as a business, particularly in New England. Wheelmakers can also be found in Amish country. Iron wheels are okay for driving on grass, but rubber is far better for roads, since it is quieter and more shock absorbent.

Antique carts can be picked up at auctions or often found in the back of a friend's barn. Driving publications and newsletters advertise used carts in their classified sections (see Appendix). If you do locate a gem of a cart tucked away in the back of someone's barn or on the auction block, make sure you check it out carefully before making a bid. Some points to consider:

- Does it fit your horse?
- Are the shafts level at the point of the shoulder where the horse is hitched?
- Can the shafts be altered in height, length, and width to suit different horses?
- Are the wheels evenly balanced when the cart is viewed from behind, and is there any looseness in the spokes, or dry rot?
- Is the cart sound? (If there is rotten wood, don't despair—it can be replaced. And loose-spoked wheels can be soaked in the creek where the moisture will swell and tighten the wood.)
- How much restoration does the vehicle need? (Is it just refinishing or major reconstruction? There are numerous publications to help the do-it-yourselfer restore old carts and buggies.)

TACK SHOULDN'T BE TACKY

The leather used in tack is expensive, and well worth the time and effort to take care of it. Most importantly, your safety may depend on it. Ideally, it's best to wipe all tack off every time you use it; big stables employ grooms to do this. But you'll probably compromise with a thorough tack cleaning once a week.

Special "horses" are available to rest saddles on for cleaning. A cheaper way is to place two high-backed chairs back to back and fold a towel, or sheet, over the tops to make a thick padding that will protect the saddle gullet. Special hooks (provided very inexpensively) that hold a bridle high enough to keep the reins off the ground make it easy to clean all bridle parts, stirrup leathers, and leather girths. You'll need the following equipment for cleaning your tack:

- A tin of saddle soap or glycerin (or spray bottle of liquid saddle soap)
- Small sponge (to apply soap with)
- Rough towel (for wiping away dirt)
- Chamois cloth (used damp for drying leather)
- Metal polish (for stirrups, bits, and metal surfaces)
- Neat's-foot oil or Lexol (for dry leather)

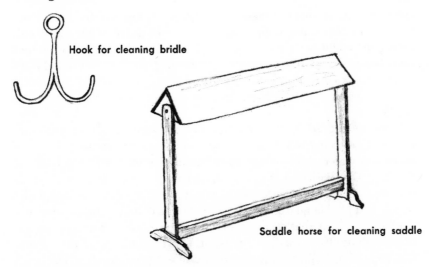

Hook for cleaning bridle

Saddle horse for cleaning saddle

- Wooden matches (to clean soap and dirt from holes of stirrup leathers, metal dees, and chains)
- Flannel rags (to shine metal with)
- Towel scraps (to apply oil with)
- Old toothbrush or nail brush (to scrub metal)
- Pail of lukewarm water (changed frequently)
- Optional equipment: saddle-cleaning stand (about fifty dollars) or tack-cleaning hook (about five dollars, depending on size)

Set aside an area in the stable or house where you can work easily. If in the house, spread out newspapers on the floor where you will be working.

Saddle

Begin with the saddle (we're talking about an English saddle here, because it involves more parts than a Western one, but the procedure is basically the same). Put it on the "horse" and remove all fittings. Hang the leather fittings by their buckles on the tack hook, which should be placed high enough so that the fittings hook at shoulder level and don't drag on the floor. Put the stirrups aside with the metal parts of the bridle (bit and curb chain if you have one) to be done later.

If the girth is made of cloth or other washable material, brush it off, making sure to get off any dried mud, then soak it in cool water and mild soap (work soap into soiled areas by hand) a few hours (overnight if badly soiled). Washable saddle pads can be handled the same way. After soaking them, wash the girth and saddle pad in the machine in cool water with mild soap or cold-water detergent. Harsh detergents might irritate your horse's skin. Remember, by the way, that each horse should have his own saddle pad so that skin conditions don't get passed from one to the other.

If you have a leather girth, treat it as you would the rest of the saddle.

Turn the saddle over on its tree (commercial stands conveniently reverse to a trough for this purpose) and wash the entire panel with lukewarm water and a rough towel. Really scrub hard to get all the dirt out. Dry with the chamois immediately. Then turn your saddle over and repeat the process on the top, under the skirt, the flaps, billet straps, and buckle guard, wiping all dry immediately with the chamois. Any leather areas that seem particularly dry should get an application of neat's-foot oil or Lexoil at this point. Don't put oil on the seat or outside flaps of the saddle, however, or it will soil your clothing. Too much neat's-foot oil on leather rots stitching and too much of a conditioner, like Lexol, will shorten leather life, interfere with shine, and rot the stitching. Water, of course, damages leather by drying it out. That's why it's important to squeeze as much water as possible from sponges before putting on saddle soap. Glycerin soap is good for keeping leather soft because less water is needed to apply it, and it promotes a longer-lasting saddle. Muddy saddles should be left to dry and brushed off rather than washed with water.

Next, apply saddle soap. Despite its name this should be thought of as a protective, waxlike covering, not a cleaner. Before applying it, the saddle should be completely free of dust and dirt or the soap will rub them in further. Wet the soap, thus keeping the sponge barely damp during the application. Don't strive to work up a lather. If you do, it's a sign that the sponge is too wet.

After soaping, your saddle should glow and smell clean. Leave it on the stand until you're through with the fittings. Then either do the fittings separately at this point or with the bridle pieces. (Martingales and tie-downs could also be soaped then too.)

Bridle

The easiest way to clean a dirty bridle is to take it apart completely. Novice horse owners should pay careful attention to the way the bridle fits together and to the holes for the crownpiece to be buckled in. Pay special attention to the direction of the bit and the way the reins are hooked to the bit.

If your bridle is brand new, soak the parts in neat's-foot oil overnight before saddle-soaping. Brand-new saddles and leather fittings should also get a coating of oil.

Hang the bridle pieces and fittings from the tack hook and wash them off one at a time with toweling, drying immediately with the chamois cloth. Then apply saddle soap, working it in well. The wooden matches can be used to remove dirt from the holes of stirrup leathers and bridle pieces. When the saddle soap is applied, the wooden matches may be used again to remove any excess soap.

All metal parts can now be washed and scrubbed with a brush, removing the dirt from the recesses. This would include bit, stirrups, and curb chain. If there are rubber treads on your stirrups, wash them with brush and laundry soap and set them aside to dry while you apply the metal polish.

Swab the metal polish generously on each piece and shine vigorously with a clean flannel cloth. When the metal is gleaming, stirrups can be replaced on the leathers and rubber treads reinserted. Stirrups and leathers can now be put back on the saddle, switching sides to equalize any stretching that may have occurred to leathers during mounting.

Lay the clean girth over the top of the saddle, each end running through the stirrups. Put it up with the clean saddle pad on top and a saddle cover over all. The bridle should be carefully put back together, adjusting the crownpiece in the same holes. Then put your bridle up as you would after a ride.

Tack *must* be cleaned regularly to keep it soft and pliable. If neglected, it will dry out, rot, and break. Reins and billet straps should always be checked before riding for worn stitching and repaired immediately. Broken leathers and worn billet straps during a ride could cause terrible accidents.

In the winter, when the temperature goes below freezing, keep your tack indoors where the temperature is between 50 and 60 degrees and cover it to prevent mildew.

Conscientiously cared for, a good bridle and saddle will last a lifetime.

10

education
and exercise—
yours and his

*It is here gentlemen that practice, example,
and experience are worth more than words.
. . . I am warning you that the horse will
use any trick he can, like tossing his head,
resisting the aids, or champing the bit.
When he resorts to this, however, or to any
such maneuver, you must reprimand him
in a stern and angry tone of voice, shouting roughly and menacingly, using whatever
words come to mind—like "come on, get on,
get going you traitor, rebel! About face,
turn, stop, turn this way, turn that." . . . !
and more of the same, and so that your
shouts are tremendously intimidating. Keep
on with this until he gets it right.*

—FEDERICO GRISONE
Rules for Riding, 1561

*The seat on a horse makes gentlemen of
some and grooms of others.*

—CERVANTES
Don Quixote

In countless romantic novels and films an aggressive, untrained equestrian leaps onto an unbroken horse—usually a stallion—and subdues him
after a brief hair-raising battle of wills. Such dramatizations have convinced a lot of inexperienced riders that bravery and power are a
winning combination in any saddle. In real life, they're not.

Brute strength and courage have almost nothing to do with good horsemanship. Some of the greatest riders in the world are lightweights who, next to strongman Charles Atlas, would look like puny, ninety-eight-pound weaklings. Petite Kathy Kusner when on the U.S. Olympic team rode burly, seventeen-hand mounts to one international victory after another. Steeplechase riders, who take high-strung racehorses over the most treacherous jumps in the world, never weigh more than 126 pounds. Of course all competitors do have an oversized share of nerve, but the basic common ingredient is talent and acquired skill.

Films and books aren't entirely responsible for all the misconceptions about horsemanship. The art of riding is often confused with the sort of activity that passes for it on public hacking trails across the country. The novice who rents a horse at a public stable often returns from the outing convinced that riding involves little more than the ability to hang on while one's mount follows his friends down the trail. A Sunday rider may feel he is in control. But if all the other horses in the party decided to return to the barn, he'd quickly discover how illusory this feeling is.

Horses at most public stables have been ridden by so many bad riders that they are numb to the aids and signals to which a well-trained horse responds. The mouths of these unfortunate animals have been pulled and their sides kicked so often that all senses are deadened. A few years at a hacking stable will drain all the spirit out of most horses. Or, in the case of a high-strung animal, the experience will make him hopelessly neurotic.

A good riding horse is the product of intensive training. He is tuned and polished like a fine violin. In comparison, a hacking stable horse is like an out-of-tune player piano, programmed to play the same tinny tune over and over.

Pleasant riding horses move forward willingly and respond to a light touch of the leg and rein. They walk and trot at a smooth, elastic, even gait. This doesn't come naturally. It has to be taught. And to teach it properly, the rider himself must be well trained. If he is not, any training the horse has had will quickly disappear, to be replaced by bad habits.

Great riders don't master their horses, they play them—much as a musician plays his instrument. The finer the rider, the better the melody. The better the instrument, the finer the harmony. Both horse and rider must work harmoniously. And like other artists, good equestrians are always striving to improve their mastery of the art.

Some riders, like some musicians and painters, are more talented than others. All have their limitations. It helps to know, through working with an instructor, what your limitations are. There's no point in spending thousands on the equine equivalent of a Stradivarius if you don't know how to play it to maximum effect.

YOUR BASIC TRAINING

To school a horse correctly there are some basic things you should know. Are you aware, for instance, that you have five natural aids at your disposal: your voice, hands, legs, seat, and weight? Can you sit comfortably and correctly at all gaits using these aids? And whether you ride English or Western, do you know something about the way a horse moves, or that his center of balance is slightly behind the withers? A horse propels himself from behind, collecting himself at different gaits by bringing his hindquarters well under him. A good rider knows how to accentuate this natural motion to achieve perfect balance or lightness and a collected gait.

None of this training can be accomplished on your own. Though books can be a helpful supplement, I don't see how anyone can teach himself to ride any more than he can teach himself to fly an airplane. Good instruction is a must. Where do you find it?

There are lots of riding teachers around, some excellent, some awful. They can be found in almost any area, in their own private stables, exclusive clubs, riding centers, summer camps, and 4-H or Pony clubs. You might begin your search by asking for a list of instructors at your local tack shop.

Youth Instruction

For children, the few **summer camps** specializing in riding are generally excellent, employing top instructors. One riding camp even takes instant replay videotapes of the class. But this sort of thing is obviously expensive, and such specialized camps run around a thousand dollars and up a month.

Make sure that the excellent rider or professional advertised in the camp catalogue is actually teaching your child. Two friends of mine, who sent their daughters to an expensive riding camp in upstate New York, found when they visited there that the professional whose praises were sung in the advertising literature was teaching only 8 of the 175 campers. The balance were being taught (or rather untaught) by unqualified counselors who knew no more, and probably less, than the thirteen-year-old students.

For children who are serious riders, an experience like this could be a big setback, not to mention the expenses. As my friends said later, "We could have spent the same amount of money and had our kids take private lessons at home three or four times a week."

Be wary of camps that offer riding along with thirty other activities. Places like this often have a few undistinguished horses tacked up half-English and half-Western with an instructor who may have taken a few riding courses sometime during his career as a tennis player.

Riding centers can be good places to begin. They are centrally located throughout the country, and advertise in most of the weekly and monthly horse journals. They are expensive but worth it.

Inexpensive alternatives for junior riders are 4-H and Pony clubs. 4-H is free. Pony clubs, which teach only English riding, require a nominal fee for registration, half of which goes to the national club. Pony, by the way, is used here in the English sense, meaning a child's mount of any size.

4-H clubs have regular horse clinics in which members learn riding theory, stable management, and horse care. Often, local vets are called in to lecture and relevant films are shown.

Sponsored by the U.S. Department of Agriculture and administered locally on a county level, these clubs have a lot of good things going for them. For instance, members are required to keep a practical yearly record of the cost of maintaining their mounts—the price and contents of feed, bedding, shoeing, pasturing, and equipment. Children must also record how often the vet comes and the cost, how many horse shows, clinics, and trail rides they've attended, and any other significant experiences with their mounts during the year. As a prerequisite for receiving prize money won at a county 4-H show, this record must be submitted.

At the beginning of every 4-H show, members are encouraged to enter fitting and showmanship classes, where they are judged on grooming, the condition of the horse, cleanliness of equipment, and personal neatness. This is a wonderful way to encourage good stable management and good grooming. All junior shows should require it as a prerequisite for further participation.

My only reservation about 4-H—which I hesitate to mention because the organization is otherwise so marvelous—is that they tend to be inconsistent about basic standards of horsemanship and horse care. 4-H has no standard way of bridling and saddling a horse, no standard riding techniques or rules for proper horse care. It all depends on the personal preference of the volunteer instructors available in any given area.

Recently 4-H has developed a topnotch horse-science program, and there is a variety of valuable literature available free by writing your County Agricultural Department.

Pony Club instructors are also volunteers, but they must work from a specific set of standards set up by the national Pony Club, which are used throughout the country. Children are rated at different levels, not only on their riding ability but on their skill at practical tasks like grooming, stable care, cleaning tack, and on their knowledge of these in a written test. It often works out that a child is more talented at horse management than at riding skills. Here he gets recognized for this.

Adult Instruction

4-H and Pony clubs are only for youngsters unfortunately. If you're married, middle-aged, and want to begin or renew your acquaintance with horse care and riding, where do you go?

For riding instruction, any competent teacher will be glad to accept older pupils, and there is no limit to the age at which you can begin. Some of my beginning pupils have been in their late sixties. Riding clubs, academies, and stables are within easy traveling distance in most parts of the country. Centers are excellent if you can spare the time.

Learning about stable management is somewhat harder. Some colleges, particularly community colleges, now offer adult education courses in the subject. I've been surprised at the large turnout at a college course I teach, and it shows what a need there is for this kind of instruction.

If the colleges in your area can't help, try calling nearby riding academies and Pony clubs to find out if you could observe some of their stable management courses. Or you might phone individual instructors and explain your plight. You'll find that most are very helpful. Riding centers are ideal for this because you do all your own stable work as part of the course.

Clinics

Although clinics are of unquestionable value, switching from instructor to instructor can often be confusing, and I don't recommend endless shopping around. But it pays to be selective in your choice of clinics. Some tips on evaluating a clinic:

- Who or what reliable organization is sponsoring the instructor?
- Does the instructor have a background familiar to you? With whom, and where, has he or she studied?
- What is the exact purpose of the clinic; what is the level of the riders accepted for it; and how many are there?
- Will it be a large group with teaching on several different levels? If so, you won't learn very much.
- Has the instructor had group teaching experience? Many teachers are great on a one-to-one basis but can't relate their ideas to a group of students.

If you have reservations about riding in a clinic, audit it from the sidelines. A receptive student can learn a lot just by watching. Take notes during the clinic and ask the instructor questions afterward.

It's helpful, riding in after clinic, to make notes on everything you can remember. Although it may mean nothing to you at the time, what you've heard may open up new vistas later. This is helpful too when you're auditing a class, particularly when the instructor is dealing with a horse or rider that has problems similar to your own.

But however favorable I am toward clinics, I'm getting less and less liberal about letting clinic instructors ride my horse. Remember that this is a personal choice—it is your horse, after all, and you don't have to allow anyone to ride him. While I'm delighted to let some instructors take over the reins, I wouldn't let some of them near my horse.

Shopping Around

Before signing up with an instructor, look around for a while. Visit riding schools and observe their classes (phoning in advance of course). Check to see whether the teacher specializes in the style of riding you want to learn—English—either hunt, saddle seat, dressage, or Western stock seat.

Explain your goals to the instructor. He needs to know whether you'll be riding for fun or show. Don't be afraid to ask what his or her background is. Riding instruction is a business and you won't be offending anyone by asking for credentials—unless, of course, there is no background, in which case you can expect a defensive reaction.

A good instructor has to be able to teach as well as ride well, and his attitude should be positive and constructive. Like math or music, riding is based on theory and a teacher should respond accordingly to any questions you ask. Any evasion, or comments like "It's that way because I say so" will give you good reason to be skeptical about an instructor's ability.

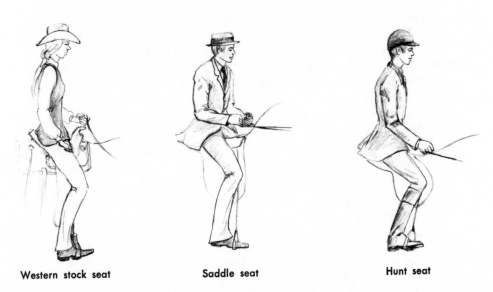

Western stock seat   Saddle seat   Hunt seat

While a teacher must demand respect, he shouldn't be authoritarian to a point where he intimidates his students. Some instructors seem to take a student's errors as a personal affront. Beginning riders are sufficiently unsure of themselves without having to contend with a temperamental teacher—particularly when rates range from ten to thirty-five dollars for a class lesson (considerably more for private ones).

Any good riding teacher will be instructing a cross section of pupils of varying ability. If there are only beginners in class after class, it may be a sign that the instructor isn't up to taking on more advanced students. A mixture of adults and children of different levels of ability is another good sign.

When you visit an instructor's stable, look at the condition of the horses, the stalls, and the tack, and the riding facilities. The surroundings need not be elegant, but the horses and equipment will be in good condition if the instructor is qualified at his job. When a stall is knee-deep in manure, the horses dull coated and underweight, and the tack dried out and held together with pins, take yourself elsewhere.

SCHOOLING YOUR HORSE—THE ESSENTIALS

No matter what work you do with your horse, he'll do it better if he's ridden consistently and schooled. That is, if he's already been through basic training before you bought him. If he hasn't, you could be in for a lot of headaches.

There are universal equine ABCs that every worthwhile riding horse should know. The days of taking a seven-year-old horse off the range, slapping a saddle on his back, and breaking him by bucking around a corral are over. Even out west these days horses are broken young, then turned out to pasture again until mature and strong enough for a full day's work.

Any well-educated horse has been voice-trained from birth. He has probably been handled and haltered since he was a few days old.

How can you tell whether your horse has received his elementary education? There are a few telling tests:

1. *Does he lead forward willingly, stopping when you stop or when you say "whoa"?*
2. *Does he stand for mounting* or gallop off like "hi-ho" Silver as soon as you get your toe in the stirrup?
3. *Will he move off at a slight pressure from the inside of the calf and from the seat,* or is it a major athletic feat to make him budge?
4. Once on the move, *does he walk on briskly and trot out in response to light seat and leg pressure?* Or do you have to flail him with a crop? And in both gaits *does he maintain a consistent speed* (4 m.p.h. at a walk, 8 m.p.h. at a trot, speeds your instruction will train you to recognize)?
5. When you try to stop your horse do you feel pounds of weight pulling on the bit, making you want to lean back in the saddle and haul on the reins in return? *Or will he halt readily when your hands stop following the motion of his head and neck and when he feels your weight drop in the saddle?*
6. *Does he lead into every turn with his nose, his spine following in an even curve with the turn?* Or is his head going in one direction and his shoulder in another? *And when you apply leg and rein pressure for the turn, does your horse move in the direction indicated, resist, or fail to respond at all?*

7. *Does he depart promptly on the correct lead at a canter*, or trot
   for twenty or thirty yards first? *Once cantering, is he light and
   collected in your hands, with hindquarters well under him? Does
   he retain a slow, rhythmic, three-beat gait*, or gain speed with
   every stride, pulling you forward and off-balance in the saddle?

I've emphasized the correct way a horse should respond in each of
these situations. If he doesn't react this way, the faults should be corrected for pleasant riding together. This means ring work under either
an experienced rider or with the supervision of a good instructor. In
some cases you may want to send your horse away to be trained. But
there are ways a rider of intermediate skill can retrain a horse and
correct some of these faults, with supervision, knowledge, and a great
deal of patience.

LEARNING HIS ABCS

Before you can correct faults or continue your horse's schooling, you
should know the specifics about his elementary education. Once you
understand what goes into training a horse, you'll be able to see what
grades he may have failed along the way. Training is a step-by-step
process. If you skip steps one and two, five and six just won't jell.

Leading

The first lesson in a young horse's schooling is learning to lead. This
is taught with a rope looped around the rump, the end brought up
and slipped through the halter ring. The trainer, standing behind the
foal's shoulder, facing forward, says "walk." Should the foal resist or
start to move backward, the trainer pulls forward on the rope, bringing

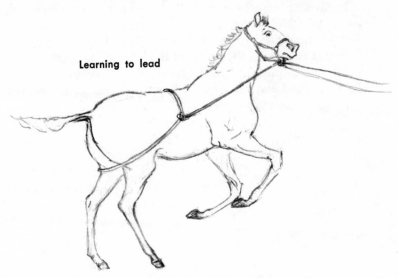

Learning to lead

pressure to bear on the rump, thereby moving him from behind. (Often the mare is led in front of the young horse at first to give him added inducement to move forward.)

If done properly, the foal never has a chance to learn that he can pull back. From the start, he's impelled forward by pressure from the rear, *never* by hauling on his head. In this initial stage of training, he's also learned his first two voice commands: "Walk" and "Whoa."

This kindergarten lesson is also a young horse's first confrontation with punishment and reward. In training a horse, punishment doesn't mean beating; it consists of applying pressure to various points on his body. Reward is the release of this pressure. In the lesson just illustrated, the punishment would be the tightened rope around the foal's rump. The reward is twofold: release of pressure and a pat on the neck or a word of encouragement, or even a little grain.

Psychologically, this is vital to later personality development, particularly with a high-strung horse. An impatient, heavy-handed trainer can create all kinds of complexes in an impressionable animal.

Early in his training, a foal is introduced to the whip. This is often done in the halter training, when the rope has been removed from his rump and replaced with a lead snapped on the halter. The trainer uses the whip as an artificial extension of his arm. As he leads the foal with his right hand, the whip is carried in his left. Should the young horse not move forward briskly enough the trainer will, without looking back, move his whip hand behind him and touch the horse *lightly* on the rump. Thus the foal never becomes aware of the whip as an entity separate from his trainer's arm, and the way this artificial aid is used is also crucial to the animal's developing personality. Used properly, there is no reason why a young horse should ever be frightened of the whip.

In his first year a yearling will also be taught the commands "stand" and "back." He will be introduced to the saddle or surcingle, to a comfortable, simplified bridle with a mouthing bit and keys (little metal bars that hang from the center of the bit, encouraging a horse to chew on the mouthpiece). The Western horse is usually introduced to the bosal first and may not have a bit in his mouth for several years.

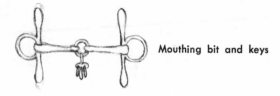

Mouthing bit and keys

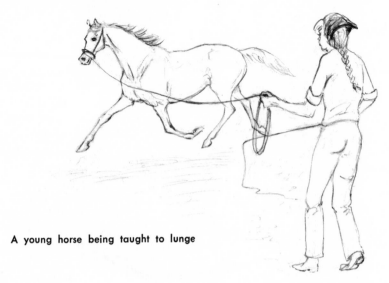

A young horse being taught to lunge

Lunging

During the next stage of training, usually at the end of his first year, the young horse is taught to lunge.

The trainer's aims in lunging here are quite different from those discussed later on in this chapter where a horse is lunged as a means of light exercise and to show how an older horse, one no doubt, who has missed being trained to lunge, can be taught to do so. Freedom of movement and obedience, not just exercise, are the trainer's main concerns here.

Once he's been lunged, the horse learns that he is expected to move in a circle in both directions around his trainer. At that point he is acquainted with more new voice commands—"reverse" and "trot," and possibly much later "canter." The trainer becomes familiar with the yearling's natural way of moving and temperament, and concentrates on helping the horse establish rhythm and balance at the various gaits.

Many well-educated horses are then put into side reins and bitting surcingle (or training roller). The elastic side reins snap to the bit and the surcingle. They are quite loose at first and gradually during weeks of training shortened up notch by notch to accustom him to the feeling of a little pressure on the bit in his mouth. Thus he learns to flex or give with the bit because the reins are elastic and give with the movement of his head and neck.

Schooling schedules at this age are consistent in duration and frequency. This is essential so that a colt or filly leaves each lesson refreshed

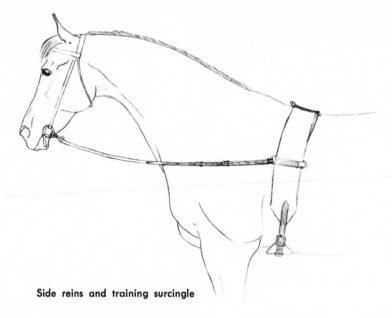

Side reins and training surcingle

and encouraged, rather than exhausted and bored, eager to return
and please his instructor.

Long Reining

The next step in a young horse's education is learning to steer. Some
trainers do this from the ground (called long reining) with long reins
slipped through the run-up stirrups of the saddle and held by the
trainer who stands four or five feet behind the horse. Some prefer to
harness the colt or filly and ride in a light braking cart (a sort of sulky).

Directed from behind by voice commands, the horse learns to walk
forward and turn to the right and left by pressure on each rein and/or
release of the opposite rein. A horse's normal reaction is to move in the
direction his head is turned. The youngster is also given rein pressure
to associate with the already familiar voice commands "whoa" and
"back."

Though long reining from the ground is a common teaching method,
many authorities frown on it, claiming it puts too uneven a contact on
the horse's mouth. These experts teach steering directly from the horse's
back either with the use of a leading rein, taking the left rein far to the
left for a left turn and vice versa, or by releasing pressure on the
right rein to release the horse's head to the left.

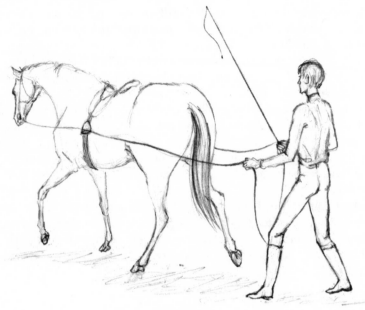

Long reining

Adding Weight

Somewhere between the first and third year, usually sooner than later, a horse will be introduced to the weight of a rider on his back. The process is not usually accompanied by the wild bucks and snorts one might expect after watching wild horses broken in TV westerns. For months the young horse has worn a saddle (as well as a bridle) while lunging, with the gradual tightening of the girth during schooling sessions. The rider leans more and more weight on a horse in stages until it reaches the point where he actually mounts. Then the rider is walked around either on a lunge or a lead.

At this final point of elementary training, the voice commands the horse has learned are coordinated with legs, weight, rein, seat, and other riding aids. When the rider says "walk," he applies calf and seat pressure as his mount goes forward. When he says "whoa," he stops the movements of his hands and braces back, sits down in his saddle simultaneously. Over several weeks, the horse is trained to go into a trot and later a canter with the rider's voice and body as simultaneous aids. Voice commands are eliminated as soon as the trainer feels they are unnecessary. More and more emphasis is put on the correct speed and balancing the horse at each gait.

Canter work is not begun until the horse is able to execute such simple figures in the ring as circles, half circles, and diagonal changes of direction and is able to maintain a good rhythm at a walk and trot.

The horse should be bending around the rider's inside leg on a circle, so that the entire spine, from the base of the tail to the poll is curved in the direction of the turn and each hind leg is following the foreleg on the circle.

This has been a highly simplified explanation of how a colt or filly is trained—a subject that requires a book in itself. Training a horse is no undertaking for anyone less than an experienced rider. But by covering these training procedures here, you will know what your horse should have learned and what gaps in his education need to be filled or corrected.

And, of course, this is just elementary equine education. From here, you may want your horse to go on to graduate and postgraduate training depending on his breeding and temperament in such specialties as cutting, reining, jumping, and, at the highest level, dressage.

WORKING HIM OUT

Your horse should be worked, or schooled, at least four times a week to keep him in condition and responsive to your commands.

An enclosure of some kind is helpful for schooling. In a fenced-in area, you can be sure your horse's attention will be completely on you and not on how to escape to the inviting pasture next door. Working rings or corrals should be level and have good footing. The cost of bulldozing a small area like this can run between $200 and $400, depending on the terrain. A flat, smooth area in which to work your horse can make all the difference in his performance. After leveling, seed the middle so that it doesn't get muddy in wet weather, and put stone dust around the working track to absorb the moisture. For simple exercises, you can get by with a ring of 45 × 85 feet. But if you'll be jumping, 75 × 100 is the safe minimum.

If you don't care about the expense, a two- or three-board fence with a wide gate looks elegant. But a four-foot snow fence tacked on to wooden posts is just as efficient at a fraction of the cost. The former can run from $400 and up; the latter as little as $225 (for 80 × 100).

Mounting and Dismounting

Before doing any kind of work on your horse he must be taught to stand for mounting and dismounting. Not only is it functional, it's a sign of good manners. It's a must in showing, whether for pleasure classes, road hack, or equitation classes, but also for hunting or on trail rides—in short, in any situation requiring frequent getting on and off.

Nothing is more annoying to a rider than a horse backing away as he tries to mount. If the horse hasn't already been taught, it's worth all of a rider's time to break the habit.

Hold the reins at the length you will be using for riding so that your horse can't move forward. Never mount a horse with long reins or with one rein longer than the other. It's helpful for a not too advanced English rider to drop both stirrups down to riding length before

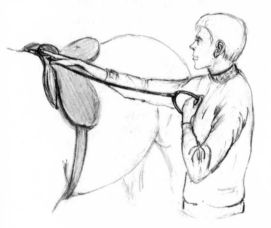

Measuring stirrup before mounting

Adjusting stirrup while mounted

getting on. You can do this by extending your arm so that your fingertips are on the safety bar of the saddle. Pull the stirrup leather taut until the bottom of the stirrup is under your armpit. This gives approximately the right stirrup length.

If you prefer to adjust the stirrups from the saddle, keep your foot in the stirrup, moving it back on the girth to allow you to unbuckle the stirrup leather and rebuckle it at the right length. In adjusting the girth from the saddle, you also keep your foot in the stirrup, putting your leg forward so you can lift the flap of the saddle and pull the billet straps up. You have better leverage for this in the saddle than on the ground.

When you mount, never allow your horse to drop his head to graze. Besides getting your bit dirty, this, too, is bad manners—and, as pointed out, a potentially dangerous habit in a child's mount. While some Western bits are especially designed for grazing—movable shanks that bend back—it only invites trouble.

In the Saddle

You are now in the saddle; your horse should remain standing until you give him a specific signal to move forward.

When a horse hasn't been worked for a long period, his reconditioning must begin slowly, the way an athlete would train. It takes anywhere from six weeks to two months of regular periods of daily exercise to get a horse fit for a hard two- or three-hour ride. Work him no more than twenty minutes daily for three to four days, beginning and ending with a period of walking.

He should **walk** along briskly and rhythmically, not shuffling with his head down by his knees, or stumbling. Use your seat and legs to push your horse's hindquarters well under him, thereby lightening the forehand and helping him to move in a longer, more rhythmic stride.

A brisk walk

Trotting is an excellent gait for training, schooling, and building muscle, either in the ring or cross-country. After walking around the ring for a few minutes in both directions, get your horse to move out into a **working trot.** This is a rhythmic, two-beat gait, with a noticeable forward energy. The hind leg should be stepping into the track of the front footprint. (This can be taught on the lunge.) The horse should be using his hindquarters to propel himself forward. This enables him to maintain a steady pace and carry himself properly. Should the horse become lazy, the rider applies pressure with seat and inside of his calf, with further assistance from the whip if the horse is slow to respond.

This is the horse's **ordinary trot** (approximately eight miles per hour). A Western horse is expected to jog, a slower, shorter stride. The horse must be balanced and maintain an even tempo, not lie heavy in the rider's hands.

An **extended trot** is not faster, but a horse should increase the length of his stride by engaging his hind legs well up under his body, which lifts the forehand, creating the second of suspension before the foot strikes the ground. When done correctly, the hind leg of the horse should overtrack the footprint of the front foot. The tempo is steady, and the horse shouldn't look as if he's trotting into the ground—a fast trot and a heavy trot are often passed off as an extended trot at horse shows. It is not uncommon to hear a Western-horse-show judge ask the entries to "trot on" and to see Western riders posting.

Ordinary trot

The **canter** (or **lope**) is relaxing for your horse when he is in condition. It is a slow, collected gallop; a three-beat gait, which takes training. Don't expect a young or green horse to do it automatically.

The ordinary canter should be a forward-swinging gait, with the rider taking care to see that the horse maintains a sure three-beat tempo —which is only possible when the hindquarters are being used correctly, driving them up under his body with each stride. The horse should not depend on the rider's hands for support. You can test this by putting your horse into a canter and dropping the reins; if he stumbles or starts to race off, you'll know you're doing something wrong. When properly balanced, a horse should be able to carry himself when the reins are dropped, maintaining a proper canter without relying on the rider's hands to hold him up. As I'm constantly telling my students, "He's supposed to be carrying you—not the other way around."

Proper balance at a canter isn't easy to achieve, but with enough work, it's an obtainable goal. If schooling is too hurried, as it often is with Western riders, a horse will be encouraged to adopt a four-beat canter—or worse. In other words, the horse is being forced to shorten his stride before the hind legs are strong enough to maintain this type of energy.

For the *canter departure,* whatever aids you have been taught should be used so as to make your meaning absolutely clear to the horse. You thereby avoid any likelihood of confusing him about which lead you want. A horse is said to be on his right lead when going clockwise in the ring; his right lateral legs move forward first. Going counterclockwise, the lead should be changed to the left. Training of the horse and rider is the key to a prompt canter departure from a walk, slow trot, or (more advanced) a halt. Wake up your horse a bit beforehand. This will help. Once you ask for a specific lead, don't settle for less, even on the trail.

Cross-cantering (when the horse is on the one lead in front and the other lead behind) is wrong any time. This is easy to feel even for a novice; it's awkward and uncomfortable. If this occurs, stop and begin again.

Ring work is essential for a horse who cross-canters frequently, leans on the bit, or goes too fast. Beginning with three-quarters of the ring and gradually making smaller circles will help. So will consistent work at the canter.

The **counter canter,** which is an advanced exercise where the horse is asked to canter on the wrong lead in the ring, should not be confused with cross-cantering. Because the counter canter is difficult (the horse has to be balanced, to bend in the direction of the lead he's on or into a turn, and not switch leads or cross-canter), it should first be done under supervision to be sure that you and your horse are ready for it.

Frequent changes of direction at a walk and trot hold a horse's attention, develop his sense of balance and agility, and steady a fast horse. Remember when turning not to jerk your horse's head around and to use the inside of your leg as well as your hands. All hand movements should be imperceptible to an onlooker.

To wake up a lazy horse and steady a hot one, it's important to vary the routine of schooling even more, with circles, turns, and half-turns. You might want to start out the session by interspersing the initial walking period with a series of halts, half halts (in which you check him), and backing.

Once he's been conditioned, try to exercise your horse in the ring at least three or four days a week, from one-half hour to an hour at a time, breaking up the sessions by taking him for a workout on the trail. Avoid too much of the same routine. Don't work him around and around in the same direction, or he'll get bored. Keep his attention by asking him to perform different turns and change his speeds at the trot and canter.

If done properly, an hour of work can accomplish a lot. Just remember not to pursue it to a point of boredom, restlessness, or weariness; he'll end up fighting you. If he does something well, don't make him do it again and again. Praise him and go on to something else, or stop for the day. Be aware, too, of his ability. If he's doing something as well as he can, don't keep hammering away for perfection. He'll get balky. With time he will gradually improve, if he is capable of it.

The Cavalletti

A cavalletti is unsurpassed as a schooling device. It can help train a horse to balance himself, maintain the correct speed and rhythm at a trot, and extend at a trot. A cavalletti is also a basic element in teaching a horse (and a rider) to jump.

Cavallettis can be simple and inexpensive, constructed of six- to eight-foot rails, or similar diameter (they can be as thick as a fence post but the diameter must be consistent), spaced equidistant to each other. Arrange them either flat on the ground or on wooden crisscrosses that lift them about six inches aboveground. The ground should be flat. If raised, the rails should be perfectly parallel to the ground. Cavallettis should be positioned in the center of the ring so as to allow a horse to turn in alternate directions after traversing them.

When starting your horse over a cavalletti for the first time, lay a single rail on the ground and let him get used to going over it. Then add another rail approximately four feet away. At a walk, your horse's feet should land between rails. If he overreaches, extend the second rail a bit farther. Strides vary from horse to horse but he should be able to walk and trot between the rails without hitting them.

When your horse can walk over two rails—straight and quietly—maintaining the same speed, add a third and fourth at the same distance. First get him to walk over them evenly at a brisk walk, progressing to an ordinary trot. Begin with three cavallettis and build up to about eight.

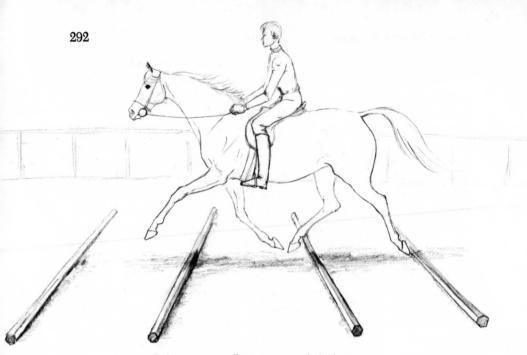

Going over cavallettis in a good rhythmic trot

You can use a series of cavallettis as a jumping exercise. Set up six rails at approximately equal distances, eliminate the fifth rail, and raise the last to jumping height, about one-half to two feet at first. The space between the fourth and sixth bar is what he'll need to take off in. Beyond the first jump, you can set up as many series of cavalletti jumps as you have room for, and can afford. The height and width can be increased and the space between jumps varied. But you should ask the help of an instructor when setting up such a complex series of jumps so as to determine your horse's stride correctly.

Cavallettis can help lengthen and shorten strides and teach a horse to adjust to sudden changes in distances between fences.

If you jump, or plan to, practice jumps that vary between two and a half and three and a half feet high, and simulate types of jumps you may face in the ring or hunt field. Also a variety of jumps will embolden your horse, so try him in as many heights and types as possible. A well-schooled horse will not hesitate to jump a strange obstacle—like those he'll encounter at shows and hunts. But never begin jumping without the help of an instructor.

DRIVING YOUR HORSE

Among the many advantages of driving, you can use a young horse a year or two before he can be ridden, depending on his build. Driving is a great way to get acquainted with a young horse and to build a sound base for later training under saddle. When taught correctly, driving develops the mouth of the horse, teaches balance, and builds muscles. Driving also allows you to use that pony the kids have outgrown.

When you're sure that a young horse (no younger than two years old) or a mature horse is familiar with all the steps of training on the lunge line, responds to all verbal commands (particularly "Halt!" and "Stand!"), and is performing all steps of long reining including circles and turns, you're ready to teach him in harness. This is done gradually, introducing no more than one or two pieces of the harness (see Chapter 9) at each schooling session (certain parts may take longer than one session), with special care and attention given to the crupper. The tail should be held carefully when you're putting the crupper on. And when in place, it should not pinch, pull, or rub if your horse is to accept it in a relaxed manner. Take your time when you're introducing a horse to harness. Many amateurs' horses are excellent for driving because the owners have taken a lot of time with each training step and have given their horses a sound foundation.

To familiarize a horse with the action of the shafts, short poles that run the length of the horse's body can be attached to the harness by slipping them through the tugs and tying them to the breeching with baling twine. After that, the horse is ground-driven, the poles flopping and slapping at his sides.

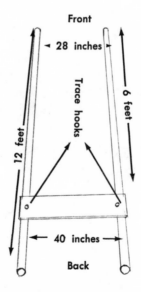

Travois or driving poles

To get her horse used to the noises of the highway, one friend of mine ties cans full of rocks to her belt, which will then rattle ominously as she steers him on the long reins. This lesson is essential to keep a driving horse from freaking out at the sound of the rumbling cart, which he is unable to see because of his blinkers.

Before actually hitching the horse to the cart (see Chapter 9), many people use a **travois,** a stretcherlike device that is easily homemade. Green wood is recommended for the frame so that the poles will have some resiliency but won't break. A travois makes a cartlike noise and slides sideways when the horse turns—but it won't turn over and won't go in reverse if the horse tries to back up. Before hitching up the travois for the first time, let your horse look it over closely. Then have a helper stand at his head as you lower the poles into the tugs. Never back a horse into the poles. Bring the poles up high, then lower them into position and slip them through the harness tugs. The same procedure is used when hitching a horse to the cart. The travois is used until the horse is completely relaxed with it and able to perform the simple exercises that he did on the long reins.

Patience and thoroughness produce a calm driving horse. It's not worth it to rush training. Once a horse runs away, say driving enthusiasts, he is no longer safe in harness. A runaway in harness is more dangerous than a runaway under saddle. So if you don't want to take the time to teach your horse carefully, be sure to find a qualified professional who will.

EXERCISE

Your horse's health and happiness—and habits—depend on regular exercise. While the casual workout he gets strolling around a pasture strengthens his legs, bones, lungs, and muscle, it can never, however vital, replace the rigor of regular workouts in the ring or on the trail. It is this that accounts for the long, hard, rippling muscles of a healthy horse; it also builds wind, and improves manners as well as discipline.

Exercise in its simplest form for a horse is the natural act of walking and grazing. Unless your horse is particularly delicate, he will therefore be much healthier if he spends most of his time outdoors. Left standing in the stall without regular exercise, he'll get irritable, soft, and may even "stock up" around the legs because of poor circulation brought on by enforced idleness.

Racing stables feel so strongly about the beneficial effects of walking that they invest thousands of dollars in walking machines (still less expensive than hiring grooms)—huge wheellike devices that lead a horse round and round before and after workouts. Long periods of walking build muscle, and they are very calming for a young, green animal.

In nippy weather, or if yours is a young or particularly green animal, you may find that in the morning he comes dashing out into the work ring, full of energy—more than you care to manage from his back. If so, you might turn him out for a few hours after breakfast to work off excess steam. Or you might want to lunge him to relax and quiet him.

Lunging as Light Exercise

Lunging is a marvelous means of taking the edge off a horse, giving him a light workout to keep him in shape, light exercise when he is recuperating from sickness or an injury, or as a routine warm-up procedure before every ride.

Twenty minutes is usually a good average lunging time; half an hour on days you won't be riding. Limit the first few learning sessions to ten or fifteen minutes, however.

Lunging can be taught very simply with a minimum of equipment. You can use either a bridle or a halter, plus a saddle; also a lunge rein (thirty feet for around seven dollars) and a whip (eight dollars and up), which are essential. A lunging cavesson (beginning at twenty dollars, but prices vary according to the materials used) is optional.

However, the cavesson is preferable to the halter or bridle because it leads the horse forward from the nose and enables him to reverse on the circle without the trainer handling him. If you invest in one, let your instructor show you how to use it the first few times. Many people

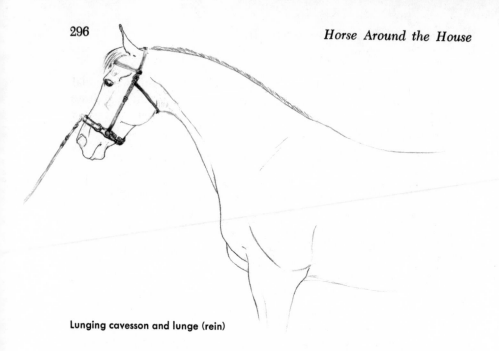

Lunging cavesson and lunge (rein)

lunge successfully with just a whip and a lunge line—and a halter or bridle and a saddle.

First tack up your horse. On an English saddle, run up the stirrups; on a western one, tie them beneath the girth with a leather thong. Making sure they're neither too tight nor flapping, secure the reins beneath the stirrup leathers.

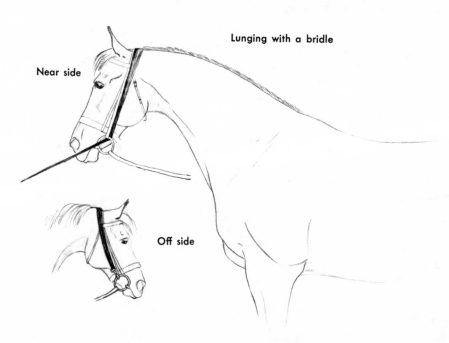

Lunging with a bridle

Near side

Off side

Put the halter on over the bridle and attach the lunge line to the dee ring under the jaw. Then you won't have to stop and reverse the line when your horse changes direction. You can lunge without a halter by clipping the line to the snaffle ring on the offside (if you're lunging him to the left) and pulling it over his poll and through the bit ring on the near side. Reverse the procedure for lunging to the right.

When lunging to the left, the line is in your left hand and the whip in your right. Stand at the center of the circle your horse is working (not necessarily the center of the ring) aligned with the center of the horse's body so that when he moves forward on the circle, he is less likely to turn toward you or pull away. Now guide him in a very small circle, gradually feeding out the rein until he has a large enough circle to move freely and still be easily controlled. With experience, the circle can be widened. The line should never be too taut and should not drop. Never pull the lunge rein, or you'll have the same damaging effect as pulling on the mouth. Nor is the whip to strike the horse with. Or waved frantically about. The whip takes the place of your legs in the saddle; it's an aid to keep your horse's hindquarters under him when he gets lazy.

Hold the whip waist high and snap it sharply when your horse fails to respond to a command. Do not overuse it, or he will eventually tune it out altogether.

At the beginning, make him "walk," "whoa," and "walk" again for several lessons before you add the trot. Make sure he's stepping out at a brisk pace and stopping on command. Should he fail to stop you can usually bring him to a halt by stepping slightly ahead of him. If he doesn't respond, thrust the whip out in front of him at waist height and repeat the command "whoa" sharply.

When you first have him trot on the lunge, make sure his gait is steady. Later, try to achieve a good working pace of eight miles an hour. Say "trot" with conviction and a snap of the whip if necessary. As with any exercise, be sure to change direction often so he doesn't get bored.

In giving commands, speak clearly, and compliment your horse when he's performed well (you'll probably speak up when he hasn't). He's more apt to learn to listen and to obey you.

After mastering the trot, your horse can go on to a canter. Cantering your horse on the lunge isn't necessary, though, unless it's for the purpose of training him to jump or for other advanced work. Getting a good canter on a lunge is difficult and you should have help from your riding instructor. However, because of the relatively small circle in which he travels on a lunge line, he usually has no trouble picking up the correct lead.

A horse that is being lunged for the first time may become balky and appear afraid of the whip. Therefore, get him used to the whip; carry it (or a crop) around in your pocket when grooming or feeding him and he should allow you to touch him with it. He'll eventually get used to it. He may also resist lunging to the right at first. This is normal because he isn't used to being led from the right side. After a few tries, he should catch on.

Don't Overdo

After a particularly hard day of schooling, halve the next working period to give your horse a rest. If you've ridden him in many classes at a show, he deserves at least a day of rest. He should be turned out to graze and relax in a pasture (a minimum pasture, not a lush one) after a show, not left to stand in a stall. If you have no place to turn him out, at least take time to lunge him at a walk for twenty minutes, or give him a short, relaxing ride.

Remember always to walk him after any kind of strenuous work to cool him out, to loosen the girth a few notches, with the saddle on as you walk, and, when removed, to rub him down or sponge him (in warm weather) all over to restore circulation. Begin at the poll on the near side and give a vigorous rubdown to all parts of the body. Many horsemen believe in slapping the horse's back vigorously to restore circulation.

A gradual increase in working time, combined with proper feeding and watering, will avoid excessive sweating. While some horses are more nervous than others and can work into quite a lather, heavy sweating on a hot day is normal.

But if it can be avoided, don't work your horse in extreme heat. Mornings and early evenings are best. Horses are subject to heatstrokes, so at shows don't keep yours out in the broiling sun too long; it's bad for his health and it saps his energy. See that he has shade and cool, not icy, water.

Trail Riding as Exercise

Even if you're not actively working your horse, never allow him to stumble along at a lazy walk or to set his own pace at a poky trot. It's how bad habits start, which will eventually have to be corrected in the ring if he is to remain serviceable. Every time you ride him, he's learning or unlearning something. The horse you take out will be a slightly different horse when he comes in—for better or worse.

Taking a trail ride and working a horse at the same time can accomplish much. It can be very challenging, in addition to improving your horse's balance and ability, to work in fields, particularly on hillsides. Keeping the same speed up and down hills is difficult; turns and diagonal lines are even harder. Don't do this type of exercise with a very green horse, and make sure to check the area out first for chuckholes and other dangers.

Uneven terrain will help your horse develop balance and agility. A few good climbs up a steep slope are excellent for his hind legs and particularly good training for a jumper or cutting horse that uses his hindquarters a great deal.

Trot him on the trail at a brisk eight miles an hour. He'll try to slow down when he's tired, but this is just the time to push him out and really make him work. He'll learn to pace himself this way.

One Western rider I know takes her horse out on ten- and twenty-mile rides the day before a show to relax him. Of course her horse is in excellent condition already and has been carefully built up to this type of work.

A long canter when your horse has been built up to it will do wonders for his wind. Remember to canter on both leads and not to

Correct riding position downhill—rider's body perpendicular to horse

Correct riding position uphill—rider's weight off seat

In both instances the horse is free to use his hindquarters to help himself

overdo it. You'll be able to tell by his breathing when he's had enough.

When riding uphill, don't be a dead weight. Raise up out of your saddle and get your seat and your weight up off your horse's back without hanging over his neck (a jumping position, if you're riding English); the horse needs his hindquarters to push himself up.

Downhill don't imitate the movies: the rider sitting back with his feet practically sticking up under his horse's nose. The proper seat for downhill riding should be perpendicular to the horse; you should be over his center of gravity in your normal riding position (your legs somewhere in the vicinity of his girth). This leaves your horse freer to move since he also uses his hindquarters to get down the hill. Allow some freedom in his head and neck, keeping only light contact with the mouth—but enough to hold him together.

Your horse should know what to do when confronted with an obstacle on a trail: he should go over it quietly. Contrary to popular opinion, a horse that has been trained to jump will not jump an obstacle unless it is big enough to merit the endeavor. He'll just walk or trot over small obstacles. A trained jumper is recognized by his ability to clear jumps with a minimum of effort and no more than a safe margin between him and the obstacle. Green horses tend to pop over fallen logs like rabbits.

RIDING IN COMPANY

If your horse is going to be used around other horses—at horse shows, in hunting, or on trail rides—part of his schooling must be done in

300

company. Nothing is more annoying to other horsemen than a horse who keeps overtaking and bumping those in front of him or who gets spooked at everything, or who is so neurotic about being left behind that he jogs all the time, or kicks out at other horses behind him.

A good trail horse should be able to follow as well as lead. He shouldn't shy at signs, garbage cans, bridges, trucks, or cars. Such commonplace things should be taken in his stride. But even quiet horses can be startled by sudden run-ins with the unexpected or in-experienced—seemingly quite ordinary things. While riding a quiet, well-mannered school horse down a country road one day, my horse froze at the sight of a woman pushing an elegant black baby car-riage. He began blowing out of his nose, trembling, and rolling his eyes. He couldn't make out the strange, black, hooded apparition ap-proaching him. It took me a while to realize what was bothering him. He'd never seen anything like it before. I should have anticipated it—and anything else that might scare him.

When riding down the road in a group, go single file, leaving about a horse's distance between each other. Be sure to observe state laws regarding traffic. If you must go on a heavily trafficked road, walk. Trotting or cantering is dangerous if there is a chance of falling in front of an oncoming car. Paved surfaces are hard on a horse's feet and legs; and if your horse slipped on macadam or concrete, it could be a disaster for you both.

Take nothing for granted on the road. Lots of riders assume that cars will slow down for them. This isn't so. Some motorists seem to get a kick out of blowing the horn or performing in some manner on the way by. Always get over as far as possible on the shoulder of the road.

Have it understood among your group that the lead rider will notify

everyone, by voice or hand signal, when they are to change gaits. When those up front suddenly break into a canter the rear riders haven't time to collect their reins and could get hurt. If someone should fall off, the group should stop immediately to investigate and give aid; the riderless horse instead of bolting will be more likely to rejoin the group or to stop and graze.

If at some point you're going to ride two abreast on the trail (never on the road), keep about three feet between you so that your stirrups won't hook or your horses bite. Be aware of your horse's mood. Remember his flattened ears and bared teeth; it's not a friendly mien. Should he seem to take offense at being passed, stop and turn him so that his head is now toward the other horse and his hindquarters are turned away. Of course you can do this with your leg pressure. When

Passing on a trail, rider at left turns his horse's head toward and rump away from other horse

you pass an unfamiliar horse, be sure to leave more than kicking distance between you. If you have a horse that kicks, place a red ribbon on his tail; it's the traditional warning to others.

Many riders fail to observe these and the simplest courtesies on the trail. Don't ever race on the trail. Your horse should become accustomed to holding steady gaits in company. And the lead horse on a trail ride should set the pace with gaits that are not too slow or too fast. Should your horse ever take off with you, you can stop him by applying a pulley rein, meaning that you set one rein short and pull up with the other. This throws a horse off balance, and he'll usually stop. An alternate and effective method is to turn him in smaller and smaller circles until he has to stop. Always punish him for this kind of behavior by making him back up—when you eventually stop (and maybe it's time to go back to the ring for a little homework).

If you plan to ride on trails or on roads that don't belong to you,

Pulley rein—setting left hand on horse's withers and pulling up on right rein

always ask permission. And be very careful to treat the land with respect, avoiding lawns and gardens and field crops. The surest way to lose riding privileges is to ride across a beautiful lawn or a newly planted field. And close gates after you. Also, it's only proper to be courteous should you encounter the owner.

11

etiquette, attire, and events

. . . On Saturdays, most everyone is well turned out: proper clothing is worn, horses are braided, tack is clean. During the week, however, only a few make an effort to be presentable. . . . Ninety percent of the members feel that they must impress someone with their bizarre equine wardrobes. Only the Master and a handful of the Field observe the dress code. The Master is always correct, her horses impeccably clean, their manes and tails meticulously braided, her person neat and attractive. . . . I appreciate her conscientiousness. . . . As for the individuals in the field, shape up or ship out.

—EXCERPTS FROM
AN ANONYMOUS LETTER TO THE *Chronicle of the Horse* BY A "TRADITIONALIST."

Just as certain bits go with certain bridles and specific trims are typical of specific breeds, particular clothes are more appropriate to one riding situation than another—for practical as well as traditional reasons.

Some instructors are very strict about riding clothes, dismissing students who appear for lessons without a jacket or who have long hair or improper boots.

Some beginning pupils of mine have turned out in dazzling displays of creativity, such as velvet bell-bottoms and sandals with a red leotard top. Almost every summer day some neighborhood kids ride by my

kitchen window, all the girls barefoot, clad either in bathing suits or shorts with halter tops, and long hair flowing. A passing motorist who didn't know much about riding once found it marvelously bucolic and romantic. But he didn't see them the day after as they limped along the road in their miniskirts, knees scabbed and blue.

I don't insist that a pupil buy a regulation outfit until he or she decides whether or not to stick with riding, but I do have requirements, even for the first six lessons, which are on the lead line: hard shoes and long pants.

Comfort and utility should be the criteria by which riding clothes are judged. In fact, most regulation attire, however elegant and expensive, originally was designed with function in mind. The scarlet coats worn by experienced members of a hunt, for example, were intended to distinguish fox hunters from harriers (rabbit hunters) and stag hunters that might be encountered in the English countryside, where the custom originated.

It takes only one set of sores on the inside of your knees to realize that shorts and baggy pants are not suitable for riding. Also, long waist sashes or elaborately fringed vests get tangled in the equipment. And a rear view of a beribboned, sequined rider jangling about has alarmed many a horse.

Sneakers or sandals have no place around a horse at all. Neither do bare feet. Wherever horses are, there are tetanus germs, which can be communicated through a single scratch. So you don't want to take a chance. Furthermore, a horse weighs a great deal, and toes are no match for a shod hoof. Boots at least offer something of a buffer. Besides, sneakers are dangerous to ride in because the heelless rubber soles slip easily through the stirrups.

Often novice horse owners forget about the cost of clothing when figuring up the expense of their new sport. But there will be a certain minimum you should budget for. Depending on your style of riding, it will range from $80 to $125. And this novice English kit will include only the cheapest of boots, pants, shirt, and hat. Each type of riding has its own basic clothing rules, which, for the most part, are sensible.

ENGLISH RIDING CLOTHES

Jodhpurs go with jodhpur boots and **breeches** with high boots. Any other combination would look silly since jodhpur boots end at the ankle and breeches at mid-calf. Saddle-seat riders wear their jodhpurs flared or bell-bottomed around the ankle (called Kentucky jodhpurs), which look good with their longer stirrups and a park saddle, but these and the saddle-seat riders' special flared jackets are inappropriate for other riding styles.

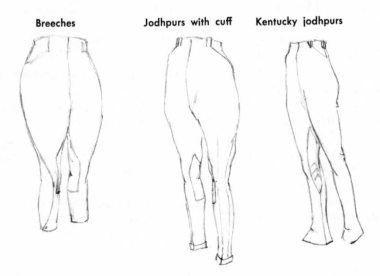

Breeches   Jodhpurs with cuff   Kentucky jodhpurs

Men's frontier pants   Exercise chaps used by
                                         English riders

Riding pants are primarily for comfort. Both with jodhpurs and breeches the traditional flared sides give a rider room in the hips and seat. (Since stretch fabrics have become popular, the fullness in the thighs has become less exaggerated.)

Jodhpurs for everyday use can be purchased either in cotton gabardine or in cotton or denim stretch fabric. For English pleasure riding, straight saddle pants are also available that are much like Western frontier pants in design. Pants of all styles run around fifteen to eighty dollars ready-made.

The traditional breeches with high boots are practical for hunting and jumping. The pants either button, lace, or tie below the knee; the boots cover the buttons or lacing. Breeches are available in denim, cotton gabardine, wool, and corduroy. For showing, there is a more expensive, custom-fitted pair.

Many types of expensive, washable—and long-wearing—stretch breeches are now available. They fit the body like a stocking, and they come in all sizes and traditional colors. The four-way stretches are priced from $44 and up.

Some pattern companies that specialize in riding apparel offer kits of these stretch fabrics, with a pattern, at reasonable prices. If you enjoy sewing, this is a great way to sidetrack a tremendous investment in riding clothes. The mothers of several of my students have copied vests, jackets, and chokers. I once made a dozen chokers in different fabrics and colors as gifts for junior riders.

Jeans as an alternative are impractical for riding because the heavy side seam rubs against the leg when pressed against the saddle. And without pants clips, jeans ride up. Often, Western riders wear frontier pants, the type that are specially designed with a smooth inside seam. Frontier pants are often used for show because of their tailored appearance.

Those who work around horses a lot wear **exercise chaps** over jeans. These keep their pants from slipping and help grip the saddle. Exercise chaps are usually made of suede. Chaps keep your legs warm for fall and winter riding, and they are also practical when riding through rough country, brush, or low branches. They are practical, good-looking, and expensive, averaging fifty to eighty dollars a pair.

Whatever the riding style, women's hair always is tied back in a braid or bun or worn in a hairnet. Some boys' hair should be worn this way too. Flowing locks may be fashionable at times among both sexes, but they are very impractical in the saddle, tending to fall in the rider's eyes or mouth when he is jumping or trying to circumvent a barrel in record time. Also, long hair looks terrible straggling out from under a hat. Most classes at shows call for a neat, workmanlike appearance.

High boots offer protection and support for the leg while jumping. Because they are expensive, junior riders who may be jumping but not immediately showing might prefer jodhpurs with a **garter strap**. It fits around the leg just below the knee to keep the pants from slipping up and wrinkling. It is used frequently in England by children as well as adults. For children their use avoids that lost-in-high-boots look.

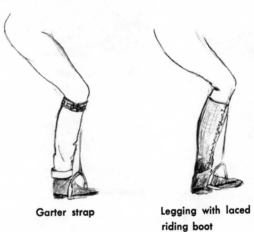

Garter strap   Legging with laced
                      riding boot

Equal in cost to high boots is a canvas legging worn over breeches with a laced riding shoe, often worn at informal hunts or shows. But high boots are more convenient and serviceable, though people who wear leggings sing their praises.

Depending on the quality of the leather and the workmanship, English high boots range from $60 to $125 ready-made and $200 and up custom-made. One can compromise by buying ready-made high boots, having the calf section fitted. But it won't look as neat as a custom-made boot, which is closely fitted down the entire leg and cut well at the top.

High boots come in several kinds. Brown field boots, originally designed only for casual riding, are now replacing the traditional black and patent-topped boots in the show-ring. Newmarket boots are made of canvas, with a leather foot and a piece stitched to the inside of the calf, for cooler summer riding.

High rubber boots for wet weather are becoming more and more popular, especially in rural areas. Rubber boots make grooming cleaner

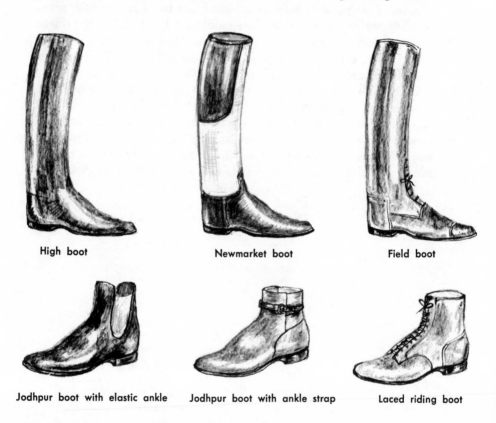

High boot   Newmarket boot   Field boot

Jodhpur boot with elastic ankle   Jodhpur boot with ankle strap   Laced riding boot

and walking around muddy paddocks easier. They cost around forty to fifty dollars and help preserve good boots for special occasions.

If you invest in a pair of high boots, be sure to include high-boot trees so the backs will get proper support and won't break down.

I prefer to use **jodhpur boots** or a laced riding shoe for casual riding. When you're on your feet a lot, they're most comfortable. Also the laced shoes can double as a good walking shoe. Jodhpur boots with elastic ankle pieces or straps that buckle around the ankle cost between thirty and fifty dollars, depending on the quality of the leather and type of fastening.

Care of boots

To keep the pores of your leather boots from clogging, be sure to let muddy boots dry thoroughly before brushing them off. Never wash mud in. Boots can be sponged off lightly so dirt doesn't become imbedded. Use castile or Ivory soap and a minimum of water. Dry the boots thoroughly at room temperature and apply a light leather conditioner like Lexol. This replaces oil, opens pores, and allows the leather to breathe. Remember that too much conditioner shortens leather life and can rot the stitching. When conditioner is dry, apply a light coat of cream polish.

Always use **boot trees.** You can buy fancy custom-made wood trees for $135 or plastic ones for $12 to $14. If the cost of the boots has temporarily exhausted your budget, improvise with crumpled-up newspapers stuffed in your boots. The goal is to keep the empty boots from sagging out of shape by reinforcing them. Avoid trees that create a lot of tensions or distort the shape of the boots.

A **hard hat** is absolutely essential for anyone who jumps or does any kind of fast work. The only safe and approved hat has a safety harness that goes around the ears and chin and has either a flexible brim or is brimless. The former keeps the hat on your head and protects you from the impact of a fall or a blow; the latter prevents a broken nose in case of a fall.

The United States Pony Club Association has set standards for protective head gear that have been adopted by the American Horse Show Association for their Junior Jumping and combined Training riders. In all organizations, including the United States Combined Training Association, where this rule is applied a rider is subject to elimination if he or she should jump a practice fence without the

Helmet with safety harness

required head gear properly secured.

A basic helmet that fulfills the safety requirements starts at $40.

Gloves protect the hands and complete the costume in the show-ring. They are an essential part of a driver's attire, whether for pleasure or show driving. I personally find them an essential part of everyday riding attire. Driving gloves should be of soft, pliable, durable leather and should be two sizes larger than the size you normally wear, to make certain they'll be long enough for your fingers. The gloves will give you a stronger grip and keep the reins from cutting into your hands. Gloves should be used always so as not to alter one's touch on the reins. String is advised for the palm of the gloves because it won't slip in wet weather as leather does. In summer, cool, hand-knitted completely string gloves are practical; in winter, pigskin gives more protection. For working around a horse, lightweight work gloves, like garden gloves, are a good idea.

In spring and fall, even for casual English riding, it's nice to have a riding shirt that fits well and a wool tweed jacket. For shows, there are appropriate seasonal jackets.

A further word on driving attire: any comfortable, practical clothes are suitable for driving around home. In shows, the type of horse you're driving and the class will determine how formal your dress is. Driving colors are traditionally conservative, and the clothes are tailored. Men wear derbies and women, floppy-brimmed hats. Except for the most formal classes, sports jackets or suits are acceptable.

Lap robes, knee rugs, or aprons are usually required in competition to protect the driver's clothes from the dust of the road, keep off the chill, and prevent clothes from being stained with harness-dressing oil. Coverings should be dark and should blend with the upholstery. In short, "ladies" and "gentlemen" are expected to live up to that description when they drive.

The leading saddlery shops have detailed charts showing what clothing should be worn and when. The *4-H Horsemanship Bulletin*, put out by the U.S. Department of Agriculture, also has a list. Appropriate clothing for each class at a horse show is indicated in the Appendix.

WESTERN RIDING CLOTHES

A cowboy's clothes are all highly functional, just like his equipment. Originally **chaps** were a must to protect the legs from prickly thorns and brush as well as to insulate them from wind, rain, and cold. These were made of a woolly material for maximum protection. Nowadays they are usually made of suede; and some can be quite elaborate. Plain chaps start between fifty and sixty dollars.

Boots used to be shorter than they are now, largely because they were easier to put on that way. The heel was also higher in the old days, to hold the foot in the stirrup and to keep it from being pulled through when roping. High heels also dug effectively into the ground when a wrangler was "running down the rope" on a steer. Today boots have a variety of heel sizes and come in different heights, colors, and styles, many of them elaborately carved. A pair of plain western boots costs about thirty to thirty-five dollars, while a carved lizard-skin **pair** could run well over a hundred.

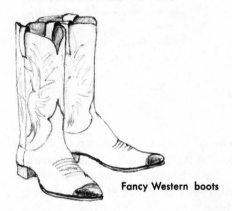

Fancy Western boots

Bandits weren't the only westerners to pull **neckerchiefs** over their noses. All cowboys did and still do in hot, dusty weather or windstorms.

Hats were designed with wide brims to act as sunshades during the long summer days on the trail. The high crown allows air to circulate underneath and keep the head cool. And the "ten-gallon hat" was so called because they were often used for drinking water—by horses as well as cowboys.

For casual riding, customary Western garb includes **dungarees,** or frontier pants, Western boots, and a Western shirt with button-down pockets. Hats are usually worn only in shows or at rodeos, as are chaps. Sometimes in shows Western riders wear an English riding jacket over a turtleneck shirt and English choker. For halter classes, exhibitors wear the dressier Western frontier suit—a tailored jacket, with straight frontier pants of the same color.

The highly decorative, spangled, sequined outfits traditionally worn by women in barrel-racing contests were originally designed to add a little sparkle to what began as a dusty, colorless men's sport in most far Western rodeos. For a while this kind of dress carried over to other

(*left*) Correct attire for horse show—

Hunt seat: hard hat, choker, shirt, jacket, breeches, high boots, gloves

(*right*) Dressy Western attire: frontier suit, shirt, tie, boots, hat

riders in the show-ring, where many contestants showed up in floppy earrings, balloon sleeves, sequined vests, and other paraphernalia more suited to a masquerade. These days the dress is more conservative, with riders favoring tailored suits and color-coordinated hats and shirts that are very similar to everyday dress.

TALLYHO

In the last century, when fox hunting was the prerogative of large English landowners, it was fashionable in London salons to make snide and witty remarks about the sport. Oscar Wilde delighted society by referring to fox hunters as the "unspeakable in pursuit of the inedible" and ever since then the sport has been maligned and joked about— usually by people who know nothing about it.

Some hunting enthusiasts feel that junior riders learn more about horsemanship in the hunt field than anywhere else. Hunting demands a high degree of equestrian skill, as much or more than riding or jumping on the flat in a horse-show ring. Hunters are all-around horsemen who know the importance of keeping a mount and equipment in top condition. And riding cross-country demands quick thinking and concentration to cope with a variety of changing situations.

Some conservationists and other citizens' groups deplore fox hunting on the grounds that it is a cruel and exclusive sport. Yet 99 percent of the time when a live animal is used, he eludes the hounds and "goes to ground." In a **drag hunt**, a type that is used where foxes are not abun-

314

dant, a burlap bag, a corner of which has been soaked in fox urine, is dragged over the grounds. The hounds follow the scent.

Hunting is exclusive in the sense that it takes money but no more so than any other expensive hobby—like sailing, skiing, golfing, or sport car racing. Membership fees are about equal to any other club's.

All hunts welcome visitors during the year. Some sponsor junior hunts for young riders and special hunts for adult novices. Those who don't want to hunt actively can follow by car or "hilltop" on horseback, led by a hunt member.

Hunts depend on their communities for their existence, and usually half the budget is raised through public events like rummage sales, hunter trials, or auctions. Members go to great effort to keep the fields up and fences mended. And during a lean winter, the huntsman even puts food out for the foxes.

Joining a Hunt

If there is a hunt in your area and you feel qualified to participate, you can call the secretary of the hunt. If visitors are welcome, tell her you would like to hunt on the next visitors' day. She will send you a fixture card, stating the time and place where the meet will start.

On the day of the hunt, arrive a half hour early and be in your saddle and ready to go before the meet is to begin. Ride up to the Master (who may in some cases be a woman) and introduce yourself. Visitors customarily pay a capping fee (it originally was collected in the huntsman's cap) to one of the staff soon after their arrival. Check with the secretary of the hunt.

During the hunt, visitors should stay to the rear of the field; juniors should be at the very end. Leave at least one horse length between riders when hacking. Never talk during a check (an interruption of the chase); the huntsman has to listen carefully to the hounds.

Hunt Attire

At a formal hunt and on opening day of the season, the horses are braided up and members and guests wear regulation attire. During midweek, members wear less formal clothes. During the cubbing season in late summer when the young hounds are being trained, they wear "ratcatcher outfits"—usually tweed jackets, brown boots, ordinary hard hunt caps, and casual (ratcatcher) shirts.

Hunt clothing is largely dictated by tradition now, but before scarlet became the customary color worn by experienced members of a hunt, the colors of the livery of the Master of the Hounds were worn. This tradition is still followed in parts of England, where yellow, blue, and other colors are in use. Scarlet coats are often called "Pink" coats, not for any difference in shade but because it was the name of a fashionable nineteenth-century English tailor. Much of the clothing and equipment originally were very functional. The stock was originally a long, white linen bandage worn around the neck of the rider in case either horse or rider was injured. The stock fastens with a plain gold bandage pin, worn horizontally. Leather sandwich cases and silver brandy flasks are carried on the saddle. On long hunts, members often have a drink to warm them or a snack at checks.

Hunt Staff

Members of the hunt staff include the **huntsman,** who carries wire cutters and a pocket knife, the **Master,** who carries the horn if he is hunting the hounds (or if a professional huntsman is employed, he will carry it), and the **whippers-in,** who carry a set of *couples* (a brace used to keep two hounds together) and spare stirrup leathers, draped over the right shoulder and buckled under the left arm. All staff members carry hunting whips, with a long thong used to control the hounds, with a horned handle on the end with which to open gates. Velvet hunt caps or hard hats, used by many English riders for schooling, jumping, and showing, are worn only by members of the staff and children during a hunt. The other riders wear derbies.

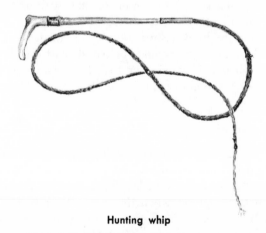

Hunting whip

There are special classes (Corinthian) in A shows that require members to wear formal attire suited to their positions in the hunt, and they are judged on their appointments. Bridles must be sewn, an extra pair of gloves tucked away under the girth, and the sandwich case and flask filled with the traditional contents. Peanut butter and Coke won't do. The sandwiches have to be ham or cheese and the flask can be filled only with brandy. All this is carefully checked out by the judge.

Guests at a hunt should wear a black melton jacket, canary vest, beige, fawn, or canary breeches, black boots, and a riding shirt with stock. The hat should be the hard hat of the correct type, mentioned above.

SHOWING OFF

Horse shows are a good place to measure your progress as a rider and to compare your horse with others. Above all, they're a challenge. Even when a class is based on the performance of your horse, it is your riding ability that will bring out his best performance. Of course winning a lot of ribbons is excellent for the ego. And it raises the value of your horse.

At its best, showing is great fun. At its worst, it's a neurotic pastime where winning becomes the only thing that counts and sportsmanship is forgotten. If you go into a show just to win, you're in the wrong ring.

Many different organizations sponsor horse shows, all with a number of classes open to different styles of riding or types of horse. Some shows are referred to as "recognized." These are given under the auspices of the American Horse Shows Association, which keeps a record of the proceedings; and they are the only shows at which points can be accumulated entitling you to enter some of the larger horse shows in the country—like the Harrisburg National and the National Horse Show at Madison Square Garden.

In horsey areas, a number of other organizations sponsor unrecognized shows, where the competition is often high and a beginning rider can pick up valuable experience. Pony clubs, 4-H, charities, horse associations, schools, and fraternal organizations all underwrite the cost of unrecognized shows. These small affairs usually last a full day, with varying entry fees in each class running from four dollars and up. At most small shows, you pay the entry fee to a secretary at the judges' stand when you arrive. It is also done at some recognized shows. You'll be asked to sign a waiver releasing the show sponsor from responsibility in case of injury.

After paying the post entry, you'll be given a number to pin on the back of your jacket. Sometimes, if you're entering classes for both horsemanship and those in which your horse alone is judged, you will receive two numbers. Of course if you are taking two horses, you'll get a number for each. If you're a parent with several children and horses, your best bet is to put horses and children's names on back of the numbers so that they don't get mixed up.

Entering a Show

To find out where local shows are being held, call or write to the various clubs and get on their mailing list. Or join the AHSA (American Horse Shows Association) and get their rule book listing all recognized shows. Before signing up for classes, be sure to go over the prize list with your instructor, who will be able to advise which entries are best for you. Don't overdo it, and try to space out the classes so as to give your horse a rest. Unless you're trying to work toward a championship, four or five classes should be enough.

When planning for a show, allow for at least an hour before the first class to get in your entries and to acquaint your horse with his new surroundings. For example, if jumps are being set up in the ring, let him walk around the enclosure and examine them. Usually you won't be allowed to school your horse inside the main ring or on the outside course, but most shows have separate schooling rings or other areas available.

If a show requires a good deal of traveling, or if it is your first experience with a particular competition, try to stable your horse overnight on the grounds. It will allow him to get used to his surroundings and give you time for a thorough workout beforehand. While most riding clubs have facilities for overnight stabling, reservations should be made well in advance.

At a one-day show you should have impeccably groomed your horse before starting out so that he'll only need warming up and a quick cleanup before the events begin. Normally on show days you'll be getting up at dawn to get everything done before the trailer arrives— assuming that if you don't own a trailer you arranged for trucking weeks in advance. Should you live fairly near the show grounds, you may decide to hack over—but be sure to leave enough time for the ride over and to cool and rest your horse when you arrive.

Small shows are the most fun as a family affair, with everyone cooperating to shampoo and braid up the horse the day before and clean up the tack. On the big day itself it's nice to take a picnic lunch along. I'd advise packing some folding chairs and some type of sunshade for searing midsummer occasions. Don't forget your rain gear for those surprise summer showers.

You'll find, as you go along, that you keep running into the same people at shows until the events become a sort of social occasion. I've met a lot of new friends at the edge of the ring. The children enjoy it more, too, when they're riding with familiar faces.

The first few shows of the season are the most exciting. By fall, when school begins, most parents—and kids—are exhausted by the weekly or biweekly routine and are eager to return to trail riding or hunting.

But, all in all, the small horse show is an occasion the whole family can enjoy—and which a child can enter confidently without a $5,000 horse.

Recognized Shows

This type of horse show, sponsored by the AHSA, is open to all breeds and has a full spectrum of divisions and classes. They are rated A, B, or C, varying by the number of classes in each division and the amount of prize money awarded. Often the A shows will last three days to a week. Sometimes a recognized show will have a combination of A, B, C divisions.

A division is a group of classes designated for a specific breed or type of horse—or type of riding. Each selects its own champion and reserve champion. You'll find divisions for Arabians, Quarter horses, and Hunters (even for half-breds), for Saddle Seat Riding, Pleasure Riding, and Western Stock. At some A shows these are broken down still further—for instance, a class for Arabian mares or green conformation hunters. And there are often age and experience limitations for riders, with classes for twelve years and under or for novice or maiden horsemen (a term that refers to both sexes).

Because the best riders in the country appears at AHSA shows, the competition naturally is stiff. And the horses are usually very expensive purebreds. Unfortunately, a judge sometimes has been known to rate a rider on an expensive horse over an equally adept horseman on an inferior mount. Thus, an intermediate rider just starting out would be better off cutting his teeth in a local unrecognized show sponsored by an area riding club or by the 4-H.

Membership in the AHSA at nominal fees a year (one-half for juniors, meaning anyone under eighteen as of January 1 of a given year—the basis also for a horse's age) entitles a member to the monthly magazine *Horse Show*. This lists results from all recognized shows, and a rule book is provided, which has a calendar of all shows, where they'll be held, and a list of recognized judges and ring stewards.

Entry fees for individual classes in recognized shows run from eight to twenty-five dollars or more in stake classes. The higher rates prevail where the cash prizes are largest and the rating is the highest (an A show). Entries often must be mailed in advance. If so, additional post entry fees might be charged at the gate if such entries are allowed at all.

4-H Competitions

4-H clubs, financed by the U.S. Department of Agriculture, run shows all over the country, ranging from small local competitions to county and state fairs. At times these are run according to the 4-H's own rules. If a show follows the rules of the AHSA or the American Quarter Horse Association, this will be noted on the prize list (sent out before any show noting the various divisions, classes, and age requirements).

Many 4-H shows use the democratic Danish system of judging, which is easy on young egos, enabling a child to compete, in effect, against himself. In any given class, for example, there might be five or six blue-ribbon winners, rated first blue, second blue, and so on—with cash prizes for each at county and state fairs. Or the judge might decide that none of the riders deserved a blue but that all were riding on a red level. This method of judging increases the chances of a child riding a swaybacked, Roman-nosed horse winning a ribbon.

The cash prizes give a child a chance to earn money for clothes and riding equipment (or maybe to pay feed bills). However, no show should be looked at as a way to make money. Usually the prizes you win barely cover the entry fees and cost of trucking.

Unfortunately many times the expense of the horse is overemphasized at large shows and proper horse care almost forgotten. It's very discouraging to note that among junior show riders, there are a few who regularly win blue ribbons at A-rated shows, who don't know how to put on a bridle or care for a horse. Pony clubs and the 4-H are very valuable in this respect.

The 4-H rules can be a little odd. Sometimes classes will be open to all children under eighteen. Consequently, a child of ten will find himself competing with a teen-ager. Or equitation classes will be split into pony and horse divisions, although equitation is supposed to be judged on the rider alone. But in general these shows are well run and fun to go to. Points accumulated at local 4-H competitions will determine whether a child is eligible for the state fair. You can get in touch with area 4-H clubs by phoning your local County Cooperative extension service.

Pony Club Competitions

Although Pony clubs sponsor horse shows, they go in more for group competitions or games like **gymkhanas.** They also hold **rallies,** at which members compete in teams. They stress sportsmanship. Children can compete equally against one another, despite the relative competence and expense of their mounts, because of the emphasis on stable management. Pony Club rallies are judged on dressage, cross-country, and stadium jumping, and stable management, in addition to a written test. After several years of Pony Club, a child will become a competent all-around horseman, not just a passenger. Also, experienced pony clubbers help teach the newcomers.

To find out what Pony clubs are in your area, write to the National Pony Club Secretary, Pleasant Street, Dover, Massachusetts 02030.

The American Quarter Horse Association

This group (not to be confused with the National Cutting Horse Association, which sponsors cutting events open not only to the quarter horse especially but to all breeds) sponsors a variety of shows and contests, and it awards points for a horse's ability and conformation.

This association has been devised to maintain the high quality of the breed. To receive a championship award or Register of Merit Listing, a horse must win a required number of points at halter and performance. The number of points awarded is determined by the number of entries in a class. Approved performance events are cutting, reining, roping, barrel racing, English pleasure, Western pleasure, Western riding, and working cow horse.

While the AQHA has its own book of rules, some of its shows are given under the auspices of the ASHA, and points can be accumulated toward association shows. A small annual membership fee includes a free rule book.

Taking a Look at the Judge

Whether a show is recognized or not, most judges will be selected from the rule book of the American Horse Shows Association. This ensures that the judge has passed an AHSA exam and has gone through a trial-judging period in the company of an experienced, recognized judge. Recognized judges are marked in the rule book with a large *R* alongside classes that are his specialty and a small *r* beside those in which he has passed a written test.

A good judge should be quick and efficient. Those who seem to take forever and keep working and working a class generally are less competent. After you've been showing awhile, you'll get to know the various judges and learn their likes and dislikes.

Obviously this is partly subjective, but all judges have their prejudices. If you are convinced that a judge is inferior, avoid his or her shows. But even if you go anyway, and lose, don't start yelling foul or have a temper tantrum. This is incredibly bad sportsmanship and in terrible taste. A surprising number of people—often adults whose children are riding—will upbraid a judge (who is getting paid to judge) for failing to place them or their children.

Granted that some judges are better than others and that subjective factors enter in, most are still highly qualified horsemen who know a great deal more than the contestants. So don't take it as a personal affront when the day isn't filled with ribbons.

Parents who take it hard when their children don't win are breeding bad sportsmanship by putting the emphasis on competition and victory, rather than on the fun and challenge of showing. Usually behavior of this sort stems from a lack of knowledge of a class and the inability to see a child objectively in it. Sometimes overenthusiastic parents will put their children in a class or show that is beyond the child's or horse's capabilities. Attending a number of horse shows and learning how and what a class is judged on would eliminate most of these hard feelings.

If you're really puzzled by the way a judge has placed a class, or if you would like some constructive criticism of your performance, there is no harm in trying to speak to him at some *convenient* moment in his schedule, and in a reasonable manner.

I've tried to encourage my pupils, when they don't understand the way a class was placed or why they failed, to speak to the judge during a break in the show. A lot can be gained by finding out what you or your horse did wrong, and good judges usually keep notes on their cards about the performance in each class. Often a criticism that the child has ignored from parent or instructor will finally sink in when the judge says it.

Avoid assailing judges after every class, however. His job is difficult enough, and he can never make everyone happy.

Remember too that shows are partly a matter of luck. Judges can't see everything that is going on in the ring at a given time. You may have seen the winning horse cantering on the wrong lead, but the rider corrected it before the judge had a chance to spot it. You'll have to learn to roll with punches like this.

And although it's difficult to accept, a child mounted on a well-bred, nicely coordinated animal looks better in an equitation class than a child of the same ability riding a homely backyard horse—even though the class is supposed to be judged on riding ability alone.

If you don't want to show, there are other events at which you can compete or demonstrate or develop your capabilities with a horse:

GYMKHANAS

Gymkhanas are like field days, a group of informal games, with classes like barrel racing or pole bending for Western riders, egg and spoon races, and even musical chairs—with burlap bags in lieu of chairs. There are saddling and bridling classes, in which riders are sometimes asked to ride to one end of the ring with a halter and lead shank, saddle and bridle their horses, and race back. The number of classes is really only limited by the imagination of the sponsors. In one California show, competitors rode bareback tandem, back to back, and were judged on their seats at a walk, trot, and canter. Gymkhanas are particularly good for children and adults who have limited riding experience, because there are always lots of strictly fun classes that everyone has an equal opportunity to place in.

ENDURANCE RACES AND COMPETITIVE TRAIL RIDES

This sport probably originated in middle Europe around the turn of the century, when members of the Prussian cavalry rode from Vienna to Berlin within a set time—the winner being the officer who came closest to the prescribed time. The U.S. Cavalry adopted the sport in the 1920s, sponsoring five-day, 300-mile endurance rides in which a horse was expected to average sixty miles a day.

In 1936, the Green Mountain Horse Association took over the sport, becoming the first civilian organization to sponsor a competitive trail ride. One of the most famous competitive rides in the country is the

Vermont 100-mile ride. In this ride, competitors cover 40 miles on each of the first two days and 20 miles on the third. Riders are expected to complete the first 40 in not less than six and a half hours and not more than seven. The 20-mile stretch—usually the most grueling part of the test—is to be completed in not less than two and a half hours and in no more than three. One of the most grueling of the dozens of endurance rides staged across the country every year is the California Tevis Cup, in which competitors must ride 100 miles from Lake Tahoe, California, to Auburn, California, in twenty-four hours or better. The trail follows an old 1849 miners' road, climbing to 9,500 feet at one point and descending 12,250 feet at another. The strain taxes the limits of any horse's capabilities. (There are many competitive trail rides over shorter distances of 35 miles to 50 miles.)

To compete in any of these rides requires an all-round horseman who knows how to put his horse in top condition before the event, how to pace him, and care for him during, as well as before, the ride. The winning horse of an endurance ride has traveled the course in the fastest time and arrived in the best condition. Competitive trail rides on the other hand are judged on the basis of timing (horse and rider must arrive at the finish line within a given time) and the condition of the horse. Each horse is thoroughly examined by a vet before starting out, and again at various points along the route and at the finish. Endurance and competitive rides are open to both English and Western riders. Awards are sometimes given to the highest-placing horse of each breed (Arab, Morgan, Thoroughbred, and quarter horse).

Traits desirable in endurance horses are in addition to soundness, conformation, and willingness to move forward the desire to eat and drink even when exhausted. This helps the animal to recuperate faster and, of course, prevents dehydration.

COMBINED TRAINING

These are events of one, two or three days in which horse and rider compete in at least three phases: dressage, endurance (which includes cross-country over obstacles), and stadium jumping. As in competitive trail riding, competitors must be able to condition, train, and pace their horses as well as be competent riders.

Combined training originated in the cavalry, where horses were expected to show obedience and discipline in dressage and close-order drill and to be bold and fast cross-country. Stadium jumping began as a way to entertain troops at Sunday horse shows. It demonstrates that the horse still has the stamina and speed to complete a course of jumps.

Since the U.S. Equestrian team won the world championship for eventing in 1975 and the Olympic gold medal in 1976, more and more amateur riders are taking up this exciting sport. It's rewarding because amateurs are allowed to compete—and feel that they have a chance—with any horse, whether he costs $400 or $4,000.

Eventing is governed by the United States Combined Training Association (USCTA) rule book and is divided into divisions, beginning with pretraining. In some areas of the country, USCTA sponsors special "chicken events" to encourage timid junior and adult newcomers and weekend riders. Jumps in cross-country chicken events are about two feet six inches and in pretraining events about three feet.

Cross-country fences are usually constructed of logs or rails or of natural obstacles like banks or water jumps or stacks of hay bales. The rider must cover the course in three hundred and fifty meters a minute (or thirteen miles an hour) at pretraining.

The pretraining dressage test is based on American Horse Show Association (AHSA) training level test one. As the rider progresses to a higher level, the dressage tests become more difficult and the endurance phase becomes longer.

In stadium jumping, riders must clear between eight and ten obstacles in a set period of time. The height and width of the jumps is determined by the rider's level of experience.

Eventing has become popular because so much depends on how well the competitors have schooled and conditioned their horses. Also, the horse is judged and competes on performance only. And it's a great way for riders to build up confidence.

HUNTER PACE AND HUNTER TRIALS

These are usually sponsored by active hunts to raise money and in most cases are for seasoned horses hunted regularly in the field. A **hunter trial** is held over typical hunting country: uneven terrain with natural obstacles. The course is generally one or two miles long, and they are great fun for competitors and spectators alike. It's a delight to watch eager riders and keen horses working over natural country.

Trials have a variety of classes for junior hunters, as well as for the field, staff members, and tandem teams of three hunters. Judging is based on riding ability as well as the way the horse goes.

In a **hunter pace**, riders go out in tandem pairs across a marked course of typical hunting country, usually five to seven miles long (sometimes there are modified courses for horses not hunted regularly). The top teams must navigate the course in an ideal time—

usually 360 yards per minute—which again requires that a rider be skillful in pacing his horse. Sometimes the course is ridden in advance by a member of the hosting hunt team whose time is revealed after all the teams have finished. Occasionally the winners are selected by taking the average time for the combined teams after they have completed the course. The winner is the team that has come closest to the average time. Hunter paces also have what is called a "race for the mask" (the mask is the face of the fox) in which the object is to traverse the course as fast as possible. This derives from the importance of staff members' staying up with the hounds during the hunt.

The type of field hunter that excels in these competitions bears no relation to the conformation hunters that win all the ribbons at A shows. The latter are usually too high strung and physically unsuited to stand up to a day in the hunt field.

For the rider who wants to demonstrate his all-round knowledge of horsemanship, there is a real challenge to be met on endurance or competitive trail rides or in the hunter paces or horse trials; the condition of the horse determines the outcome, and riding skill involves much more than the ability to sit and look pretty on a horse.

While large recognized shows offer a lot of top competition, to do well requires excellent instruction, lots of experience, and a well-bred

horse. All this takes money, as does the high entry fees and expense of vanning. Although there are a few talented youngsters who have made it without money, by working part-time and depending on their clubs to supply them with horses, they are rare exceptions. Entering the National Horse Show at Madison Square Garden is not within the reach of every good rider of modest means.

You may decide that you don't wish to compete at all but are amply rewarded by frequent riding and daily care of your horse and the development of a rapport between you and your equine friend.

12

getting
along
together

In the days when horses were man's most popular and dependable
mode of locomotion, persons who had an above-average rapport with
them were credited with supernatural powers. Known as "whisperers"
because of their practice of mumbling supposedly secret words in the
ears of obstreperous mounts, these pied pipers of the equine world
were supposed, generally, to be able to tame and charm any horse, no
matter how wild. Among the tools of their trade were talismans like
toad bones (blanched and dried in an anthill), oil of burdock, and
hoofs from dead horses nailed above the stable door. Citizens with
problem mounts paid high rates for the services of these sorcerers.

A whisperer could probably make a pretty good living today. There are thousands of ill-mannered horses across the country that a little patience, understanding, and discipline disguised as witchcraft could correct. Anyone who keeps a horse around the house will eventually have to learn a little bit of such sorcery if he wants a happy relationship with his mount.

One key to getting along well with a horse is to view him as a fellow creature rather than an object for entertainment.

While sympathizing with your horse and respecting him, you must also establish that you are the boss. He may be stronger, but you have the edge on brains. Just as good stable manners should always be rewarded with a pat or kind word, or, in the case of a young horse, an occasional treat, when a horse behaves badly, he must immediately be punished. A spoiled horse is as annoying as a spoiled child—and twenty times as dangerous.

BAD MANNERS

Some of the more common bad manners not to be tolerated in any horse:

Biting. Pupils at times complain that their horses bite. When I ask if they ever hand-feed them, the answer is always yes. Hand-feeding is a sure way to teach a horse to bite you, and if you've been doing it, stop.

A horse that is hand-fed learns to look for a snack and starts to nuzzle, push, and beg whenever you come around. At first this may seem like a cute and endearing trait, but sooner or later, your horse will become irritated at not finding a snack in your pocket and give you a nip. Around children, this is particularly dangerous.

Should your horse try to bite you, the immediate punishment is a smack on the nose, accompanied by a sharp "no." If done fairly (obviously not too frequently), this won't make a horse head shy. The next step is to get your horse accustomed to eating snacks out of a feed dish or bucket. Even when you're only offering him a few carrots, cut them into strips and put them in an aluminum pie pan, not in the palm of your hand; and don't carry them around in your pocket.

Young horses, particularly colts, tend to be more oral in their greetings than adults; and biting is often an expression of affection. So if a one- or two-year-old tries to nip you, his intentions are probably good. However, whatever the age, if his ears are flat back, he's not being affectionate. With young horses, you may find that any punishment becomes sort of a game; the horse will try to get in a nip and pull back before you can smack him. About the only thing to do with this sort of youthful behavior is to stay out of biting range and warn others to do the same. Your horse will eventually outgrow it.

Cow-kicking. When a horse cow-kicks (kicks out sideways with a hind leg when you are grooming or mounting), he should be hit hard across the rump with a crop, as well as reprimanded verbally. Some authorities advise an even more extreme punishment—returning the kick with the side of the foot in the stomach. But a crop is just as effective. If you've been kicked while saddling or grooming, it may be partly your fault or someone else's. You'll have to punish the horse in any case, but in the future slide the saddle easily into place on his back and tighten the girth gradually. When grooming with the curry, remember that he might be ticklish or sensitive. Watch his ears and expression.

Cow-kicking

Not standing for mounting. A horse that won't stand for mounting is a nuisance in the show-ring and on the trail. This habit would disqualify him in a hack or pleasure class, but apart from that it is simply inconvenient and undignified to have to hop after a horse with your foot up in the stirrup. Teach your horse to stand until you have

adjusted your stirrup, gathered up your reins, and mounted. Only then should he move out, and only because he's been asked to. Difficulty here could be caused if you tug on the saddle, or stick a toe in the horse's side when you mount, thudding down in the saddle, or trying to mount with long, loose, or uneven reins. If you're having difficulty mounting, let your stirrup down three or four more notches than usual rather than pull on the saddle. Then adjust to proper length when mounted. This is an acceptable procedure even in the show-ring.

Rubbing or butting the rider. When leading a horse after coming in from a ride, he is usually hot and itchy and will, if allowed to, try to scratch his head against your shoulder. This can be hard on you, as well as your clothes. A horse's head has a lot of weight behind it, and an emphatic rub of the head can knock a child down and throw an adult off balance. Any pleasant riding horse should be taught not to treat people like trees and fence posts. If your horse tries this, say "no" sharply and slap him on the neck.

Grazing during a ride. I've already mentioned this but it's worth elaboration. Many ponies have particularly strong necks, and when they stop suddenly in the midst of a ride to graze, a young rider is apt to be catapulted off. You can prevent this sort of behavior by always keeping a firm hold on the reins and maintaining a light contact with your horse's mouth. A horse should not be allowed to graze, even when standing, and should be punished by voice, or, if he persists, with a smack on the rump with the crop. Ponies with this habit should wear an antigrazing sidecheck.

Crowding in a stall. Crowding is extremely disagreeable and potentially very dangerous. In a straight stall, after you pat your horse on the rump and say "over," he should immediately move over. Don't enter the stall until he does. Should a horse indicate by the set of his ears (or a leg) that he has other ideas, speak firmly to him and carry a crop where he can see it. When a bad actor like this finally does obey you, give him a pat to encourage continued good behavior or put a treat in his feedbox.

In a box stall your horse should be taught to face you when you enter. Swinging the rump around toward you or crowding—habits that can develop through rough or careless handling—are unfriendly acts. In most cases, behavior like this is a bluff. But if it isn't, you don't want to be on the receiving end. So move out of the way with alacrity, yet not in a frightened, jumpy manner that will scare your horse or give him the idea that you are afraid.

In the future when you enter the stall, take your horse by the halter and tell him to "back," with a hand on his chest, before bringing in the grain. Then hold him back from the feed dish as you pour the grain in. When leaving the stall, turn him to face the doorway as you exit. Some trainers feel very strongly about stall behavior and its relationship to a horse's entire manners. In one large stable that has three hundred head of purebreds, the horses are taught to stand in the middle of the stall as the attendant pours the grain, and they don't approach the feed dish until he has left. The trainers consider it routine good manners.

Frequently, bad stall behavior is inadvertently caused by the owner. One horse I board, who has the best stable manners of any I've ever known, came back from a summer at home with the habit of kicking out when his feet were picked up. It turned out that the boy who owned him had been picking up his feet in the pasture without first tying him. Naturally, with nothing to stop him, he eventually tried to walk away (reasonable behavior under the circumstances) and became annoyed when the boy pursued him trying to pick up his feet.

If the boy had just taken a few minutes to tie his horse properly, the habit wouldn't have developed. After three or four sessions, we managed to correct the situation and the horse became his normal, well-behaved self again.

Pulling away while being led. If your horse tries to pull away as you lead him or while you're unsnapping the lead rope, he's learned the habit through poor handling. Review the chapter on leading from the near side.

When leading your horse into a pasture, take him all the way inside and turn him to face you before unsnapping the lead or removing the halter. Children often unsnap the lead before a horse is through the gate. This creates problems when the animal decides halfway through that he doesn't want to go in. With his rump toward you, it will be difficult to change his mind.

Running off in the pasture. The practice of slapping a horse on the rump and yelling "yah" after unsnapping the lead will encourage him to try to break away as soon as you open the gate of the pasture, often kicking up his heels as he departs. This can be dangerous if you happen to be in his way. When you unsnap the lead, say "easy" and encourage the horse to leave you in a quiet manner. This will make it easier to catch him again, too, because he will be more apt to trust you.

If you have bars across the pasture instead of a gate, slide the bottom one first. Otherwise you will encourage your horse to rush through as you bend over to undo the bottom bar.

Never lead a horse with anything but a regulation lead rope in good condition. Old clothesline and baling twine are out of the question.

A horse can be trained to come to you. It's a question of proper handling and winning his confidence. If your horse is difficult to catch, teach him to approach you by offering treats or grain in a bucket for a few weeks. You should also have a little foresight about what time you go out to fetch him. When a horse knows he will be ridden at a certain time of day, he'll get accustomed to being caught at that time.

The sure way *not* to catch a horse is to chase him around and shout when he eludes you. Yet this is the method employed by a lot of junior riders I know, who sprint around the pasture, yelling and waving carrots. Any horse will immediately sense that a child who behaves this way is just treating him as an object to ride. He's frightened by the noise and running around, and he won't trust his pursuers. The idea of being led away by one of them will seem most unappealing.

A horse that trusts his owner will enjoy the daily routine of being ridden and groomed, and he will either stand while you walk up to him or will approach you himself. (Some horses can be trained to come to a whistle.) Whenever my husband or I go out in the pasture to repair a fence, it's hard to keep a friendly muzzle from peering over our shoulders to see what's going on. Horses are by nature gregarious and curious animals, and they like the company of friendly humans and others. But they are also naturally nervous; in the wild, their reaction to strange sights or noises is to flee in fear, a trait that ensures their survival. So it isn't surprising that they should run from a posse of screaming children trailing lead ropes.

Leaving a halter on a pastured horse makes him easier to catch, but it also loses a lot of halters—which get buried in the mud or chewed off. Some horses make a game of chewing each other's halters. Halters can also get caught on trees or brush in the pasture; horses who scratch themselves behind the ears with their rear hoof—like dogs—might get a foot caught in a halter. I leave my halters on in the winter and take them off in the summer, which seems to work out pretty well.

VICES

Some horse habits go beyond bad manners and are serious personality problems. These are called vices, and they nearly always stem from a single cause: boredom.

Stall walking, weaving, digging, kicking, cribbing, striking, charging, chewing, and eating dirt are all habits that develop in horses who are stabled for long periods without enough exercise and diversion. Some of the vices are merely damaging to property; others are dangerous to horse and owner. High-strung, nervous horses are usually more prone to vices.

Stall walkers are in the habit of pacing or sometimes even trotting around their stalls for hours at a time. In a dirt or clay floor, this will wear a circular track, and it dirties all the bedding. It won't happen if your horse is let out to pasture daily or exercised regularly. Racehorses with this vice can be impeded in their tour of the stall by your placing obstacles in their paths—like rubber tires or bales of hay. Sometimes horses seem to enjoy the noise they make stall kicking, and if one horse in a stable starts doing it, the others are likely to follow suit. One boarder of mine who started stall kicking during an ice storm when he had been stabled several days was quickly cured of the habit after I resumed riding him every afternoon.

Weaving horses stand in front of the stall door or window and rock or weave back and forth on their front legs. I had one really neurotic

Thoroughbred boarder who did this all the time, and one of my pupils used to say she was dancing. It's a common vice among high-strung fillies, caused by nerves and excess energy. Weaving horses will lose weight from the increased exercise, and other horses can pick up the habit through observation. One veterinary authority recommends hanging tires, chains, or water-filled cans above the heads of weaving horses, rigged so that they will bump into them. But he concedes that severe weavers will become accustomed to the bumps and drips and work it into their routines. The best remedy is plenty of daily exercise and a window opening on the paddock yard to allow a horse to see what's going on.

Digging fortunately is a rare vice. It can be eliminated by putting the horse on wood or asphalt floors. A digger will scoop out huge holes in a dirt or clay floor, sometimes as deep as three feet. This is obviously dangerous because the horse can fall into the holes. A classic remedy is to fill the holes with water. I think it would be easier to change the flooring—or sell the horse.

Kicking at the stall walls can become a vice unless it is corrected early. As mentioned before, it can be corrected by striking the horse with a crop on the rump. Usually, careful attention to his daily exercise and keeping grain rations regulated to the amount of work he's doing will stop this symptom of boredom. The horse usually likes the sound of the noise. It should be immediately discouraged since others in a barn are quick to learn, and, aside from being rough on your stable, it can develop blemishes on the horse, or damage his hocks and tendons.

Cribbing, or wind sucking, is the most common of all the vices. It occurs when a horse grasps an object with his front teeth, pulling back and up with an arching movement of the neck and gulping in air at the same time. Often horses will chew the wood off their hay cribs—hence the name cribbing. The vice can develop with horses that need their teeth floated, and it can be learned from watching others. But the usual cause is boredom. Cribbing is obviously dangerous because the horse might swallow a splinter of wood, or he may get too much air in his stomach. To discourage the activity, put a strap around his neck when he's idle. It will press on his throat when he pulls his neck up.

Striking with one of the front legs often starts as simple pawing and can develop into rearing—a very undesirable and dangerous habit. Punish the horse by striking him across the offending leg with a whip or crop—making sure to stand to the side.

Charging. Some nasty horses will charge you when you enter their box stall or pasture. Again a whip is helpful in discouraging this bad behavior symptom. Trying to build up the horse's trust in you will cure the ailment.

Chewing, not to be confused with cribbing, is also dangerous because the horse may swallow sharp particles, get colic, wear down his teeth, or develop an infection from a splinter, or turn into a cribber. There are unpalatable liquids that can be painted on fences, stall doors, and hay cribs to prevent this.

Eating dirt in the pasture can indicate a mineral deficiency or parasitic infection, and the vice often leads to colic. The favorite dirt spots the horse chews on can be soaked with pine oil to discourage him.

When you know your horse will have to be stabled for an extended period, stall toys can be a useful diversion. A half rubber tire, a knotted burlap bag, a rubber ball, or a plastic bleach bottle with paper removed and some pebbles inside—any of these things hung from an elastic

string from the ceiling will give your horse something to butt around and chew on. Some breeding stables pamper their horses with all kinds of diverting toys. One trainer even put a mirror in a high-strung filly's stall to give her the illusion of company. A stable in Arizona soothes its occupants with piped-in music and keeps them cool with air conditioning.

But remember not to leave anything around the stall that you don't want chewed or played with.

Whether working in the stable or in the field, always remember to place valuable equipment, tack, and possessions out of reach. Once when my husband and I were out mending fences on an overcast day, he hung up his new expensive mackintosh over a fence post in case of a sudden downpour. A few minutes later we froze to the unmistakable sound of tearing cloth. Looking around we saw our two colts, each with a severed section of raincoat in his teeth.

HORSE SENSE

Some horses are smarter than others. But even those of relatively large intellect are not, compared to humans, very bright. Horses have tiny brains, with approximately the same reasoning capacity and attention span as a child in nursery school. But, fortunately, what they lack in logic is made up for in memory; and for this reason horses are fairly easily trained.

Apart from intelligence, a horse's senses are much more developed than ours. Their **vision,** for example, is superb. Like cats, they can see well in the dark. And except for a small blind spot, they have a much wider span of vision than humans, being able to see somewhat to the rear and side as well as to the front. (Some trainers believe that horses have a blind spot in front as well as behind, and for this reason many racehorses are equipped with nose or shadow rolls. But this has never been scientifically established.)

As any horseman knows, loud or unexpected noises will frighten any horse. Their **hearing** is particularly sensitive—the reason why it's important to speak in low tones when working around them. A horse confronted with a shouting child will react with visible annoyance.

Because horses have a highly developed sense of **feeling,** they can be trained to respond to various subtle riding aids—like seat, leg pressure, and hands. A horse's sense of **taste** is also quite refined, and some racehorses have been very discriminating about changes in water and their favorite foods—favoring things like sardines and artichokes. Others have more common tastes, going in for things like ice cream and hot dogs (a favorite of Kelso).

Probably the least developed of all his senses is that of **smell**. But it is still keen enough to enable stallions to scent mares in season, wild horses to smell water, and any horse to detect a rider's fear.

While novelists, savants, and farmers are fond of crediting horses with a sixth sense—claiming they can sense danger, sense a rider's fear, and predict weather changes—their skill at ESP will probably always remain a subject of fascinating conjecture.

Once you understand your horse's intellectual and sensory capabilities and limitations, you can see why certain human behavior is more appropriate in the stable than others. In addition to no sudden movements or loud or harsh tones of voice, in strange surroundings, always let your horse become familiar with the area by sight and smell before making demands on him. Before riding a strange horse, walk up to him and let him see and smell you, and when working with your horse, remember that he can't concentrate for long; so try to introduce as many diverting variations into his schedule as possible.

LEARNING TO LOAD

There are times in any horse's life when he will have to be transported. Should you be going on a lot of trail rides or to hunts or shows, these occasions will be quite frequent, and if you want to retain your sanity, it's essential that your horse be trained to load easily. Otherwise, you'll spend frustrated, anxious hours trying to get him in the trailer.

With a new horse that you know doesn't truck well or a young horse that has never been taught, it's a good idea—if you don't own one—to try to borrow a two-horse trailer from someone who would be willing to park it in your pasture for a few weeks. If this is impossible, rent one for the same purpose. It's time and money well spent.

Set the trailer up so that it's stationary, with the ramp down and the partition either open or pushed to the side, so that only one stall is accessible—but not allowing enough room to turn around in. Then begin feeding your horse all his meals on the ramp of the trailer. (Obviously this will work better in the summer when you keep your horse outside most of the time.) Nine times out of ten the horse will go up the ramp to eat. Every day, move the feed dish and hay farther and farther up the ramp until they are in the recesses of the trailer. By the end of two weeks, he should be willing to walk in and eat his meals out of the crib at the front of the trailer. One friend of mine trained her horses so well this way that they walk right in the trailer without even being led. She opens the back door and they walk in unattended.

It's important to follow up this kind of training with a quiet solo trailer ride. If a horse is banged around in the van by an incompetent driver, it will really turn him against getting into a trailer. So be sure, if you are paying someone to truck your horse, that he is a competent driver. Try to get someone who can be vouched for to be sure of a safe trip. Never allow your horse to be transported in an open truck or a homemade trailer, or one with a steep loading ramp.

If you will be driving the trailer, practice for a few days before you put your horse in it. It's tricky to maneuver a trailer when you're backing up. Make sure, too, to check that the brakes and brake lights are working.

When you are ready to load a horse, be sure everything is ready for him before you bring him around to the ramp. The doors should be open, the hay in the crib, and the escape door, if there is one, open. Don't rush your horse inside. Take time to walk him around the trailer and let him look the scene over. Then pause for a moment at the foot of the ramp so that he understands what you want him to do. Get him lined up straight and ask a friend or family member to be ready to hook the chain and close the doors behind him as soon as the horse is inside. If not done immediately, the horse will be able to back right out again should he change his mind. Then walk in, leading the horse, tie him with a slipknot, and go out the escape door. If there is no escape door, walk into the vacant stall when heading him in.

A very important safety measure: don't tie the knot or snap the horse in until the chain or bar is up. If you tie a horse first, without the chain up behind him, he can pull back and panic, break his halter, his lead—or both—and quite possibly injure himself. For the same reason, you always untie a horse before undoing the back chain.

If your horse shows a tendency to balk, avoid pulling him in. Have two assistants come from behind him, holding a rope across his rump, even with the base of his tailbone, pushing him gently forward (with a particularly difficult horse make sure they have a good grip on the rope). You might also, for extra leverage, want to attach a rope to each side of the back of the trailer, while someone holds each end of the rope to create a sturdy crisscross at the same point of the horse's rear as above. This way, the horse can almost be lifted into a trailer. But only resort to this method if yours absolutely refuses to move on his own. If your horse hesitates on the ramp, it may help to pick up a hoof and put it in the trailer.

Remember that the push and propulsion must come from behind. It won't do any good, although I've seen a lot of people do it, to stand in front of a horse and whip him across the face and neck. Losing your temper doesn't help either. If done properly and with patience, even the most difficult horse will learn to load. After a while, he will simply realize that he can't win.

Difficult loaders should always be rewarded with carrots or a few handfuls of grain when they get inside. Avoid feeding whole meals while your horse is on the road, however, because he will be too nervous to get the most nourishment out of it.

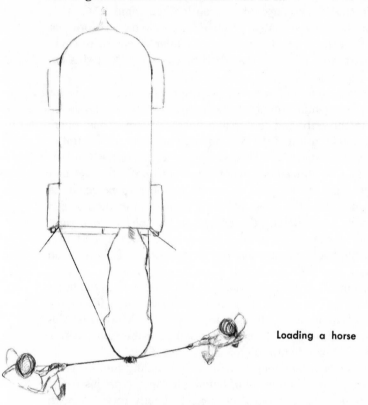

Loading a horse

When **unloading** your horse, untie him through the escape door first, toss the rope over his neck, open the back door, and then drop the back bar, or unhook the chain. If you drop the bar or chain first, he will pull back on the rope.

Have someone stand at the door to guide him down the ramp as he comes out and to grab the lead rope. If you're alone, move around very quickly to the ramp after starting him back. To get him moving backward, put your hand on his chest and say "back." Guide him down the ramp so he won't step off in an awkward position.

TIPS ON TRAILERS

In this day and age, the owner of a horse usually becomes the owner of a trailer. New trailers are expensive ($1,800 and up) and there are many types and styles to choose from: wide, long, high, or heavy. When you go out to look for a trailer, consider the size of your horse. Also, what will be pulling the trailer? A pickup truck or a car? How powerful is it? If you're using a car, I would suggest getting antisway bars as well as load levelers, which keep the back of the car from settling too low from the weight of the trailer.

I've discussed the pros and cons of various types of trailer fittings with friends, and they seem divided in their tastes about what they do and don't like. Floor-length center partitions, for instance, which I prefer, as do some friends. Others avoid them because they want their horses to be able to spread their feet. Some horses, on the other hand, will climb walls, but I think this is the fault of the driver.

Many trailers have a solid partition in front with a tray for hay. Others have a breast bar, and a hay net can be hung from a ring in the roof. I prefer breast bars because I have a horse who likes to bang his front feet against immovable objects, and a partition gives him a good target.

Opinion varies on ramps or step-in trailers. Some horses load more easily on ramps, while others are terrified by stepups. Horseowners who dislike ramps claim that their equine charges may take a crooked step off the ramp and be injured. If you use the proper precautions— either you or a helper stand and guide your horse away from the edge of the ramp with your hand after he's untied—such catastrophes can be prevented. One point on which everyone seems to agree is that every trailer should have an escape front door for the person who leads the horse in—ideally one on each side.

Two-horse trailers have ruled the road since the late 1940s. Though they're still popular, limitless options from which to choose now exist (with your imagination and budget controlling the limits). Today's trailers and stall areas generally run larger than they did in the World War II period.

Goosenecks are four- or six-horse trailers. They look like a two-horse trailer but they're longer and can be drawn by a pickup or a small truck, and in many places they're taking the place of vans. Many goosenecks and some two-horse trailers are equipped with a two- by four-foot dressing area, and some with luxurious living areas.

Keeping Your Secondhand Trailer in Shape

To keep your secondhand trailer in top condition, store it indoors in winter, and—if you can—give it a light coat of silicone wax before putting it into hibernation. Remove the rubber mats and recreosote the floorboards. Always remove all straw, hay, and manure to keep bacteria from accumulating and rotting out the floorboards (this should be done after every use anyway). Hose down the floorboards after cleaning.

As trailers age, they begin to leak in the seams. You can stop this deterioration by applying a latex caulking compound in the seams.

Used trailers range in price from $800 to $1,500, and they don't depreciate quickly. In other words, they are a good investment, if you take proper care of them.

Some tips on what to look for in a secondhand trailer or van:

- The floor: Remove the mats and see if the floorboards are rotten and require replacement.
- Check the metal underframe to make sure that it's not bent.
- Check crucial places around escape doors, ramp, attachments, the hitch, and any hinges, doors or rungs for rust. Make sure none of these essential parts is rusted through.

Trailers usually rust from the inside out, so be sure to make a thorough check of the inside, particularly near the center and the front partitions, on the sides near the tires, and—if it's metal—on the bottom near the ramp. When a trailer is rusted out, a horse could easily kick through, not only wrecking the trailer but tearing himself up badly. A friend of mine had a horse who did just this, kicking through the wall of the secondhand trailer just above the rear tire. His thick leg wrap was the only thing that saved him. My friend traded in that trailer the same afternoon, figuring after the vet's bill that a safe trailer was a less-expensive route.

When you're buying a secondhand trailer, it's advisable to take it to a mechanic who can check the electrical fittings, fixtures, and the bearings behind the wheels, which have to be removed and examined for soundness. Incidentally, this should be done regularly every year.

Always pay attention to the pressure in your trailer tires. A slow leak in one tire will put the trailer out of balance, and this can be a very frightening experience if you're heading downhill, since the trailer will lurch and weave and could turn over. So make it a point to take your trailer for regular garage checkups. And, when driving, be aware that you can't stop as quickly with a trailer behind you as you can with a car alone. Keep a distance of three or four car lengths between you and the car ahead. Always keep your brakes in good condition for just this reason. People who don't drive trailers are forever pulling out suddenly in front of you or are quickly jamming on their brakes.

GOING AWAY

I've mentioned that it's often a lot harder to find a horse sitter than a babysitter when you want to go away for a few days or on vacation.

But if you do find someone to come in, make sure that he is competent, and able to follow a feeding schedule, mend a fence if necessary, and recognize unnatural behavior in your horse. Have the horse sitter come by for a few days before you go away to go through the routine with you to make sure he knows what to do.

You may prefer to ship your horse to a stable for the time you'll be away. The cost of boarding out in the Northeast will run from around a hundred dollars a month (less if they grow their own hay) for private, rural farm to two hundred dollars and up for a stable in a suburban area. This will vary according to the kind of accommodations you want your horse to have. It's less expensive to have him turned out to pasture, more if he's stabled, exercised, and groomed.

When you leave your horse with someone, always leave the number of the vet and, to be on the safe side, a neighbor who would be willing to help catch your horse if the fence breaks down and he escapes.

THE SCENE SOCIALLY

Like all other animals, man included, horses observe a social pecking order. In any large stable, one horse will be the acknowledged king of the pasture with a descending hierarchy of lords, ladies, and serfs. As long as all the stablemates know their place, things will work out fine. But occasionally you'll find two horses competing for top billing, and then there's trouble. Usually this sort of situation is resolved in a day or two. But if it drags on longer than that, the two horses must be separated—for their own protection.

If you're introducing a newcomer to a pasture with two or three (or more) others, it's best on the first day to segregate him with your most dependable (friendliest) horse so the gang won't pick on him. After a few days move him in with the others, watching carefully for any signs of an uprising. Often the trouble comes not from the kingpin but from the low man in the pasture who sees the new horse as an opportunity

to improve his social standing. One of my horses, who is exceptionally mild mannered, with no status at all among his peers, and no apparent pretensions, recently spent a happy week lording it over a short-term boarder. The poor visitor cowered in a far corner of the pasture all day while my horse, mad with newfound power, stalked up and down imperiously to make sure he stayed there.

Occasionally a horse who has had the room at the top in one stable finds himself demoted socially when sold to another. A beautiful sixteen-hand Thoroughbred gelding who once reigned supreme in my pasture ended up at the bottom of the equine ladder in his new home, where he was chased mercilessly around the paddock by a Shetland pony.

GAMES HORSES PLAY

Horses are herd animals, and they naturally like company. With very close stablemates, this can present a problem, particularly when one is left behind. Some horses get hysterical when their friends leave, breaking down stall doors and fences to follow them. I had one hunter who used to jump over the gate whenever his stablemate was taken out on the trail. He came from a big stable where he had had constant company and had developed a real neurosis about being left alone.

Actually, since he demonstrated that he could get out any time he wanted to, he was quite reasonable about it, only hopping over the fence to follow his friend, and at mealtime, after popping a fence, he'd amble over to the stable and stick his head over the feed-room door as I fixed his dinner.

If you have more than one horse, one way to avoid this kind of situation is to separate stablemates frequently when young, and not always take them out together. On the trail, a horse that constantly looks back and balks at moving out won't be a pleasant ride. And it's no fun when you're miles from home to have a galloping stablemate suddenly appear on the horizon.

If you have only one horse and he looks lonely, you may want to get him a companion. Horses are fond of cats, dogs, chickens, ducks, goats—and, at my stable, even a racoon. One friend of mine has two stable cats that leap from the rafters to her horse's back, where they often nap. It doesn't bother her horse at all.

The racehorse Portico II was more renowned for her mascot than her prowess on the track. Her companion was a goat called Fainting Bill, so named because he often swooned from fright. Portico II was very protective of her horned friend, carefully covering him with a blanket of straw every night when he lay down to sleep. If anyone disturbed the goat's blanket, Portico II would get very angry about it, tear it apart, and make another one.

The famous Kelso shared his stall with a dog named Charlie, with whom he rubbed noses every morning. Nashua, a well-known track star in the 1950s, had a well-publicized friendship with a pony named Bill. Nashua's trainer recalls that the racehorse liked to come up behind Bill, grab the pony's tail in his teeth, and pull up until his hind legs left the ground. Then he'd suddenly let go.

Horses amuse themselves in all kinds of curious ways. In midwinter, it's not uncommon to see two stablemates basking in the sun on a snow-covered pasture with muzzles touching. Most horses also enjoy playing the "scratching game" in which they stand head to tail and scratch each other's withers or backs with their teeth, stopping every once in a while to break into a contented horse laugh.

In a group, horses like to play running games like racing and tag. At game time, they huff and snort and carry their tails high, making a docile, ordinary horse suddenly look like a graceful dressage horse. Sometimes two horses will line up side by side and race to the end of a field and back. Or one will tag the other with a bite on the rump and then race around the paddock until he is nipped in turn.

When you see two normally friendly horses rearing up at each other, don't be alarmed. Horses, particularly colts, often stage ritual fights modeled after the real fights that stallions have. They may try to grab a front leg with their teeth, coming down on their knees so that they look as if they are bowing to one another. Or they will strike out with their front feet as they rear up.

One yearling quarter horse filly I know likes to chase her tail. Even more remarkable, considering the short length of a yearling's tail, is that she occasionally catches it.

One of the greatest delights in having a horse around the house is the pleasure you'll get from watching him cavort with his stablemates in your pasture—or, as you sit on the terrace in the morning or the evening, watching him quietly graze.

Add to this the daily antics your friend will dream up to surprise you with, the satisfaction you'll have in working with him, giving him a good grooming or serving him a meal, and the pleasure you'll get from his nicker of greeting every morning. You'll no doubt agree with Robert Surtees that there "is no secret so great as that between a rider and his horse."

appendix

EVERYTHING YOU WILL NEED FOR A NEW HORSE

Sturdy lead ropes (2) with strong clips
Halter
Bridle
Saddle

Grooming tools (*See* chapter 6)
Stall cleaning tools (*See* chapter 5)

Feed dish
Fortex water bucket
Hay net for barn

Hay crib for pasture
Hay fork

First aid kit (*See* chapter 8)
Tack-cleaning equipment (*See* chapter 9)

Hay, grain, bedding (*See* chapter 4)

Stable and fence maintenance equipment (*See* chapter 5)
Inside stall or open shed (12 x 10 per horse)
Pasture area (preferably 1 acre per horse)
Enclosed working ring

Riding clothes (*See* chapter 11)

Optional
Heavy blanket
Cotton "sheet"
Leg bandages
Crossties

DO-IT-YOURSELF RIDING APPAREL

Where to send for catalogues, kits, etc.—Riding Togs (Division of Sewing Knits, Inc.), Box 1493, Boulder, Colorado 80306.

For English and Western riding apparel for men, women, and children; also saddle seat and hunt seat—Country Carriage Originals, CCO, Inc., Box 1192, Grand Forks, North Dakota 58201. Catalogue: $1.00

Saddle seat, hunt seat, English and Western; also horse blankets, and chaps, men and women—Lola Gentry Originals, Box 970, Dell City, Texas 79837. Catalogue: $1.00

MAKING YOUR OWN HORSE AND PONY BLANKET

Materials

4 yards (3.7 meters) of 45 inch (114.5 cm) wide machine washable fabric with firm body (denim is a good choice)
1 spool of thread of matching or coordinating color

5 to 6 yards (4.6 to 5.5 meters) of webbing for girth straps (available at some tack shops)

Twill or bias tape (doubled) or webbing made for upholstering or for hooked rug bindings

6 to 8 yards (5.5 to 7.4 meters of 2.5 cm) twill or bias tape for edges blanket (optional)

2 overall buckles

Supplies

Scissors	Iron and ironing board
Straight pins	Tracing wheel and dressmaker's carbon
Pencil and chalk	Large sheets of brown wrapping paper
Sewing machine	Transparent tape

Making your blanket

1. Enlarge the pattern shown below, then tape together sheets of brown wrapping paper to make a rectangle at least 6 feet (1.9 meters) long by 4 feet (1.2 meters) wide. Mark the paper into a grid of 6-inch (15 cm) squares and then mark a series of dots on the grid to duplicate the outline of the blanket as shown on the pattern. Connect the dots to make a smooth, continuous line.

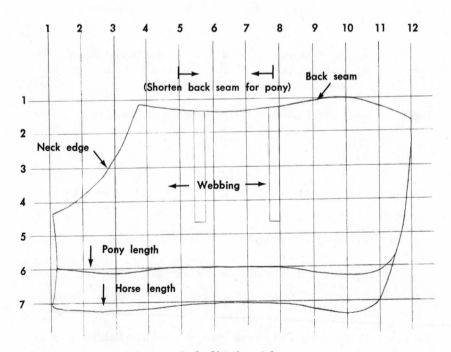

Scale: ⅜ inch = 1 foot

2. Fold the fabric in half, lengthwise. Pin the pattern on the wrong side of the fabric, with the long edge of the pattern along the selvage of the fabric. Using a tracing wheel and dressmaker's carbon, trace the outline of the blanket onto the wrong side of both layers of fabric. Mark the position of the webbing.

3. Before cutting, check to see if the back curve fits the horse's back. Machine baste across the back seamline. Drape the blanket wrong-side-out over your horse to see that it lies smoothly on his back (if not, pin a new curve that fits). Check the rest of the outline of the blanket directly on the horse to see that the size is correct. Any changes can be marked with a piece of chalk.

4. Add a half-inch (1.3 cm) seam allowance and cut along the correct outline.

5. Sew the two pieces together along the correct back seamline. Press the back seam to one side, and finish it with a flat felled seam, or zig-zag stitch both raw edges in place. Stitch slowly and carefully to make a smooth seam along the curve.

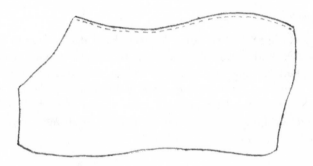

Blanket edges

1. Turn the edges twice (about ¼ inch or 6 mm) each and stitch in place. Use a straight, zigzag, or decorative stitch.

2. Finish the edge with double-fold bias tape. Fold the tape over the edges of the blanket and pin in place. Using a straight or zigzag stitch, stitch through both layers of tape and blanket.

3. Finish the edge with ½ inch (or 1.3 cm) of twill tape. Fold, press, and pin edges of the blanket ¼ inch (or 6 mm) to the right or wrong side, depending on whether or not you want it to show. Pin the tape flat along the fold, covering the blanket's raw edge. Stitch along both edges of the tape, using a straight, zigzag, or decorative stitch.

**How to make a horse and
pony blanket**

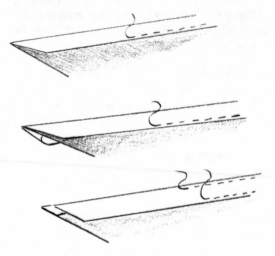

Attaching the webbing

Cut the webbing into two equal lengths. Fold each piece in half, and
mark the fold with a pin. Place the pin mark on the back seam at the
place marked for the webbing. Pin along the placement line to 15
inches (38 cm) from the bottom edge of the blanket. Do this for both
webbing strips on the left and right sides of the blanket. Sew in place,
stitching down both edges of the webbing and straight across at the
15 inch (38 cm) marks.

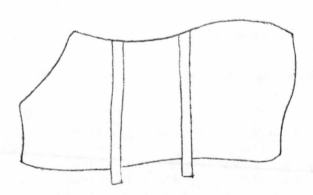

Attaching the overall buckles

1. Slip the ends of the webbing strips through the slots in the buckles and pin in place. Put the blanket on your horse. Fasten the buckles and adjust the webbing length to fit your horse. You might want to attach a strip of elastic tape between one end of the webbing and the buckles to allow more adjustment. Stitch the buckles in place.

Making chest ties

1. By using leftover fabric, leftover tape, decorative trim, or velcro, you can make ties to hold the blanket in place over your horse's chest. Buckles made just for this purpose are also available in tack shops. To tell how long the ties should be and where they should go, you'll need to try the blanket on your horse.

2. When making ties from leftover fabric, cut the material in strips 3 inches (or 7.5 cm) wide in the desired length. Press strips in half lengthwise with an iron. Then open and fold the long edges in to meet the center crease and press. Fold again, press, and pin. Topstitch along both edges and across one end.

MAKING A COOLER

You can make a cooler for practically nothing by using an old blanket and dyeing it to freshen the color, or by buying a kingsize blanket on sale. (A wool blanket isn't a good idea because you want to be able to throw the cooler in a washing machine.) Several friends have picked up new, full-sized acrylic blankets at white sales for around ten dollars to fifteen dollars. The only other materials they added were bias seam binding and cotton roping. (Binding can be used instead of roping if you're using a contrasting color and want all your trim to match.)

1. If you're using a blanket, remove the satin binding at the top and

bottom. Then place a saucer-sized plate on each corner to give a uniform curve to them. Trace with a pencil or pen and cut on the line.

2. Start in the center of one of the short sides and pin the binding around the edges of the blanket until you reach the beginning, making sure to leave enough binding to overlap the beginning by one inch. Cut off the excess, then turn the raw edge under ⅛ inch, overlap the start of the binding and stitch as close to the edge of the binding as possible, making sure you catch both sides.

3. Fold blanket, or cooler, lengthwise and mark the center front (head) and the center back (tail). For durability, it's a good idea to overlap the tail end of the blanket. Use cotton cord or binding for the brow band and tail tape. Cut one piece 14 inches long for the brow band and a piece 24 inches long for the tail.

Diagram of a cooler

4. Lay the blanket out flat and pin the ends of the cord to the blanket 6½ inches from the center front for the brow band and 11½ inches from the center back for the tail, on the wrong side of the fabric. Overlap the cord 1 inch over the edge of the blanket so the end can be stitched securely. Flatten out the cord slightly, cut 4 pieces of binding 1½ inches long, fold over the ends ¼ inch and place over the ends of the cord. Stitch in place following the pattern indicated.

5. For the ties, cut 4 pieces of binding 8 inches long. Turn under the

raw edges ¼ inch and stitch. Place one set a third of the width from the bottom of the blanket and the other set a third of the width from the top. And that's it.

6. Rain coolers are also simple to make, following the same directions as above but substituting heavy-duty sheet plastic (like that used for covering windows in the winter). Hem it on itself around the outside edge using a zigzag stitch. The hem can be sewn with a thread of your stable colors and match the cording of the head and tail. Also, felt initials can be added easily to give an all-over chic effect.

MAKING A SADDLE COVER

An easy-to-make waterproof, slipover saddle cover with heavy-duty elastic all around is the best protection for your saddle when it isn't in use.

1. Waterproof canvas, nylon, Naugahyde, or a similar vinyl material is easily obtained at larger fabric stores and often can be bought as remnants at big savings. A friend of mine used an old vinyl tablecloth. Whatever your choice of fabric, you'll need a yard of 60-inch material and 3 yards, 8 inches of heavy-duty elastic (less than ½ inch wide). Take your saddle pad, lay it out flat on a 60 × 36-inch sheet of paper. Trace around the pad with a bright-colored chalk or crayon, then add another 6 inches all the way around.

2. Place the pattern on the wrong side of the material, then trace around it with a crayon and cut on the crayon line. *Do not pin* the pattern to the material because the holes will make it less waterproof.

3. Fold the edges over ¾ of an inch and stitch very carefully ⅝ of an inch from the edge to form a casing for the elastic. Use heavy-duty polyester or nylon thread, leaving a 2-inch opening to insert the elastic.

4. Pin a large safety pin to one end of the elastic and insert into the opening. Push the elastic through the casing until it comes out the other side. Do not let the loose end go through the opening. You should now have both ends of the elastic outside the opening. Tie the loose ends together temporarily and place the cover over your saddle. Now pull the elastic until the cover fits snugly and knot again permanently. Remove from saddle, push knot into casing, fold over edge and stitch. You now have a saddle cover—and it needn't have taken you more than 45 minutes.

	ENGLISH RIDING			WESTERN
Informal, Morning or Afternoon Classes	Semi-Formal, Afternoon or Evening Classes	Formal, Evening Five-Gaited Classes	Formal, Evening Three-Gaited Classes	Western
COAT: Tweeds, checks, gabardine, or cavalry twill. Brown coat with tan, brown, or green jodphurs; black with gray jodphurs; or blue with blue tweed or dark blue jodphurs. Any conservative color is acceptable. Two- or three-button coat.	COAT: Gabardine, worsted, or other men's wear materials. Inverted pleats in back and one or two buttons in front. Dark colors preferred. Linen or tropical worsted for summer.	COAT: One button, inverted pleats. Tuxedo mode in black or midnight blue gabardine or dress worsted; soft pastel colors can also be used.	COAT: One button, inverted pleats. Tuxedo mode in black or midnight blue gabardine or dress worsted; soft pastel colors can also be used. Summer — white coat with shawl collar, satin lapels.	COAT: Men — stockmen's coat. Women—coat; suede or leather jacket can be, worn for pleasure riding. Where a coat is worn, it matches the frontier pants, making a western outfit.
JODPHURS: Gabardine, whipcord, or cavalry twill in colors to match or contrast with coat. Kentucky style—no flare at hip, bell bottoms.	JODPHURS: Same material and color as coat. Kentucky style — no flare at hip, bell bottoms, no cuffs.	JODPHURS: With black coat — black jodphurs in matching material. With pastel coat—black or midnight blue jodphurs.	JODPHURS: With black coat — black jodphurs in matching material. With white or pastel coat — black or midnight blue jodphurs. Satin stripe down outside of jodphurs.	PANTS: Frontier pants of gabardine, whipcord, cavalry twill, or cotton twill.
VEST: Optional—light solid color or tattersall check.	VEST: Solid color or tattersall check.	VEST: White pique.	VEST: White pique.	VEST: Optional — leather or beaded vest.
SHIRT: Man's shirt, white or colored broadcloth or oxford cloth; or plain or fancy ratcatcher shirt in pleasure riding.	SHIRT: Man's shirt, white or light color to match suit.	SHIRT: White dress shirt with wing collar and starched or pleated front; or man's shirt.	SHIRT: White dress shirt with wing collar and starched or pleated front; or man's shirt.	SHIRT: Western shirt in solid color or plaid to match or contrast with frontier pants.
TIE: Contrasting four-in-hand tie or bow tie.	TIE: Matching or contrasting four-in-hand tie.	TIE: With dress shirt — white bow tie; or black, maroon, or midnight blue bow tie and matching cummerbund. Continental tie is also acceptable. With man's shirt — dark four-in-hand or bow tie.	TIE: With dress shirt — white bow tie; or black, maroon, or midnight blue bow tie and matching cummerbund. Continental tie is also acceptable. With man's shirt — dark four-in-hand or bow tie.	TIE: String tie or Reno-type rolled silk scarf.
HAT: Semi-hard or hard derby to match jodphurs or coat. Soft felt is also acceptable.	HAT: Hard derby to match suit.	HAT: Hard derby.	HAT: Silk top hat.	HAT: Western hat.
BOOTS: Strap or elastic jodphur boots to match jodphurs.	BOOTS: Black or brown jodphur boots to match suit.	BOOTS: Black jodphur boots.	BOOTS: Black jodphur boots.	BOOTS: Western boots.
GLOVES: Optional — natural color pigskin or string gloves with leather palms.	GLOVES: Optional — natural color pigskin or same color as suit.	GLOVES: White gloves.	GLOVES: White gloves.	GLOVES: Optional—buckskin roping gloves.
ACCESSORIES: Cuff links, tie pin, belt, riding whip.	ACCESSORIES: Tie clasp, cuff links, belt, riding whip. Optional—spurs.	ACCESSORIES: Cuff links, formal shirt studs, riding whip.	ACCESSORIES: Cuff links, formal shirt studs, walk-trot stick of cane or hickory.	ACCESSORIES: Hand-carved belt or silver belt buckle. Follow show rules in regard to carrying rope or reata, romal, and hobbles. Optional—spurs and chaps.

SIDE SADDLE FORWARD SEAT OR HUNTING—Dark melton habit with matching skirt; black boots without tops; hunting silk hat, hatguard required; white or colored rain gloves. Neckwear, coat collar, vest, sandwich case, and flask same as Member of a Hunt. Optional—spurs. SIDE SADDLE SHOW SEAT—Habit of dark blue, black or oxford gray

RIDING	HUNTING AND JUMPING			
Western Horsemanship	Hunting	Hunt Seat Equitation	Member of a Hunt	Jumping
COAT: Western-cut coat.	COAT: Black hunt coat of melton, heavy twill, or shadbelly. Men may wear "pink" coat and, if members in good standing of a recognized hunt club, the club insignia on coat buttons.	COAT: Black hunt coat of tweed or melton. If members of a recognized hunt club, men may wear metal buttons with the club insignia and women may wear black bone buttons with the club initial carved in the button.	COAT: Black hunt coat of melton, heavy twill, or shadbelly. Men may wear "pink" coat or scarlet cutaway hunt livery. Collar should be same material and color as coat unless member has been invited to wear hunt colors. Buttons should conform to hunt livery.	COAT: Hunt coat in any color, solid or checks.
PANTS: Frontier pants, conservative in color.	BREECHES: With black coat—brown, tan, or buff breeches. With "pink" coat—white breeches.	BREECHES: Buff breeches.	BREECHES: With black coat — buff or brown breeches. With "pink" coat—white breeches.	BREECHES: Color to match or contrast with coat.
VEST: None.	VEST: Hunting yellow or hunt colors of member.	VEST: Yellow or hunt colors of member.	VEST: Buff, yellow, or hunt colors of member.	VEST: Solid color or checks.
SHIRT: Western shirt, matching or contrasting color with frontier pants.	SHIRT: Shirt with collar band.	SHIRT: Shirt with collar band.	SHIRT: Shirt with collar band.	SHIRT: Stock shirt with stock, ratcatcher shirt, or man's shirt.
TIE: String tie or Reno-type rolled silk scarf.	STOCK: White stock, fastened with plain gold safety pin.	STOCK: White stock, fastened with plain gold safety pin.	STOCK: White stock, fastened with plain gold safety pin.	TIE: Four-in-hand tie or stock.
HAT: Western hat.	HAT: Hunting derby or silk hat. If you have your colors and are not a master, professional, whipper-in, or huntsman, you have to wear a top hat when you wear a "pink" coat.	HAT: Hunting cap or derby, depending on age.	HAT: Hunting silk hat, hatguard required.	HAT: Hunting derby or hunt cap.
BOOTS: Western boots.	BOOTS: Black boots with tabs flying free. Tabs sewn on. Black boot straps; or white boot straps with white breeches.	BOOTS: Black hunt boots with tabs sewn on.	BOOTS: Regular hunting boots with tabs. Black calf.	BOOTS: Black or brown hunting boots.
GLOVES: Optional—buckskin roping gloves.	GLOVES: Yellow or white leather. String gloves under girth for rain.	GLOVES: Optional.	GLOVES: Heavy wash leather or brown leather. String gloves for rain.	GLOVES: Natural color pigskin or brown or yellow string gloves.
ACCESSORIES: Follow show rules in regard to carrying rope or reata and hobbles. Optional — spurs, chaps, shotgun chaps, or chinks.	ACCESSORIES: Stock pin, belt, hunting crop, spurs with black straps.	ACCESSORIES: Stock pin, unrowelled spurs. Optional —crops or bats.	ACCESSORIES: Boot garter, spurs, whip, sandwich case, flask.	ACCESSORIES: Belt, hunting crop, spurs, stock pin.

with matching or contrasting skirt; black jodphur boots; bow or four-in-hand tie; white shirt; hard derby; white or pigskin gloves. PLANTATION WALKING HORSE OR TENNESSEE WALKING HORSE—Attire should be same as listed for five-gaited, except that a pork pie hat should be substituted.

Courtesy United States Department of Agriculture

357

USEFUL BOOKLETS AND PLANS TO SEND FOR

Horse Barns and Equipment—5 barn plans. Publication #M-26. Available from the University of California Extension Service, Public Service Division, 140 Mark Hall, Davis, California 95616. *Cost:* $1.00.

1½-Story Horse Barn. Plan No. 6024 (1968). Order #M-1102. U.S. Department of Agriculture, Office of Information, Washington, D.C. 20250. *No cost.*

Saddle Horse Barn. Plan No. 5994 (1966). Order #M-1029. U.S. Department of Agriculture, Office of Information, Washington, D.C. 20250. *No cost.*

Barns and Equipment for Horses. U.S. Department of Agriculture, Office of Information, Washington, D.C. 20250. *No cost.*

Horse Equipment for Field Events. Plan No. 6014 (1968). Order #M-1085. U.S. Department of Agriculture, Office of Information, Washington, D.C. 20250. *No cost.*

Partial List of Horse Training and Horsemanship Schools. Order #CA 44–71. U.S. Department of Agriculture, Office of Information, Washington, D.C. 20250. *No cost.*

The Light Horse. (This has an excellent section on feeding, covering types of feed common to the West and Southwest; also two pages of illustrations of different types of knots.) Order #AXT 212. University of California, Agricultural Extension Service, Davis, California 95616. *Cost:* 50 cents.

Horsemanship and Horse Care. U.S. Department of Agriculture, Office of Information, Washington, D.C. 20250. *No cost.*

POISONOUS PLANTS

More than 700 species of plants in the United States and Canada are known to have caused illness at one time or another. No pattern of relationship, geographical distribution, habitat, season, or plant part can be successfully used to separate poisonous plants from those that are harmless.

Poisonous plants are everywhere and trying to eradicate them from a particular spot is usually impractical. Therefore, one should learn to recognize the most dangerous plants and be aware of the way in which they may cause trouble. Whether or not poisoning takes place is usually determined more by the management of animals than by the presence of a harmful plant.

Plant	Poisonous Part	Symptoms
Wild Plants		
Black locust	Bark, sprouts, and (less often) foliage	Nausea, weakness, and depression
Cherries, wild and cultivated	Foliage and twigs	Released cyanide acts within minutes to produce gasping, excitement, and prostration
Elderberry	Roots mostly, berries least	Nausea, digestive upset
Oaks	Fallen leaves and acorns or felled oaks	Gradual kidney damage from large amounts
Wooded Areas		
Baneberries	Foliage, irritant sap	Intensive digestive upset
Braken fern	Foliage mixed in hay or bedding	Nervousness characteristic of deficiency
Mayapple	Foliage and roots	Severe digestive upset
Wild Dutchman's breeches, jack-in-the-pulpit	Foliage	Chemically related to opium. Oxalate crystals embed in tissues of the tongue and mouth, resulting in intense burning and irritation. Death may occur if it causes base of the tongue to swell enough to block air passage
Swamps or Moist Spots		
Cocklebur	Seeds, burs	Nausea, depression, and weakness
Marsh marigold	Irritant sap	Intensive digestive upset
Water hemlock	Fleshy roots	Violent and painful convulsions
Fields, Meadows, Pastures		
Buttercups	Foliage contains irritant juices	Digestive upset

Plant	Poisonous Part	Symptoms
Common agricultural crops	When spoiled: sweet-clover hay, sorghums, sudan grass, and some clovers	
Corn cockle, bouncing vet, cow cockle	Seeds and foliage	Injury to the wall of the digestive system, destruction of red blood cells, severe digestive upset or death
False hellebore	Leaves contain alkaloids	Depressed blood pressure
Horsetail	Foliage	Vitamin B deficiency and nervousness
Nightshade, all members, including henbane, jimsonweed, and others	Foliage, particularly vines and green tissues, contains complex alkaloids	Intensive digestive disturbances, nervousness
Poison hemlock	Foliage and seeds contain at least five alkaloids	Nervous excitability, staggering, depression of vital functions, and death
Pokeweed, dogbane, celandine poppy	Foliage, roots, and berries (least)	Severe digestive disturbances
Pond scums (algae)	Blooms: dense masses of tiny organisms; water becomes paint-like, with millions of green or blue particles	Death
Sensitive fern	Foliage mixed in the hay	Brain damage and death
St. Johnswort	Foliage contains pigment	Reacts with sunlight and causes blood vessels to leak; blood serum collects under skin producing watery swelling and even killing skin, leaving raw, painful exposed areas

Plant	Poisonous Part	Symptoms
Yard Plants		
Christmas rose	Whole	Severe purgation
Dumbcane, caladium, philodendron	Needlelike crystals of plant	Intense burning and irritation; death if swelling of the tongue blocks air passages
Foxglove	Whole, fresh, or in hay	Increased contraction in heart, irregular heart-beat and pulse, digestive upset; mental confusion
Iris	Fleshy underground portions	Severe digestive upset
Larkspur and aconite, or monkshood	Cuttings thrown to animals	Digestive upset; nervous excitement or depression
Lily and the amaryllid groups: hyacinth, narcissus, or daffodil, autumn crocus, star-of-Bethlehem, lily-of-the-valley, snowdrops	Bulbs (lily-of-the-valley is not bulbous)	Intense digestive upset, nervous symptoms; lily-of-the-valley may also affect the heart
Lupines (wild in New York state)	Alkaloids of plant	Death
Oleander and poinsettia	Leaf	Affects heart; severe digestive upset
Ornamental sweet pea	Seeds	Skeletal deformities from large amounts
Poppies and bleeding heart or Dutchman's breeches	New growth in early spring before other foliage arrives	Similar to that from morphine and opium; death from Dutchman's breeches
Vegetable Garden Plants		
Box and privet hedge	Clippings	Mild to severe digestive upset that may result in death
Horse chestnut, buckeyes	Plant or nut	Irregular gait, excitement, loss of coordination

Plant	Poisonous Part	Symptoms
Mountain laurel, rhodo-dendron, pieris	Leaf	Nausea and vomiting, depression, difficult breathing, prostration, and coma
Onions (in large quantities)	Whole	Destroy red blood cells
Potato	Sprouts, vines, and rotted potatoes	Intensive digestive disturbances; nervous symptoms
Rhubarb	Leaf	Toxic oxalic acid crystalizes in kidneys, ruptures the tubules of that organ
Tomato	Vines	May be poisonous to livestock in large amounts
Yew	Foliage	Depressed heart action; sudden death

From *Common Poisonous Plants*, Information Bulletin 104, by John M. Kingsbury. Courtesy Cornell University, Cornell Cooperative Extension, Ithaca, New York.

BREED ASSOCIATIONS AND REGISTRIES

American Albino Association, Inc.
P.O. Box 79
Crabtree, Oregon 97335

American Andalusian Horse
   Association
Glenn O. Smith, Registrar
P.O. Box 1290
Silver City, New Mexico 88061

American Association of Owners &
   Breeders of Peruvian Paso Horses
P.O. Box 2035
California City, California 93505

Appaloosa Horse Club
P.O. Box 8403
Moscow, Idaho 83843

Appaloosa Horse Club of Canada
Box 3036, Postal Station "B"
Calgary, Alberta, Canada

Arabian Horse Club Registry of
   America, Inc.
One Executive Park
7801 Belleview Avenue,
Englewood, Colorado 80110

American Bashkir Curly Registry
Sunny Martin, Secretary
Box 453
Ely, Nevada 89301

American Connemara Pony Society
Mrs. John E. O'Brien, Secretary
R.D. #1
Hoshiekon Farm
Goshen, Connecticut 06756

American Buckskin Registry
Association, Inc.
P.O. Box 1125
Anderson, California 96007

American Donkey and Mule Society
Carl A. Wilson II, President
2410 Executive Drive
Indianapolis, Indiana 46241

American Fox Trotting Horse Breed
Association, Inc.
100½ S. Crittenden
Marshfield, Missouri 65706

American Gotland Horse Association
Mrs. Robert Lee
R.R. 2, Box 181
Elkland, Missouri 65644

American Hackney Horse Society
Paul E. Bolton, Jr., Executive
Secretary
P.O. Box 630
Peekskill, New York 10566

American Horse Shows Association
527 Madison Avenue
New York, N.Y. 10022

American Indian Horse Registry, Inc.
Rocking LJK Ranch
Rt. 2, Box 127
Apache Junction, Arizona 85220

American Morgan Horse Association
Inc.
Box 29, W. Lake Moraine Road
Hamilton, New York 13346

American Mustang Association, Inc.
P.O. Box 338
Yucaipa, California 92399

American Paint Horse Association
P.O. Box 13486
Fort Worth, Texas 76118

American Part-Blooded Horse
Registry (APB)
4120 S.W. River Drive
Portland, Oregon 97222

American Paso Fino Horse
Association, Inc.
Mellon Bank Building, Room 3018
525 William Penn Place
Pittsburgh, Pennsylvania 15219

American Quarter Horse Association
Amarillo, Texas 79168

American Quarter Pony Association
Harold Wymore, Secretary
New Sharon, Iowa 50207

American Saddle Horse Breeders
Association, Inc.
Charles J. Cronan, Jr., Secretary
929 South Fourth Street
Louisville, Kentucky 40203

American Saddlebred Pleasure Horse
Association
Irene Zane, Executive Secretary
801 S. Court Street
Scott City, Kansas 67871

American Shetland Pony Club
P.O. Box 468
Fowler, Indiana 47944

American Tarpan Studbook
Association
Ellen J. Thrall
Route 2, Highway 78
Liburn, Georgia 30247

American Walking Pony Association
Route 5, Box 88
Upper River Road
Macon, Georgia 31201

Cleveland Bay Society of America
A. MacKay-Smith, Secretary
Middleburg, Virginia 22117

Colorado Ranger Horse Association,
Inc.
John E. Morris, President
7023 Eden Mill Road
Woodbine, Maryland 21797

Galliceno Horse Breeders
  Association, Inc.
Mrs. Mary Stubblefield
111 E. Elm Street,
Tyler, Texas 75701

Gliding Pony and Horse Registries
19100 Bear Creek Road
Los Gatos, California 95030

Half-Arab and Anglo-Arab Registries
224 East Olive Avenue
Burbank, California 91503

Half-Saddlebred Registry of America
Roberta M. Busch, Secretary
660 Poplar Street
Coshocton, Ohio 43812

International Arabian Horse
  Association
224 East Olive Avenue
Burbank, California 91053

International Buckskin Horse
  Association, Inc.
Richard E. Kurzeja, Executive
  Secretary
P.O. Box 357
St. John, Indiana 46373

The Jockey Club
300 Park Avenue
New York, N.Y. 10022

Kanata Pony Association
35388 Hallert Avenue
Matsoui, British Columbia, Canada

Missouri Fox Trotting Horse
  Association
P.O. Box 637
Ava, Missouri 65608

Morab Horse Registry of America
P.O. Box 143
Clovis, California 93612

National Appaloosa Pony, Inc.
112 East Eighth Street
P.O. Box 297
Rochester, Indiana 46975

National Chickasaw Horse
  Association
% Mrs. Roy Hughes
Route 2
Clarinda, Iowa 51632

National Cutting Horse Association
P.O. Box 12155
Fort Worth, Texas 76116

National Quarter Horse Registry,
  Inc.
Cecilia Connell, Secretary
Raywood, Texas 77582

National Reining Horse Association
Kaye Potts
R.R. 3
Greenville, Ohio 45331

National Trotting Pony Association,
  Inc.
Ronald R. Moul, Executive Secretary
575 Broadway
Hanover, Pennsylvania 17331

Original Half-Quarter Horse Registry
I. M. Hunt, Secretary
Hubbard, Oregon 97032

Palamino Horse Association, Inc.
P.O. Box 324
Jefferson City, Missouri 65101

Palamino Horse Breeders of America
P.O. Box 249
Mineral Wells, Texas 76067

Paso Fino Owners and Breeders
  Association, Inc.
P.O. Box 764
Columbus, North Carolina 28722

Peruvian Paso Horse Registry of
  North America
P.O. Box 816
Guernville, California 95446

Pinto Horse Association of America,
  Inc.
P.O. Box 3984
San Diego, California 92103

Pony of the Americas Club, Inc.
P.O. Box 1447
Mason City, Iowa 50401

Hacking Horse Breeders' Association
    of America
Headquarters: Birmingham,
    Alabama
Mailing Address: Helena, Alabama
    35080

Spanish Barb Breeders Association
Peggie Cash, Secretary
Box 20
Farwell, Minnesota 56327

Spanish Mustang Registry, Inc.
Mrs. Leana Rideout, Secretary-
    Treasurer
Route 2, Box 74
Marshall, Texas 75670

Standard Quarter Horse Association
4390 Fenton Street
Denver, Colorado 80212

Tennessee Walking Horse Breeders
    & Exhibitors' Association
P.O. Box 286
Lewisburg, Tennessee 37091

Thoroughbred Owners & Breeders
    Association
P.O. Box 4038
Lexington, Kentucky 40504

Thoroughbred Racing Associations
5 Dakota Drive
Lake Success
Hyde Park, New York 12538

United States Trotting Association
    (Standardbreds)
William Hilliard, Secretary
750 Michigan Avenue
Columbus, Ohio 43215

United States Trotting Pony
    Association
P.O. Box 468
Fowler, Indiana 47944

Welsh Pony Society of America
Gail Headley, Secretary
P.O. Drawer A
White Post, Virginia 22663

glossary

For those terms covering the parts of the horse not included here, see the endpaper illustration. For those terms covering ailments not included here, see chapters 7 and 8.

Aged. A horse past the age of nine as of January 1 of a given year. The term means "fully mature," not elderly.

Anglo-Arab. The offspring of a Thoroughbred sire and Arab dam.

Appointments. Equipment and clothing required for a specific class, event, or style of riding.

Bag. The breast or udder of a mare.

Balance seat. English seat that can be used for all types of riding. The rider sits on seat bones in center of saddle with legs hanging in a natural, bent position, inside of legs against saddle, ankles flexed, balls of feet resting in stirrups, feet close to the inside. Arms are bent at elbows and reins held over the horse's withers slightly angled inward at top.

Bald. A large, uneven white mark on a horse's face that includes one or both eyes; referred to as a "bald face."

Barrel. The trunk of a horse, the area between the fore- and hindquarters.

Bars. Black, horizontal marks on legs, desirable in certain color breeds like buckskins. Also called "zebra striping."

Bay. A horse of medium brown color with a black mane and tail. There are light bays and dark bays.

Bearing rein. See Neck rein.

Bedding. Materials used to bed down the floor of a stall, such as straw, peat moss, wood shavings.

Billet straps. Straps on English saddle that attach saddle to girth. Sometimes called girth straps.

Blaze. A wide white mark running from between the eyes down to the muzzle.

Blemish. An unsightly mark or scar that does not interfere with service-ability of a horse.

Blistering. Application of a heating ointment to an inflamed area, usually a tendon, to heat it and draw blood to the injury, thereby speeding recovery.

Bloom. A term used by horsemen to describe an exceptionally healthy-looking horse with a good coat.

Boggy (Spongy). A "bog" spavin is a soft swelling caused by inflammation of the bursa in the joint capsule at the front and sides of hock.

Bone spavin, or jack spavin. A bone enlargement that can be felt through skin in and around the hock joint. Usually causes lameness.

Bottom line. The line of the pedigree in which the dam of a horse is described. The "top line" describes the sire.

Breastplate. Leather piece across a horse's chest that attaches to the saddle and the girth to prevent the saddle from slipping back.

Breed. Any horse with a distinct bloodline that can be traced through a registry, such as Arab, Thoroughbred, or Morgan.

Bridle. A head harness used to control a horse and usually including a bit, reins, crownpiece, cheek straps, throatlatch, headband, and cavesson (or noseband).

Bridoon. Small snaffle bit used in combination with a curb bit.

Brood mare. A female horse used for breeding.

Brown. A color often mistaken for black. The difference is in the flanks and muzzle, both of which are brown in a horse of this color.

Brushing. A faulty way of going in which the inside of a hoof brushes or interferes with the opposite leg, causing cuts and abrasions.

Buckskin. A beige color with a black mane and tail, sometimes black points and dorsal and eel stripes.

Bursa. A fluid sack which surrounds joints, ligaments, and tendons.

Canter. A slow collected gallop, a three-beat gait originally called the Canterbury gallop.

Cantle. The rear of the English saddle.

Capped hock. Enlargement on the point of the hock caused by an injured bursa which secretes excess fluid like "water on the knee."

Capping fee. Fee for the privilege of hunting paid by a guest when arriving at a meet.

Caste. The term applied when a horse lies down in its stall and is pinned in such a way that he is unable to get up without help or injury.

Cavesson. The noseband and its adjoining headpiece on an English bridle.

Chaff. The husks of grains and grasses, separated by threshing.

Cheek strap. Straps on the bridle, or the cavesson, that run down the side of the cheek to hold either the bit or noseband in place.

Chestnut. A color similar to bronze or copper, often referred to in the west as "sorrel." *Liver Chestnuts* are dirty bronze or pewter in shade. Chestnuts also are little knoblike calluses on the inside of a horse's front legs just above the knee.

Cinch. Girth of Western saddle.

Cold back. Referring to horses that have probably not been properly broken to the saddle or who have been mistreated sometime in their training so that the sudden weight of a saddle on the back or tightening of the girth will cause them to bolt, plunge, rear, or buck.

Cold-blooded. A horse with draft blood evident in his appearance.

Colic. A painful, sometimes fatal, stomach ailment usually caused by overeating, overheating, or overwork.

Collected. An ideal way of going in which a horse is perfectly balanced with hindquarters well under him, which lightens the forehand.

Color breed. A breed registered according to strict color qualifications, such as Appaloosas, albinos, and palominos. May also be double registered with another breed: i.e., a palomino quarter horse.

Colt. A male horse under the age of four.

Combination horse. A horse used for both riding and driving. Shown in classes in horse shows under saddle and in harness.

Conditioning. Working a horse like an athlete to put him in top physical condition so he's fit in wind and limb.

Conformation. A horse's build or physique—the sum total of his parts and their relationship to each other.

Conformation faults. Faults of build, like pigeon toes or knock-knees, some of which are less important than others. Others may interfere with horse's way of going.

Conformation hunter. A hunter, usually a Thoroughbred in this country, which is judged in the show-ring on his looks and way of going as well as on performance.

Cooling off. Walking out an overheated horse to cool him off gradually after a workout. Essential to prevent illnesses like colic and founder.

Coupling. The brace used to couple two hounds together. Also, a region of the lumbar vertebrae.

Cow-hocked. Conformation fault where hocks are too close together.

Creasing. Firing a bullet next to the withers of a horse to daze but not kill him—an uncertain method introduced by the French, used by cowboys of the Old West to cut mustangs out of a wild herd, resulting in a lot of dead horses.

Crest. The top of a horse's neck.

Cribbing. A stable vice in which a horse chews the wood of his stall or pasture fence and swallows air, dangerous because wood splinters may be swallowed, and it can lead to digestive disorders. It is considered an unsoundness.

Crossties. Two chains or rubber leads each about four feet long hung from rings on opposite sides of a stable aisle, used to secure a horse on each side of his halter for grooming or medical treatment. More efficient than tying by a single lead because the horse is less mobile.

Crownpiece. Piece of bridle leather that goes over horse's head and attaches to the cheekpieces.

Curb. A type of bit used on both Western and English bridles, only in combination with a bridoon in the latter. Also a swelling of the plantar ligament just below the hock, usually caused by overwork or poor conformation.

Curb chain (or Strap). Chain or strap used under chin of horse with either curb, Pelham, or Kimberwick bit, which gives a fulcrumlike action to bit.

Cutting. Also called brushing—a faulty way of going in which the inside of a horse's hoof strikes the opposite leg and injures it.

Cutting horse. A western riding term for a horse that is trained to cut cattle out of a herd.

Dam. The mother of any horse, referred to on a pedigree as the "bottom line."

Dapples. Patterned color variations on a horse, usually the size of a fifty-cent piece.

Diagonal. A term in English riding that refers to the rider's posting when trotting on the inside of a ring, when the diagonal hind leg and foreleg of the horse strike the ground together. When the horse and rider are moving clockwise around the ring the rider posts in rhythm with the horse's left front leg and therefore is on the left diagonal.

Direct rein. Displaces horse's weight from the forehand to the hindquarters. Is most frequently used in English riding to decrease speed, turn, or back a horse. Pressure is *never* increased when used correctly.

Dishing. A faulty way of going, usually occurring in pigeon-toed horses, where the feet swing sideways at a trot. Also called "paddling" and "winging."

Draft horse. Horse originally bred for farm work, especially plowing. Characterized by their powerful builds.

Drenching. Giving a horse liquid medicine by elevating his head and pouring liquid down his throat in a bottle or syringe.

Dressage. Considered the most refined form of flat riding, in which a horse is trained to move in perfect balance with the utmost lightness and ease. This type of riding is often referred to incorrectly as high school work.

Driving horse. A horse trained or bred to pull wagons, gigs, and sulkies— such as Hackneys, Cleveland Bays, and Standardbreds.

Dun. A beige color with similarly colored or brownish mane and tail. Sometimes with an eel stripe.

Eel stripe. A dark stripe down the spinal column extending from the withers to the base of the tail.

Eohippus. The most ancient ancestor of the modern horse.

Equus Caballus. The scientific Latin name of the modern horse.

Ewe-neck. Neck curved upward like a "u" or upside-down neck, a conformation fault that often interferes with performance.

Far side. The right side of the horse viewed from the rear; also called the offside.

Faults. In a jumping class, points taken off one's performance.

Field hunter. A hunter of any breeding or cross who regularly hunts with a recognized pack of hounds.

Filly. A female horse under the age of four.

Fittings. Accouterments of an English saddle that can be separated from the saddle, such as stirrup leathers, stirrups, girth.

Flat saddle. Saddle with a low or cut-back pommel and no knee rolls used for saddle-seat riding.

Flats. Term usually referring to Thoroughbred racing tracks. Short for flat racing.

Flaxen. An unusual color. A chestnut with either a white or cream-colored mane and tail.

Flexion. The degree to which a horse can relax his jaw, thus bend at the poll.

Floating. Filing down of rough, irregular molars to give a smooth grinding surface to these teeth.

Foal. A newborn horse of either sex.

Forage. All types of horse feed, including hay, grass grain, concentrates, and vegetable snacks.

Forehand. The forequarters of a horse, including head, neck, shoulders, and front legs.

Forelock. Hair from horse's mane that hangs down over its forehead between his ears.

Forequarters. See **Forehand.**

Forging. A faulty way of going in which the rear hoof strikes the toe of a front hoof, most likely to occur at a trot, causing a clicking noise. This is caused by poor balance or overextending.

Founder (or Laminitis). An inflammation of the sensitive laminae in the foot. In acute cases the sole drops down and separates from the wall. It is caused by overheating, overfeeding, and overworking; it can be chronic.

Gaited. Refers to American saddle breds, who can be either three-gaited or five-gaited.

Gaits. Ways of moving forward, characterized by the sequence and speed with which a horse's feet leave the ground. The basic gaits are walk, trot, canter, and gallop. Other gaits, which certain breeds are either born with or easily trained to do, are slow gait, rack, pace, running walk, and fox-trot.

Gallop. The fastest gait a horse is capable of—a full run.

Gelding. A castrated or gelded male horse.

Get. The progeny of any stallion.

Girth. A band of leather or other material that encircles the body of a horse so as to fasten the saddle to his back.

Grade. A horse of unregistered and/or uncertain ancestry.

Grain. The seed or seedlike fruit of cereal grasses like oats, corn, or barley fed alone or in combination.

Green horse. An unschooled or partially schooled horse, usually a young one.

Green jumper. A horse that has just learned to jump. In most horse shows there are special classes for green jumpers or hunters.

Ground tie. The method by which a Western horse is trained to stand still when the rider dismounts and drops the end of one rein on the ground. The horse is taught to remain stationary and not graze or move around.

Gymkhana. A riding meet consisting of informal games like egg-and-spoon and relay races on horseback.

Hack. A horse used for pleasure riding or one ridden to a hunt meet. Trail and pleasure riding are often referred to as "hacking."

Half-bred. A horse with a purebred sire or dam.

Halter. A rope or leather headpiece with noseband, cheek strap, and occasionally a headband, used for tying or leading a horse.

Hand. A standard of equine measurement. Four inches equal one hand. Therefore a seventeen-hand horse would be five feet eight inches, measured from the bottom of the front hoof to the top of the withers.

Hard mouth. A mouth in which the nerves on the main bone or "bar" of the jaw have been deadened by harsh bits and mishandling.

Harness horse. A driving horse trained to pull a cart or sulky rather than to be ridden.

Hay. A variety of different regional grasses and legumes, such as timothy and alfalfa, that have been cured, dried, and baled to serve as the bulk of a horse's diet.

Hay crib. Trough-shaped, slatted, wooden structure used to hold hay in the field or stall.

Hay fork. Three-tined fork used for handling hay, not to be confused with a five- to ten-prong manure fork.

Hay net. Rope or plastic fiber bag hung in stall to keep hay at shoulder height of a horse.

Headband. Piece of bridle over the horse's forehead to prevent the bridle from slipping back.

Headstall. The leather pieces of a bridle, not including bit and reins.

Heat. The period of time during which a mare may be bred. Occurring at approximately three-week intervals and lasting from four to six days.

Heavy in the forehand. A horse that pulls with his head and neck so that he's putting more than a normal amount of weight toward front of his body. Often a fault of conformation, caused by an oversized head and neck.

Heavyweight hunter. One capable of carrying a rider weighing over 205 pounds.

Herring gutted. A barrel that slants sharply upward from the forehand. A conformation fault that is unattractive but doesn't interfere with function.

Hindquarters. That portion of the horse situated behind the barrel.

Horse. Any member of the species Equus caballus that measures over 14.2 hands. Anything under that size is a pony.

Hot-blooded. A horse with Arab or Thoroughbred blood in his ancestry, usually a purebred. The term is usually synonymous with "high-strung."

Hunter. A horse of any breed used for fox hunting—usually a Thoroughbred or Thoroughbred cross, although Arabs, Morgans, and even saddle breds have been successfully used in the field.

Hunter classes. Horses who enter are judged either in the ring over fences, or over an outside course with fences that might be found in the hunt field. These hunters are judged on their manners, sometimes conformation, and way of going.

Hunter seat. A style of riding that is supposed to be workmanlike in appearance and suited for jumping and hunting. The biggest differences between this and the balance seat is that there is less ankle flexion in the hunter seat, and a slight bend at the rider's hips at the trot, so that he's posting with the motion of the horse. (Sometimes called forward seat.) The heel, seat, and shoulder should be in line when the rider is seated in the center of the saddle. The hands are carried in a closed but relaxed position slightly tilted in off the vertical and the line between the bit, rein, hand, and rider's lower arm is straight.

In foal. A pregnant mare. The gestation period is usually 340–400 days.

In season. Sometimes referred to as in "heat." A period when a mare is able to conceive a foal if bred. This usually varies with individual horses, lasting about a week and recurring every three. Often, during the winter months in northern climates, a mare will not come into season until spring.

Indirect rein. Used to displace a horse's weight laterally from one side to the other. It is also used to put a horse into canter and to make turns.

Inside. Refers to inside of circle when working a horse on a circle or in a ring.

Interference. A faulty way of going in which the horse's legs brush or interfere with each other at various gaits.

Irish hunter. Usually a cross of seven-eighths Thoroughbred and one-eighth coldblood (a draft breed like a Percheron) to produce a rugged mount with a suitable temperament capable of taking the rough terrain encountered on Irish hunts.

Jog. A very slow trot—required in Western classes and most comfortable for Western riding where the rider doesn't post but sits the trot.

Jointed snaffle (broken snaffle). The mildest type of bit, consisting of two bars, joined in the center. The mildness depends on the thickness of the bars.

Jumper. Any horse who has been trained to jump, either in the ring, on the hunting field, or over a steeplechase course.

Jumper classes. In a show, classes judged on a horse's faults over jumps, such as knockdowns with the front or hind legs, ticks, or refusals. Sometimes speed is a factor, but a horse's style of jumping is not considered. As long as he clears the jumps, he's ahead. In the case of a tie, jumps are raised or spread.

Knee roll. Leather or foam-rubber padding in a forward seat saddle to help keep rider's knees in place.

Laminitis. See **Founder.**

Lead. A horse is said to be on his right lead when going clockwise in the ring; his right lateral legs move forward first. Going counterclockwise changes the lead to the left.

Lead line. A rope, leather, or chain shank with a snap end used to lead and tie a horse by the halter.

Leading. Walking a horse forward by standing at his shoulder, lead line or reins in your right hand, and moving your left foot simultaneously with his right leg.

Leading rein. Puts horse's weight in the direction of movement and is used as a simple way to turn a young or green horse.

Legumes. Leafy grasses high in protein and vitamins, like clover and alfalfa, which make the highest-quality hay. Most horses find legumes the most palatable form of hay.

Light horse. Any horse not of draft ancestry. Originally it meant light-legged.

Lightweight hunter. A horse that can carry up to 165 pounds.

Limit class. Class at a horse show in which entries may not have won more than six blue ribbons at a recognized show.

Lope. Although a contraction for the word "gallop," it refers to the canter in Western riding, which is a slow, balanced three-beat gait.

Lunge (or Longe). A rein or rope, usually made of canvas, about thirty feet long. It attaches to a halter or lunging cavesson and is used for training or breaking a horse.

Lunge whip. The long whip used as an aid in training a horse on the lunge line. It never actually touches the horse but is snapped to reinforce spoken commands. It has a small "popper" on the end that sounds like a cap gun when the whip is snapped.

Lunging (or Longeing). Training a horse with a lunge line and lunge whip and voice by working him in a circle. Horses are usually taught to walk, trot, canter, halt, and reverse on the lunge line before being mounted.

Maiden class. A class at a horse show open to entries who have never won a blue ribbon at a recognized show.

Manger. A wooden feeding box or slatted trough attached to the stall wall to hold feed and hay.

Manure fork. Five- to ten-pronged fork used to remove droppings from a stall.

Mare. A mature female horse (over the age of four).

Martingale (or Tie-down). A device used to aid in keeping the horse's head in the correct position so he can be controlled. Some attach directly to the noseband (or cavesson) and some attach to the reins. They terminate at the girth and usually have a piece that goes around the neck.

Mature horse. Any horse over five years of age.

Medicine hat. Rare coloration found on certain mustangs, consisting of chestnut or black speckling around the ears, chest, barrel, legs, and rump on an otherwise white coat. The Indians considered it extremely lucky.

Middleweight hunter. A hunter who is up to carrying 185 pounds.

Milk teeth. Equivalent to baby teeth in a human. In a young horse they are lost and replaced by permanent teeth in a consistent order.

Muzzle. That part of a horse's head that includes his nose, nostrils, lips, and chin.

Navicular disease. Disintegration of the navicular bone of the foot, usually caused by overwork on hard surfaces.

Near side. The left side of the horse, viewed from behind. Schooled horses are accustomed to being approached, mounted, led, haltered, and saddled from the near side (as opposed to the off- or far side). Stems from cavalry officers' carrying their swords on the left hip, making mounting on near side a must.

Neck rein. A method of turning a western horse or polo pony with reins in one hand, laying reins across side of neck to turn in opposite direction. Rein on left side of neck would cause horse to make a right turn. The advantage is that the rider can change direction without decreasing speed. Also called a bearing rein.

Noseband. Strap that goes over the nose as part of the Western bridle.

Novice class. Open to entries who have not won more than three blue ribbons at recognized shows.

Offside. Right side of the horse when viewed from behind; also called the far side.

Open class. One open to any horse and rider in a given division.

Open jumper. Horse capable of high jumping in competition. The horse is scored only on faults.

Outside. Refers to the outside of the circle when a horse is turning in a ring or on a circle.

Paddling. Faulty way of going in which the feet at a trot paddle like an eggbeater. See **Dishing.**

Paddock. Small, fenced area directly adjoining the barn where the horse can go in and out at will.

Parasites. Referring to hundreds of worms, flies, lice, etc., which live on or in the horse and, if uncontrolled, can permanently damage the animal's health.

Park horses. Refers to horses with animated gaits originated with horses used for riding or driving in the park.

Park saddle. Flat saddle with low or cut-back pommel and no knee rolls, used by saddle-seat riders.

Park trot. A slow, animated, very collected trot with a lot of leg action called for in the show-ring. Seen in all harness classes where Hackney or saddle breds perform.

Pellet concentrates. A horse feed comprised of small compressed pellets which can contain concentrated hay, grain, vitamins, and minerals, or a combination of these, with a high nutrient value.

Piebald. A horse whose color is black and white. Sometimes called a pinto.

Pigeon-toed. A horse who stands with his toes pointed inward.

Plantar ligament. A deep short ligament extending from the point of hock to the point below.

Pleasure horse. Usually applies to a horse who is quiet, tractable, and performs willingly at all three natural gaits.

Pointing. Way of standing, with weight on the back feet, indicating unsoundness, particularly founder.

Points. Color of muzzle, legs, and mane and tail.

Poll. The uppermost point of a horse's neck behind the ears.

Polo pony. Any small, agile horse between 15 and 15.2 hands capable of the speed, endurance, and quick turns needed in polo. Usually one-half to three-quarters Thoroughbred.

Pommel. That part of the English saddle in front that fits over the withers.

Pony. Any horse under 14.2 hands. A small pony measures up to twelve hands, a large one runs to 14.2. In England, however, a pony is any child's mount, no matter what size.

Post entries. Entry fees paid on the day of a horse show as opposed to entries mailed in advance to meet a deadline.

Posting. In English riding, the action of the rider as he rises and descends with the rhythm of the trot.

Pulley rein. A severe rein aid used for a sudden stop.

Purebred. A horse whose sire and dam are registered in a studbook.

Quarter horse. A breed developed to race the quarter mile.

Racehorse. Any breed developed for racing, like the Thoroughbred and Standardbred.

Rack. A four-beat gait done at speed; also called the single-foot. It is an acquired gait that is difficult for the horse.

Refusal. In showing or schooling, when a horse stops at or refuses to go over a jump.

Reining. A skill in Western riding where the horse performs complex patterns of turning at the lope.

Ringbone. A bony enlargement high or low on pastern bones, often resulting from overwork.

Roan. A coloration that can be either bay, black, or chestnut, consistently intermingled with white hairs over the entire body.

Roaring. A defect in the respiratory system caused by paralysis of a vocal nerve, resulting in a roaring noise.

Rose gray. A gray horse with chestnut hairs mixed in. Most common in horses of Arabian breeding.

Running walk. A slow gait which resembles the regular flat-footed walk, except it is faster. The sequence of hoof beats is a diagonal four-beat. It is the gait developed primarily in the Tennessee Walker.

Saddle seat. A style of riding in which the rider sits close to the cantle of the saddle, with very little bend of the knee. Toes and knees are in line with feet parallel to horse's sides. Hands are held even with waist over horse's withers.

Schooling. A training regime that begins at birth in which a horse is taught to lead, tie, respond to voice commands and riding aids to all gaits.

Scratches. Skin disease usually caused by unclean stalls and paddocks or excessive moisture.

Season. See **Heat.**

Seat. When used with "proper" or "good" it refers to the way a rider correctly sits his horse.

Shank. A lead line of half leather or rope and half chain.

Sire. Father of a horse. The "top line" in a pedigree.

Skewbald. Like a piebald except that the colors are bay, chestnut, and brown on white, or vice versa.

Slow gait. One of the slower of the two artificial gaits performed by an American saddle-bred five-gaited horse. It is usually a slow pace or stepping pace. Taken from a walk, it is a slow ambling lateral, almost four-beat gait—very easy and comfortable. Other slow gaits are the running walk and fox-trot.

Snip. A white mark along a horse's nostril.

Sock. White on the leg below the fetlock joint.

Sorghums. A genus of cereal grasses used as animal feed, of which there are four distinct types. One of the best known is milo. Molasses is made from sweet sorghum.

Sorrel. See **Chestnut.**

Soundness. Free from any abnormal deviation in structure or function that would interfere with usefulness.

Splayfoot. A horse who stands with his toes pointing outward.

Spook. A high-strung, unpredictable horse given to shying and bolting for no apparent reason.

Stake class. A class at a horse show that offers money prizes. Entry fees depend on the amount of the stake.

Stallion. A mature male horse used for breeding.

Star. Small white mark between a horse's eyes. Also marks on the biting surface of a horse's teeth that help determine age.

Stock seat. The correct **Western seat,** where a rider sits on seat bones with a slight bend at knee, toes under knee and feet parallel to horse's sides. Reins are held in one hand in a comfortable position over horse's withers.

Stocking. White on the leg from the knee down.

Stocking up. Swelling of the legs or filling of the tendons.

Straight stall. Usually an 8 × 5-foot enclosure in which a horse is tied, with manger and bucket at his head. Also called a tie stall.

Stud. A place where stallions and mares are kept for breeding purposes.

Studbook. The registry where all the purebred ancestors of a breed are recorded.

Switches. A matching hairpiece that ties into a horse's tail, matching his own color and texture, to add length or fullness.

Tack. Bridle, saddle, and other equipment used in riding and handling a horse.

TDN. Total Digestible Nutrients in any feed. In oats, for example, the TDN is the highest of all feeds—80 percent.

Thoroughpin. Swelling of lubricating sheath surrounding tendons on sides and back of hock. Soft and spongy. Doesn't usually cause lameness.

Throatlatch. The strap on the bridle that goes under the throat. This part of the anatomy is also called the throatlatch.

Thrush. A disease of the hoof characterized by black flaking of the sole and frog and a foul odor.

Ticks. In jumping, when horse's hind legs or front legs nick a jump without knocking down the obstacle.

Tie-down. A Western martingale. It runs from the cinch to the noseband to keep horse's head down in its normal position when working.

Tie stall. See **Straight stall.**

Top line. On a pedigree, the description of a horse's sire.

Trail horse. A horse used exclusively for pleasure riding or trail riding, not show. Often called a hack or hacking horse.

Tree. The wooden or metal frame on the inside of the saddle.

Trot. A natural two-beat gait where legs move diagonally.

Unsound. Unhealthy or unsuitable in wind or limb, not serviceable.

Walk. A natural slow (flat-footed) four-beat gait.

Watch eye. A blue eye circled with white, sometimes called a glass eye. The other eye is usually brown. This unusual coloration doesn't affect vision.

Weanling. A foal that has been weaned and is not yet a yearling.

Weaving. A stable vice in which a horse weaves rhythmically back and forth in his stall.

Western seat. See **Stock seat.**

Whistling. A milder form of **Roaring.**

White coronet. White bands on the coronet just above the hoof. Sometimes a horse will also have white heels.

Wide behind. A horse whose hocks are not parallel, making him look bow-legged when viewed from the rear.

Wind puffs. Puffy, spongy swellings around fetlock joints caused by pockets of fluid secreted from bursa.

Wind sucking. A stable vice in which a horse swallows air by tucking in his chin. This can develop into an unsoundness because it can lead to indigestion.

Winging. See **Dishing** and **Paddling.**

Yearling. A horse of either sex that is a year old on January 1 of a given year.

magazines and periodicals

PUBLICATION	ADDRESS	FREQUENCY
Appaloosa Journal	P.O. Box 8403 Moscow, Idaho 83843	Monthly
Arabian Horse Times	R.R. 3 Waseca, Minnesota 56093	Monthly
Arabian Horse World	P.O. Box 60910 Palo Alto, California 94306	Monthly
Blood Horse, The	P.O. Box 4038 Lexington, Kentucky 40544	Weekly
Carriage Journal, The	R.D. 1 Box 115 Salem, New Jersey 08079	6 issues a year
Chronicle of the Horse, The	P.O. Box 46 Middleburg, Virginia 22117	Weekly
Dressage & Combined Training	Sport Horse Publ., Inc. 211 West Main Street New London, Ohio 44851	Monthly
Driving Digest	P.O. Box 467 Brooklyn, Connecticut 06234	6 issues a year
Eastern Horse World, The	P.O. Box 249 Huntington Station, New York 11746	Monthly

PUBLICATION	ADDRESS	FREQUENCY
Eastern & Western Quarter Horse Journal	Drawer 690 4 Abbey Lane Middleboro, Massachusetts 02346	Monthly
Equus	P.O. Box 932 Farmingdale, New York 11737	Monthly
Florida Horse, The	P.O. Box 2106 Ocala, Florida 32678	Monthly
Hackney Journal, The	P.O. Box 200 Crawfordsville, Iowa 52621	6 issues a year

Harness Horse, The	The Harness Horse,
	    Inc.
	P.O. Box 1831
	Harrisburg,
	    Pennsylvania
	17105
		Weekly

Horse Bits	R.D. 1 Box 50 Durhamville, New York 13054	Monthly
Horse Digest	3 Royal Street South East Leesburg, Virginia 22075	Monthly
Horse Illustrated	P.O. Box 6040 Mission Viejo, California 92690	
Horseman	P.O. Box 1990 Marion, Ohio 43305	Monthly

Horseman's Yankee Pedlar	785 Southbridge
	    Street
	Auburn,
	    Massachusetts
	01501
		Monthly

Horse Play	11 Park Avenue P.O. Box 545 Gaithersburg, Maryland 20877	Monthly
Horse Show	A.S.H.A. 220 East 42nd Street New York, New York 10017	Monthly

PUBLICATION	ADDRESS	FREQUENCY
Maryland Horse, The	Maryland Horse Breeder's Assoc. P.O. Box 427 Timonium, Maryland 21093	Monthly
Modern Horse Breeding	656 Quince Orchard Road Gaithersburg, Maryland 20878	Monthly
Morgan Horse Magazine, The	P.O. Box 1 Westmoreland, New York 13490	Monthly
N.R.H.A. Reiner	P.O. Box 36 Minster, Ohio 45865	Monthly
Paint Horse Journal	The American Paint Horse Assoc. P.O. Box 18519 Fort Worth, Texas 76118	Monthly
Palomino Horses	P.H.B.A. Inc. 15253 East Skelly Drive Tulsa, Oklahoma 74116	Monthly
Performance Horseman, The (Western & English)	Gum Tree Corner Unionville, Pennsylvania 19375	Monthly
Pinto Horse, The	The Pinto Horse Assoc. 7525 Mission Gorge Road Suite C San Diego, California 92120	6 issues a year
P.O.A.	P.O.A. Club Inc. 5240 Elmwood Avenue Indianapolis, Indiana 46203	Monthly
Practical Horseman	P.O. Box 927 Farmingdale, New York 11737	Monthly

PUBLICATION	ADDRESS	FREQUENCY
Quarter Horse Journal, The	Box 32470 Amarillo, Texas 79105	Monthly
Show Horse	P.O. Box 1270 Bangor, Maine 04401	Monthly
Spur	P.O. Box 85 Middleburg, Virginia 22117	6 issues a year
Thoroughbred of California, The	201 Colorado Place Arcadia, California 91006	Monthly
Thoroughbred Record, The	P.O. Box 1959 Newmarket Road Marion, Ohio 43305	Monthly
Trotting Bred, The	International Trotting & Pacing Assoc. 575 Broadway Hanover, Pennsylvania 17331	8 issues a year
U.S.D.F. Bulletin	United States Dressage Federation Inc. P.O. Box 80668 Lincoln, Nevada 68501	Monthly
Washington Horse, The	P.O. Box 88258 Seattle, Washington 98188	Monthly
Western Horseman, The	P.O. Box 7980 Colorado Springs, Colorado 80933	Monthly
Whip, The	American Driving Society P.O. Box 160 Metamora, Michigan 48455	6 issues a year

The Whip	% Robert G. Heath Secretary 1230 Nepperham Avenue Yonkers, New York 10703	Monthly
Your Pony	1040 W. James Street Columbus, Wisconsin 53925	Monthly

This list from the U.S. Department of Agriculture, Animal Science Research Division, is not complete. No discrimination is intended against those publications that are not included.

index

Note: page numbers in italics refer to illustrations